UNDER THE MARCH SUN

UNDER THE MARCH SUN

THE STORY OF SPRING TRAINING

CHARLES FOUNTAIN

OXFORD
UNIVERSITY PRESS

2009

OXFORD
UNIVERSITY PRESS

Oxford University Press, Inc., publishes works that further
Oxford University's objective of excellence
in research, scholarship, and education.

Oxford   New York
Auckland   Cape Town   Dar es Salaam   Hong Kong   Karachi
Kuala Lumpur   Madrid   Melbourne   Mexico City   Nairobi
New Delhi   Shanghai   Taipei   Toronto

With offices in
Argentina   Austria   Brazil   Chile   Czech Republic   France   Greece
Guatemala   Hungary   Italy   Japan   Poland   Portugal   Singapore
South Korea   Switzerland   Thailand   Turkey   Ukraine   Vietnam

Published by Oxford University Press, Inc.
198 Madison Avenue, New York, New York 10016

www.oup.com

Oxford is a registered trademark of Oxford University Press

Library of Congress Cataloging-in-Publication Data
Fountain, Charles.
Under the March sun : the story of spring training / Charles Fountain.
p.   cm.
Includes bibliographical references and index.
ISBN 978-0-19-537203-8
1. Spring training (Baseball)   I. Title.
GV875.6.F69 2009
796.357'64—dc22   2008052713

Printed in the United States of America
on acid-free paper

FOR BOB AND BETSY

No father has ever been more proud.

Contents

Under the March Sun

Under the March Sun

On a chamber of commerce February morning in 2005, under a postcard-blue sky, Tommy Lasorda finished a quiet conversation on the sidelines and walked out amid three dozen or so pitchers and catchers playing long toss on Dodgertown's field number 3. The eyes of the fans followed Lasorda across the field. A spring training that had begun with only the snap of ball hitting glove was about to get a new and noisy soundtrack. "You gotta love it boys," Lasorda shouted, his public-address-system voice washing across the grounds like a freshening breeze. "You gotta love it out here! It's the only place to be, boys! Right here! Right here on this baseball field! There are billions of people who want to be where you are right now! Right here on this baseball field! Billions!"

And who would argue with him? Oh, there'll be a bit of amused snickering at the bombast of his "billions"—but there is little quarrel with his underlying thought. Spring training draws us all. The March sun warms and refreshes both body and soul. Nothing in American sport, few things in American life have come to symbolize hope and new beginnings and the possibilities inherent in both. "Spring training is the best event in all of sport," gushed New York Yankee scout Joe Caro in 2005. "Baseball is the only sport I know that begins each year at its peak and goes downhill from there," is how Furman Bisher of the *Atlanta Journal-Constitution* put it back in 1981.

Spring training is as timeless as baseball itself, and its appeal is as evident as the sun in the sky. Starting a century ago, every year in late February, men left their winter jobs on the farm, or at the lumberyard or hardware store, or driving a cab in the city, and made their way south—to Florida, mostly, though also to Texas, Georgia, or Arkansas. There, under the March sun, they sweat out a winter's lethargy and fried foods, harden once again muscles and calluses that have grown soft, and ready themselves for another season of baseball.

It is the same today—and it is different. They still gather each spring under the March sun. They are millionaires now, fresh off a winter in the gym, tweaking the precise and finely tuned asset that is the modern athlete's body. They arrive in little need of six weeks of conditioning. Indeed, for many, the languid pace of spring training interrupts a rigid training regimen; and these players today work out individually, before and after the public sessions on the field, to guard against the genuine threat of leaving camp less fit than when they arrived. But for six weeks, just as their forebears did, they go through drills and practice games, absorb instruction in fundamentals like bunting and sliding and hitting the cutoff man. And they do it, particularly in the early days of camp, with unmistakable joy. It's how all of the game feels in the spring. Are there any words that are as sweet to a baseball fan as "Pitchers and catchers report in…"?

Spring training is sunshine—therapeutic, inspiring, been-too-long-without-ya sunshine. Major league baseball today is played from southern California through Arizona and Texas and into Florida, and vast numbers of major leaguers today grew up without winter, in places like Latin America and the American Sun Belt. But for three-quarters of a century, when baseball was being woven into the fabric of America, the major leagues were confined to the northeast quadrant of the country. St. Louis and Washington were the game's southernmost outposts, and these are both cities with honest winters. The beginning of spring training each year has always been a moment of hope, a reassurance that the landscape of snow and gray skies and barren trees will soon pass, and the world will again be green.

Spring training is anticipation realized—like the arrival of the weekend after the long workweek. But spring training, too, is anticipation heightened; it is Saturday afternoon with thoughts turned to Saturday night, because for all of the sensory pleasure of spring training itself, it leads ultimately to the climax of opening day.

Spring training is the *game* again, after an off-season during which baseball news is increasingly as dispiriting and confining as winter itself. "Each year, it becomes clearer to me that my purpose in touring the spring-training camps is not to deepen my appreciation of the sport, or to report on teams and trades, phenoms and veterans," wrote the *New Yorker*'s Roger Angell, who's been visiting spring training and giving eloquent voice to its pleasures for more than forty years. "It is to rid myself of the aftertaste of winter baseball news—the bitter flavor of money, litigation and failed imagination."

Spring training is two middle-aged men playing catch in the parking lot outside Al Lang Field in St. Petersburg as they wait for the gates to open. It is two brothers, maybe four and six, in too-big baseball hats, approaching Rays catcher Dioner Navarro and asking for an autograph in a whisper so soft and nervous it is barely audible. Navarro signs and flashes a 100-watt smile. Fans of all ages get autographs. Very few get smiles. "What do you say, boys?" chides the father after Navarro signs for his sons. "Thank you," they whisper, still staring at their baseballs. Thank yous are even rarer than smiles in the autograph world, but they are far more prevalent in spring training than they are anywhere else.

Spring training is millionaire, rock-star major leaguers playing catch and eating lunch with $1,500-a-month minor leaguers who are hoping to maybe play at Double A, and who may never get any closer to the show than this. The ballparks are small—minor league size—and the crowds, though swollen tremendously since the 1980s, are still only a fraction of those at a regular season game. This gives a proximity that allows for not only autographs and pictures, but eye contact and conversation as well. "Spring training is as human and as close to baseball's core as you can get at the major league level," says Charles Steinberg, the executive vice president of public affairs for the Los Angeles Dodgers. "This is where you come and you gather and you see [the players] up close, and they might sign an autograph. Or they might just high-five you. You know, it's enough if they just look at you, acknowledge you, and smile." This intimacy is much greater in some camps (Orioles, Twins, Pirates) than in others (Red Sox, Yankees, Cubs), and it is vanishing everywhere, year by year. But it is still sufficient to send fans home with the notion that they have made a genuine connection with a player or two, and this will sustain them through a long summer of seeing those players only from the second deck or through a television lens.

Spring training is three generations of one family filling a whole row in the stands in Clearwater, Port St. Lucie, or Mesa. Even more, it is baseball's generational family, gathering every year for one of the game's grand holidays. It is Bob Feller in Winter Haven, once again wearing Cleveland Indians uniform number 19, having a catch along the first-base line minutes before game time, looking at eighty-seven like he's itching to once again take the mound. It is Sandy Koufax in Vero Beach, chiseled and trim at seventy, looking like he absolutely could take the mound. Koufax remains in the background at Dodgertown, keeping a distance from the fans and an even greater distance from the media. He'll have animated conversations with old Dodger-family friends and quiet, earnest conversations with young pitchers. But there's not a soul in the house who is unaware that Koufax is there. His very presence sends a buzz through the camp and brightens everyone's day.

Spring training is eighty-six-year-old Johnny Pesky in Fort Myers, rapping out fungos to Red Sox players young enough to be his grandsons. "I get a little sore now and then," he admits, "because I think I'm twenty-five years old, and I'm not. But that's what spring training does. It makes you believe you are young all over again." It's Yogi Berra and Whitey Ford, enlisted each spring as special coaches, their duties ill defined because their real purpose in camp is to remind players by their simple presence that wearing the pinstripes carries an obligation. Today's Yankees are expected to write the next chapter in the continuum of excellence that runs from the Yankee teams of Ruth, Gehrig, and DiMaggio through the teams of Mantle, Berra, and Ford to the Yankees of Jeter and Rivera.

Will the Hall of Famers in today's game—who play three, four, or five years with one club and then move on, retiring with a closet full of jerseys—feel enough of a sense of connection with any one team to return to spring training when their careers are through? A small matter to fret about perhaps, but spring training gives time to understand that small things are often special things.

Players and coaches, as on the first day of school, greet friends old and new—more new than old, given big league transience—with bear hugs and knuckle-bump handshakes and the resumption of conversations suspended in October. The small irritations that come when men work, travel, and live in close proximity for eight months have been forgotten and will not manifest themselves again for several months. There's little heckling or booing from the stands in spring training; fans have a patience with imperfection in March that will be but a memory in July. Even players and reporters manage to get along in the spring.

During spring training, baseball's history gets told in full again, as ex-players and writers and radio guys sit around bars and restaurant tables and dugouts and tell not only the stories of their youth, but the stories they *heard* in their youth, from those who were old before them. Fans have yesterdays too, of course, and these too come alive in conversations overheard in the stands and along the ropes at the practice fields. "Oh sure. I saw Babe Ruth play many times." "DiMaggio. Now that was *my* guy." "When I played semipro..." "It happened right over there. It was 1956, and I was seven years old. He signed it: Mickey Mantle, #7. And I've been a Yankee fan from that day forward." "I still have my mitt from 1934. It was a Gus Triandos model. He was a pitcher for the Phillies." Gus Triandos actually was a catcher in the 1950s and would have been just four years old in 1934. But does that really matter?

The Grapefruit League. The Cactus League. Even the names have a lyrical quality, not only beautifully bespeaking a sense of place, but also evoking a certain perfume of the outdoors and a freedom from care. In comparison, "American League" and "National League" sound like a day in the office.

Spring training moves at the speed of a bicycle—always figuratively, sometimes literally. For thirty years, Dodger coach Manny Mota pedaled his Schwinn Cruiser from field to field and from dining hall to clubhouse along the paths of Dodgertown in Vero Beach. When they were both with the Twins, pitchers Johan Santana and Carlos Silva, fellow Venezuelans who made their off-season home in the Twins' spring training city, pedaled through the early morning fog of Fort Myers, up the bicycle path along Six Mile Cypress, commuting to work at Hammond Stadium. In Tucson, a couple in their sixties rode a bicycle built for two to a Rockies–White Sox game at Hi Corbett Field.

Maybe most of all, spring training is ritual. It's the newspaper photo of the equipment truck leaving the frosty North for Florida or Arizona, a week or so in advance of the players. The public address announcers at games in Fort Myers, Winter Haven, Lakeland, and elsewhere giving the game-time temperatures not only at the ballpark—generally in the eighties—but back home in Minneapolis, Cleveland, and Detroit as well: seldom above freezing. The local television sportscaster from those same cold-weather cities doing his evening news live shot dressed in shorts and a Hawaiian shirt and standing in front of a palm tree, bantering with the anchors back home, who never fail to tell him how jealous they are.

The ritual includes pitchers' fielding practice—PFP in clubhouse shorthand—particularly the pitchers-covering-first-base drill that's become almost an opening ceremony for spring training. This is an astonishingly low-tech, plebian drill. Pitchers pantomime a throw to the plate, a coach raps a ground ball fungo to first, and the pitcher breaks for the bag, taking an angle that brings him to the inside edge, on a parallel, not a crossing plane, to the imaginary runner. This is not ballet; it is not even particularly physical—each pitcher's turn comes up every ninety seconds or so and requires just a fifty-foot dash at maybe three-quarter effort. It can be quite stupefying to watch. Yet from Fort Lauderdale to Scottsdale, groups of fans, ranging in size from the dozens to the hundreds, will cluster and sit transfixed for an hour or more as pitcher after pitcher cycles through. To a first-time spring training visitor, this appeal might seem a head-scratcher. The cynic might liken it to sitting in the dayroom at the asylum, staring at nothing for hours on end. The romantic knows it's more like sitting on the beach and watching the waves. Little happens and nothing changes. But it is a pleasing vista nevertheless, and there is an ineffable inner comfort in being there.

Dr. Charles Steinberg is the P. T. Barnum of Dodger Stadium. As vice president of marketing and public relations, he's in charge of the lump-in-the-throat moments, such as the 2008 opening-day ceremony that celebrated the Dodgers' fiftieth anniversary in Los Angeles by bringing fifty former Dodgers back to throw out the first pitch. Before joining the Dodgers, he did the same thing with the Boston Red Sox for six years, and with such enthusiasm and élan that he brought about the seemingly impossible: he helped to intensify the already white-hot relationship between the Red Sox and their fans, which has burned for generations. He is very much of the Field of Dreams, baseball-as-poetry school. "Spring training is the essence of baseball's core," he says. "Baseball itself is pristine and divine. Everything you needed to play baseball was in the Garden of Eden. You had the grass. You had the dirt. You had a branch from a tree to make a bat. There had to be a cow somewhere to give you the ball and the glove. I was telling this story once and some wise guy said: 'Yeah, they even had a snake for the media.' But you had everything you need. Out in the sun. You don't need a manufactured court; you don't need a metal-rim basket. You just need a bat and a ball and the good Lord's earth to play on."

Steinberg switches from the rabbi that he is not to the doctor he is (he is a dentist and was for a time the Orioles' team dentist while simultaneously working in their front office in the 1980s) to explain further. "There is a biological resonance when things repeat through the years by starting from their original beginnings," he says.

"In medicine it's been pretty thoroughly discredited, but it works here, I think.

"It's called *ontogeny recapitulates phylogeny*, and it's when the human being, in its development, goes through stages similar to the worm and the fish and each level of the animal kingdom—you go back to the single-cell animal and you're ultimately the most complex animal, the human.

"Now that may not be a metaphor or a parallel that's been drawn before," he acknowledges with a smile, as behind him the Boston Red Sox begin to take the field for their first workout of 2006, with more than 2,000 true believers bearing noisy witness. "But it's the same thing with these early days of spring training. They play catch, which is the atom of baseball. A catch is the atom of baseball. These days of baseball start with the players doing that which we could do too. And then as these days reach their finality before the exhibitions begin, they take off. In the first days of spring training, that's where we watch the development of the game from the atom—the cell—to the magnificent art form that is the best in the world."

Those early atom-of-baseball practices Steinberg loves are free. Drive up, park for free, and walk out onto the field to within feet of the players. Listen to the coaches' instructions or eavesdrop on the players' conversations about restaurants and golf.

When the exhibitions start, the ante goes up and the access goes down. Parking is five bucks, a ticket somewhere between ten and twenty. Spring training seats are always close to the players and the action, but there's a wall between fan and player now. The sounds of the game on the field must compete with the public address announcer reminding you to "visit our sponsors" or to visit the concession and novelty stands "located throughout the park for your convenience."

Then, the regular season begins, and parking can be as much as $20 or $30. To sit as close to the action as in spring training will cost $75 or more. The chances of sitting close to the field are slender, however; those seats go to longtime season ticket holders and folks with connections. And come October, even some of the folks with connections and money will find themselves on the outside with their noses pressed against the glass.

In the spring, however, all the chaos, cost, and frenzy seem far away. Spring training is so pleasingly quaint. License plates from around the country fill the parking lots, from Fort Lauderdale northwest to Dunedin, from

Viera southwest to Fort Myers, from Tucson up I-10 to Phoenix. Young families come in rented minivans. College kids on a spring break road trip—baseball and beaches by day, bars by night—come in ten-year-old SUVs. Retirees arrive in Cadillac, Buick, and Chrysler sedans. The baseball they see—perfect weather, friendly gregarious players, games where the outcome can be immediately forgotten because it doesn't count—may be fantasy. But that's just the point. These are baseball theme parks, places of make-believe no less than Disney World—which, not surprisingly, has a spring training complex all its own.

The market is booming. Spring training games attracted just under 3 million fans in 2007 and 2008, a higher percentage of capacity than for the regular season. Studies by the Florida Sports Foundation put the economic impact of spring training in Florida at more than $500 million annually. That's the equivalent of two Super Bowls and a figure that has doubled in the last fifteen years. The estimated impact on Arizona is smaller—$250 million—but growing swiftly, as the state aggressively pursues teams from Florida. In 2000, twenty teams played in Florida compared to just ten in Arizona. By 2010, the numbers will be fifteen and fifteen.

With so much money at stake, nothing happens by serendipity. Gushers of public money prime this $800 million pump. In Florida, state and local governments have spent more than $300 million in public money since 2000, upgrading existing and building new spring training facilities, in an attempt to keep their big league tenants happy and where they are. But they're finding it hard to outspend Arizona. Since the mid-1990s, when the Cactus League began poaching teams from Florida, Arizona has also spent more than $300 million in public money, building springtime palaces for *its* big league tenants. The story of spring training has always been as much about the host communities as about the baseball teams. National identities and significant economies have come to communities with a spring training connection, and getting or losing a franchise can be a boost or a blow to the local psyche.

Investing in spring training is a mercurial endeavor in the twenty-first century. The lifespan of a complex would appear to be less than twenty years. In 1987, the Texas Rangers moved into a new state-of-the-art facility in Port Charlotte. "They asked what our ideal facility would be," said Rangers general manager Tom Grieve at the time. "This is it." Yet by 2002, the Rangers had left Port Charlotte for a state-of-the-art facility in the Phoenix suburb of Surprise, Arizona. Four years later, Port Charlotte had to commit

$30 million in improvements to the Rangers' old facility to get the Tampa Bay Devil Rays to bring spring training back to town. Four other stadiums built in the late eighties—in Sarasota, Plant City, Haines City, and Port St. Lucie—have been abandoned, razed, slated for replacement, or undergone major renovations.

Baseball old-timers lament the changes. The vulgarity of big-time commerce is stripping spring training of its innocence and its charm, they say. Yet while spring training is decidedly more crowded than ever, and would be unrecognizable to players from the flannel-uniform days, it has changed less than it might appear. Teams have been asking host communities to make improvements to municipally owned facilities since the time of Connie Mack and John McGraw. Spring training is a profit line for major league teams today, where in the past it was always a cost item, but money has always been an overarching concern. The stakes are just higher now. Spring training baseball is now played in the spotlight as well as the sunshine.

In the beginning, it was a much more private affair. More private, but every bit as colorful.

ONE

Myths, Madcaps, and Misbehavior

Spring Training in the Nineteenth Century

Baseball loves myth, and in the absence of fact, myth swoops in to fill the void, then stays for generations, an obdurate squatter with a mulish sense of entitlement.

Spring training myth credits Cap Anson with being the first to bring a team south to sweat out the winter's sins in the warmth of the sun, as he brought his Chicago White Stockings to Hot Springs, Arkansas, in the mid-1880s. Cap Anson was both player and manager, the signature figure of nineteenth-century baseball. It was said in his day that his name was better known across America than that of any statesman or soldier. He played twenty-two seasons—at the time, a major league longevity record—all of them for the Chicago White Stockings, batting .329 and amassing an even 3,000 hits. He was player-manager of the Chicago club for nineteen of those years, 1879–1897, winning five championships and finishing second four times. His most profound impact on the game, however, is not a happy one. More than any other single individual, Cap Anson was responsible for making baseball a whites-only province between 1887 and 1947. He let it be known that he would refuse to take the field for a game against Newark if Newark insisted on playing Moses Fleetwood Walker and George Stovey, its two black players. Anson and money trumped Walker, Stovey, and principle; the blacks did not play. Resistance to black players by both teammates and patrons had been making team owners nervous to begin with. Anson's open defiance doomed the black players' opportunities and kept major league baseball all white for the next sixty years.

But for all of his real historical relevance, Cap Anson no more started spring training than Abner Doubleday invented the game of baseball. Baseball teams had been traveling south in the spring for at least fifteen years before Anson got the notion. In his seminal study of the game's early history, Harold Seymour claims that newspaper records from 1869 show that no less a figure than William Marcy "Boss" Tweed, the head of New York's Tammany Hall and the man who would come to define political corruption in America, may have been the first to come up with the idea of spring training, when he sent his New York Mutuals, a team of amateurs, to New Orleans to ready themselves for the 1869 season. One year later, the Cincinnati Reds, which in 1869 had become the first fully professional team, began their second season with a spring training of sorts, starting their season in New Orleans and playing their opening dozen games or so across the South. That same year—1870—the White Stockings, six years prior to Anson's joining the team, also began their season in New Orleans.

Throughout the 1870s, any number of teams from the newly formed National League and other professional and amateur clubs started their season with a trip south. Following the lead of the Mutuals, Reds, and White Stockings, other teams flocked to New Orleans; the city remained the most popular early destination, with Savannah and Charleston also hosting early camps. A town in Florida inquired of the Philadelphia Phillies as to their interest in training in the Sunshine State, but Phillies manager Harry Wright judged travel to Florida too expensive and opted for Savannah instead. Trips south were by no means universal, and more often than not, "spring training" in the 1870s and 1880s consisted of gathering the troops a few days before the first game and putting them through a regimen of calisthenics, medicine-ball work, and maybe a game of catch in a local YMCA, armory, or barn. New York Giants teams of the 1880s trained under the wooden grandstand at the old Polo Grounds, suffering the winter temperatures but protected at least from the rain, snow, and wind.

The Anson legend has the Chicago player-manager bellied up to a Windy City bar during a February snowstorm in 1885, when one of his pitchers comes in, bursting the buttons on his vest from a winter of living the good life. The pitcher then proceeds to quaff six or eight beers in the presence of his boss, and Anson, it is said, resolved then and there that he would take his players to the baths at Hot Springs, where he would sweat the winter fat off them.

Anson's boss, Chicago owner Albert Spalding, enthusiastically endorsed the plan. "I have written to a professor down there, and he is making arrangements to build a vat in which he can boil the whole nine at once," Spalding told a newspaper reporter prior to the trip south. "You see, the beauty of this scheme is that I get a brand new nine on April 1. I boil out all the alcoholic microbes, which may have impregnated the systems of these men during the winter while they have been away from me and Anson. Once [I] get the microbes out, the danger of a relapse is slight. If that don't work, I'll send 'em to Paris next year and have 'em inoculated by Pasteur."

Cap Anson did two things that his spring-trip predecessors had not. He won championships in his first two seasons after bringing a team south, which convinced him to make spring training a regular affair. And he brought along a newspaper reporter to publicize the trip. Both played no small part in building the legend that he had been first, a legend that has been kicking around since at least the time of the First World War, competing with another fable that credits the idea of spring training to Ned Hanlon, the manager of the Baltimore Orioles during the 1890s. The Anson story was given permanence in 1936 by Dan Daniel, a widely read and highly influential columnist for the *New York World-Telegram* and the *Sporting News*. Daniel wrote about major league baseball for more than sixty years; he went to his first spring training in 1909 as a cub reporter for the *New York Herald*, covering the Brooklyn Dodgers' camp in Macon, Georgia. The Dodgers were sharing training facilities that year with the Sparks Circus, also readying itself for the coming season, and the irony of the inept Dodgers training side by side with circus clowns was not lost on even a teenaged reporter.

By 1936, Daniel was the "Arnold Toynbee of baseball," a reference to the British historian who was then in the midst of compiling his twelve-volume history of the world. The 5,000 words that Daniel wrote each week in the *Sporting News* delved frequently into the game's history, and in a column calling 1936 "spring training's golden jubilee," Daniel quoted outfielder-turned-evangelist-turned-temperance-crusader Billy Sunday as his source for the Anson legend. The conversation had taken place some years earlier; Sunday had died three months before Daniel wrote his 1936 column. A .248 hitter in eight seasons with the White Stockings, Sunday had apparently been peeved by an article he'd read which had credited Hanlon for starting spring training. "You baseball historians keep insisting that Hanlon was the first to get the idea," Sunday chided Daniel. "Well, it was Cap Anson, and not Hanlon, and Cap beat Ned to it by a clean ten years. I was with the Chicago club in 1886, and Anson took us to Hot Springs to boil out. It was considered a startling, expensive innovation."

The fact that Anson first took a team south in 1885, not 1886, was a detail apparently lost in Sunday's memory and never checked by Daniel. The word of the outfielder-turned-man-of-God was good enough for Daniel, and the word of Daniel—who sometimes wrote as if he were delivering the Sermon on the Mount—was good enough for everybody else. For the better part of the next forty years, brand-name sportswriters, including Red Smith, Arthur Daley, and John Lardner, echoed Daniel's assertion so frequently and so unquestioningly that it became canon. Any story that delved into spring training's past began with Cap Anson. Harold Seymour was the first to puncture the Anson myth, and a host of historians have subsequently followed. But myths die hard. Google "Cap Anson and spring training" and a host of sites at the top of the list still credit Anson with being first.

By the late 1880s, spring training trips were becoming more common than not. Florida first joined the roster of hosts in 1888, when Washington Senators manager Ted Sullivan brought his team to Jacksonville. One of the most enduring, detailed, and colorful descriptions of early spring training comes from Connie Mack, a twenty-five-year-old catcher with the Senators on that trip, and Mack's account does not suggest the building of team harmony and the development of baseball efficiency that teams were hoping trips south would bring. Sullivan was pinching pennies; he rented seven Pullman berths for the trip, and the fourteen players slept two to a bunk for the two nights it took to get from Washington to Jacksonville. Moreover, the players were rousted out of their berths at seven in the morning and moved to a day coach, so that Sullivan might save a few pennies more. "By the time we arrived in Jacksonville, four of the fourteen players were reasonably sober," remembered Mack. "The rest were totally drunk."

When they arrived in Jacksonville, the players sobered up by schlepping their luggage, on foot, from the train station to the hotel that Sullivan had booked for them. "But the manager was horror-stricken when he found we were ballplayers," said Mack, and turned the team away. They were turned away at other hotels as well, before Sullivan finally found a boardinghouse on the outskirts of town, where, for a dollar a day per player, the proprietor agreed to provide food and two-to-a-bed sleeping accommodations for the players, so long as they agreed not to mingle with the other guests. The prisoner-of-war-like treatment did not inspire the players to conduct themselves with any degree of decorum. "There was a fight every night, and the boys broke a lot of furniture," said Mack. "We played exhibitions during the day and drank most of the night."

Ballplayers were unwelcome for reasons other than their reputation for boorish behavior. America was still a country of regions in the late nineteenth and early twentieth centuries; the Civil War was not long in the past, and in many parts of the South the wounds were still raw. Not a single team in the National League represented a city that had been part of the Confederacy, and players in those early days came predominantly from the Northeast and the Midwest. The reception they received in the South was frequently rude, which was a trigger to more boorish behavior. One season in the early 1890s, the Cubs, told they would be unwelcome in Jacksonville, were scheduled to train in Waycross, Georgia. The townspeople received the northern interlopers coolly and warily, and the players exacerbated the tension with untoward and persistent advances on the young women of Waycross. The players were already in a foul mood because the club refused to spend more than a dollar a day for their accommodations, and, even in nineteenth-century Georgia, a dollar didn't buy much. The ill feelings and frustration came to a head one night as the players stood outside their hotel watching an acrobat get set to perform his high wire act. As the tightrope walker climbed to the top of his tower, something moved Cub shortstop Bill Dahlen—his nickname was "Bad Bill"—to tug on the guy wire, which sent the aerialist tumbling to the street. That brought the cops and the hotel manager, all brandishing their pistols. The Cubs were invited to leave Waycross, not, as it turned out, for the assault on the aerialist—circus performers and actors had no more standing than ballplayers, apparently—but because the hotel manager claimed that his wife had been insulted by the ballplayers. The team left the next morning for Savannah.

The baseball conditions were as spartan as the living conditions in nineteenth-century spring trainings. Southern towns had baseball weather but not always did they have baseball facilities. Teams practiced on whatever open patch of ground they could find; seldom was it actually a baseball diamond. This was less of a disadvantage than it might seem, for early camps were more fat farms than baseball camps. The players of the day were given greatly to off-season dissipation and frequently showed up in the spring "looking like aldermen." The degree to which the off-season had eroded players' baseball skills was of less concern to managers, owners, and newspaper reporters than the degree to which the winter had eroded their conditioning. "The Men Are All Overweight," read the headline in a *Brooklyn Eagle* story on spring training in 1896. "With their chins crowded into the collars of their heavy overcoats, a dozen members of the Brooklyn base ball club boarded the 3:30 annex yesterday afternoon and their trip to the South was begun." Though there was some throwing and some hitting, much of spring training in those years was given over to long morning hikes of two to seven miles, medicine-ball and Indian-club workouts—an Indian club is something akin to a weighted bat—with maybe some hot baths thrown in to boil out those alcoholic microbes. All of this was exactly what teams had done in the armories and barns back in the North. From the first, club owners pondered whether the baseball value of a trip south justified the expense. Cap Anson's Chicago teams won championships after preseasons in Hot Springs. But Connie Mack's Washington Senators finished dead last after their spring in Jacksonville, and Brooklyn was deep in the second division during the season that the *Eagle* reported the players all showing up fat.

Team owners—*magnates* in the newspaper argot of the day—kept careful track of spring training expenses. And, like good businesspeople everywhere, they looked to cut expenses and squeeze out revenue wherever they could. In 1908, the Boston Red Sox took a young outfielder named Tris Speaker to camp with them in Little Rock. Speaker did little to impress, and when the Red Sox left camp they assigned his contract to the Little Rock Travelers of the Southern League as payment for the rental of the Travelers' field during training camp.

Records from the Philadelphia Phillies' spring training in 1892 showed a bottom-line expense of $469 for the team's month-long trip to Gainesville. Manager Harry Wright left Philadelphia with $200 in expense money. Train fare for fourteen players cost the team $404.60; Pullman berths were another $89. (Unlike the Senators of 1888, the Phillies' players were not forced to share a berth with a teammate.) The tickets were billed to the club; the Pullman berths came out of Wright's $200, as did breakfast in the Richmond train station—seventy-five cents per player for a total of $10.50—and lunch and dinner aboard the train (each meal, fifty cents a player for a total of $14).

In Gainesville, room and board at the team's hotel ran $10 per week per man, a total of $325.64. Wright soon ran out of money, wired back to

Philadelphia, and received an additional $375. Two local exhibitions put some money back in the till. The first of these, against a local team, brought in $17.50 in gate receipts; the second, against the National League's Brooklyn Bridegrooms, brought in $44.80. The only added expense involved in these games was fifty-five cents for groundskeeping. Three games on the road in Florida brought in over $100—$106.97—but room, board, and travel took an $82 chunk of that. The mother lode, insofar as single-game gate receipts were concerned, was an exhibition against the New York Giants in Richmond as the team made its way home. The teams split a gate of $219.25, with each team realizing $95.62 after paying out $20 in advertising, $3 for a license, and $5 for the rental of the field.

When the team got back to Philadelphia for the start of the regular season, expenses had totaled $1,131.78, around $80 per man. Total gate receipts were $662.09 (there had been other exhibitions against the Giants as the teams made their way north) for a net loss of $469.69.

Teams made their spring training plans based on cost. They also made them at the very last minute. In 1900, the Brooklyn club still had no firm plans in place as late as March 1. The team's manager was unconcerned; he planned a trip to Augusta, Georgia, sometime in the next week or so to scout out hotel space in advance of the start of camp, that year scheduled for March 20.

By the turn of the twentieth century, the question of whether a spring trip was necessary—whatever the cost—had been settled pretty conclusively by Ned Hanlon and the Baltimore Orioles. Hanlon had been the thirty-four-year-old player-manager of the Pittsburgh club in 1892 when he snapped a tendon in his leg chasing a batting-practice fly ball on opening day. The injury ended his playing career; Pittsburgh cut him loose, and Baltimore owner Harry Vonderhorst hired him to manage the last-place Orioles. Hanlon kept the Orioles in last place in 1892 and moved them up only a couple of notches in 1893. But he was busy making trades, putting together a starting lineup in which six of the eight position players would ultimately find their way to the Baseball Hall of Fame.

Before the 1894 season, Hanlon took the Orioles to Macon, Georgia, and put them through a new and entirely different kind of spring training. For eight hours a day over eight weeks, Hanlon drilled the Orioles in the hit-and-run, the squeeze play, the double steal, and driving the ball into the ground when the defense was playing deep—the hit that would forever after be known as the "Baltimore chop." Hanlon also drilled his boys in some extralegal ploys, including running across the diamond from first to third when the single umpire's attention was directed elsewhere and grabbing a base runner's belt for a second or so after a ball was hit. He also instilled in the Orioles the notion that they were the toughest sons-of-bitches ever to take the field. "We'd spit tobacco juice on a spike wound, rub dirt on it, and get back out there and play," remembered John McGraw, Hanlon's third baseman and most devoted pupil.

The results of Hanlon's innovative spring training were immediate and decidedly dramatic. The Orioles opened the 1894 season against the New York Giants, sweeping a four-game series and bedazzling the Giants by successfully executing thirteen hit-and-runs over the four games. "It's a new game they're playing," acknowledged New York manager Monte Ward. "It's just not baseball." Playing their brand of what would come to be called "inside baseball," the Orioles won the 1894 pennant and the next two thereafter. The swagger and the precision teamwork that marked their game was something all clubs now began imitating. It was the tacit consensus of magnates and managers alike that the place to make this happen was training camp in the spring.

In the years subsequent to Hanlon and the Orioles, no one epitomized the Hanlon philosophy more than John McGraw. Spring training stories in the first quarter of the twentieth century invariably featured McGraw front and center. He took over as manager of the New York Giants in 1902, transferring that old Oriole swagger to Broadway, where his star would quickly eclipse not only that of his mentor (who'd moved to the Brooklyn Dodgers) but that of everyone else in the game. McGraw was the face and the personality of baseball until Babe Ruth emerged after the war. McGraw told everyone who would listen—and he was never without an audience about inside baseball and the Oriole way. His spring trainings were every bit as long and as disciplined as Hanlon's. But while he worked his charges just as hard as his mentor had worked him, he also treated them like the kings he expected them to be. McGraw made spring training a spectacle. The players loved it; the press waxed poetic. All of baseball and no small number of southern towns and cities benefited, as America grew more intimate with spring training and the places that hosted it.

Prior to McGraw's arrival, the Giants had always trained at home— the farthest they'd traveled was to the Jersey shore for a couple of years in the 1890s. McGraw took them to Savannah. After the Giants defeated the

Athletics in the 1905 World Series, he moved the Giants' camp to Memphis, in part because he had persuaded a high-end Memphis hotel to house his players. The Giants' boardinghouse days were over, and the boardinghouse days for the rest of major league baseball were numbered. That 1906 Memphis camp marked the beginning of spring training as the spectacle it remains to this day. McGraw arranged for the Giants players to be driven from their hotel to the practice field each morning in open coaches drawn by horses draped with yellow blankets with the words "World Champions" embroidered in blue. He boasted to the reporters that the team would repeat as World Series champions in 1906, and it was all dutifully and breathlessly reported to the snowbound newspaper readers back in the North. McGraw understood that, while spring training was an opportunity to prepare a team to play baseball on opening day, it was also a place to sow the seeds that would allow the ticket office to be in full flower by opening day. "You can't expect a man in New York with his nose in his coat collar to get excited about baseball overnight," he said. Dan Daniel explained John McGraw's marketing genius this way: "The fan, no less than the player, must be prepared for the major league championship season," he wrote. "The turnstile-clicker must be warmed up after the long winter. [The fan's] baseball appetite must be whetted afresh, his curiosity intrigued.

"Years ago [Daniel was writing this in 1947], before baseball went in for this annual springtime enterprise, the pennant campaign was at least three weeks or a month old before the fans began to show signs of real interest. Now your customer comes into the opener agog and aglow."

McGraw drove his troops in spring training because he also understood the box office importance of a quick start to the season. "You have to get that money in the till before the Fourth of July," he said. "If things go badly after that you're at least sure to break even. But if you go badly in the first half and lose those early big attendances, there's absolutely nothing you can do in the second half to get it back."

McGraw took the Giants to Memphis just that one year; in the years following, he would take his teams farther south and west—to Marlin and San Antonio, Texas; to Gainesville and Sarasota, Florida; and across the country to Los Angeles. But Memphis, together with Marlin, Texas, remains the city most identified with the John McGraw Giants. Every year, wherever he trained, McGraw would invariably bring the Giants to Memphis on their way back to New York, stopping for at least a weekend and sometimes for a week or longer. Memphis was a good exhibition town; the games the

Giants played there, be they against another major league club or the hometown Memphis Chicks, generally put a lot of money in the till. Second, an extended stay in one town got the players out of their Pullman berths and into a comfortable hotel. The norm in those days was to travel to the next town by train overnight as teams barnstormed north, arriving on a siding in the early morning—and reaching home and the start of the regular season exhausted and irritable from living on a train for two weeks. McGraw sought to break that up. Finally, he thought that Memphis's climate provided the ideal transition from the March warmth of Florida or Texas to the April chill of New York, Boston, Philadelphia, and Chicago. "If the weather [in Memphis] was warm, it wasn't as warm as it had been where the Giants had trained," explained Frank Graham, the New York columnist who covered the Giants for virtually all of McGraw's thirty years with the team. "And if it was cold, it wasn't as cold as it would be...wherever they were going to open the season."

John McGraw was an odd mix of Marine drill sergeant and fraternity prankster at spring training. If he felt his players were loafing or underperforming, he wouldn't hesitate to keep them running drills for an extra two or three hours. If they displeased him on the field, he could unleash a stream of epithets and insults so blue it made ordinary ball field vulgarity sound like prayer. What seemed like slave driving was part motivation, part cunning. At day's end, he wished to leave his players too tired for carousing. "Sure, [a player's] afternoon workout will not be as lively as his pre-luncheon drill," he said. "But an alert manager will keep his players on the move and get them into a mood for bed long before the midnight curfew."

But for all of the discipline of McGraw's days, he is also remembered for the decidedly different bent he brought to his nights, keeping the Giants loose over the long weeks of spring training with practical jokes and steady carousing. One spring in San Antonio, he traveled with a wildcat kitten he named Bill Pennant, carrying it into hotel lobbies in a small cage and setting it loose and laughing as the other guests fled in horror. Sometimes, the writers who traveled with the club were his victims; sometimes, they were his confederates. He delighted in spending the evening drinking with the writers and then feigning ignorance and innocence when the writers would stumble back to their rooms to find all of the furniture piled on the bed.

During the ten years that the Giants trained in Marlin, Texas, before World War I, McGraw would barhop at night with a four-piece band in tow. At evening's end, he would pay off the band with all of the change and loose bills he had in his pocket, invariably a good night's pay for the musicians. One night, he instructed a writer to turn off the light as he paid off, and in the darkness he slipped the trumpet player a nickel, three pennies, and some folded paper. When the lights came back on, he retreated to a dark corner to watch the trumpeter try to explain to his mates that eight cents was all he'd been given. "Don't tell us that's all he give you," shouted one. "Mr. McGraw ain't cheap. He give you plenty." And with that, he cracked the trumpeter on the head with a bull fiddle, setting off a melee that destroyed all of the instruments by the time it was over and tickling McGraw's misshapen funny bone no end. He and his rather dark sense of humor no doubt felt the amusement well worth the price of the instruments, for which he reimbursed the band the next morning.

The Giants players lived in such fear of their manager that he was seldom the butt of any jokes himself. But nobody who instigated as much as McGraw did could get away without at least some retaliation. One year in Marlin, the Giants jury-rigged a steam room in a hotel bathroom, plugging the gaps in the doors and windows with towels and running the bathtub's hot water to create the steam. They'd sit on the hot radiators, protecting themselves by laying towels on top. As McGraw came in and blindly made his way through the clouds of steam, someone removed the towels from the radiator and McGraw sat down, "wearing nothing but perspiration." He howled in pain and threatened vengeance upon the perpetrator. Suspicions always centered on pitcher Bugs Raymond, but, knowing McGraw always meant what he said, the players with knowledge of the incident took the secret to their graves.

McGraw visited most of his pranks upon writers, locals, and other hangers-on, like the unfortunate band; he seldom directed pranks at his players, which was almost certainly by design. Like Ned Hanlon with the old Orioles, McGraw instilled an us-against-the-world ethos in his players. He alone would mete out discipline. The result was that the Giants players came to fear McGraw and nobody else, knowing their manager had their backs. One year in Marlin, pitcher Rube Marquard, another of the Giants' blithe spirits, got the notion to shoot up a burlesque-show billboard within sight of his room with a handgun. The gunfire greatly unnerved the locals, and the Marlin constabulary came for Marquard's head. McGraw said he'd handle the discipline, but the local sheriff insisted on arresting Marquard. "Dammit, we put this town on the map," roared McGraw, "and we can just as quickly put it off by leaving." Marquard never left his room, and the Giants stayed in Marlin for ten years. The town had great appeal for the Giants players. The burlesque show whose sign Marquard had shot up was only one of several in the town; there were also a great many saloons and gambling halls during the pre–World War I decade when the Giants wintered there.

McGraw's Giants camps were probably no more rambunctious than any other. Spring trainings during the prewar years tended to be madcap, undisciplined affairs, filled with snipe hunts, food fights, water balloons tossed from hotel windows, sneaking in after curfew, then playing with a next-day hangover, and other benign and time-honored misbehavior. One of the most famous spring training stories from the twentieth century's early years involves Philadelphia Athletics catcher Ozzie Schreck, who grew increasingly frustrated with the poor quality of the steak he was served at the team's hotel and with the hotel's seeming indifference to his complaints. Somewhere along the way, he secured a hammer and nails, and when another steak displeased him, he rose from his table and nailed the steak to the dining room wall.

McGraw's spring trainings were the best chronicled, and that is perhaps the reason for the enduring quality of the stories and for the profound influence he had upon the practice of taking a team south. When McGraw took the Giants to Los Angeles in 1907, the trip captured the imagination of all of baseball. As the colorful, competitive New York newspaper writers spread the legend of McGraw, other team owners and managers sought to create the same buzz around their spring trainings. Sports editors took note of the circulation potential of spring training stories, and soon every American newspaper covering major league baseball was sending a reporter south in March.

Local mayors and chambers of commerce took note of what a month's worth of national datelines could mean for a city's burgeoning hotel and tourism business. Baseball players were no longer seen as the incorrigible degenerates they had been in the 1800s. Now, they were celebrities of the first order, and as America returned to business after the Great War, southern cities began clamoring to keep company with these new celebrities and grabbing for themselves a bit of the money to be had by being a part of baseball's spring training.

TWO

St. Petersburg's
Mr. Baseball

Al Lang came to St. Petersburg to die.

It was 1910; Lang was thirty-nine years old and the proprietor of the largest laundry in Pittsburgh. He'd recently been diagnosed with a respiratory disease—maybe tuberculosis, maybe not; in all that was later written about Lang, it was never made clear—and doctors told him he had six months to live. The Rx for respiratory afflictions in 1910—whether to enhance one's chances of recovery or simply to make the final days just a trifle more comfortable—was clean air. Mountain air, sea air, warm air, cold air—it didn't matter. Anything but Pittsburgh air.

Lang sold his laundry and left Pittsburgh to spend his final days in the salt air and sunshine at the southern edge of Tampa Bay. He had initially intended to move to Fort Myers, but along the way he'd stopped in St. Petersburg for a visit and within five days had bought a house. It would turn out that the prognoses of those Pittsburgh doctors as to his life expectancy would be off by forty-nine and a half years. And when Al Lang died in 1960, 1,000 people would fill Christ Methodist Church for his funeral, and 2,000 more would stand outside.

St. Petersburg in 1910 was a community scarcely two decades old; it had been incorporated and christened in 1888, after the arrival of the Orange Belt Railroad. The Russian-born builder of the Orange Belt named its new terminus after the city of his birth. According to the census of 1910, St. Petersburg was home to 3,100 people, an increase of 20 percent, or about 600 people, from the census of 1900, but still very much a community where the locals took pride in knowing their neighbors, indeed in knowing everyone in the community. New citizens were arriving every day, and the city was poised for a boom that would make it among Florida's largest, most prosperous, and best-known cities a decade later. And the dying laundryman from Pittsburgh would play a big part in that boom.

As Lang's health improved, he became an evangelist for the miracles of St. Petersburg. He also became involved in civic life. He told his new friends that the only thing keeping St. Petersburg—"Spearsburg," he called it-short of perfect was the absence of baseball. He took it upon himself to fix that. Lang had never been a part of the game, but he'd never been far from it. He and his boyhood friend Barney Dreyfuss had had their own particular knotholes in the fence of Exposition Park, where the Pirates played, and they would defend their turf with particular vigor on game days. When he was a teenager, Lang took a job at a restaurant frequented by members of the Pirates and members of the visiting clubs. "Your Al will never amount to anything if you don't keep him away from those swearing, tobacco-chewing, whiskey-drinking ballplayers," Lang's mother was told by a well-meaning friend. But if his mother ever passed on the message, young Al didn't listen.

By 1913, his old boyhood chum Barney Dreyfuss owned the Pittsburgh Pirates, and Lang thought that St. Petersburg, the Pirates, and spring training would be a perfect combination. He was wrong. "Al Lang, you must think I'm a damn fool, suggesting training in a little one-tank town that's not even a dot on the map," wrote Dreyfuss in a letter. Lang had told Dreyfuss of all the opportunities the players would have to swim, boat, and fish in their free time in St. Petersburg; he later thought that had been a mistake. Dreyfuss, Lang felt, didn't want to hear about diversions that would take his players' minds off the task at hand. It is likely the opposite is true, however, for the Pirates returned to Hot Springs, Arkansas, in 1914, a town with a much greater range of off-field diversions than those of St. Petersburg.

Undaunted and convinced that spring training would make St. Petersburg a tourist mecca, Lang recruited other civic leaders and formed the St. Petersburg Major League and Amusement Company. The group raised somewhere between $20,000 and $50,000—reports varied—in a stock issue to buy land on which to build a baseball field suitable for major league spring training. But first they needed a team, and the job of finding one fell to Lang. He struck out with the Cubs but interested the St. Louis Browns, the most woebegone franchise in all of baseball. And even the Browns wouldn't come cheaply.

The Browns' general manager at the time was Branch Rickey, a man legendary for both his ability and his eagerness to squeeze a nickel, and Rickey sensed a willingness to please in the St. Petersburg men that gave him an advantage in the negotiations. The St. Petersburg folk promised to pay the expenses of the Browns' travel to St. Petersburg, as well as their living expenses while they were in the city. They also agreed to pay the expenses of five reporters to accompany the team. The newspapermen were key. If spring training were going to be a spur to paying visitors, those potential visitors needed to know about it. The St. Pete Major League and Amusement Company took an option on some land in Coffee Pot Bayou, land that is today part of a string of parks that runs along the water north of the Vinoy hotel. The group chose the land partly because they could get it on a lease agreement—meaning, they did not have to commit to buying it until they were confident that their experiment would succeed—and partly because it was near the water, which would give the players recreational opportunities in their off-hours. Those recreational pursuits—and the St. Petersburg waterfront—would be featured prominently in all of the newspaper stories making their way back to St. Louis and other places where the winters were cold.

That first St. Petersburg spring training was a qualified success. Four thousand fans turned out for the first and only exhibition game, between the Browns and the Chicago Cubs. Men in bowlers, dark suit jackets, and starched paper collars sat in rows five deep on the grass along both foul lines. Reports on the finances of that first spring varied. One said the enterprise had lost $1,000. Another pointed to a dispute over $6,500 in charges run up by the Browns that the St. Petersburg businessmen refused to pay. It was one year and done for the Browns; they moved camp to Houston, Texas, in 1915.

Al Lang wasn't concerned. He now had a ball field and a track record to sell to major league teams. The Pirates were still not interested, but he used his old Pennsylvania political contacts to approach the A's and the Phillies. That worked. The Phillies agreed to come in 1915; and they followed their spring in St. Petersburg by winning fourteen of their first fifteen regular season games and then continuing on to the National League pennant, the first championship in their history. The Phillies gave credit for their fast start to the perfect weather they'd had in St. Petersburg, and Al Lang had another arrow for his quiver. See, said Lang to all who would listen—and his audience was constantly growing—see what training in St. Petersburg will do for a team?

See too what a winning team will do for St. Petersburg. "That [championship] was the greatest advertisement we could have received," said Lang during the 1920s. "Famous Philadelphia sporting writers...made our city famous."

That same year, a month after the Phillies lost to the Red Sox in the World Series, the citizens of St. Petersburg elected Al Lang as their mayor. He served two terms, a mere four years, 1916–1920. But in those short years, he helped to transform St. Petersburg from "our village" to a modern vibrant city. Nearly ninety years after his term ended, nearly fifty years after his death, he still casts a long shadow over his adopted town. "St. Petersburg probably owes more to Al Lang than to any other single individual after the founder," wrote the *Evening Independent* following Lang's death. "In retrospect, one may now see that in his mind the burgeoning growth of [the 1950s] was as logical as a mathematical formula. It was as though he had laid out a mental blueprint years before and had helped unceasingly to bring it into physical being."

Lang's mission as mayor was to burnish St. Petersburg's image and appearance and to spread the word, so that St. Petersburg might become Florida's leading tourist destination. As the city grew—the population would double during Lang's four years as mayor—Lang feared it was also in jeopardy of turning into a seaside honky-tonk. He was particularly offended by the appearance of the city's benches. St. Petersburg's benches were legendary, even in that early hour. In the twentieth century's first decade, a flamboyant real estate man and future mayor named Noel Mitchell noticed that the bench outside his downtown office was always full. He added a couple more, with his name on them, so weary foot travelers would know to whom they should be beholden for their resting place. Those benches filled. Soon, Mitchell had benches all over the city, hundreds of them, each painted a garish orange and bearing the words: "Mitchell, The Sand Man. The Honest Real Estate Man." The benches were always full, and so was Mitchell's real estate office. Success breeds nothing so much as imitation, and soon there were hundreds of more benches across the city, advertising druggists, victualers, and competing real estate firms. At the height of the bench craze right before World War I, there were reported to be more than 3,000 benches throughout the city. On Central Avenue, the heart of St. Petersburg's business district, they were lined up in rows, like seats on a school bus. Each batch of new benches was painted more brightly than the last, trying to stand out amid the cacophony. The crazy-quilt of colors and advertising all abraded Al Lang's sensibility; it was inconsistent with the image of St. Petersburg he was trying to cultivate and sell. He pushed an ordinance through the city council that decreed that all benches must be of a uniform size and that all must be painted green. The merchants who'd paid for the benches groused a bit but complied. In paint stores throughout St. Pete, the shade of green on the benches became known as "Lang green." Green benches became the city's signature. They then became the city's public relations cross. As St. Petersburg became a haven for retirees through the twentieth century, the elders would make full use of the benches, particularly in the downtown and waterfront areas. The sight of so many dozing senior citizens filling the benches would earn St. Petersburg a tough-to-shake reputation as "God's Little Waiting Room."*

Lang didn't stop at green benches. Garish storefront signs were replaced; pushcart and peanut vendors and "other bowery aspects" were chased from the city's downtown. Most important, the city seized control of the waterfront, putting it in public hands and guaranteeing access for generations yet unborn. The reclamation of the downtown waterfront had already begun by the time Lang became mayor. As early as 1907, it was described in a public report as having "an unsanitary and unsightly condition" that did not "well compote [sic] with a live, progressive city such as St. Petersburg aspires and claims to be." When Lang left office, the downtown waterfront consisted of a string of parks, and a city ordinance was in place to ensure the space would remain public.

Lang's years as mayor and the booming twenties that followed were a feel-good, can-do time for St. Petersburg. It took to calling itself the Sunshine City. The *Evening Independent* proclaimed: "This Newspaper Free on Rainy Days." Lang hired a publicity agent, said to be the first on any public payroll. John Lodwick's job was to get posters, brochures, press releases, and photographs into the hands of travel agents and newspaper editors and into

---

* In 1969, the city council would pass another ordinance, this one ordering that benches be of different colors and shapes, in an effort to shake the city's tired image.

store windows in the frosty Northeast and Midwest. During the tourist season, Lang and his wife would meet every arriving Atlantic Coast Line train and personally welcome the visitors. Tourists tripled in number every year during Lang's time as mayor.

Lang had come to St. Petersburg a wealthy man from the sale of his laundry, and real estate investments in St. Petersburg made him even wealthier. When he left office, he had both the means and the time to pursue and nurture baseball spring training for his adopted home, and baseball became his life's work. In St. Petersburg, he became known as Mr. Baseball. In the baseball world, he was known as Mr. St. Petersburg, or Sunshine Al. Encouraged by the success of the Phillies camp in 1915, Lang went to New York in the fall of 1920 with the notion of bringing not just one but two teams to St. Petersburg. "We laughed at him," remembered sportswriter Dan Daniel, "and said, 'Go back to that dump if you like it so well.'" But Lang's enthusiasm could not be blunted by insult. Six feet tall and rail thin, with angular features—he looked a bit like a cross between Connie Mack and Judge Kenesaw Mountain Landis—he was gregarious, active, energetic, a put-his-hand-on-your-shoulder, look-you-in-the-eye conversationalist. "He loved to talk with [people]," remembered a business associate. "He liked people. People liked him." Lang networked; the word in this context was decades away from coming into the language, but that was exactly what he was doing. He returned to Pittsburgh each summer to watch baseball and talk with baseball people. When the Chicago White Sox and New York Giants toured Europe in 1924, Lang went along as a guest of Charles Comiskey and John McGraw. He knew Grantland Rice, Ring Lardner, Damon Runyon, and virtually every other baseball writer from any newspaper worth reading. Those New York writers who had laughed at him in 1920 made him an honorary member of the National Sportswriters Association five years later. Back in St. Petersburg, he would prowl the press box, the dressing rooms, even the outfields during spring training workouts. He would talk to players, coaches, managers, owners, writers, and fans. "I thought I knew as many men in baseball as anyone," said Commissioner Landis at one point in the mid-twenties, "but Al Lang's friendships are deeper and wider."

St. Petersburg was without a spring training team when Lang left the mayor's office in 1920. The Phillies had left during World War I, the ball field at Coffee Pot Bayou was turned to parkland. Only the Indianapolis team from the American Association made its way to St. Petersburg in 1920. But in 1921, Lang helped to secure, on behalf of the city's park board, a ninety-nine-year lease on a piece of land at the water's edge at the foot of First Avenue South. It was one of the last parcels of waterfront property to be secured for public use. Spring training baseball would be played there for more than eighty-five years.

Lang spearheaded a private fund-raising campaign under the auspices of the St. Petersburg Athletic Club, the group that ran the minor league St. Petersburg Saints of the Florida State League. The campaign raised $20,000 for the construction of a wooden grandstand at what was already being called Waterfront Park. Lang had already exacted a promise from the Boston Braves' owner, George Grant, to bring his club to the new facility in the spring of 1922. Despite a devastating hurricane in the fall of 1921, Waterfront Park was ready in time for the Braves' arrival on March 5, 1922. The park was hailed as "the finest athletic field in the state, if not the entire South." But its most remarkable feature—on opening day in 1922 and for the eight decades that followed—was its setting. Just beyond the outfield grass were the sparkling waters of Tampa Bay. The grandstand had seats for 1,200, with "twenty private boxes, wide and convenient entrances and exits, two box offices [and] retiring rooms and toilets for both sexes." In a nod to modernity, the grounds of the park even contained "parking facilities for twenty-five automobiles, directly back of first base." The clubhouse, too, was state of the art, with locker, shower, and lavatory facilities.

No community had ever done more for a major league team than St. Petersburg did for the Braves. Lang and his brethren in the city's business and civic community clearly expected the community's investment to be returned many fold, in the increasingly precious coin of good publicity. Waterfront Park, explained the St. Petersburg Athletic Club in an open letter to the community prior to the park's opening, would bring free advertising that no amount of money could buy:

> There can be no cleaner, no more penetrating, no more exhaustive, no more honest advertising for your city and its marvelous climate, than the letters and telegrams to their home papers, sport journals, etc...., written from this city by the high-class competent correspondents and writers who always accompany these major league ball clubs during their spring training trips....
> Already the great journals of Boston and New England, New York, Brooklyn, Philadelphia, Washington and Baltimore,

Chicago, Detroit, Cleveland, Cincinnati and Pittsburg[h] and other cities . . . [and] all the sporting magazines and journals of the country at large, have carried column after column telling the story of the rapidly approaching visit of this Boston league team to St. Petersburg and what this city has done and will do for its reception and entertainment.

When the Braves came to St. Petersburg in 1922, there were only three other teams taking spring training in Florida. The Senators were across the bay in Tampa, the Phillies near the center of the state in Leesburg, and the Dodgers in Jacksonville. The rest of major league baseball was still scattered about Georgia, Louisiana, Texas, and California. Lang was determined that Florida would become the center of the spring training world. Year after year, he continued proselytizing on behalf of not only St. Petersburg, but Florida in general. He delighted in calling attention to every frost in Georgia or to a freak snow squall that canceled a White Sox game in Shreveport in 1926. Al Lang would help to bring Florida cities and major league teams together, and while he probably gets more credit than he deserves for fathering Florida spring training—he became a darling of his new friends in the newspaper game, and some 1920s clippings call him the man responsible for bringing virtually all of major league baseball to Florida—the fact is that in the years Al Lang worked to make Florida the center of the spring training world, Florida became just that, and nobody played a more central role. From four teams in 1922, the Grapefruit League grew to nine teams in 1925. A decade later, twelve of the sixteen major league teams trained in Florida, and people in the state talked about the day in the near future when every team would set up springtime camp in the Sunshine State. (That never quite happened. The closest Florida came was during the late forties and early fifties, when fourteen of the sixteen major league teams trained in the state.)

Less than four decades after Ted Sullivan, Connie Mack, and the rest of the 1880s Washington club had been turned away from every respectable hotel in Jacksonville, baseball was now ensconced in as opulent and as socially genteel a setting as Florida could muster. Each year during spring training, Lang would host a dinner at the Jungle Country Club and Hotel, one of a series of elegant, new luxury hotels that rose in the 1920s—the Rolyat, the Don CeSar, and the Vinoy Park were among the others—to serve the growing number of wealthy northerners who'd begun spending all or part of their winters in St. Petersburg. At first, Lang's dinners were just for the baseball people and the writers—most particularly, the writers. "When the baseball scribes come, Al gives them the freedom of the city and in entertainment and refreshments he furnishes everything a sport writer could desire," wrote one observer in the mid-1920s. "As a result, columns of publicity for St. Petersburg flow from the Coronas and the north reads again of the man who has even been accused of starting the Florida boom." As the years passed, the baseball dinners became a highlight on the St. Petersburg winter calendar. St. Petersburg rivaled St. Augustine, Palm Beach, Miami, and Key West as Florida's top tourist destinations.

And then Babe Ruth and the Yankees came to town.

After five years of tireless effort, Al Lang finally realized his dream of bringing a second team to St. Petersburg when he convinced Yankees owner Jake Ruppert to move the Yankees from New Orleans for their 1925 camp. Ruppert wanted out of New Orleans, and Ruth was the reason. The brothels and speakeasies of Bourbon Street were proving a counterbalance to the daily workouts when it came to the Yankees star and too great a distraction to the franchise. While not exactly bereft of temptation—and Ruth could find an opportunity for sin in a church—Lang's green-bench St. Petersburg was more in keeping with the sort of image Ruppert was trying to cultivate for the Yankees. It was also the off-season home of Yankees manager Miller Huggins. Huggins would become as much of a salesman for St. Petersburg as Lang. "Think of me" when you're covering those football games, Huggins said by way of goodbye to the sportswriters after the World Series one year. "I'll be in a small boat away out in the bay, a fishing pole in my hands.... I'll be smoking my pipe and catching fish and I'll think of you and feel sorry for you." An extra six weeks in St. Petersburg every year was exactly to Huggins' liking.

With the Yankees' arrival, St. Petersburg became the unquestioned center of the spring training universe; for wherever Babe Ruth went, newspaper writers followed.

Babe Ruth was the first baseball player that American newspapers paid their own money to cover. Before Ruth, and in many cases for many decades thereafter, baseball writers traveled on the ball club's dime. It was a simple, sound investment on the part of the club owners: the cost of an upper berth, a $3-a-night hotel room, and a handful of fifty-cent meals was a small price to pay for the column after column of free publicity their business was getting in the newspaper every day. But Babe Ruth was a story that could not be contained within the parameters of a simple, single game story. "Laughing but earnest men in fedoras and off-the-rack suits, sportswriters, watched the sun rise and fall on his big head and were moved to grand statements," wrote biographer Leigh Montville. "They typed the legend into place, adding layer upon layer of adjectives until often the man in the middle couldn't even be seen." The new kid on the New York newspaper block, the tabloid *Daily News*, seized the Ruth initiative better than the older papers. It assigned one reporter—a Great War veteran by the name of Marshall Hunt—to cover not the game but the Babe. "What was more important," asked Montville, "how the runs were scored or where the great man went to dinner? The double that won the game or the raccoon coat the Babe wore when he left the clubhouse? He was the object of public fascination. He was the star, everyone else on both teams only bit players in this daily tragedy or comedy. He was the one who sold papers."

And now, for six weeks every year, the datelines these stories would carry would be: St. Petersburg, Fla.

The dispatches back to the big city's dozen or so daily newspapers, with their millions of readers, told of alligators in the outfield and tape-measure home runs, of contract demands and the hotels where the contract details were finally agreed to: the Princess Martha, the Yankees' team headquarters, where Colonel Ruppert stayed, and the Rolyat, where the Babe stayed. They talked of golf games at the Jungle Club and fishing excursions out on the bay. They did not, however, mention the bathtub in the Babe's suite at the Rolyat, filled every night with the finest in Prohibition liquor, nor the Babe's midnight tryst with a waitress in the sands of St. Petersburg beach. It was as if Al Lang had edited the copy.

The Babe gave way to Lou Gehrig, who gave way to Joe DiMaggio, who stepped aside for Mickey Mantle. Joe McCarthy replaced Miller Huggins, and Casey Stengel ultimately replaced him, as the Yankees and St. Petersburg became almost as synonymous as the Yankees and the Bronx.

The Braves left St. Petersburg for Bradenton after 1935, but were replaced the following year by the St. Louis Cardinals, an infinitely more appealing team. These were the Gas House Gang Cardinals of Dizzy Dean, Pepper Martin, Frankie Frisch, and Joe Medwick, winners of four National League pennants since 1926, three times the World Series champions. The Cardinals were a team still very much at the top of their game. Four more times in the coming decade they would play in the World Series, winning another three of them.

Not only was St. Petersburg the only city with two spring training teams, but it had what were arguably the two most appealing teams in all of baseball. And Lang was determined to keep them happy. In 1939—the most melancholy of all St. Petersburg springs because it was during spring training that baseball saw the first, unmistakable signs and writers began reporting to readers that something was seriously wrong with Lou Gehrig—the Cardinals and Yankees came to the city with a list of concerns about Waterfront Park. The park was too small to handle the crowds now coming to spring training games. But Yankees general manager Ed Barrow and Cardinals owner Sam Breadon were more concerned about fire. There had been eleven fires in the Waterfront Park bleachers in 1939. None were serious, but they were ominous warnings of what might happen when thousands of people—a majority of them cigar and cigarette smokers—crowded into a structure that was effectively built of kindling. The time had come, the clubs told the city, to build a modern concrete-and-steel ballpark.

No one disagreed that a new park was necessary. There was, however, much disagreement about where it ought to go. The St. Petersburg Women's Club and a group calling itself the Southside Improvement Association wanted the ballpark off the waterfront. Citing the early twentieth-century civic mandate that the waterfront "must be held inviolate," the groups proposed a site near Woodlawn Park, about a mile away. The Cardinals and Yankees wanted the park to stay right where it was, arguing that the waterfront was where the people were and that attendance would suffer if the park were moved. Downtown businesspeople sided with the ball clubs. Naturally reluctant to support anything that took potential customers away from downtown, the business owners argued that, if the clubs were right, and attendance dwindled, the Cardinals and Yankees would inevitably look elsewhere for their spring training.

The waterfront preservationists carried the day. The city council voted in May 1939 to build a new ballpark at Woodlawn Park, and they further voted that it should be called "Al Lang Field." But events intervened, and Al Lang Field in Woodlawn Park was never built. The city had worked out arrangements with the federal government to have various Works Progress Administration crews provide the labor for the new ballpark, but red tape delayed the start of the project by more than two years, and by that time World War II had begun. The first season after the war ended was a time for baseball and its spring training cities to become reacquainted and, in some cases, was a chance for teams to find new homes. Once St. Petersburg was assured that the Yankees and Cardinals wished to resume their springtime visits, work finally began on getting them their new ballpark.

There was no discussion this time around of siting the park anywhere but where it had always been; it was built just 100 yards south of the old Waterfront Park, with the same intoxicating view of the bay. And there was never any question but that it would be named for Al Lang. Construction started after the close of the 1946 Grapefruit League season, and on March 13, 1947, baseball and St. Petersburg gathered on the waterfront to honor Al Lang. The new ballpark had 4,300 seats, but temporary bleachers from all over the west coast of Florida were brought in to handle the opening-day crowd of more than 8,000. In addition to the Yankees' and Cardinals' organizations, those on hand that day included baseball commissioner Happy Chandler; Connie Mack, a longtime Lang friend even though the Athletics had never trained in St. Pete; Honus Wagner, the Hall of Fame shortstop whom Lang had known since his Pittsburgh days; and Grantland Rice, the ubiquitous sportswriter who made his spring training headquarters at the Vinoy Park hotel, just a short way up the waterfront from the new field. The Cardinals beat the Yankees in that first game. Stan Musial hit a home run. Lang was in the press box during the game, talking to the writers. He was in the locker room after the game, talking to the players. Just as always.

Al Lang died on February 27, 1960, just a few days before the beginning of another spring training season. He was eighty-nine. The Cardinals and Yankees postponed the openings of their camps by one day so players and team officials could attend the funeral. Musial, baseball commissioner Ford Frick, Yankees general manager George Weiss, Cardinals owner Augie Busch, and sportswriters Arthur Daley and Dan Parker were among the 1,000 mourners. Sharing newspaper space with the stories of Lang's death that spring were rumors that the Yankees might soon take their spring training out of St. Petersburg. Fort Lauderdale—a fast-growing outpost on the Atlantic coast, then best known as the raucous home of spring break, the annual loosing of the college students—was luring the Yankees with promises of a new stadium. The Yankees owners, Del Webb and Dan Topping, both had Fort Lauderdale ties; Webb had business interests there, and Topping berthed his yacht in Fort Lauderdale. These facts alone made the move inevitable; baseball teams have always trained where their owners wanted them to. But no one in 1960 St. Petersburg could believe it. "I know they're the Yankees and all that, but they've made a mistake or two, too, ya know," said Casey Stengel, "and in my opinion, moving out of St. Petersburg would be a mistake. I'll take it over any place they ever put a club."

Save for the war years, when no one traveled, the Yankees had been in St. Petersburg for thirty-five years. No team had ever had a longer association with one community; no one was even close. The next longest running affiliations—the Senators and Orlando, the Tigers and Lakeland, the Cardinals and St. Petersburg—were shorter by some ten years. But the Yankees did leave, and an era ended.

A year later, though, the Mets came to town, and they brought Casey Stengel with them. Nobody was ever a bigger friend to the newspapermen than Casey Stengel; he'd always called the writers "my boys" when he was with the Yankees. His return to St. Petersburg kindled a fresh bonfire of the baseball-gods-are-in-their-heaven-and-all-is-right-with-the-world stories bearing St. Petersburg datelines. St. Petersburg no longer really needed the newspaper writers to spread the word; it was a major city by the early sixties, with a stable tourism trade. But the baseball people still kept track. In the spring when Al Lang died, E. C. "Robbie" Robison, Lang's longtime friend, sometime rival, and now the chair of the city's baseball committee, reported to the board of governors of the Greater St. Petersburg Chamber of Commerce that the recently concluded spring training season had generated 1,145,000 words in the nation's newspapers. Additionally, there had been thirty-nine hours of radio broadcasts devoted to St. Petersburg spring training baseball and one telecast of a Yankees game back to New York that was seen by an estimated 2.5 million people. A survey of patrons at Al Lang Field showed that 71 percent gave spring training baseball as their primary reason for wintering in St. Petersburg; another 19 percent gave it as their secondary reason.

Al Lang was gone; the Yankees were gone. But St. Petersburg would remain the capital of spring training baseball for another third of a century.

THREE

Spring Training Takes Root

Right around the time that Al Lang's evangelism was beginning to bear fruit, and a critical mass of major league teams were taking their spring training in Florida, the phrase *Grapefruit League* began to enter the language. The earliest known use of the term was in 1923, when a Syracuse, New York, newspaper referred to Commissioner Kenesaw Landis "touring the orange and grapefruit league." Sporadic references followed; they became more common by the end of the decade when some newspapers began capitalizing the term. But it did not come into general use until after World War II. Not coincidentally, this was also when exhibition games began to increase in number. Before the war, teams were more inclined to keep to themselves, perhaps playing a few exhibitions against local college, semipro, or minor league teams before partnering with another major league team at the end of camp and barnstorming north together. The Grapefruit League in the twenties and thirties was less a league than it was a collection of individual outposts, each conducting its own business in front of its own small colony of reporters.

It was also during these years that fans and newspaper readers back north began to feel a connection to a handful of Florida cities because of the datelines—the same datelines now, year after year—that would appear in the newspapers of the great cities. In addition to St. Petersburg, New York newspapers regularly carried stories datelined Sarasota, Fla.—where John McGraw and the Giants trained beginning in 1924—and Clearwater, Fla., where Charles Ebbets brought his Brooklyn Dodgers from 1923 to 1932. Readers in Cincinnati and then Washington learned of a small central-state city named Orlando. Bradenton became a part of the vocabulary for baseball fans in St. Louis, Philadelphia, and Boston, as the Cardinals, Phillies, and Red Sox followed one another in succession to that Manatee County town. Philadelphia fans also knew of Fort Myers—where Connie Mack and the Athletics had found a home—and of a central Florida hamlet filled with lakes, with the melodic name of Winter Haven, where the Phillies trained for a decade after leaving Bradenton. Another small central Florida town—Lakeland—became familiar to Cleveland readers in the 1920s, though it would soon be Detroit readers who would come to know that town the best.

These articles contained stories of veteran pitchers trying new pitches and hitters finding their batting eye; journalists wrote of young prospects, their contracts just purchased from Nashville or Newark or Louisville, kids with live arms who were befuddling the veteran hitters, or kids with sure hands and quickness around the bag, the likes of which the local nine had not seen in many seasons. They quoted managers expecting to improve upon last year's record, unless last year had produced a pennant, in which case the managers' quotes talked of repeating.

But these stories contained other things too. Writers wrote of hotel porches that looked out upon the shimmering aqua waters of the Gulf of Mexico; of bath-like gulf waters, sport fishing, boating, and golf; of palm trees, exotic flowers, and birds. And for some readers, these now-familiar places of which the newspaper writers wrote became more than datelines in a newspaper. For the affluent—and in the booming twenties, affluence was decidedly more egalitarian than it had ever been before—these spring training towns became winter vacation destinations. The boom times wouldn't last, but these towns retained their cache in the chilly North through the Depression and into the war years.

By the late 1930s, after some musical-chair moving in the twenties and thirties—generally to the same cities—exactly one-half of major league teams had settled into long-term Florida homes. The Yankees and Cardinals were in St. Petersburg; the Braves in Bradenton; the Red Sox in Sarasota; the Reds in Tampa; the Dodgers back in Clearwater after some mid-decade jumping around; the Senators in Orlando; the Tigers in Lakeland. Seven of the other eight teams were transients, moving throughout Florida, Georgia,

Alabama, Louisiana, Texas, and California and seldom staying more than a year or two in any one spot, as there was always a better deal to be had up the road. The sixteenth team was the Chicago Cubs, which would spend nearly thirty years on Catalina Island off the coast of California.

World War II took away all of spring training's hard-won stability.

In the early weeks of 1942, just after the holidays, when baseball officials and players normally began turning their thoughts to spring training, the game and its people were instead paralyzed by uncertainty. The nation's industrial complex was going through a wholesale changeover from the production of consumer goods to filling the voracious and far-reaching needs of the military. Rationing of food, clothing, and gasoline would soon be in effect. Within days of the declaration of war in December 1941, a German U-boat sank a freighter just twenty miles off the coast of Long Island. Where did baseball fit into this new reality? Would there even be anyone to play baseball? Recruiting stations and draft boards were turning thousands of civilians into soldiers every day.

In their annual winter meetings during the week after the bombing of Pearl Harbor, major league owners tentatively drew up a normal schedule for the 1942 season. But a month later, they had no idea whether they would be able to play it, or if they should. They went to Commissioner Landis and asked him to seek clarification from the government. In a handwritten letter, dated January 14, the commissioner asked President Franklin Roosevelt for direction. "The time is approaching when, in ordinary conditions, our teams would be heading for spring training camps," he wrote. "However, inasmuch as these are not ordinary times, I venture to ask what you have in mind as to whether professional baseball should continue to operate."

Roosevelt answered the next day. His letter, later known as the "green-light" letter, has become one of the most famous pieces of correspondence in baseball history; a poster-sized reproduction hangs in the Hall of Fame in Cooperstown. "[T]he final decision about the baseball season must rest with you and the Baseball Club owners," the president wrote, "so what I am going to say is solely a personal and not an official point of view":

I honestly feel that it would be best for the country to keep baseball going. There will be fewer people unemployed and everybody will work longer hours and harder than ever before.

And that means that they ought to have a chance for recreation and for taking their minds off their work even more than before.

Baseball provides a recreation which does not last over two hours or two hours and a half, and which can be got for very little cost. And, incidentally, I hope that night games can be extended because it gives an opportunity to the day shift to see a game occasionally.

As to the players themselves, I know you agree with me that individual players who are of active military or naval age should go, without questions, in the services. Even if the actual quality of the teams is lowered by the use of older players, this will not dampen the popularity of the sport.

Roosevelt was a baseball fan, a regular at Griffith Stadium in Washington, and he had apparently been lobbied in advance of Landis's letter by his friend Clark Griffith, the Senators' owner, who urged him to let baseball go forward. But Roosevelt was also an astute politician and an intuitive leader who understood that Americans were going to need all the normalcy they could get in the years ahead. Major league baseball was an anchor of American life. How much Roosevelt's decision may have helped morale at home is not measurable. But in letters home to their families and in interviews with newspaper reporters, there is considerable testimony from soldiers abroad that following the pennant races—in *Stars and Stripes* or in the local papers that came in packages from home—buoyed spirits at the front.

Baseball would continue, but it would hardly be the same. Of the 400 players who had been on a major league roster at the close of the 1941 season, 61 had either been drafted or enlisted by the start of spring training in 1942. More would leave during the season. One hundred rookies played major league ball in 1942, the most in baseball history. At the close of the 1942 season, there was a wholesale exodus of ballplayers to the military, led by the enlistments of Ted Williams and Joe DiMaggio. By opening day the next spring, 219 men from the 1942 rosters were in active service. Still, 1942 was something of a last normal season. The clubs all traveled south for spring training, and most teams played the season with recognizable rosters.

By 1943, everything had changed, including spring training. Gas rationing had taken effect in December 1942. Americans were limited to four gallons per week, allowing about sixty miles of driving, enough it was determined, to get an American back and forth to work, the grocery store, and church. Roosevelt banned all driving for pleasure or recreation. Rationing on business travel was no less onerous; businesses had to justify their travel costs to the federal Office of Defense Transportation. In December 1942, Joseph B. Eastman, the director of that office, had asked Commissioner Landis and the league presidents to present a plan as to how major league baseball could meet its travel requirements "without waste in space or mileage." A month later, Landis delivered his response. For the duration of the war, major league baseball teams would take their spring training in the North. Landis decreed that all camps must be north of the Mason-Dixon line and east of the Mississippi and must be as close as possible to each team's base of operations. The two St. Louis teams, already west of the Mississippi, were not bound by the map but were told they must find facilities equally close to home. Eastman made the announcement: "I approve of baseball's cooperation with the war effort, and I'd say baseball's cooperation with us might serve as a pattern for the nation." Not only was baseball a morale booster, it was a role model for self-sacrifice as well.

Teams looked first to local colleges with indoor training facilities. *New York Times* columnist Arthur Daley noted that the Midwest teams were at an advantage in this search. "The baseball fathers have been searching throughout the East for colleges with field houses which may be available for spring training," he wrote. "Although no self-respecting Midwest school would think of doing without a field house, the Atlantic seaboard has mighty few of them." In the end, only a handful of teams would opt for school field houses, and three of those would be in the East. The Red Sox trained at Tufts University in suburban Medford, Massachusetts, the Senators at the University of Maryland; the Braves found a home at the Choate School in Connecticut. In the Midwest, the Reds trained at Indiana University, and the Indians went to Purdue. Four teams trained in Indiana. Newspaper stories noted that a "Limestone League" was taking over for the Grapefruit League. The Cubs and White Sox trained together in the resort community of French Lick; the Tigers were in Evansville; and the Pirates in Muncie. The two St. Louis teams traveled south along the Mississippi; the Browns trained in Cape Girardeau, the Cardinals across the river in Cairo, Illinois. Back east, everyone found spring homes within fifty miles of their cities. The weather was predictably lousy. The Dodgers, training at Bear Mountain, New York, had some limited access to the field house at West Point. They needed it, for the field at Bear Mountain was snow covered and in the shadow of a ski jump; the newspaper photos of the day of their arrival showed the players in topcoats, throwing snowballs for the camera.

Some made the best of it, such as Cardinals manager Billy Southworth. "That occasional indoor drill is a good break, rather than an interruption in our routine," he said. "You see, the early outdoor work makes the muscles sore and the indoor work warms them up and takes out the soreness. I believe we have hit upon an excellent way of getting into condition." Others grumbled. "I am getting ready a club for play in sunlight, on a field. I am not training a basketball team or a track squad. I am dead set against training indoors," said Yankees manager Joe McCarthy. Some of the few veterans still playing rebelled against trying to play baseball in the midst of a northern winter. Carl Hubbell of the Giants, forty years old, refused to go outside and, according to the *Sporting News*, did nothing but play Ping-Pong all spring. He still managed to go 11–8 during the regular season, and in 1943—his last season in the majors—he skipped spring training altogether.

Reflecting all of life on the home front, most simply coped. With meat, butter, sugar, milk, shoes, tires, gasoline, and dozens of other consumer goods all rationed; with 12 million Americans serving in uniform; with the manufacture of baseballs themselves threatened by a shortage of horsehide and a rationing of cork, the 400 men still playing major league baseball— veterans like Carl Hubbell, career minor leaguers past draft age, and assorted 4-Fs, including one-armed outfielder Pete Gray—were not about to complain too loudly about not being able to go to Florida. They prepared the best they could in the gyms and chilly fields of the North, knowing that everyone they'd be playing during the season was doing the same.

When the war ended in 1945, Americans craved a return to prewar days, to have everything be just the way it was. That, of course, was quite impossible. America was moving forward. Veterans were going to college on the G.I. Bill, or heading to the fresh air and open spaces of the suburbs, into greater affluence, into a gradually more integrated society. Yet Americans wished to begin that move forward from the point where things had stopped, not so much to forget the war as to compartmentalize it. With its military veterans back in the fold, baseball in 1946 picked up where it had left off in 1942. After three springs in the North, twelve of the sixteen major league teams returned to the Florida cities they had left behind in 1942, many of them cities that were already becoming identified with their teams: Orlando and the Senators; Tampa and the Reds; St. Petersburg and the Yankees and Cardinals; Sarasota and the Red Sox. And there was Lakeland and the Tigers, a connection that continues to this day.

Lakeland was a bustling little midstate city of 25,000 when the Tigers first arrived in 1934. Born as a railroad hub in the 1880s, it quickly became a center for citrus farming and even tourism for a time in the 1920s. It had a picture-postcard downtown; hotels and offices and shops sprouted on the edges of Lake Wire and Lake Mirror. By the time of the Tigers' arrival, the Depression had taken its toll on Lakeland, but the Tigers and Frank Lloyd Wright—brought to Lakeland by Florida Southern College to build a "great education temple in Florida"—are credited with reversing Lakeland's decline almost before it began. The eighteen buildings that Wright designed for Florida Southern remain the greatest concentration of Wright buildings in the world. And the Tigers have been a part of Lakeland's identity for more than seven decades.

Lakeland had a nice, city-built stadium when the Tigers came to town. Clare Henley, a local druggist, for whom the field would ultimately be named, and a big baseball buff (he would own the Florida State League's Lakeland Highlanders during the 1920s), had urged its construction in 1922 as a means of attracting spring training. In the stadium's first year, Henley was able to attract only the minor league Louisville Colonels, but the Cleveland Indians followed one year later and stayed for five years in the mid-twenties. Then, Henley convinced Detroit owner Walter Briggs to bring the Tigers there in 1934. Henley Field accommodated 1,000 people, and there were small but modern clubhouses under the stands. The manager's office was more of a cage, set off from the rest of the clubhouse by chicken wire and big enough only for the manager himself. Reporters wishing to speak to the Tigers' manager through the years had to stand outside and speak to him through the chicken wire. The field was a ten- or fifteen-minute walk from downtown and the New Florida hotel, where the Tigers stayed.

From a baseball management perspective, Lakeland was an ideal place to train. Restaurants were limited. Bars were nonexistent; Lakeland was a dry town until the early sixties. "Lakeland was so quiet in those days that the only places open after eight o'clock were the phone booths," wrote Joe Falls, who covered spring training in Lakeland for a half-century for three different Detroit newspapers.

Lakeland was also segregated. Because it wouldn't take their black players, the Tigers left the New Florida hotel in the early sixties, moving up the road to a Holiday Inn that would. But the black players were still barred from most of Lakeland's restaurants. They generally ate with families in their homes in the black section of town. But a couple of times during each camp in the 1960s, outfielder Willie Horton would set up a barbeque outside his room at the Holiday Inn. He got a fifty-five-gallon drum, cut it in half, and filled both halves with charcoal, roasting ribs, chickens, steaks, and anything else "that wouldn't fall though the grate."

"The parties would go on until midnight," reported Joe Falls, "and then, at the crack of dawn, there'd be Willie in his rubber suit running around the lake, trying to work off the extra pounds from the night before."

Marcus Marchant got to Lakeland at about the same time as the Tigers. He had nothing to do with the Tigers coming but everything to do with their staying for more than seventy years. Marchant was "Joker" Marchant to one and all. Nobody used his given name; few in Lakeland even knew it. A gregarious, unpretentious man with an ever-present cowboy hat and a sense of humor that left no doubt about how he came by his nickname, Marchant had come to Lakeland to play football for Florida Southern College and stayed around, taking a job as a lifeguard with the city of Lakeland in 1939 and eventually being named director of the city's Parks and Recreation Department in 1946, the year of the Tigers' return. As the director of parks and recreation, Marchant nurtured the Lakeland-Tigers relationship and helped it grow. By the early 1950s, the Tigers needed more space than Henley Field could offer. They wanted to spread out for their workouts; they especially wanted to bring their minor leaguers to camp with them. Marchant took them out to the site of the former Lodwick School of Aeronautics, which, under contract to the government, had trained thousands of pilots for service during World War II. A mile or so north of Henley Field, it had barracks and lots of flat land, and it now belonged to the city. In the spring of 1953, this became "Tigertown," with major and minor league practice fields and buildings for meals and meetings. The Tigers continued to play their exhibition games at Henley Field but shifted everything else to Tigertown.

A decade later, Henley Field finally grew too small to serve the needs of a major league spring training game. Again it was Marchant, still the parks and rec director, who brokered the construction of a 5,000-seat, $500,000 stadium adjacent to Tigertown. When the new stadium was ready to open in 1966, the Tigers and the city were in full agreement that the stadium be named Marchant Stadium. Marchant was properly touched by the honor, but too much the joker to acknowledge it with a straight face. "Y'all put the peanut shells in your pockets and don't be messing up my new stadium," he warned the crowd in his dedication-day speech.

Finally, there was Vero Beach and the Dodgers. Nothing in spring training has so burrowed itself into the hearts and minds of all of baseball as Dodgertown and Vero Beach. Born in 1948 out of surplus war buildings, segregation, and the singular and peculiar baseball genius of Branch Rickey, Dodgertown has a heritage that is matched only by its physical beauty. Royal palms line the outfield berm, framing the ever-pleasing green-brown-white geometry of the field, providing a perfect theater for the chatter of the players, the crack of the bat, and the snap of ball hitting glove. The orange trees are gone now, but for years the fragrance of citrus blossoms from an adjacent, Dodger-owned orange grove permeated the grounds. During its heyday, Dodgertown comprised more than 400 acres consisting of orange groves, golf courses, and quiet pathways and streets named for Dodger Hall of Famers. There were accommodations for 200 and a full-service kitchen, a conference center, tennis courts, a swimming pool, and a movie theater. It had six practice fields long before six practice fields were fashionable, a modern clubhouse, and the exquisitely unmodern 6,500-seat Holman Stadium, a reach-out-and-touch-the-players throwback that *Baseball America* called "the most fan friendly" park in all of baseball. It had, moreover, the ghosts of Rickey and Robinson; Campanella, Hodges, and Snider; Koufax, Drysdale, and Wills; the Walters Alston and O'Malley; Garvey, Lopes, Cey, and Russell. The past permeated the present at Dodgertown as at almost no other spring training site; it always had a Yankee Stadium, Fenway Park, Wrigley Field kind of allure. And it had permanence. From Brooklyn to Los Angeles, from Don Newcombe to Derek Lowe, Dodgertown was a constant, something that became a part of everyone who ever wore the Dodgers uniform. "We have a college campus atmosphere, here," said former shortstop and longtime instructor Maury Wills. He referred not only to the pastoral setting, but to the sense of place and time and the shared camaraderie that Dodgertown engendered in all who spent a springtime there.

Like so very much in modern Dodger history, the story of Dodgertown is inextricably linked to the story of Jackie Robinson. Robinson's first spring training in organized ball, with the International League's Montreal Royals in 1946, was an awkward beginning to Branch Rickey's great experiment. Rickey had chosen Daytona Beach for the 1946 camp after exacting a promise from the mayor of the city that Robinson and African American teammate John Wright would be welcome. But "welcome" was relative for blacks in postwar Florida. Members of the Brooklyn club and Robinson's teammates on the Royals all lived at the oceanside Riviera hotel; Robinson and Wright stayed at a private home near Bethune-Cookman College. Their teammates dined together at the Riviera; Robinson and Wright ate alone with their wives at black-owned restaurants. The Royals canceled a game in Jacksonville after being told by local authorities that they could not field their black players; in Sanford, the local chief of police came onto the field during the third inning of a game and ordered Montreal manager Clay Hopper to remove Robinson from the field.

Robinson bore the indignities in steely silence, but Rickey seethed. The Dodgers' president wished to protect his black players, certainly, but he was also interested in building a cohesive team. He understood that was impossible with 90 percent of the team living together, and the black players notably elsewhere. Rickey in 1947 took spring training to Havana, a mixed blessing, for while the black and white players still lived in separate hotels, there was a long Cuban heritage of blacks and whites playing on the same field. But training in Cuba also meant the team was forced to fly to Florida for exhibition games. The compromises of Florida seemed less onerous than the compromises of Cuba, so Rickey resigned himself to working around Jim Crow and began looking for a site in Florida for 1948. Word of Rickey's search reached a Vero Beach businessman named Bud Holman, who called Rickey in the fall of 1947. Holman told Rickey what he had to offer, and suddenly Rickey began thinking that perhaps he wouldn't have to compromise too much after all.

Holman wanted Rickey to look at an abandoned naval air station. The navy had trained 3,500 people in Vero Beach during the war, greatly expanding the city's small airport and building barracks, a dining hall, and an auditorium/recreation building across the street. Surrounding these buildings, Holman explained, were large tracts of flat ground that could easily be transformed into baseball fields.

Bud Holman was the proprietor of the Vero Beach Cadillac Company, but automobiles were not all he sold. After helping to get the Vero Beach airport launched in the late 1920s, he persuaded his friend Eddie Rickenbacker, the World War I flying ace and the head of Eastern Airlines, to make the tiny airfield a refueling stop on Eastern's Jacksonville-to-Miami run. By 1935, Eastern had established a small passenger terminal at the airport, and Vero Beach also had direct airmail service. It was the smallest community in the country to have either. Holman became Eastern's local manager and, later, airport manager. He was still airport manager in 1947, seeking a money-generating use for the 1,000 acres of airport land that the federal government had recently returned to the city of Vero Beach.

Vero Beach in 1947 was largely agricultural, home to dairy farms and beef ranches and the heart of Florida citrus country. It had long been a stop on Henry Flagler's Florida East Coast Railroad, but it was not a stop where many visitors got off. The fifteen miles of the city's barrier island were largely sand and jungle and were connected to the mainland by a one-lane wooden bridge that swayed in the wind and shook violently when a car crossed it.

On November 2, 1947, Buzzie Bavasi, then thirty-one years old and general manager of the Dodgers' Nashua, New Hampshire, club, took the Florida East Coast train to Vero Beach and was met at the station by Holman and newly elected Vero Beach mayor Merrill Barber. Bavasi had been charged with inspecting the Vero Beach facilities, as well as possible sites a little farther south in Fort Pierce and Stuart. Holman and Barber showed Bavasi the air station facilities and then showed him an evening's hospitality at Holman's cattle ranch in the westernmost reaches of Indian River County. They monopolized his time to the point where he never did get back on the train to look at what Fort Pierce and Stuart had to offer.

The old naval air station appealed to Rickey on two counts. First, the barracks and dining hall would be under the Dodgers' control and therefore free of the local segregation ordinances. Second, the barracks had enough beds for all 600 men under contract to the Dodgers organization, and the virtually unlimited land in Vero Beach would allow Rickey to formalize what he liked to call the Dodger Baseball School and what the writers had taken to calling "Rickey University." Rickey, who started life wanting to be a Latin teacher, believed that baseball wasn't just learned, it could also be taught. "Men can imitate. Men can learn," he wrote. "They do, but sometimes, and very often indeed, men who rely upon their own observations, initiatives or adaptations do not improve very rapidly. Learning by imitation is a slow process. We really want to contribute something to the baseball education of boys, apart from what they get by their own observation."

In 1948, the Brooklyn team spent time in the Dominican Republic and played most of their exhibition games in Miami; the major leaguers did not get to Vero Beach until the end of camp and played a couple of exhibition games on a hastily built "Ebbets Field #2." It was 1949 before the major leaguers would take their full camp in Vero Beach. Nonetheless, Dodgertown—the name was established by the close of that first camp in 1948—was full of minor leaguers in 1948 and a source of media fascination. *Life* magazine devoted a cover story to this new sort of spring training. Jimmy Powers, a columnist for the New York *Daily News*, marveled at the sense of order in the small and sleepy community the Dodgers now called their spring home. "The Dodgers have an excellent rookie camp in Vero Beach," he wrote. "Vero Beach is much farther north than Miami, as a result too decent and too quiet for the hoodlum element to bother with."

Everybody who visited Dodgertown was fascinated by a web of poles and string that stretched in front of a row of home plates. Together with track meets, sliding pits, and other innovative training techniques, Rickey established what he called the "visible strike zone." The "strings area" became one of Dodgertown's signatures. Rickey explained its construction and its purpose as follows:

> Drive two six-foot poles twelve inches into the ground, fifteen feet apart. Place a home plate mid-way between the poles with the right angle apex of the plate exactly in line with the poles. Connect the poles with two parallel small strings, one shoulder high, the other knee high (top and bottom of the strike zone). Attach two very light strings to the top lateral string seventeen inches apart, and wind the string's bottom extensions one or two loops around the lower lateral string, the two loops also seventeen inches apart. The strings attached to the poles can be moved up or down to simulate the batsmen's various strike zones. A catcher, without any equipment, can safely work behind the strings. Regardless of where a batsman stands, the strings create a visible strike zone in the pitcher's mind. Pitching to the strings will accelerate the mastery of control, and pitchers, particularly the younger ones, should be given ample opportunity to use them.

Both on and off the field, conditions at Dodgertown in those early years were pretty spartan. The fields were more akin to those in sandlot ball than to the major leagues. Players would traverse the grounds carrying bats, lest they be surprised by a snake. The barracks, free of segregation ordinances, were bereft of heat and air conditioning as well. Players slept six or eight to a room, with the bathroom down the hall. Herman Levy, the Dodgertown mailman and night watchman, would blow a whistle each morning at six, rousting the players from a chilled or sweaty sleep. From their barracks, the players would follow a military-like regimen throughout the day. Breakfast, morning calisthenics en masse, a day of station-to-station drills—batting cages, sawdust sliding pits, bunting field, running track, lecture halls, pitchers and catchers in the strings area—all of it evaluated and graded by coaches with clipboards. In the evening, it was dinner—served on military surplus metal trays and eaten at one of three long, length-of-the-room tables—and back to the barracks. There were few cars on base (to Dodger old-timers, Dodgertown will always be "the base") in the early years, so there were few forays into town. Not that town was much of a draw. It didn't take long for players to give their spring home a new name: Zero Beach.

Dodgertown grew to be its own self-sufficient community and developed its own rhythms of life. Rickey asked the city to add a swimming pool to the grounds in 1949. When the city balked, Bud Holman fronted the money himself against proceeds from future spring training games. Pool tables, jukeboxes, and Ping-Pong tables were added to the barracks' rec rooms. Shuffleboard and tennis courts were added outside. A canteen— "Take All You Want, But Eat All You Take"—satisfied between-meal munchies. A laundry, post office, photo service, and barbershop followed in quick order. The barracks themselves, weed-strewn and paint-weary from three years of dormancy when the Dodgers first arrived, began to take on a more appealing luster.

One building was given over to the major league club and converted into two-man rooms with private baths and curtains on the windows. For the hundreds of minor leaguers, who still lived like World War II naval airmen in the barracks next door, the big league barracks were like Oz's Emerald City. Maury Wills spent nine springs in the minor league barracks before finally being called up to the big club in midseason 1959. "You wanted to get to the big club, not just to make more money, but to get to those big league barracks," he said. After starting all six games in the 1959 World Series, he anxiously awaited the beginning of spring training in 1960. "I wanted to get to those big league barracks." But when he arrived in camp in 1960, he found himself assigned once again—for the tenth straight year—to the minor league barracks. He asked Fresco Thompson, the Dodgers' vice president of minor league operations, why. "Just keep bustin' your ass," Thompson told him. While Wills had finished the '59 season in Los Angeles, there was no guarantee he'd start 1960 with the big club. There were four other shortstops in camp, including the erstwhile starter Don Zimmer, whose toe injury in 1959 had given Wills his chance. Thompson used the minor league billet as a motivating tool. You haven't proved anything yet, it told Wills. Just keep bustin' your ass. However comfortable and convenient the Dodger organization sought to make life for the players, nobody ever lost sight of the fact that Dodgertown was about growing baseball players. Just keep bustin' your ass. If you don't, one of those other 600 guys in camp is going to grab your job.

And some players, of course, faced pressures other than baseball. While life on base may have been a sanctuary, for the African American players it was also a necessity. Whatever their standing in the Dodger organization, beyond the gates of Dodgertown they were still in a segregated South. Jackie Robinson called it "like being confined to a reservation." He remembered bitterly when his wife and young son were denied a cab on base and told to wait instead for the "colored cab," a dilapidated school bus that ferried the domestic workers from their homes in the black neighborhood to their jobs in the kitchens and laundries of Vero Beach. Some of life's indignities even crept onto the base. The Dodgertown barbershop either would not or could not cut the hair of the black players; each spring, they chose one of their own for the task.

FOUR

A Sportswriter Helps to End Separate but Hardly Equal

Young men and women of principal have long been attracted to journalism because they believe it just might give them the chance to help change the world. Few ever do. It's a big world and largely resistant to change.

Wendell Smith helped to change the world. Twice.

Smith became a baseball writer because he couldn't become a baseball player—although he may have been good enough. In the presence of a Detroit Tigers scout in the early thirties, Smith pitched his American Legion team to a 1–0 win in a district playoff game. The Tigers' scout signed his battery mate* to a pro contract. He signed the pitcher that Smith had outdueled in the 1–0 game. And he told Smith, "I wish I could sign you too, kid. But I can't."

Wendell Smith, who had grown up in a largely white neighborhood, was the only African American in his high school class and on all the baseball teams he'd ever played on. He had never thought much about race. His father had been a chef for Henry Ford, and as a young boy he'd spent the days playing baseball with the Ford grandsons, Edsel, Benson, and Henry. Watching his catcher and the pitcher he had beaten be given a chance that

---

* Smith's catcher was Mike Tresh, who would play twelve years in the big leagues with the White Sox and Indians.

he could not have was his first brush with America's prejudice. "That broke me up," he said years later. "It was then that I made the vow that I would dedicate myself to do something in behalf of the Negro ballplayer."

Smith went to play baseball at West Virginia State College in Charleston, where he also started writing for the student newspaper. When he graduated in 1937, it was his writing skills that got him his chance. He was offered a job at the *Pittsburgh Courier*, the nation's leading black newspaper. He worked a year as a general assignment reporter and was then promoted to sports editor. The *Courier* was a crusader; during World War II, it pushed a "Double V" campaign—victory over fascism in Europe and victory over racism in the United States. Smith too had a crusader's heart, and he fit right in at the *Courier*.

While his primary responsibility at the paper was covering the Negro League's Pittsburgh Crawfords and the nearby Homestead Grays, Smith wrote about the major leagues when he could. The Pirates didn't make it easy for him; he was not welcome in the Forbes Field press box because he was not an accredited member of the Baseball Writers Association of America. In one of the most perfect examples of a Jim Crow Catch-22, he was denied entry into the writers association because he did not cover major league baseball on a daily basis. But Smith's interests were less with the Pirates' wins and losses than with the major league players' attitudes toward the Negro League players. So he haunted the lobby of the Schenley hotel, where the visiting National Leaguers stayed. He began every conversation with the question, "Have you seen any Negro ballplayers who you think could play in the major leagues?" During the 1938 season, he spoke with all eight National League managers and more than forty players. He reported to *Courier* readers that, contrary to the popular belief that there was widespread opposition among white major leaguers to playing with blacks, 75 percent of those to whom he'd spoken favored integrating the game. Smith's stories were picked up by the *Sporting News* and other white papers, which helped to put the subject of integration on baseball's agenda, where baseball, quite bluntly, did not wish it. In 1939, *Courier* publisher Ira Lewis was able to talk himself onto the agenda at the annual baseball owners meeting in New York, where he presented Smith's findings. "Gentlemen," he told the owners and the white reporters covering them, "there is a wealth of baseball talent out there and contrary to what people say, we believe these men can play major league baseball and that the majority of the players would tolerate them on their teams."

To no one's great surprise, the matter died there. But for the next decade, Wendell Smith was in the center of the fight to integrate the game. During the war, as part of the *Courier*'s Double V campaign, he repeatedly called for the integration of the game and slowly began to feel as though he were making progress. "People were becoming more conscious of this question," he said. "The public, the general public, was on our side. And baseball began to find itself mildly on the defensive. The owners began making excuses." Smith's incessant drumbeat was echoed by heavyweight white writers, such as Jimmy Powers and Dan Parker in New York, Shirley Povich in Washington, Warren Brown in Chicago, and Dave Egan in Boston. "It would seem as though every time there was a lull in the baseball news, these men would bring up the issue," said Smith. "Three or four times during the off-season. Hot stove stuff. The matter of integrating the game suddenly became a topic that baseball owners started finding difficult to ignore."

Smith complemented his writing with an active back-channel political campaign. During World War II, he came close to persuading Pirates owner Bill Benswanger to scout some Negro Leaguers with an eye to offering a tryout, but Benswanger got cold feet and backed out. Most notably, Smith got a Boston city councilor—under the threat of vetoing the teams' special permit to play Sunday baseball—to force the Red Sox and Braves to hold a tryout for three Negro League players in April 1945. Smith selected the players: Sam Jethroe, a twenty-three-year-old outfielder for the Cleveland Buckeyes; Marvin Williams, a twenty-five-year-old second baseman with the Philadelphia Stars; and Jackie Robinson, a twenty-six-year-old shortstop from the Kansas City Monarchs. The *Courier* paid the players' expenses to Boston.

That notorious tryout has entered the annals of history for the farce that it was; the Red Sox had no intention of integrating and were merely doing what was necessary to continue playing Sunday baseball. But it was the event that served to bring Wendell Smith and Branch Rickey together. At Rickey's request, Smith stopped in Brooklyn on his way home to Pittsburgh, and in Rickey's office the morning after the Fenway Park tryout, the two men talked about Negro League baseball players and specifically about Jackie Robinson. Rickey wanted to know what Smith knew of Robinson's temperament: was he "belligerent"? Rickey seemed more interested in the fact that Robinson went to UCLA, where he'd played on integrated teams, and grew up in an integrated world in California, than he did in the particulars of his baseball accomplishments. Rickey never told Smith that he was thinking about integrating organized ball; the cover was always that Rickey was thinking of linking up with the nascent United States League, a planned third Negro major league, and fielding a team called the Brooklyn Brown Dodgers, who would play at Ebbets Field while the white Dodgers were on the road. Nevertheless, Smith intuited from the beginning that Rickey had other plans. He flat out asked him if there was a chance that he was looking at Robinson for the Dodgers. Rickey was evasive; he didn't say yes, but he didn't deny it. Throughout the summer, as Brooklyn scouts followed Robinson and the Monarchs about the country, Rickey and Smith stayed in touch on the subject. In their letters and phone conversations, they never mentioned Robinson by name; he was always "the young man from the west."

Smith wrote not a word of what may have been the century's biggest baseball story, which he had exclusively. There would be time enough to write of Jackie Robinson, Smith knew. Doing so prematurely, he understood, could well ruin Rickey's delicate plan. For his part, Rickey also understood that the way the story was covered in the newspapers might well determine how things played out. In 1947, he persuaded Arthur Daley of the *New York Times* to sit on the story of Robinson's promotion to Brooklyn. "I must hold you to your solemn world of honor," he told him. "This is the most important thing I ever did in my life and a premature leak could destroy it." But throughout the process of scouting, signing, and getting Robinson to the majors, when Smith was privy to every development weeks before any public announcement, Rickey never had to tell him how or when to write the story. Newspaperman though he was, Wendell Smith was far more concerned with seeing this through than he was in getting the word out. He was at the threshold of realizing the promise he'd made to himself as the disappointed teenager unable to pursue a career in pro baseball: "I would dedicate myself to do something in behalf of the Negro ballplayer."

After Robinson signed in the fall of 1945, Smith immediately understood that his organized baseball career would begin in the Jim Crow South and that, unless measures were taken to anticipate and address the oil-and-water challenges of playing integrated baseball in a segregated world, the noble experiment might collapse before it even began. Smith suggested to Rickey that he sign a black teammate for Robinson, so that at the very least, Robinson need not endure his trials alone. Smith suggested Kenny Washington, Robinson's UCLA football teammate. "I understand that he is a much better ball player than Robinson and that he plays in the outfield and infield," wrote Smith to Rickey. "He is a very intelligent person and, I understand, has a wonderful personality." Rickey decided instead on a pitcher named John Richard Wright. Wright was a twenty-seven-year-old New Orleans native who'd gone 30–1 with the Homestead Grays in 1943.*

But while Rickey did not take Smith's counsel on Washington, he did actively seek it in other areas. Knowing that the black players would not be allowed to stay in the Riviera hotel in Daytona Beach with the rest of the Dodgers and Montreal Royals, and knowing that finding suitable accommodations for a black man in the South would be a task largely beyond the experience of his white staff, Rickey asked Smith to find living arrangements for Robinson and Wright. "Most certainly I don't want to find ourselves embarrassed on March 1st because of Robinson's not having a place to stay," wrote Rickey on January 8. Rickey would in effect ask Smith to chaperone Robinson through his first spring training. "It is my understanding that you will be able to stay in Daytona Beach during the training period of about four weeks," he wrote to Smith. "This whole program was more or less your suggestion, as you will recall, and I think it had a good point because much harm could come if either of these boys were to do or say something or other out of turn." Smith eagerly accepted Rickey's entreaty. "I am most happy to feel that you are relying on my newspaper and me, personally, for cooperation in trying to accomplish this great move for practical Democracy in the most amiable and diplomatic manner possible," he responded in early 1946. "Now, Mr. Rickey, I want you to feel as though the publishers of the *Pittsburgh Courier* and I are a distinct part of this undertaking. We do not want you to take all of the responsibility with regards to help[ing] to strengthen these boys spiritually and morally for the part they are to play in this great adventure."

When Jackie Robinson and Rachel, his bride of just two weeks, had completed a tortured and humiliating trip from Robinson's home in Pasadena to his first spring training in Daytona Beach—the trip took more than

---

* There were a number of stories by white writers that first spring which suggested that Wright, who bore the unfortunate sobriquet "Needle Nose" from his Negro League days, was actually the better prospect. But he never made the big leagues, and in fact played just two games for the Montreal Royals in 1946 before voluntarily returning to the Homestead Grays. Smith felt that Wright was intimidated by the integrated game, and he would later write that the pitcher had "a tendency to choke up while laboring among the Caucasians" (nlbpa.com/wright_john; see also Rampersad, *Jackie Robinson*, p. 165).

thirty-six hours, during which they were bumped from a connecting flight in New Orleans, bumped again from a connecting flight in Pensacola, then forced to the last seat of the bus on a sixteen-hour bus ride across the state—Wendell Smith, together with *Courier* photographer Billy Rowe and John Wright were at the bus station to welcome them. Robinson was seething from the humiliation he and his wife had endured. "I never want another trip like that one," he said. Smith talked him down and told him to focus instead on the task at hand. For the next month, the four men—the two ballplayers and the two journalists—would be inseparable.

Smith had arranged lodging for the Robinsons at the home of Joe Harris, a local pharmacist and social activist known as "the Negro mayor of Daytona Beach," on a quiet, tree-lined street near Bethune-Cookman College. Robinson's isolation from his teammates was mitigated somewhat by the warmth of his hosts, the gentility of the neighborhood, and the celebrity status he enjoyed among the middle-class blacks of Daytona Beach.

The morning after his arrival, Robinson, Wright, Smith, and Rowe all left for Sanford, where the Royals would conduct their first week of workouts. Things turned bad very quickly. On the evening of the players' second day in Sanford, Smith was sitting on the porch of the home in the black neighborhood where the four men were staying when a white man approached and announced he had been sent by a delegation of 100 other whites. "We want you to get the niggers out of town," he told Smith, making it clear there would be trouble if they didn't. Smith called Rickey; Rickey told him to bring the players back to Daytona. Rickey had chosen Daytona Beach for baseball's first integrated spring training because he had been assured by city officials that there'd be no trouble from the community. Prior to the Dodgers' arrival, the mayor of Daytona Beach, William Perry, had made a public statement supporting the black players training in his city. "The city officials and the population in general simply regard them as two more ballplayers conditioning themselves here. We welcome them and wish them luck," said Perry. He equated Robinson and Wright with entertainers, and Daytona had always welcomed black entertainers. "No one gets excited when Cab Calloway comes here," he said. Daytona Beach was no cradle of enlightenment; it was just slightly less hostile than other southern cities. "Blacks lived a second-class existence there versus the third-class existence they lived elsewhere in the South," wrote historian Chris Lamb.

Wendell Smith never wrote of the Sanford threat to Robinson and Wright, and there were no similar incidents in Daytona Beach during that first spring. There were, instead, the day-to-day indignities. The black players could not go out to dinner with their white teammates; Smith and Rowe could not go out to dinner with the white writers. Smith was not allowed to sit in most of the Grapefruit League press boxes (he was allowed in Daytona). Instead, he would sit with Rachel Robinson and Billy Rowe in the Jim Crow bleachers and tell *Courier* readers of the history unfolding before him. Players and journalists alike bore these daily indignities stoically. Jackie Robinson's making the Montreal Royals was what mattered right now. The grandstand and Main Street could come next.

Smith was a crusader, not a bomb thrower. His approach was to push very hard against the door that was closed. Once the door opened, however, he entered with humility and a sense of appreciation rather than entitlement. Smith knew that, while he and his race most assuredly belonged, they were also most assuredly not warmly welcomed in those early days. If this great adventure were going to succeed, he believed, it needed to go off free of trouble. Toward that goal, he ended his spring training reporting with an epistle to black fans, explaining to them their role:

> Robinson and Wright [have] had pressure from two sides—the Negro fans and the job of making good. Now that they have made the team and are set for the long pennant grind, the Negro fans can help by taking some of the pressure off them. Cheering is all right at the proper time, but it is unnecessary before something has happened. It simply causes them to strain and tighten up.
>
> The Public Conduct item, however, is even more important. Drinking in the stands and rowdy deportment will only embarrass Robinson and Wright and hamper their efforts to reach the big leagues. Every owner in baseball will be watching Robinson and Wright—and also how you react, Mr. And Mrs. Negro Baseball Fan!
>
> Let's help these two players make the grade—good Public Conduct is the way to do it!

Readers flocked to the *Pittsburgh Courier* to read Wendell Smith's stories about Jackie Robinson. By the start of the 1947 season, the paper's circulation was 250,000 per week, the highest in its history.

The special relationship between Smith and Robinson that began during the 1946 spring training continued through the end of Robinson's rookie year in the majors in 1947. Smith traveled with Robinson for the entire 1947 season, from spring training in Havana to the World Series in New York, where he subtly but ever so proudly let *Courier* readers know that Jackie Robinson was not the only black man who had arrived by datelining his story "Press Box, Yankee Stadium, New York." He also was Robinson's ghostwriter for a column in the *Courier* that summer. Here too—in his writing under both Robinson's name and his own—he was still much more social activist than journalist. Determined to portray Robinson's presence in the major leagues as completely normal, he downplayed the death threats that Robinson received during his rookie year, never mentioned the tremendous strain that Robinson felt from carrying the weight of integrating the game. On the road, he was Robinson's roommate and traveling secretary, making all the arrangements for accommodations in cities where the team hotels still did not welcome blacks. He was paid $50 a week by Rickey, over and above his *Courier* salary. But he would have done it for nothing. He sought neither fame nor credit for his contributions. He was, above all, Robinson's confidant and friend, a steadying presence in Robinson's turbulent life, forever reminding him that he was a part of something bigger than himself.

Smith and Robinson grew apart after the 1947 season. Neither man ever spoke of the reasons for the rift, but Robinson biographer Arnold Rampersad speculates that the cause may have been Robinson's dissatisfaction with Smith's ghostwriting on Robinson's 1948 autobiography. Written in great haste and under enormous deadline pressure to capitalize on Robinson's high-profile rookie season, there were a number of errors in the book, including Robinson's own birth name (Smith wrote it as John Roosevelt Robinson instead of Jack) and his mother's name (Smith wrote it as Mollie instead of Mallie).

Nonetheless, the two men remain forever linked in baseball history, the accomplishments of each impossible without the work of the other. Smith's behind-the-scenes work to integrate baseball changed Robinson's life, and the visibility that came from his association with Jackie Robinson changed Smith's life as well. He broke a color line of his own in 1948, moving from the *Courier* to *Chicago's American* to become the first black sportswriter on a major metro newspaper. He applied yet again for admittance to the Baseball Writers Association of America and was accepted. His beat at the *American* was boxing, but he still followed baseball and would from time to time write a progress report for *American* readers on the status of the black man in the game. On the field, it was pretty rosy, particularly for the two Chicago teams; off the field, it was forever improving. But by the beginning of the 1960s, there was still one intractable pocket of baseball segregation: spring training. And for the second time in his life, Wendell Smith found himself in a position to do something about it.

Curt Flood grew up in Oakland in a multiethnic society, where his baseball coach and other role models were white and where he had played on integrated baseball teams. Flood's boyhood was consumed with drawing and baseball, not civil rights. The segregation of the South was a vague and distant concept when he arrived in Tampa in February 1956—barely eighteen years old and a recently signed rookie with the Cincinnati Redlegs.*
He arrived at the Floridian hotel, the team headquarters, identified himself, and asked for his room key. Before the desk clerk could insult him, a black porter stepped in, hailed him a cab, and Flood was taken to Ma Fletcher's Boarding House. That was where all of the black Cincinnati players stayed during spring training—minor league rookies like Curt Flood and major league all-stars like Frank Robinson.

By the middle of the 1950s, major league baseball was more than 10 percent African American, and in the National League in particular most of the brightest stars were black: Jackie Robinson, Roy Campanella, Willie Mays, Monte Irvin, Henry Aaron, Roberto Clemente, Ernie Banks, Frank Robinson—Hall of Famers all. Gradually, housing barriers had fallen during the regular season, formerly "all-white" hotels in Philadelphia, St. Louis, Kansas City, Washington, and, finally, Baltimore had grudgingly allowed blacks into their rooms. Some still forbade blacks from entering the dining room and discouraged them from sitting about the lobby. Still, their "presence in the hotel, even under ground rule conditions that are not pleasant to take, [was] important as an icebreaker," noted Sam Lacy of the *Baltimore Afro-American*.

Ten years after the first integrated spring training, however, Florida remained solidly segregated. The only integrated spot in all of spring

---

* At the height of Senator Joseph McCarthy's anti-Communist hysteria in 1953, the Cincinnati ball club formally changed its name from Reds to Redlegs. The change lasted throughout the rest of the decade. Davis, "Baseball's Reluctant Challenge," p. 158.

training was the dugout. Black players were barred from team hotels, restaurants, beaches, and golf courses and from community social events organized to honor the players. Black fans entered the ballparks through separate entrances and sat in segregated bleachers. In West Palm Beach, the ballpark didn't even have a gate for the black fans; they entered through a hole in the fence. Inside, blacks drank from the "colored" water fountains and used the "colored" facilities, if the park even had them. Sam Lacy once asked where the "colored" restroom was in one Florida ballpark and was directed to a tree some thirty or forty yards beyond the right-field fence. The only team whose players lived and ate together was the Brooklyn Dodgers, on their former air base in Vero Beach. Yet when the Dodgers went on the road for a Grapefruit League game and stopped for food, their black all-stars had to stay on the bus and have their food brought to them.

Many of the black players had known segregation long before they knew the major leagues. Some, like Mays and Aaron, had grown up in the South; others, like Campanella and Irvin, had played in the Negro Leagues and barnstormed the South. They all accepted segregation as a part of the price of admission into the organized baseball fraternity. That was how it was explained to young players like Curt Flood. "Putting up with separate spring training facilities was not about being an Uncle Tom," he was told, "it was about getting to the big leagues."

After the end of what would be his final spring training in 1956, Jackie Robinson spoke out against the segregation in spring training. "After ten years of traveling the South, I don't believe the advances there have been fast enough," he told the *Sporting News*. "It's my belief that baseball itself hasn't done all it can to help remedy the problems faced by those players in O[rganized] B[aseball]." Economic pressure was the answer, he said. Without the men of organized baseball exerting pressure of some kind on the Florida segregationists, however, nothing would happen. Black major leaguers would instead absorb five more years of boardinghouses, second-class motels, and meals eaten on a bus.

Change was slow in coming, and partly this was because the players themselves were of different minds on how hard to push. Some of the older black players actually expressed a preference for the segregated life. "To tell you the truth, I liked it better than I did staying at the hotel," said Chuck Harmon, a utility man who played four seasons for the Reds and Cardinals from 1954 to 1957. "[The housekeeper] could cook, and she washed our clothes and did everything for us." Many other black players were simply resigned to the way it was. "[It was] degrading as hell," said Monte Irvin of the Giants, "but what the hell else could we do? We wanted it so badly that it didn't bother us that much." In those days of the reserve clause, players were in constant fear for their jobs and never anxious to be seen as some sort of agitator. When Sam Lacy asked Elston Howard of the Yankees to help him persuade the Yankees' management to put pressure on Baltimore hotels to integrate in 1957, Howard simply walked away from him. This avoidance was particularly true for the second-line players, the guys fighting for a spot on the roster, and the second-line black player was doubly vexed. While major league baseball welcomed black all-stars, black utility players and relief pitchers found those jobs going to the white players every time.

Still other players felt that their job was baseball, not civil rights. "I regret, in a way, that I can't be more active, more stand-up [on race]," wrote Frank Robinson later in his career. "But it would take away from my game. The way I play the game I can't be distracted."

Others coped by using humor. Told by a waitress that she didn't serve Negroes, Cleveland Indians first baseman Vic Power quipped: "That's all right. I don't eat them." Stopped for jaywalking once, Power told the cop he thought the Walk sign was for whites only, and he was to wait and cross after it was off.

But throughout the late 1950s, a growing number of black major leaguers, men whose racial frame of reference was *Brown v. Board of Education* and Rosa Parks—and, yes, Jackie Robinson—were refusing to stifle their humiliation any longer. Robinson continued to call for the baseball owners to pressure business and civic leaders to relax their segregation ordinances. Henry Aaron and, particularly, the St. Louis Cardinals' trio of Curt Flood, Bob Gibson, and Bill White all voiced their frustration at indignities large and small. Many others, talking off the record with black reporters, echoed the words the all-stars were saying on the record.

The first public broadside in what would become the decisive battle in the long-overdue war on spring training's segregation was fired on January 23, 1961, in a front-page article in *Chicago's American* written by Wendell Smith. Headlined "Spring Training Woes," it was vintage Smith—reasoned and calm, yet soberly indignant and morally indisputable. It was time, he argued, to put this issue on the baseball and the civil rights agenda. "At the moment [the Negro ballplayer] is not belligerent," Smith wrote. "He is merely seeking help and sympathy, and understanding, and a solution. There is concrete evidence, however, that his patience is growing short."

Smith cited no names in his article; players had spoken to him in confidence, but he was clearly relaying the fruits of his reporting and not speaking in his own voice when he referred to the "growing feeling of resentment in the Negro player" over the "embarrassment, humiliation and even indignities" he was forced to endure in Florida every spring. And he also quoted players directly, if anonymously, as he did with the story of black players trying to get a meal after an exhibition game. "We went to a store and bought a loaf of bread and some cold meat. We didn't have a place to stay, either. So we walked around the streets and ate the bread and cold meat like a bunch of vagrants. That was quite a sight, believe me—about $250,000 worth of precious baseball talent walking down the street eating bread and cold meat in the broad daylight."

Though now writing for *Chicago's American*, Smith still contributed to the *Pittsburgh Courier*, and he repeated the story there, this time in his own voice and even more passionately:

> If you are [Minnie] Minoso, [Al] Smith or [Juan] Pizarro...you are a man of great pride and perseverance....Otherwise you would not be where you are today, training with a major league team in Sarasota, Fla. Yet despite all your achievements and fame, the vicious system of racial segregation in Florida's hick towns condemns you to a life of humiliation and ostracism.
>
> You are horribly embarrassed each day when the bus returning the players from the ballpark stops on "this side of the railroad tracks" and deposits you in "Colored Town," and then proceeds on to the plush hotel where your white teammates live in splendor and luxury.
>
> You suffered a bruised leg sliding into second base, but you cannot receive immediate treatment from the club trainer because he is living in the "white" hotel. If he can get away during the night and come to your segregated quarters, he will, of course, but for obvious reasons he prefers to wait until daylight.
>
> Your wife cannot call you in case of emergency from your home because the place where you are incarcerated does not have phone facilities available at all times.
>
> That is what it is like to be a Negro big leaguer in Florida during spring training....And the story has only been half told.

The story would quickly become more fully told.

A week after the Smith column, Ralph Wimbish and Robert Swain, two leaders of the St. Petersburg chapter of the NAACP (National Association for the Advancement of Colored People), called a press conference and announced that they would not assist in finding housing for the black players on the Cardinals and Yankees as they had in the past, telling reporters that it was time for all players to stay together and calling upon the Cardinals and Yankees to see that it happened. "They needed to be together," said Swain years later, "because there was just no other way to discuss the day's events, or share information." Swain, an oral surgeon, owned an apartment building next to his dental office that was filled with players every March; his principled stand cost him $650 a week. Following the Wimbish-Swain press conference, the president of the Florida chapter of the NAACP sent a letter to every major league team then training in Florida, asking them to take the lead in ending segregated housing.

The NAACP action was not triggered by Smith's article; Wimbish and Swain had been planning the action for more than a year and had told their guests at the end of spring training the previous March that they would be taking this step in an effort to accelerate integration. They pointedly did not tell the Yankees' and Cardinals' team management, not wishing to give them time to make arrangements for the black players that somehow preserved the status quo. After the announcement, Yankees owner Dan Topping issued a statement, saying the black players on the Yankees "mean as much to our ball club as any other players and [we] would like very much to have the whole team under one roof," and instructed his people to make it happen. The Soreno hotel, the Yankees' team hotel during those years, responded within a day, refusing to alter its policies. A year later, the Yankees would leave for Fort Lauderdale; reporters at the time and historians subsequently claimed St. Petersburg's rigid segregation as the reason. Dan Topping insisted at the time that it wasn't. The Yankees had been in talks with Fort Lauderdale for more than a year at the time of the 1961 integration issue; they were getting new and better facilities in Fort Lauderdale than they had in St. Petersburg; Topping and Del Webb had business and social ties in Fort Lauderdale. And if the Yankees had been concerned about the spirits and welfare of their black players in St. Petersburg, they could have done much more in the years before their hand was forced.

Some of the Cardinals' biggest stars, meanwhile, had been renting beachfront houses during spring training. The rest of the team had been staying at the Vinoy Park, one of St. Petersburg's oldest and grandest hotels, and it, too, refused to welcome blacks. When the Cardinals had difficulty finding another hotel to take them, blacks in St. Louis began calling for a boycott of the Anheuser-Busch Company, the team's owners. Anheuser-Busch subsequently starting making noises about taking the Cardinals out of St. Petersburg. Here, finally, was the economic pressure that Jackie Robinson had been calling for. For the 1962 season, a St. Petersburg businessman purchased two motels out by the northern end of the Sunshine Skyway, and this became the Cardinals' headquarters. "[W]hen Stan Musial and Ken Boyer gave up their private accommodations to move in with the rest of the team—blacks included—the Cardinals had successfully broke[n] down the local custom," wrote Bob Gibson. "The Cardinal motel became a tourist attraction. People would drive by to see the white and black families swimming together, or holding one of our famous team barbeques."

While the changes in St. Petersburg could not be attributed to Wendell Smith's writing, what happened in Miami and Sarasota could. Bill Veeck, the White Sox owner, who had integrated the American League when he had signed Larry Doby to a Cleveland Indians contract in early 1947 and whose support for the black player went back even further than that, wrote a letter to the Sarasota Terrace hotel, the team's spring training headquarters, and to the McAlpin hotel in Miami, where the team had reservations for its exhibition games against the Orioles near the end of spring training. When the McAlpin refused to accept blacks, Veeck canceled his reservation and secured lodging for black and white players at the Biscayne Terrace. The Sarasota Terrace indicated at least a willingness to talk.

Smith reported on this, as well as on the St. Petersburg developments and other signs of progress in a lengthy piece on February 6. He cited a statement from Florida governor Farris Bryant, who was elected on a segregationist platform, admitting that he knew of no Florida law that would be violated by blacks and whites sharing hotel accommodations, but adding, rather defensively, that he believed in "the freedom of association."* Other positive developments since Smith's January article included statements of support from Commissioner Ford Frick and American League president Joe Cronin

* There was in these years a Florida law, state statute 509.092, which allowed hotels and restaurant managers "to refuse accommodations or service to any person who is objectionable or undesirable to said owner or manager."

and another from Orioles general manager Lee MacPhail, who was quoted as insisting upon, and expecting to find, integrated accommodations for the Orioles players in Miami that spring.

Balancing these, as Smith wrote, were a number of other indicators of how much work remained to be done. National League president Warren Giles issued a statement saying he was aware of no problems or complaints regarding spring training housing. The Kansas City Athletics said they had no plans to force the issue of integration in West Palm Beach. "If it has been accepted in the past that Negroes use different hotels, then we have to subscribe to what has been done in the past," said Kansas City general manager Frank Lane. Milwaukee Braves vice president Birdie Tebbetts stepped in it when he told reporters that the black players on the club were "satisfied with their spring training housing arrangement." Henry Aaron was quick to refute him, both personally—telling him, "Hell, no, I'm not happy. It's about time you all realized that we're a team and we need to stay together"—and publicly through Wendell Smith's column. "There is really only room for four men, and last year there were eight to ten living there," he told Smith, referring to the rooming house where the Braves' black players stayed in Bradenton. "Beds have to be put in the hall and if players don't hustle to the bathroom in the morning, the last man up doesn't get any hot water."

The white press picked up the story. The Chicago papers followed the *American*'s lead and reported the pressure Bill Veeck was bringing upon the owner of the Sarasota Terrace hotel; the *New York Times* followed the Wimbish-Swain story as it related to the Yankees. And then in March, every newspaper in the country took up the story after Cardinals first baseman Bill White decided he had had enough.

Born in Florida, raised in Ohio, educated at Hiram College, the twenty-seven-year-old White was about to begin his third season as the Cardinals' starting first baseman. The future National League president took umbrage that the invitation list to the chamber of commerce's annual Salute to Baseball breakfast at the St. Petersburg Yacht Club included more than forty members of the Cardinals and Yankees, including many reserves and rookies, but not a single one of either team's black players. White shared his anger with UPI sportswriter Joe Reichler. "How much longer must we accept this without saying a word?" White asked rhetorically. "This thing keeps gnawing away at my heart. I think about this every minute of the day." Reichler put it on the wire the day before the scheduled breakfast; it ran in newspapers across the country, and suddenly what had been quiet resentment became "our own little civil rights movement," according to White. The Cardinals issued an awkward statement, saying that the invitation omissions had been an oversight on the part of their public relations director. The chamber of commerce was forced to extend invitations to the black players. Under pressure from the Yankees' front office, Elston Howard of the Yankees attended, but after much discussion among themselves, the Cardinals' three black all-stars—White, Bob Gibson, and Curt Flood—determined that there was greater dignity in refusing the invitation than in accepting.

Wendell Smith spent the spring in Sarasota with the White Sox and kept the pressure on from there. Given the southern racial climate in 1961, the magnitude of what the players were asking for was made evident in a feature Smith wrote about the newly integrated hotel where the White Sox's black players were staying. Still barred from the Sarasota Terrace, the black players—and Smith—found rooms at the DeSoto motel, run by a retired couple from New York, who were keenly aware of the statement they were making by integrating their previously all-white motel, located in the middle of a white neighborhood. They paid a high price for making it, as Smith made clear, calling them the "loneliest people in Sarasota."

"We received calls from men who said they were members of the Ku Klux Klan," Smith quoted motel owner Edward Wachtel as saying, "and that they were going to burn a fiery cross on my front lawn. There were calls from merchants who said they would refuse to serve me in their stores. All but one or two of my neighbors quit speaking to me."

Veeck made clear to the chamber of commerce that he was considering leaving Sarasota if the whole team could not stay together—that meant in the Sarasota Terrace, the team's headquarters. With that, the Sarasota Chamber of Commerce became an unlikely ally in the fight to integrate the hotel. The owner of the Sarasota Terrace, however, remained intractable, believing that not only would his hotel be hurt, so too would be his construction business. "My clients throughout Florida and other sections of the South would reject my business, I believe," he said to Smith. So the Sarasota Terrace, at least for spring training 1961, was a standoff.

But Smith was making progress. He encouraged the Major League Players' Association to put spring training integration on its agenda during its summer meeting at the all-star game and was successful. He became increasingly militant in his columns in the *Courier* when it came to black players remaining silent on the subject of segregation in the South, calling them

"Fat Cats" and "Uncle Toms" for refusing to jeopardize their place on a team. He became particularly outraged when a Baltimore player requested segregated housing, saying he was "more comfortable" there and only interested in making the team. "[Didn't he] realize the consequences of his decision?" Smith asked. "[Didn't he] recognize what people like Martin Luther King and hundreds of Negro college students are trying to do?"

When Veeck sold the White Sox in the summer of 1961, Smith's first question to new owner Arthur C. Allyn concerned his plans for spring training housing, reporting to *American* readers that the new owner was "unequivocally opposed to segregation during spring training" and had promised to consider seriously taking the team elsewhere if he could not integrate Sarasota. "My position on this issue is the same as Bill Veeck's," said Allyn. "Segregation serves no purpose and I want it terminated as far as the White Sox team is concerned." Allyn's pockets were considerably deeper than Veeck's and that allowed him options unavailable to Veeck. When the Sarasota Terrace again balked when approached in the fall of 1961 about admitting black players the following spring, Allyn bought the hotel, and in the spring of 1962, the White Sox players—black and white—stayed together. So, too, did the Cardinals, Yankees, Mets, and Pirates. By 1964, the entire Grapefruit League was fully integrated.

The integration of spring training housing, coming so long after the integration of the game and so small a piece of the civil rights struggle, seems so inevitable when viewed from the distance of nearly a half-century. But it was truly a complex moment, fraught with peril for the players, the teams, and activists like Wendell Smith.

The campaign to integrate spring training came rather early in the civil rights movement. It followed Rosa Parks, Little Rock, the start of the lunch-counter sit-ins, true. But it also came the spring before the freedom rides had begun; a year and a half before federal troops were necessary to help integrate the University of Mississippi; two years before black schoolchildren were firehosed in Birmingham; three years before civil rights workers were murdered in Mississippi; and four years before the violence on the bridge in Selma. It was an emotional issue during an incendiary time, and it may have been an even greater triumph than the integration of the game itself. And not only did it happen; it happened peacefully.

Wendell Smith was an extraordinarily self-effacing writer; he never sought attention nor claimed credit for all he had done. But when the integration of spring training became a national story in the spring of 1961, and any number of sources other than Smith—Bill White and Joe Reichler, the St. Petersburg

NAACP people, the *New York Times* among them—were cited as the cause of it, Smith became, ever so slightly and ever so briefly, just a tad defensive. In his February 6 story, he quoted both Ernie Banks of the Cubs and Larry Doby of the White Sox, and both were a little obvious in their praise of Smith and his newspaper; their quotes have the feel of having been fed to the ballplayers. "I am sure I am speaking for every Negro player in the big leagues when I say we are very grateful to *Chicago's American* for bringing this situation to the attention of the American public," said Banks. "We are particularly pleased with the sane and dignified way it has been presented. There has been nothing inflammatory about the stories, and for that we especially are grateful." Larry Doby sounded much the same. "The campaign started by *Chicago's American* to secure equal treatment for Negro big-leaguers in the South is a great contribution to the nation's sports scene. Everyone who believes in justice and fair play will, I am sure, endorse the newspaper's efforts wholeheartedly."

Smith even felt it necessary to punctuate those quotes. "Some newspapers in other cities, in fact, have realized that there is so much merit in the campaign that they have attempted to take credit for the progress made thus far," he wrote. "Most readers agree, as well as most sports writers, that there is justification for the campaign. As a Negro, this reporter, who himself has experienced many of the humiliations Negro ballplayers suffer in the South, believes *Chicago's American* merits all the commendation it already has received in this effort."

As we have come to more fully understand Jackie Robinson's role in transforming twentieth-century America—and not just on the ball field—we have come to know and appreciate too the role Smith played in baseball's racial legacy. Both men were gifted, passionate, and keenly attuned to the nuances and ramifications of their actions—partners in hastening the integration of America.

Wendell Smith died on November 26, 1972, just four weeks after the death of Jackie Robinson. He was fifty-eight years old. In 1993, the Baseball Writers Association of America, the group that had blackballed Smith for more than a decade—honoring primarily the work Smith had done during that decade—posthumously awarded him the J. G. Taylor Spink Award. It is the highest honor the association can bestow upon a fellow writer, for with it comes a place in the writers and broadcasters room at the Baseball Hall of Fame in Cooperstown.

FIVE

Mr. O'Malley's Dodgertown

However much Branch Rickey may have given birth to the concepts and ideas of Dodgertown and however much his presence always permeated the place—the strings disappeared long ago, but the pitching practice area at Dodgertown was always known as "the strings area"; the workouts in the twenty-first century still have the station-to-station personality of Rickey's postwar workouts—the Dodgertown of lore and romance is not Branch Rickey's. It is Walter O'Malley's. The bane of Brooklyn, who took over as the Dodgers' owner after the 1950 season, took a place and made it a place in baseball's heart. He made Dodgertown better. He made it special. He made it—it always seemed—permanent.

The early upgrades to the barracks were O'Malley's. The fields got notably smoother and greener after O'Malley took over, though the Brooklyn team still played the great majority of its exhibition games in Miami, a three-hour bus ride to the south. Just a game or two each year was played in Vero Beach, on what was christened Ebbets Field #2, a rustic diamond across Airport Road from the rest of the complex, with temporary wooden bleachers enough for about 1,000 spectators. But as soon as a new, twenty-one-year lease was finalized in 1952, O'Malley announced plans to build a 5,000-seat concrete stadium in Vero Beach. This not only signaled a commitment to Vero Beach. To O'Malley and his architect, Emil Praeger, it was also intended as a trial run for the construction of the new stadium O'Malley planned to build in Brooklyn, a domed marvel at the confluence of Atlantic and Flatbush avenues. The Brooklyn stadium never happened of course, but a decade after Vero Beach, O'Malley and Praeger did work together in building Dodger Stadium, using some of the same engineering techniques they had developed in building the spring training park.

The stadium was built by excavating 20,000 cubic yards of "sand, marl and muck" from a site adjacent to the new stadium and fashioning it into a berm that would circle the entire field. The earth around the infield and the shallow outfield, short of the foul poles, was packed and shaped to receive the concrete for the grandstand. Construction took fifty-five days in the fall of 1952. In a letter that fall to architect Norman Bel Geddes, O'Malley put the cost of construction at $30,000. In a letter to St. Louis Cardinals president William Walsingham two years later, he claimed the total cost was more than $60,000. The hole from which the earth had been excavated was fashioned into a heart-shaped pond that O'Malley dedicated to his wife, Kay. Mae Smith, the widow of former Dodgers minority owner John L. Smith, donated fifty royal palm trees in memory of her husband. They were planted along the outfield's perimeter and were the only delineation of the field's edge until Dick Allen crashed into one chasing a fly ball in 1971. A fence was constructed soon thereafter, but the trees still ring the outfield embankment beyond that fence. The stadium was dedicated with a game against Connie Mack's Philadelphia Athletics on March 11, 1953. At O'Malley's insistence, it was named in honor of Bud Holman, by now a very close friend of the O'Malley family, who continued as a quiet facilitator in dealings between the team and city.

O'Malley worked Dodgertown much like a big-city Irish pol worked his turf. He was fond of pomp and ceremony: each year, the Vero Beach High School band would be at the airport for the arrival of the Dodgers' plane from Brooklyn and, later, from Los Angeles. O'Malley was solicitous of constituent needs at Dodgertown, asking players what he might do to make things better and constantly adding amenities to improve life on the base. The pond created by the dredging for Holman Stadium was stocked with fish and became the Dodger fishing hole, a favorite spot for Carl Furillo and Carl Erskine, among others. A small pitch-and-putt golf course sprouted along the shores of the pond in 1954, foreshadowing grander golf to come.

Every year of his stewardship of the Dodgers, Walter O'Malley was the first to arrive in Vero Beach and the last to leave, often skipping the freeway exhibition series against the Angels in order to have another seventy-two hours in Florida. At Dodgertown, O'Malley was ubiquitous. There he was, standing in line with his tray at the dining hall, in among the Brooklyns and the minor leaguers. There he was in his golf cart, driving about the grounds, squiring guests and friends, team officials and reporters. There he was in a green plastic derby, presiding over Dodgertown's annual St. Patrick's Day party. There he was amid the grounds crew, helping to rake the infield on the day Holman Stadium was to be dedicated. There he was playing poker with team execs and sportswriters in the Dodgertown press room, which doubled as an after-hours, off-limits-to-the-players lounge. There he was with his wife, Kay, playing golf, walking the grounds, keeping score of a game at Holman, or retiring to their private suite by the swimming pool. And there he was in the Vero Beach *Press Journal*, posing with the key to the city in one photo, surrounded by a half-dozen comely women in bathing suits in another, disembarking from the Dodgers' plane in a third, shaking the hands of little leaguers and local leaders in an endless series of those tired old newspaper grip-and-grins.

O'Malley would greet practically everyone with a hearty slap on the back and a warm "How are you? How's your family?" He would tell every one, from players to groundskeepers, to "Call me Walter," though many players who knew him as the signature on the bottom of their paychecks were largely reluctant to do so, preferring "Mr. O'Malley." He'd host a predinner cocktail party every night for the writers covering the team. "Spring training was never the same after my Vero Beach experience," said Jack Lang, who covered the Dodgers for the *Long Island Press* and would later serve as the longtime head of the Baseball Writers Association of America. "There it was family." Not all writers fell under O'Malley's spell, however. Roger Kahn, the *Boys of Summer* author, who covered the team for the *New York Herald Tribune*, claimed that "as with an under-boiled potato, O'Malley's warmth was mostly external." But the affection of so many in the Dodgers family for O'Malley was deep and genuine. "He was a wonderful man," recalled Manny Mota. "I remember Kay and Walter were just wonderful people," said Lee Lacy, who played for the Dodgers in the seventies. "They were so hospitable and so polite and so kind to everyone. They were actually hands-on 100 percent. They communicated with all of the players. They made everyone feel so close and we had such a family back in those days."

And O'Malley's affection for Vero Beach was palpable. "Mr. Walter O'Malley, and later his son Peter—they loved this place," said Jaime Jarrin, the Dodgers' Spanish-language broadcaster and a Dodgertown fixture since 1960. "He was always very proud of this place, always improving it."

"Dad was a planter," said Peter O'Malley. "He had a green thumb, and he enjoyed planting trees and landscaping and all the flowers. He deserves the credit for making the place as beautiful as it was—is."

In 1964, after four years of political wrangling and infighting in Vero Beach—wrangling in which the Dodgers were sometimes players and sometimes helpless bystanders—O'Malley got the opportunity to consummate his affection for Dodgertown by buying the land.

The story of the Dodgers' purchase of their spring training site—they were the first and remain the only team to have ever owned their spring training facilities—begins in 1960, when the proprietors of a Vero Beach flight service and Cessna dealership applied for space on the airport flight line. Bud Holman, still the airport manager, refused to rent them space, claiming he held an exclusive lease on flight line operations. The spurned flight-service operators appealed to the Federal Aviation Administration (FAA), which still had oversight on the airport, even though it had given ownership of the airport to the city, which in turn had given control of its operations to Bud Holman. The FAA came in for a look around and didn't like what it saw. It didn't like Bud Holman's management on a lot of levels. It particularly didn't like the terms of the Dodgers' lease, which paid the city $1 a year and the proceeds from one predesignated spring training game, the so-called Airport Fund Game. Money from the Airport Fund Game was notoriously unreliable—one year, it brought in only $100—and the FAA said the Dodgers were paying a "mere pittance" of the true value of the lease, which it suggested should be $12,000 per year.

In November 1960, the FAA ruled that the city needed to fix the leases to the FAA's satisfaction within sixty days or the federal government would retake control of the airport. The FAA stayed its deadline while the Vero Beach City Council first fired and then sued Holman—fired him from his job as airport manager and sued to void the leases he still held at the property. They also put all leases on a month-to-month basis—of particular concern to the Dodgers, who had a lease through 1973, with an option for twenty-one years after that. By the fall of 1961, when there was still no resolution, the Dodgers began to grow concerned. Publicist Red Patterson tried to help Vero Beach understand what it had in the Dodgers by saying that he hoped Vero Beach wouldn't throw the team out. If it did, he made clear, there were cities in Florida, Nevada, California, and Arizona that had all expressed interest in having them. O'Malley sent a telegram to members of the city council in which he suggested they "go fishing and relax." He also defended the lease the Dodgers had, pointing out that the city had spent a mere $19,000 on Dodgertown through the years, most of that on the swimming pool built at the very beginning of the Dodgers' stay. The Dodgers, meanwhile, had spent $3 million building Holman Stadium and otherwise improving the property, as well as $250,000 each year in costs. "Do you think the City of Vero Beach has strained itself in any way in spending $19,000 in fourteen years in order to have in its midst the finest, biggest major league winter training quarters in the U.S.A.?" he asked in November 1961.

But even the O'Malleys understood that the lease they had was difficult for the city. "A dollar a year and the proceeds from the Airport Fund Game really wasn't fair to the city," said Peter O'Malley, who was Dodgertown's director at this point. "If the game got rained out a day or two before the team left, there was no rent. And if the game was scheduled against a team other than the Yankees, or if it was a cloudy day and the attendance was low, the rent was low."

Former Vero Beach mayor Merrill Barber, who'd helped to bring the Dodgers to town, was brought in to help find a solution. He was the first to raise the possibility of the Dodgers' buying the property they trained on. The FAA had to sign off on any sale, and the Dodgers' lease was only one part of an increasingly complicated airport puzzle. It would take another three years to sort it all out. Meanwhile, the Dodgers stayed loyal to Vero Beach. They had been a California team for a half-decade now; moreover, since the start of the controversy surrounding their lease in Florida, the Cactus League had grown from four teams to six, with the addition of the expansion Angels and the Houston Colt .45s. A move to the desert made perfect fiscal and baseball sense for the Dodgers. Yet it never even came up for discussion.

"Our roots were so deep there that leaving Vero Beach was impossible," said Peter O'Malley. "Yes the team was in California. But the friendships that we had established were too important to all of us to leave behind. Leaving Vero Beach was really never seriously considered."

In September 1964, four months after Bud Holman's death at sixty-three, the deal to buy the property was finally done. The team and city had three appraisals, picked the one in the middle, and on March 16, 1965, Walter O'Malley presented the city of Vero Beach with a check for $133,087.50 for

Holman Stadium, the barracks and other buildings, and the sixty-odd acres the team had been training on for more than a decade and a half. Included in the sale were an additional fifty-plus acres of land just beyond the outfield of Holman Stadium, bringing the total purchase to 110 acres. O'Malley had no sooner closed the deal than he broke ground on the Dodgertown Golf Club on the new land beyond the outfield. He built the course largely to give the African American players in the organization a place to golf; they were still excluded from the Riomar and Vero Beach country clubs, the two local private courses. Vero Beach beyond the base was still quite an inhospitable place for the black players. It had only been a couple of years before, in 1962, that the O'Malleys had finally ordered that the restrooms and grandstands at Holman Stadium be integrated. "When they put that golf course up there, that was a highlight," remembered Lou Johnson, who played with the Dodgers in the mid-sixties. "I didn't know one place we [the black players] could go to play golf. That made a big difference, I think, in the African American players in their appreciation of Walter O'Malley."

But O'Malley took as much pleasure from that golf course as any of his players; he did most of the designing and played practically every day during spring training. He also took notice of where his regular opponents hit the ball, and when he discerned a pattern, he ordered his grounds crew to build a bunker in just that spot.

The purchase of the land triggered a decade-long building boom that transformed both the dimensions and the physical appearance of Dodgertown. O'Malley liked his nine-hole golf course so much that he soon bought another 230 acres diagonally across the street from Dodgertown at the corner of 26th Street and 43rd Avenue. There, he built an eighteen-hole course, first called Safari Pines, for his interest in African big-game hunting—some of the trophies from those hunts hung on the walls of the clubhouse—but soon changed to the Dodger Pines Country Club. Little by little over the next ten years, O'Malley would buy up smaller parcels of land between Dodger Pines and King's Highway. He planted citrus trees on forty acres of land just north of the barracks and the practice fields. The oranges would eventually provide fruit and juice for the dining hall. By the time O'Malley was finished, Dodgertown totaled 465 acres.

The biggest physical change came after spring training in 1971, when construction began on ninety "villas"—motel buildings, really—a long-anticipated upgrade of the living conditions in camp. The world-weary state of the barracks had been one of the driving reasons to buy the property.

"The city didn't have the money to rebuild the place," said Peter O'Malley. "It was logical that if we owned it we would improve it."

With their 600 beds, the barracks were dinosaurs; by the late 1960s, Dodger minor leaguers numbered no more than 200. Nobody had ever really liked living in the barracks, but they were a part of the commonality of Dodgertown. "In the beginning, and when the team first came to California, it was like camping out, and it had some appeal to it," said Peter O'Malley. "My own view is this brought everyone together, and did it at the most key time, the beginning of the season."

There was a little melancholy when the barracks were razed a year after the villas opened: a faux Save the Barracks campaign, with posters and bumper stickers, popped up during the spring of 1972, and everyone had a little fun with it. For the barracks were filled with a quarter-century's worth of Dodger memories—conversations, card games, and more than a few late-night, boys-will-be-boys moments. It was in the barracks that manager Walter Alston broke his 1955 World Series ring banging on the door of Larry Sherry's room after catching the relief pitcher sneaking in after curfew. It was in the bushes outside the barracks that Fresco Thompson used to wait with a flashlight, trying to catch players coming back from Lennie's bar, the shot-and-a-beer joint over on the corner of 43rd Avenue and 20th Street, a short walk along dark paths from Dodgertown.* It was outside the barracks that Thompson was waiting in a tree one night, when Lou Johnson grabbed a grapefruit from a nearby tree and splattered him with a perfect throw, made all the sweeter—for Johnson, clearly not for Thompson—by the fact that he never got caught. To those who were there in the beginning,

---

* Lennie's, which closed a few weeks after the Dodgers completed their final spring in Vero Beach—the two events were not related—may be at least as responsible as Branch Rickey's strings for a couple of the Dodgers' world championships during the 1960s. Sandy Koufax was having a beer at Lennie's one night in 1961 with fellow pitcher Ed Roebuck, catcher Norm Sherry, and scout Kenny Myers. Sherry and Myers persuaded Koufax, who was struggling mightily with his control after six seasons with the Dodgers, to shorten his delivery and to "take the grunt off [his] fast ball." Don't try to throw it through a concrete wall, they told him. Just try to get it over the plate. The next game following that advice, Koufax pitched seven hitless innings. He went 18–13 that season, a breakout year, and for the next five years, before an elbow injury ended his career at age thirty, Sandy Koufax was as dominating a pitcher as modern baseball had ever seen. Jane Leavy, *Sandy Koufax: A Lefty's Legacy* (HarperCollins, 2002), pp. 102–103.

the barracks will always be a part of Dodgertown. "The wooden door and the steps that creaked as you went up to the barracks. These are the things that stick to your ribs," remembered announcer Vin Scully, who slept in the barracks for twenty-two springs.

In the barracks' place rose a modern conference center that included a new dining hall, new major and minor league clubhouses, and conference and meeting space not only for the Dodgers, but also for the conferences and groups that would begin to visit Dodgertown during the forty-five weeks each year that the Dodgers weren't there. The Dodgers had always sought ways to offset the operating costs of Dodgertown. While Holman Stadium was still on the drawing board, O'Malley wrote to the Chicago Cubs and asked if they'd be interested in sharing the training facilities in Vero Beach. Nothing came of it, but the team did generate some money with a summer boys' camp in the fifties and sixties. Off-season activity exploded during the 1970s. The summer boys' camp gave way to twice-a-year adult fantasy camps. The New Orleans Saints brought their preseason training camp to Dodgertown for a time in the seventies and eighties. The Kansas City Chiefs and Philadelphia Eagles made shorter visits to ready themselves for playoff games. The biggest off-season addition came in 1980, when the Dodgers based their Single A, Florida State League team at Dodgertown. "After all these years, the marriage between the Los Angeles Dodgers and Vero Beach has produced its first baby," said the Vero Beach *Press Journal* in announcing the birth of the Vero Beach Dodgers.

From the first, Dodgertown had emphasized family and community. The very first spring, in 1948, homemade street signs appeared along the pathways at Dodgertown—Flatbush Avenue, Rickey Boulevard, Durocher Trail. As the pathways became more defined and paved over, the Dodgers made it official. In the 1970s, they began formally naming the streets after Dodger Hall of Famers. Jackie Robinson Boulevard leads into the center of the complex, and there are streets for all Dodger Hall of Famers, including announcers Scully and Jaime Jarrin. The streetlights are twelve-inch baseballs—white globes with the red stitching painted on. Over the years, flowers, other plantings, and palm trees complemented all of the new construction to the point where *Sports Illustrated*'s Tom Verducci called Dodgertown "a baseball training facility disguised as an arboretum."

By the time Walter O'Malley died in 1979, Dodgertown was as it would be for the next twenty years, a baseball theme park. Peter O'Malley, whose love for Vero Beach was perhaps even greater than his father's, made sure that little changed.

"When you've got only two people, father and son, and you have all these traditions—the St. Patrick's Day party that my father started, the memorial mass [for members of the Dodgers' family who'd died since the previous spring] that my mother started—all this meant a lot to our family," said O'Malley. "It meant a lot to the people who went there. So maintaining it was important to us."

Like the theme parks up in Orlando, Dodgertown attracted visitors from across the land. They all came in search of America as it once was and would never again be. Except here. Unlike most other spring training sites, Dodgertown was not dominated by regular season Dodgers fans looking for a peek at the forthcoming edition of their team and for a few soothing moments in the Florida sun. Vero Beach is a long way from Los Angeles, and unlike fans of the Red Sox, Yankees, Tigers, Twins, and the rest of the Frost Belt teams, Dodgers fans have no real need to flee their winter weather. Dodgertown was, rather, universal in its appeal. Cardinals fans who vacationed in Jupiter, Mets fans who made the trip to Port St. Lucie, Indians fans from Winter Haven, families on a week at Disney World—all made a side trip to Dodgertown. That would become Dodgertown's special appeal and also its ultimate curse. When spring training became so much about the bottom line, there were too many pilgrims and tourists on the property. Not enough Dodgers fans.

Dodgertown's appeal is both evident and intangible. There is a serenity and tranquility to the grounds—Maury Wills's college campus meets Tom Verducci's arboretum. The aesthetics of the grounds are enhanced by the expansiveness. It's ten minutes to walk from fields five and six, where the minor leaguers practice, past the villas, the conference center, and the major league practice fields, to Holman Stadium and the major league clubhouse. Yet for all of the feeling of space, there is also an undeniable intimacy. Fans have unmatched access and proximity at Dodgertown. They walk side by side with the players as the players make their way from the clubhouse across the bridge to the practice fields. On the practice fields, only a thin rope separates fan from player. The truly fortunate might catch a glimpse or score an autograph from a Dodger legend like Wills or Sandy Koufax, because the Dodgers are fond of the notion of "once a Dodger, always a Dodger," and the Dodgers of the past are invited back to Dodgertown to talk to the kids of today, just as the Dodgers of the distant past had at one time talked to them.

Finally, there is the signature stature of the Dodgers' franchise—its long and rich history, yes, but also its utterly unique dual identity. After a half-century in California, they are the *Los Angeles* Dodgers surely, the Dodgers of Hollywood and Chavez Ravine. But no sports franchise has ever had a continuing identity with its abandoned city like the Dodgers have with Brooklyn. Probably because the Dodgers of the 1950s belonged not just to Brooklyn, but to all of America. That last glorious Dodgers team is frozen in time and in America's mind; the *Brooklyn* Dodgers will always be Robinson taking that taunting lead off third, a healthy Campy chattering behind the plate, Reese making graceful and effortless pivots at short, the stalwart Hodges at first, Furillo forever in right, Snider standing at plate, and the Ebbets Field crowd tingling with the anticipation of the Duke's fluid-as-ballet swing putting yet another baseball out onto Bedford Avenue. This is, moreover, the team that taught America that blacks and whites would live and play together and that America must come to grips with a new racial dynamic. They belong on the history pages not with John McGraw's Giants or Babe Ruth's Yankees but with *Brown v. Board of Education* and Rosa Parks.

On the baseball field, meanwhile, the Brooklyn Dodgers' story had the dimensions of Greek tragedy. Between 1941 and 1956, they won seven National League pennants and lost four others either in playoffs or in the final at-bat of the final game of the season. In those seven World Series matchups—all of them against the Yankees—they lost all but one. The Yankees were both privileged and fortunate. The Dodgers were flawed and constantly befallen with bad luck. The Brooklyn Dodgers, in other words, were like us. To walk the grounds at Dodgertown is to feel this history and connect with it.

Like the rest of coastal Florida, Vero Beach has grown tremendously since the mid-1980s. The barrier island, those fifteen miles of white sand oceanfront and jungle when Branch Rickey and the Dodgers arrived in 1948, is now an unbroken stretch of high-end homes—condos that start at a half-million dollars and estates that can cost as much as $20 million. Still, Vero remains a sleepy community, very much "Zero Beach" when stacked against bustling ports-of-call such as Fort Myers, Tampa, or Phoenix. It is the smallest community to host a major league spring training, and its identity beyond Indian River County remains inextricably linked to the Dodgers and the "Vero Beach, Fla." datelines that appeared so reliably in the nation's newspapers every March for so many years. Like a retired couple on their daily walk along the shoreline, Vero Beach had grown comfortable and secure in its marriage to the Dodgers. There was faith and permanence to the union; certainly no sign of disquiet or unrest as the twentieth century neared its close. The outside world, too, saw it as that ideal marriage—the one everyone else admires and envies.

But in the spring of 1998, as the Dodgers were beginning to celebrate their fiftieth anniversary in Vero Beach, the tranquility of that marriage was shattered. The Dodgers announced they were considering a move to Arizona. It was numbing news—not only to Vero Beach but to all of baseball. We were all reminded that, while a piece of land can become a part of a person's, or a family's, soul, as Dodgertown had with the O'Malleys, to a large corporation it is nothing but an asset.

SIX

The Bottom Line
Crowds Out the Box
Score

For more than seventy-five years, every news story that dealt with the financial side of spring training involved the costs to the team. From a cost of $1,100 in the 1890s, the price of spring training rose to an estimated $9,000 by 1913, when owners like Connie Mack of the Athletics, Barney Dreyfuss of the Pirates, and Frank Navin of the Tigers called for a scaling back of the spring trips, claiming they were not only expensive, but that beyond a certain point—Dreyfuss suggested cutting back to three weeks from a month—they were counterproductive, threatening to make a player stale before the season even started. By the mid-1930s, the tab for a club's spring training travels had grown to an estimated $20,000. That was for an average team, with a typical spring itinerary. The Chicago Cubs' excursion to Catalina Island and then home to Chicago via California and Florida for exhibition games cost an estimated $50,000. By 1960, the number had grown to $38,000 for hotel, food, and per diems alone—the number did not include travel. A decade later, the number had jumped to $150,000, a big chunk of the jump attributable to inflation and the rise in the standard of spring training living, but a bigger chunk of the increase coming because more and more teams were now bringing along their minor leaguers. By the end of the eighties, the estimate was $400,000.

Insofar as anyone attempted to judge the economic impact of spring training on the host communities, it began and ended with these costs.

Most of that money, it was reasoned, was spent in the local economy, on hotels and meals and in bars and nightclubs. The value of the city's name in the dateline of faraway newspapers was always talked about, but impossible to quantify. And there was the vague sense that baseball was benefiting from the publicity that spring training generated. "There are millions who yammer: 'The whole thing is 100 percent commercial,'" wrote Dan Daniel in 1947. "'Training, with its daily stories and features in the newspapers, its radio repercussions and its newsreel demonstration, is nothing but a gigantic advertising stunt.'" No one ever thought long or deeply about the economics of spring training.

This started to change in the late 1970s, as baseball began to enjoy a resurgence in popularity after a couple of decades of playing second fiddle to the National Football League. As Grapefruit League and Cactus League crowds began numbering in the thousands instead of the hundreds, people started taking a closer look at the money generated by spring training. The Grapefruit League building boom in the mid-eighties—five new complexes rose in a span of three years—peeled the lid off stories about the economics of spring training. Even Yankees owner George Steinbrenner, just then beginning a search for a new spring home that would take the Yankees from Fort Lauderdale to Tampa, called the money being tossed around by Florida cities vying for spring training "unbelievable." That Steinbrenner would find any sum of money "unbelievable" was headline making in and of itself.

At first, the talk of economic impact was quite anecdotal: reports of a restaurant in St. Petersburg serving more than 200 meals a night in March, fewer than 100 a night in April; a travel agency in Cincinnati that had been running a spring training trip for more than thirty years suddenly finding itself selling a great many more trips and selling them earlier. There were some primitive attempts to quantify matters. Newspaper reporters interviewed fans at games and reported what they were spending. The *St. Petersburg Times*'s research department undertook a study in 1978 that estimated that out-of-state spending by tourists came to roughly $3 million per team for each of the nineteen teams then training in Florida. There were other guesses at the economic impact of spring training in Florida, ranging from $54 million on up, none of them backed by terribly convincing data. There were also a number of off-the-cuff, eyebrow-raising comments, like the one from Florida governor Bob Martinez, who told the annual Governor's Baseball Dinner in St. Petersburg in 1987 that spring training "conservatively has a $1 billion" impact on the state.

In 1987, the Florida Department of Commerce commissioned a study to determine the financial impact of the Grapefruit League. Delivered in the fall of that year, it showed a $295 million windfall as a result of March baseball. Pinellas County, with four spring training teams—the Phillies, Blue Jays, Mets, and Cardinals—received the lion's share of the money, some $67 million. The study showed the Red Sox as having the biggest Grapefruit League following, trailed closely by the Yankees. Suddenly, big money and small became story fodder for the journalists. When the lockout of 1990 delayed the start of camp by more than a month and cut the number of exhibition games in half, the city of Dunedin went looking for a way to recoup the $3.2 million it had spent in expanding and upgrading Grant Field, the Blue Jays' training site. It asked the citizens of Toronto to contribute $1 each to help the city out in its revenue-less spring. Dunedin received one check for $100 and 250 individual contributions, each for one (Canadian) dollar.

Attendance at Grapefruit and Cactus league games has grown steadily, from an average of roughly 2,500 per game in the mid-seventies, to 3,500 per game by the early eighties, then jumping to 4,500 per game in the mid-eighties and over 5,000 per game in the late eighties, when the first rush of new Florida parks opened. By 1993, per game attendance topped 7,000, and, with many teams at or near their park's capacity, it has remained relatively steady ever since.

Total attendance topped 1 million for the first time in 1981. It topped 2 million ten years later and 3 million just three years after that, in 1994. It took baseball the rest of the nineties to recover from the self-inflicted damage of the 1994–1995 strike; attendance numbers did not top 3 million again until 2000. It has dipped below 3 million just once since, during an abnormally wet 2003. Grapefruit League attendance records were set in 2006 and 2007 (1.7 million fans attended games in 2007 alone). The 2008 season would have easily set another record, but both the Dodgers and the Red Sox left Florida more than a week early for games in China and Japan. After four rainouts left the Cactus League a few hundred fans short of a record in 2007, it did set attendance records in 2008, with more than 1.3 million fans.

The states of Florida and Arizona are heavily invested in spring training. Every stadium and complex save one—Disney's Wide World of Sports—has been built (or, in Dodgertown's case, purchased and upgraded) with public money. Since 2000 alone, Arizona has spent more than $250 million in public funds on spring training construction and upgrades, Florida nearly $150 million. Roughly half this money has come from state coffers (a bit more in Arizona's case), the balance from local funds.

The estimated return on this investment, in 2007 dollars, has grown to nearly $1 billion a year. The Cactus League Association completed a survey in 2007 that showed spring training fans spending $310,775,015, up a jaw-dropping 54 percent from a similar study completed just four years earlier. The Florida Sports Foundation's most recent figures are from the year 2000. A survey conducted that year to bolster the argument in support of the legislative appropriation for spring training funds set the economic impact at $450 million. A parallel study by the Indian River County Chamber of Commerce in 2000 showed the economic impact of the Dodgers on the local economy to be right around $30 million, consistent with the Florida Sports Foundation's numbers for the Dodgers and Vero Beach.

These studies reflect both direct and indirect impact. Direct impact includes salaries to local employees, taxes, and the purchase of local goods and services by the teams and the people who come to watch the teams play. Indirect impact is calculated using what economists call the multiplier factor. Very simply, the multiplier factor says that, when a team pays a local employee $1 in salary, that dollar is going to be respent in the local economy and will thus equal $2 of total impact. Different multiplier factors apply to different categories of revenue. For every dollar a tourist spends in a local restaurant or hotel, for example, ninety cents is calculated to be respent in the local economy.

The Cactus League numbers do not include spending by the teams; the Florida figure is aging rapidly. If Florida's numbers jumped anywhere near what Arizona's did between 2003 and 2007, the total impact is easily over $1 billion.

If you want to believe the numbers.

"Politicians are making these claims, not economists," said Phillip Porter, a professor of economics at the University of South Florida and the most oft-quoted critic of the economic impact claims of spring training. "There's a group of sports economists, people who teach at universities and do very very legitimate, frontline, historical, archival research in sports economics—people with no irons in the fire—and among that group of economists you'll find uniform agreement that spring training and the presence of sports teams in a community have very little impact on jobs, on employment, on income and earning, and very little on spending."

Porter and his colleagues in the academic community express open contempt for the process used in the economic impact studies that have been done on spring training, and only a slightly veiled contempt for the people who've done them.

"These people may have some economic training, but they're not professional economists, they're not Ph.D.-level economists that are looking at how these models are built or how the models are done," said Porter. "They're the kind of people who do government consulting jobs or work in government offices, like the Florida Division of Tourism."

The economic impact studies that have been done use what is known as input-output models. There are a number of commercial models available. "They're very user-friendly models," said Porter. "[Y]ou pay a few thousand dollars for the software and you can use the model. And you put numbers in the beginning of this model and out the other end comes impacts." The problem, insists Porter, is that these models were not made to study events like spring training.

"The models are flawed. They're good models for long-run, steady-state activities," he said, citing the opening or closing of an air force base as an example. "The model makes good sense if you're talking about something that's permanent. But if you're talking about something for six weeks? Nobody builds a hotel for six weeks. Nobody builds restaurants for six weeks.

"But the guy that's using this model probably's got a bias anyway. So essentially what he does is hire a bunch of [college] kids and they'll go out to a spring training game or any sporting event and they'll ask the people: 'Why are you here?' 'Well I'm here to watch spring training.' 'Where are you from?' 'I'm from Ohio.' 'How many days are you in Florida?' 'My family and I, four of us, we're here for a week.' And all of a sudden because he was at that game, a whole week's worth of demand for Florida vacation is attributed to that event. In the model, what goes in is a week's worth of spending by four people. It's really not the case that these people only came to Florida because of spring training. They came to Florida because it was a great vacation place and, oh, one of the things they did one afternoon was go watch the local team in a spring training game.

"You've got a model that is really inappropriate to the application, so what you've got coming out the other side is really meaningless."

But Porter and his brethren cannot convince the tourism industry that there is no impact. "I disagree with [Porter] 100 percent," said Jeff Mielke, the executive director of the Lee County Sports Authority. "Because we see it. We go as a county staff to the Twins Fest in Minneapolis every January, and we set up this huge booth in the Metrodome, with a sign saying 'Come to Lee

County for Spring Training.' And there's thousands of people who come up to our booth and start planning their trip or say: 'I've already got my tickets. We're coming down there.' And they're coming down specifically to see the Twins play. There's no other reason they're coming here. Spring training drives its own individual tourism. And I know what [Porter's] argument is. He says: 'Well it's just another activity; it's people that are in the town anyway and are just finding another activity to do.' Well it's not true. And we know it. We're up in Minnesota talking to thousands of people who are specifically coming down here for this reason, creating their vacation to come see the Twins. They're going to do the beach because they're here. But their primary purpose is to see spring training."

As long as there is winter in places like Minneapolis, Chicago, Cleveland, Detroit, and Boston, and America remains the land of disposable income, Florida and Arizona are going to be full in March, spring training or not. But if major league baseball were to move its spring training to an aircraft hangar in Alaska, there would be fans who'd travel to Alaska to watch. Even Porter admits that spring training has some economic impact. But the only way to be certain of its real impact, he believes, is to look at what happens when spring training goes away. "Wait until somebody moves," he says. "These are the things that provide natural tests for whether or not spring training provides the economic kick it is said to provide. If a team moves out of Winter Haven, say, what happens to Winter Haven? If next year it's business as always with the same sort of sales and income and employment, then you gotta conclude that the presence of the team didn't add anything to the community because its absence didn't take anything away."

That research has yet to be done. No one studied the impact on Cocoa, Pompano Beach, Plant City, Yuma, Chandler, or Port Charlotte when spring training left. Perhaps Winter Haven, or Vero Beach, should it fail to replace the Dodgers, will provide interesting case studies for the economists in the years ahead. For now, the only spring training–specific research of the academic sort that Porter espouses was a study by University of Akron sociologist John F. Zipp, who looked at the economic fallout, or more specifically the lack thereof, from the strike-season/replacement-player spring training of 1995. Proceeding from the premise that out-of-state baseball fans stay in hotels, eat in restaurants, and otherwise partake of goods and services that are taxable, Zipp compared taxable sales in Florida counties that hosted spring training for the strike year of 1995 against the average in those counties for 1993 and 1994. He found no discernible difference. "How these counties did in the spring of 1995 is largely a function of how they did previously," he wrote. "This seems to indicate that, even in the relatively small economies of these Florida counties, professional sports can produce rather limited economic benefits."

However much Zipp, Porter, and their colleagues may be in agreement in this view, they have a difficult time making their voices heard in the city, county, and state offices and legislative chambers where decisions are being made. The Grapefruit and Cactus league economic impact studies are what have generated the headlines. Pseudo-economics, scoffs Porter.

"The economic impact studies are never subject to review," he said. "They are never even open to criticism by outsiders. It's only ever the press release that makes it into the public eye. We don't get to see the underlying data. We don't get to see how the model was calibrated; we don't even know what model was used. We don't even have a way to critique them. And yet the politicians consistently listen to their in-house people, who have been paid to generate tourism. None of them ever cite any of the literature—which has been burgeoning and growing, there's a huge literature out there—that says sports has very minimal impact and one-time-only events, like spring training and Super Bowls, have practically no impact.

"If no communities subsidized sports, we'd still have pretty much exactly the same sports we have now in exactly the same locations," he argues. "What the teams are doing is playing one city against the other. They're not going to go away if we don't pay them a subsidy. They'll simply go someplace else."

Porter's doubts are nothing new. Economists have long mustered arguments against the wisdom of investing public dollars in professional sports franchises. But the keepers of the public purse strings have ponied up nonetheless, and will likely continue to do so. Both the Arizona and Florida legislatures have twice passed bills that would provide state money for spring training facilities. The second piece of Arizona legislation, Proposition 302 in 2001, also passed a public referendum. Florida governor Jeb Bush twice signed legislation that made a total of $150 million in state money available for spring training construction. But the first time he had such legislation on his desk, he vetoed it, and he was a tough sell each of the times he did sign.

"I believe he felt, somehow, some way, the money that the state was going to give these communities was going to filter to the teams," said Larry Pendleton of the Florida Sports Foundation. "Which it doesn't. When I sat down and talked to him about it, I think he believed me, but I'm not sure. I don't think he thought I was lying to him, but somewhere down there, he felt in some sinister way the teams are going to be able to get some of this money through the locals." The governor still sounded like a man with doubts even when he finally did sign the bill.

"I want to help communities," Bush said in 2006. "And I know people think these things are important. But my libertarian gene kicks in when people come to discuss these things."

Former governor Bush is not alone in his reservation. The facilities may be publicly owned, but they are hardly public property in the same sense as a park or a city-owned museum. Access is controlled and limited. Except on game days, spring training stadiums appear more as fortresses of exclusivity and privilege than as egalitarian public assets.

And they are money losers. In every city or county with a spring training facility, the bottom-line number on the public ledger for that facility is red. Every lease is different; the one constant is that they are written to favor the ball club. Communities once had more favorable terms, but when they started building new facilities and competing for teams in the 1980s, the balance of negotiating power shifted to the teams, and the leases reflect that. Many leases call for teams to pay the municipalities somewhere between $100,000 and $300,000 per year. Some split revenues from ticket sales, concessions, and parking between the team and the city/county; some give all that money to the team. Virtually all leases call for the municipality to absorb all operations and maintenance costs. The only team maintaining their own spring training facilities is the Los Angeles Dodgers; their deal with Indian River County called for a $1-a-year lease, with the team retaining all revenues and absorbing all expenses; and they will have the same arrangement, this time in partnership with the White Sox, in their new facility in Arizona. Two-team facilities are a better deal for the community than a single-team complex. The two-team facilities in Peoria, Surprise, and Tucson all break even, or very close to it. For the rest, the number most often cited is $1 million: when all is said and done, that's what it costs a community to own and manage a spring training facility. Lee County, Florida, which manages two individual complexes for the Red Sox and Twins, loses about $2 million a year maintaining the two facilities. Yet, despite the drain on the municipal budget, there is not a single spring training community that does not believe that the money spent is a sound investment and that the spring training stadium is a jewel of a community asset.

Why?

Part of it goes back to name recognition. A national dateline six weeks every year is an asset difficult to quantify but impossible to disregard, particularly for a community steeped in the travel and tourism industry, or a new community looking to grow its business and residential base. Most spring training communities in Florida and Arizona fit into one or both of those categories, and an association with major league baseball and spring training gives them instant cachet, just as it did for St. Petersburg in the 1920s.

"For years I would travel and go to conferences and people would ask where I was from and I'd say: 'Kissimmee, Florida' and they'd say: 'Where's that?'" said Larry Whaley, the clerk of courts for Osceola County, who as county commissioner in the 1980s helped to bring spring training to Kissimmee. "Now I tell people I'm from Kissimmee, Florida, and there's instant recognition. They all go: 'Oh yeah, Astros spring training.'"

A second reason that communities are willing to look past the red ink is the conviction that a spring training stadium is a revenue generator for the community as a whole.

"This stadium [Mesa Hohokam] loses a million and a half dollars a year," admits Robert Brinton, the Cactus League Association's vice president and the executive director of the Mesa Convention and Visitors Bureau. "But what we aren't counting is what comes in off of hotels, what comes in off of restaurants. It's millions of dollars of revenue that's coming in to businesses, which translates back into taxes for the city. None of those factors are ever included in the city analysis. All they do is say it costs this much to plant the seed and mow the lawn and turn the water and power on. You need to look at the bigger picture."

Most spring training facilities have some life beyond spring training. Ten of the seventeen Grapefruit League stadiums are used for Class A Florida State League games, seventy home games a year. Only one Cactus League stadium—Tucson Electric Park, home to the Tucson Sidewinders, the Triple A affiliate of the Diamondbacks—plays host to a minor league team, but five of the nine Cactus League parks are used for the Arizona Fall League, the six-week, thirty-game-long developmental league run by major league baseball each October and November. While Triple A baseball draws well, the Florida State League and the Arizona Fall League are not big revenue generators. The crowds are small, and the local communities don't see a lot of tourism fallout. "In the Florida State League half the teams commute and go home," said Don Miers of Osceola County. "So of your seventy games you only get thirty-five hotel nights." Fifteen of the Grapefruit

League complexes and seven of the Cactus League facilities host rookie league teams. The Gulf Coast and Arizona leagues both play their games on the backfields before crowds of seldom more than a dozen people, who pay nothing to get in. Still, according to the local spring training boosters, there is benefit in having even these low-key activities. "We do see a benefit from that point that major leagues are consolidating more activities here," said Brinton. "Scouts are still coming in, and the teams are still paying for people to stay in hotels. So there's still a benefit. Not hundreds of millions, but still [money] coming in."

The most lucrative out-of-season use of these facilities is as a sort of convention center for amateur sports. When the Houston Astros left Cocoa for Kissimmee in 1985, the city sold Cocoa Stadium and the adjacent fields to a group of local businesspeople, who reinvented the complex as Cocoa Expo and began renting out the fields and staging tournaments in the stadium for high school and college teams needing a place to play on their spring break trip south. The early Cocoa Expo people were British, and so soccer tournaments and training opportunities were added to the Cocoa Expo menu. Football, basketball, softball, volleyball, lacrosse, swimming, and even band camps followed in rapid order. Athletes stayed in the old 400-bed Astros dormitory, their parents in one of the many nearby Cocoa Beach hotels, and together they visited the family-friendly honky-tonk of Cocoa Beach or nearby Cape Canaveral when the games were over. By the turn of the twenty-first century, Cocoa Expo, once home to forty-five days of Astros spring training, was humming year-'round, with more than 25,000 athletes playing on its fields.

Such success did not go unnoticed. Across Florida and Arizona, communities found that spring training complexes could have some lucrative nonspring uses as well. The Lee County Sports Authority brings in 60–80 events a year to the Red Sox and Twins complexes in Fort Myers; one tournament alone, the adult Roy Hobbs World Series, for players twenty-eight and over, attracts 190 teams over a four-week span and accounts for 10,000 room nights. "This is a November event, before Thanksgiving, which is a really dead time for us," said Jeff Mielke. "So that's 10,000 hotel rooms that wouldn't be sold unless this tournament was here."

In Osceola County, the United States Specialty Sports Association, which generates tournaments and training opportunities in a dozen different sports, has been given free rent on the grounds of Osceola County Stadium, so long as it sponsors events in the Osceola Stadium complex that generate a minimum of 20,000 room nights per year in the county. In recent years, it has doubled that number.

Plant City Stadium reinvented itself as a softball mecca following the Reds' departure in 1998. Down in Port Charlotte, the county bided its time between the Rangers leaving in 2002 and the Rays' arrival in 2009 by hosting independent leagues, spring break college tournaments, and even spring training for a professional team from Korea.

There is perhaps no surer sign of the viability of spring training complexes as economic engines than private money following public. In the early nineties, Walt Disney World entered this game. Based on the same principles that were driving the public complexes—that cold-weather athletes will pay for a temporary place in the sun, and spring training is a good brand to be associated with—Disney's Wide World of Sports quickly become the gold standard for all such complexes after its opening in 1997. With more than 200 acres of playing fields, gyms, and fieldhouses, Disney hosts some 180 mostly multiday events in over forty different sports every year and has hosted more than 1.5 million athletes since its inception. Most of these athletes stay at a Disney hotel, and most add theme-park tickets to their sports competition packages.

And from the first moments, spring training was central to Disney's vision for Wide World's success.

"We basically had two main pillars of the business before we announced Disney's Wide World of Sports," said Reggie Williams, who came to Disney after a career as a Cincinnati Bengals linebacker to build and oversee the Wide World of Sports complex. "The first pillar being a long-term relationship with the AAU [Amateur Athletic Union], and the second pillar was signing a spring training agreement with the Atlanta Braves."

The spring training piece was critical, said Williams. There was never any talk of a Wide World of Sports without it.

"We were going to have spring training," he said. "In order to launch the vision of being the number one destination in the world for kids who love sports to compete, you have to be able to tap into the existing tradition of sports, and the longest running, deepest-rooted tradition of sports in the state of Florida is the Grapefruit League. We wanted a piece of that rich legacy to pass on to our guests and our athletes. Whatever their sport was, they knew that this place was tied into the most tangible, traditional fabric of sports in the state."

Sunshine has always been Florida's most lucrative commodity. And Florida is finding that sunshine that comes with a vicarious connection to major leaguers can be sold at a premium.

SEVEN

Red Sox Nation
Flies South

They begin arriving before nine o'clock on a weekday morning in mid-February, and take their places in a long queue along Broadway in front of City of Palms Park. It is school vacation week back in New England, and the line pulses with children loosed from the confines of both school and bulky winter clothing. They leave the line to play catch amid the palms, to run up and down Broadway. They dart in and out of the stadium souvenir store, though it is difficult to imagine there is anything in there that these kids don't already own. They assert their individuality by wearing the same things: navy blue or red T-shirts with the names and numbers of David Ortiz, Jason Varitek, and Curt Schilling; white game jerseys with Manny Ramirez's number 24 or Ted Williams's number 9; leftover T-shirts displaying a continued affection for the departed Nomar Garciaparra and Pedro Martinez; T-shirts proclaiming "Yankees Suck." Conspicuous by their absence this year are the Johnny Damon jerseys so popular in recent springs. Damon has signed with the hated Yankees over the off-season, and the Red Sox fan's attitude is unequivocally and universally: he's dead to me.

The line knows no clear demographic. The schoolchildren are mixed in among laidback teens, twenty-something and thirty-something couples, parents and grandparents. Maybe two-thirds of the line wear some form of Red Sox cap—blue, red, white, tan, green, pink, and other pastels; wool game caps; unstructured cotton caps; visors; and oversized straw sun hats—all bearing the distinctive red Boston *B*. By ten o'clock, the line has swollen to more than 300 people, and finally the first buses arrive. Red Sox fans clamber aboard like rush-hour passengers on the "T" back home, filling seats, laps, and every square inch of aisle space. They pay a buck a head for a two-mile ride out to the end of Edison Avenue.

As vacation bus rides go, this is not exactly a trip along the Seine. The landscape out the bus windows is gray and brown. Yet for more than three hours, the buses rumble in a continuous stream down Edison Avenue—past a pawnshop; a school that could pass for a prison, with iron bars on its windows; low-rise public housing with similar iron bars on the windows; and a number of different warehouses, trucking companies, and auto body shops. But, at the terminus of Edison Avenue, tucked right behind the equipment yard for the Fort Myers Department of Public Works, the bus rider's world suddenly changes from gray and brown to a Technicolor sweep of green and blue and otherworldly white. The end of Edison Avenue has brought these travelers to their own little Oz.

The sign at the entrance reads "Boston Red Sox Player Development Complex," and it is where at 1 p.m. on this brilliant February Thursday, the Red Sox will hold their first full-squad workout of the spring. Development of the players on this day will involve nothing more than stretching, throwing, and a bit of hitting and fielding. But 2,900 fans have taken the buses from the stadium and parking areas in downtown Fort Myers (there is no public parking at the Red Sox's minor league complex) to watch. For the season has arrived, and these witnesses believe that they are nothing less than the chosen ones, the lucky surrogates for the millions of absent citizens of Red Sox Nation. They shout raucous greetings to coaches and players—even new players, in their first day in a Red Sox uniform, are family—to front office personnel like rock-star general manager Theo Epstein and principal owner John Henry, even to media members like Dan Shaughnessy, the fiery *Boston Globe* columnist Red Sox fans love to hate.

There is nothing in all of spring training quite like the circus that follows the Boston Red Sox around Florida. The New York Yankees rival the Red Sox in spring training appeal. They, too, sell out every home game at Legends Field and are likewise a popular draw as a visiting team. But Yankee and Red Sox spring training fans give off decidedly different vibes. Yankee fans at Legends Field are like art lovers at the Louvre, realizing a life's dream maybe and drinking it all in with keen appreciation. Red Sox spring training fans are like pilgrims at Lourdes, convinced that their lives have been touched by something spiritual and life affirming.

Taking nothing away from the very real passion that fans of the Cardinals, the Cubs, the Yankees, and others have for their teams, it is different with the Red Sox. Being a Cardinal or Cub fan involves a three-hour-a-day, 162-days-a-year commitment. They have jobs and families and lives outside the game. In Boston and New England, the Red Sox are never out of season; they are a 24/7/365 obsession. In the years the Patriots were marching through the NFL playoffs on their way to winning three Super Bowls in four years, they were sharing the front page of the January sports sections with Red Sox trade rumors. The Red Sox so dominate social intercourse that even the most disinterested are aware of whether things are going well or poorly, as judged by the mood swings of the people around them. During the season, even the most casual fan is preoccupied with the Red Sox; the serious fans are obsessed. More than a small percentage of Red Sox Nation is flat-out nuts, still prone to agita at the memory of Aaron Boone, plunged into depression at the thought of Bill Buckner, convinced that their lives would be somehow different and richer had Darrell Johnson not gone to Jim Burton in the ninth inning of game seven back in '75. This perpetual dark cloud above the heads of some Red Sox fans brightened notably in the wake of two world championships in four seasons. But it is still there

The Red Sox are also, forever, a part of the fan's DNA. You take a kid who grows up in Philadelphia as a Phillies fan, in Detroit as a Tigers fans, or maybe in Chicago as a White Sox fan—anything but a Yankees fan. This kid comes to Boston for college and settles down in the area afterward. At some point during the time between college commencement and the day he takes his child to Fenway Park for the first time, this expatriate has become a Red Sox fan. The Phillies, Tigers, or White Sox may always hold a place in his heart, as first loves do. But the conversion to Red Sox fan is real and absolute.

It does not work in reverse. Take a New Englander suckled on the Red Sox and have him make his way as an adult to Baltimore, Cleveland, or St. Louis. He is still a Red Sox fan, part of the crowd that buys tickets to the local park whenever the Sox are in town, part of that boisterous, vocal few (and sometimes many) that make the Red Sox feel as though they are among friends wherever they go.

"I'd love to put my finger on it and give it to you in some verse of poetry," said Dr. Charles Steinberg, of the deep-rooted, unshakable connection that Red Sox fans have with their team. Before leaving for the Los Angeles Dodgers in 2008, Steinberg was for six years the team's executive vice president for public affairs, and thus on the front lines of the team's connection with its fans and its heritage. "It is based on love; I do believe that. Two kinds of love. It's based on the love of baseball, and the love of family and family lore. Boston and New England are places so proud of traditions, so proud of the interconnecting of generations."

Love of the Red Sox is thus a sort of family heirloom. To trifle with it is somehow a form of betrayal.

The phrase "Red Sox Nation" entered the language because of Dan Shaughnessy, a columnist for the *Boston Globe*. Shaughnessy also wrote *The Curse of the Bambino*, giving Red Sox fans a rationalization and catchphrase for their generational misery. He was not the first to use "Red Sox Nation" in a newspaper story; he searched the *Globe* archives a few years ago and discovered that feature writer Nathan Cobb had used the phrase once in 1986. Shaughnessy was unaware of this when he began regularly using the phrase in his column in the early 1990s. Red Sox Nation remained Shaughnessy's domain more or less exclusively for about five years, but by the time he put it in the title of a book in 1996—*At Fenway: Dispatches from Red Sox Nation*—his colleagues in the Fenway press box were beginning to use the phrase with some regularity too, sometimes crediting Shaughnessy, sometimes not. By the end of the decade, the phrase had become a pretty familiar part of the conversation; it had passed into the public domain, so to speak. Today, it's become an official Red Sox marketing campaign. "Make your membership official," goes the advertising copy. Players do promos holding Red Sox Nation membership cards, urging fans to sign up for one of three levels of citizenship in Red Sox Nation, ranging from $14.95 to $199. At the start of the 2008 season, there were over 45,000 dues-paying members of Red Sox Nation, from all fifty states and forty-seven foreign countries.

"I guess I'm less comfortable with it now than I was," said Shaughnessy in 2006 of the phrase he made a part of the language. "It's become so trendy, it's taking in non-baseball people now." Shaughnessy never meant it to be trendy. Red Sox Nation, he insists, was meant to describe those who are born in New England and raised on baseball, those for whom the Red Sox are "in your genes."

The Red Sox and spring training are the perfect storm. At the vortex is the fans' fixation with their team. Swirling about the edge is the fact that Boston in March is a good place to get the hell out of, and Fort Myers is a sweet place to visit. Bostonians love their Christmastime snows and take a fierce pride at being able to persevere through their frigid Januarys. But by March, even the heartiest New Englander is sick of slushy streets and dirty, crusted snow and wind chills that give no hint of an imminent spring. Fort Myers is a perfect antidote. It's less than three hours by air, with a wide range of cheap, direct daily flights from Boston. In addition to the Red Sox, Fort Myers has beaches, golf, and fishing in abundance and hotels and restaurants for every budget. For the self-flagellating Red Sox fan, Fort Myers in March even has oppressive Boston-like traffic. So each February, Red Sox Nation decamps for Fort Myers; those who don't make the journey physically make it in spirit, living vicariously through the men and women of the New England Fourth Estate.

Just as there is no other team with fans that are quite as suffocating in their love, no team—save for *maybe* the two New York teams—has a press cadre anywhere near as large or as voracious. The City of Palms Park's press box is twice as large as anything else in the Grapefruit or Cactus leagues except for the Yankees' Legends Field. And, like the press box at Legends Field, it is always filled. More reporters cover a March exhibition game between the Red Sox and Rays than a G-8 summit.

The Red Sox have rewarded their reporters with a century's worth of headlines. Spring training stories tend to leak off the sports page and onto the front page and the gossip page.

The first spring training example is the strangest and the saddest. In the middle of spring training in 1907, manager Chick Stahl committed suicide. Stahl, the centerfielder on Boston's first World Series championship team in 1903 and the manager since late in the 1906 season, tried to quit as manager after the team had broken camp in Hot Springs and began its barnstorming north, saying the pressure of managing was too much for him. Owner John I. Taylor persuaded him to stay on until a replacement could be found. But a day later, on March 28, when the team was in West Baden, Indiana, Stahl drank a bottle of carbolic acid he'd been given to treat a bruise on his foot. Newspapers reported that his last words, to teammate Robert Unglaub, were: "It [the pressure of the manager's job] drove me to it."

The newspapers reported that Stahl was a practicing Catholic, a regular mass-goer, a devoted son who had just bought his elderly mother a house. They reported that he'd been married less than six months earlier and quoted his widow, Julia, as saying that their life together had been "one long honeymoon." News stories told of how popular he was with teammates and fans, his love of life, and the belief that until he was burdened with the manager's mantle, "Stahl had never known a care in the world." Teammate Cy Young had tears in his eyes when he told reporters: "It is mighty tough boys. Players may come and go, but there are few Chick Stahls." Pretty standard 1907 *de mortuis nil nisi bonum* newspaper fare.

Soon, however, Boston newspapers began reporting a different story. Stahl's love of life, these stories said, often took the form of partaking in the delights of the "Baseball Sadies." Some years earlier, one jilted lover had taken a shot at him on the streets of his hometown of Fort Wayne because he'd refused to marry her. At the time of his suicide, he was reportedly being blackmailed by a Chicago woman who claimed the child she'd borne over the off-season was the product of a midseason tryst with Stahl. Moreover, in addition to a child, this woman reportedly gave Stahl a case of syphilis, which he in turn had passed along to his new bride. And because of that, the couple had lived apart for all but the first month of their marriage.

And then it gets even curiouser. Julia Stahl, who lived just around the corner from the Red Sox's first ballpark on Huntington Avenue, was herself found dead in the vestibule of an apartment building less than two years later. The cause of death was edema of the brain, a symptom of syphilis. She'd been out partying with a group of college boys on the night of her death, and speculation was that she'd been working as a prostitute since her husband's suicide.

Much of the early reporting on the sordid angles of the Stahl story was done by Fred O'Connell of the *Boston Post*. At some point during the reporting of the story in West Baden, Indiana, O'Connell came down with pneumonia and died two weeks later. Some jaded readers saw O'Connell's fate as just desserts. For Boston fans have long had a love-hate relationship with the reporters who cover their team. Tell us everything you know and tell us in infinite and intimate detail, the fans demand of the Boston press. But don't you ever say anything bad about our boys.

Nothing has ever quite topped the Chick Stahl story for drama and pathos. But Boston reporters, the "knights of the keyboard," as Ted Williams liked to call them, have never wanted for good spring training material. Williams was introduced to newspaper readers in 1938 as self-confident to the point of arrogance, plainspoken to the point of rudeness. Some writers questioned his emotional stability. Williams sniffed at the rainy Florida weather on his first day in camp and told the Boston writers that he was disappointed that the Pacific Coast League's San Diego Padres had sold his contract to the Red Sox. Fenway Park, he knew, was not conducive to left-handed pull hitters. "When I first learned I'd been sold to Boston, I was going to quit," he told reporters. "New York or Detroit, that's where I belong. I could have gone to Southern Cal on a baseball scholarship, too, dammit. Hell, if I'd of known I was going to end up at Fenway Park, I'd of taken it."

"Wait until you see [Jimmy] Foxx hit," one of the writers reportedly said to Williams, referring to the Red Sox first baseman who hit fifty home runs in the 1938 season. "Wait until Foxx sees me hit," Williams reportedly said in response. This exchange became famous, igniting the spark of mistrust between Williams and the press that persisted for two decades. Williams insisted throughout his career and afterward that he never said anything of the sort, and he is utterly believable on this point. Williams freely admitted that it was how he felt as a nineteen-year-old, and he was never one to try to deny anything he said to the press or anybody else. Nonetheless, "wait until Foxx sees me hit" became a part of the Williams legend.

But through a quarter-century in Sarasota, where a pitcher once injured himself falling off a circus elephant in a publicity stunt; to a brief sojourn in Scottsdale, where another pitcher injured himself falling off a horse in a publicity stunt; to a quarter-century in Winter Haven; and now for more than fifteen seasons in Fort Myers, Boston writers have seldom needed to resort to invention for their headlines. "I've said it before and I'll say it again: Covering this team is like doing lay-up drills on an eight-foot rim," said Dan Shaughnessy, who's been covering Red Sox spring trainings for a quarter-century.

Civil rights activists protested the Red Sox during the waning days of spring training in 1959, when the team optioned infielder Pumpsie Green to the minors. The Red Sox were then the only team in major league baseball to have never put a black player on the field, and sending Green back to the minors ensured they would still be the only all-white team come opening day.

"Send money, guns and lawyers," said pitcher Bill Lee as he ran up to a gaggle of loitering reporters one March day in Winter Haven in 1978. "The shit has just hit the fan." The Sox had just traded for Dennis Eckersley.

Red Sox history in Winter Haven can almost be demarcated by the stories generated; in among the normal holdouts and trade demands, there was the Earl Wilson restaurant spring; the Elks Club spring; the slugger-and-the-front-office-exec-fight-it-out-over-a-parking-space spring; and the Wade Boggs–Margo Adams spring.

In the team's first spring in Winter Haven in 1966, pitcher Earl Wilson, the best on the Red Sox staff, was refused service in a restaurant/bar called the Cloud 9 in Lakeland because he was a black man. He asked that the team make a statement of protest about the incident. The team's statement was to trade Wilson to the Tigers.

Six years later, in 1972, newly acquired Tommy Harper noticed that free guest passes to the Elks Club lodge had been placed in the lockers of the white players but not those of the black players. He did nothing about it at the time, but when he returned to the team as a coach in 1980, he asked the team to discontinue its association with the Elks. The club did nothing. When Harper was dismissed as a coach in 1985, he claimed as part of a wrongful termination suit against the club—filed during spring training— that the club promoted racism by tolerating the Elks Club's whites-only policy. It was not a comfortable spring for the Red Sox management, but the team's relationship with the Elks Club was finally over.

Not all of the Red Sox's off-field stories in Winter Haven were fraught with great social significance, of course. In 1981, Jim Rice arrived late one morning for an away game in Lakeland and grabbed the parking spot nearest the locker room. It happened to be the spot reserved for public relations vice president Bill Crowley. Rice made the bus, and when Crowley showed up for work a bit later he not only found Rice's yellow Cadillac in his spot, he found his "Reserved for Bill Crowley" sign in the grass in an adjacent orange grove. When the sixty-two-year-old Crowley—a World War II bomber pilot who never shrank from an argument—got to Lakeland later that morning, he found Rice in the batting cage and started giving him the what-for. The two men scuffled and Crowley's hand was bloodied. The writers feasted for days.

Margo Adams was not a spring training story at first. Wade Boggs's long-time paramour had filed her explosive palimony suit against the future Hall of Famer during the summer of 1988. This prompted a huge clamor, which then subsided. But as the Red Sox were gathering in Winter Haven in 1989, Margo Adams was telling the world her story in the March issue of *Penthouse* magazine, accompanied by photographs. She painted Boggs as petty, venal, and a borderline racist. Boggs gave an interview to a local Boston television station, and another to ABC's Barbara Walters, saying he was recovering from an "addiction to sex." As if that were not surreal enough, in the middle of camp, the Red Sox tried to trade Boggs, the five-time

American League batting champion. There were no takers. Later in camp, Margo Adams was arrested for shoplifting in a California Nordstrom's.* That summer, the story line would be Wade Boggs winning a sixth American League batting title.

Lay-up drills on an eight-foot rim indeed.

The off-field stories that emanate from Red Sox spring training in the twenty-first century are decidedly less flamboyant and more likely to be found on the business page than the gossip page. In the spring of 2005, following their first world championship in eighty-six years, the Red Sox added 300 seats to City of Palms Park in Fort Myers in order to sate a bit of the demand that, even before the World Series triumph, had been running impossibly far ahead of supply. One hundred and ninety of those new seats were in what had previously been a part of the playing field, a strip of foul territory running from dugout to dugout, land where the on-deck circles had been. The Sox priced these new seats at an eye-popping $44. All around major league baseball, people rolled their eyes and shook their heads. Forty-four dollars was more than twice the average price for spring training tickets in 2005; it was $19 more than the second-highest spring training ticket—the $25 the Phillies were charging for the best seats in their new stadium in Clearwater. Of the other twenty-nine major league teams, only nine had tickets that topped out above $20. The $44 the Red Sox would be getting for their best spring training tickets was more than twice the average price for *regular season* tickets in 2005. It was higher than the highest-priced regular season ticket of more than a dozen teams. The Red Sox's $44 ticket was not only in a rarified atmosphere, it was an Apollo moon shot in a world where everyone else was still marveling at Lindbergh. "Naked greed" is what the *Boston Globe*

---

* It must be noted here, especially in light of the Red Sox finishing second to the Yankees so many times throughout history, that they finish second to the Yankees in bizarre spring training stories too. In 1973 Yankee pitchers Fritz Peterson and Mike Kekich announced that they had "swapped lives." After some months of consenting-adult wife swapping the previous season, the two men announced that Peterson had moved into Kekich's home with Kekich's wife and children, and Kekich had taken Peterson's place in his home. "We didn't do anything sneaky or lecherous. There isn't anything smutty about this," said Susan Kekich-Peterson. See espn .go.com/page2/s/list/baseball/shocking/moments.html.

called it. Yet the Red Sox sold every one of those $44 tickets—together with every other ticket they had for a 2005 spring training game—in just six and a half hours.

Sensitive to the criticism, the Red Sox took pains to point out that the $44 seats did not reflect a price increase. The top-priced seats at City of Palms had sold for $24 in 2004. Those same seats would sell for $24 in 2005. Only now the fans in those seats would be looking over the heads of the fans in the new field-level seats in front of them. Dr. Charles Steinberg told reporters that the team was "humble and grateful" that spring tickets had sold out as quickly as they did. It is hardly surprising, given the frenzy that surrounds the team, that the Red Sox are the hottest ticket in spring training. Tickets to Red Sox spring training games sell out within hours of going on sale each December. Since 2002, the Red Sox have played to more than 100 percent of capacity at City of Palms Park. They could have charged $88 for those new seats and gotten it easily; for that and more is what scalpers often get for lesser seats on the streets outside City of Palms. Scalper prices for a Red Sox–Yankees game have topped $200 in the twenty-first century. And it doesn't stop at tickets.

The Red Sox have tripled the size of their team store at City of Palms since their world championship, and on game days it's still not large enough. Maximum occupancy limits require a gatekeeper at the door to watch over a waiting line. Once the place fills, which is not long after the gates open, fans are let in only as others leave. The Sox report that the average sale inside is $200. Citizens of Red Sox Nation give as freely of their purses as they do their hearts.

Despite the stratospheric ticket prices, the long lines at the team store, the ubiquitous ballpark advertising, and the other evidence of commerce, the Red Sox employ a remarkably soft sell when it comes to separating their fans from their money. "I don't believe in the focus being on the selling," said Steinberg. "Appeal to the hearts of your market."

The Red Sox have certainly done that. The on-the-field success speaks for itself, but since taking over in 2003, the ownership group headed by financier John Henry has also gone out of its way to make the citizens of Red Sox Nation feel that they are truly a treasured piece of the Red Sox phenomenon. This is a dramatic reversal of the puritanical reserve of the previous ownership. Henry et al. have worked hard at dressing up beloved Fenway Park, widening concourses, upgrading concessions, putting seats in exotic and heretofore unreachable parts of Fenway (most notably and most dramatically on top of the left-field wall). It remains the basilica it has always been for baseball fans, but now it's taken on an organic we've-gotta-go-and-see-what's-new energy as well. The organization has also reached out to the community in ways large and small. The Red Sox Foundation has donated millions to New England charities. When they won the World Series the first time, in 2004, they took the championship trophy on a four-month tour of New England cities and towns. Tens of thousands of family photo albums now feature grinning Red Sox fans standing happily next to the trophy.

"The Red Sox finally have an ownership that embraces the fans the way the fans have always embraced the team," said the *Globe*'s Shaughnessy.

The Red Sox have taken this same sense of community with them to Fort Myers, becoming involved in local charities and civic organizations and giving what chief operating officer Mike Dee sees as a New England feel to Fort Myers and southwest Florida. "It's amazing. You see *Boston Globe* newspaper boxes on the streets, Dunkin Donuts are all around the area," he said. "There's just a New England flavor to this region, and the local politicians and the people who have put their hearts and soul into spring training baseball will tell you that the Red Sox really played a big role in that." Whether fans have followed the Red Sox to Fort Myers as year-round residents, seasonal residents, or winter vacationers, they feel an undeniable bond. There is little they won't do for their team. They may raise their eyebrows at the high prices. But they don't balk at paying them. "I can't tell you why you should give us your money," said Steinberg. "But I can tell you why I think this is the greatest game in the world. Now if you love it so much, you're just gonna take out your money."

Red Sox Nation does not spend all of its money in Fort Myers, either. The exuberance that follows the Red Sox south from New England follows them about Florida as well, much to the delight of the rest of the Grapefruit League. The Red Sox and Yankees are on everyone's wish list when schedule requests are made the previous summer. Red Sox and Yankees games sell out across the state and are generally the first games to sell out for the various home teams. In Vero Beach in 2006 on the January morning that Dodgers tickets went on sale, the line began forming at five o'clock, five hours before the ticket windows opened. The first people in line were New

England expatriates, looking to buy Red Sox tickets. So were the 100 people behind them.

"I'd take fifteen Red Sox games every year," said Dodgertown director Craig Callan, who every year requested a home-and-home with the Red Sox.

The Red Sox games in Vero Beach over the Dodgers' last four springs there averaged more than 9,000 in attendance. That's 3,500 more fans than the Dodgers' Grapefruit League average. The Red Sox visited eleven different Grapefruit League parks in 2007; in eight of them, their game represented the largest crowd of the season for the home team. By contrast, the Yankees, though they led the Grapefruit League in attendance—due to the 10,000-seat Legends Field—represented the largest crowd in only four of the parks where they played as visitors.

The Red Sox could easily sell out a 10,000-seat stadium for their spring training games. They could probably fill a 20,000-seat stadium. But the team is conflicted on what to do about the disparity between spring training supply and demand. "It's a fine line that we walk in terms of having enough capacity in the ballpark," said Mike Dee, the Red Sox's chief operating officer. "We've expanded the ballpark over the last three years and people say, well, you should expand it more. People say it's 7,500, it would be great if it were 10,000. But if it were 10,000, you'd have people saying it's too bad it's only 10,000, it should be 14,000. Where does it stop? Because what's special about spring training is that it is a different environment.

"And we do worry about losing that. I think we're close to the point that we don't want to go beyond in terms of size. We don't want to take one bite out of the apple and put it back in the basket. It's a very special time for fans. And if it becomes too big and too commercial, I think you reach a point of diminishing returns."

Spring training, and particularly Red Sox spring training, is at a crossroads. You keep the ballpark small because it affords access and proximity, and with exhibition baseball, access and proximity are what you're selling. But keeping the park small limits the access. With no team is this more acute than with the Red Sox. Every game is a sellout. The team has more than 400 names on a waiting list for spring training season tickets. There is a thriving scalper and eBay market for spring game tickets, which can be the most expensive and problematic pieces of spring vacation for Red Sox fans.

Ten teams, nine of them in Arizona, play in spring training stadiums with capacities of 10,000 or more. Is the access and proximity of Cubs,

Yankees, or Giants fans any less special for the extra 2,000 spectators? If spring training is about access, isn't opening that access to greater numbers the right answer? But what is that number? By 2008, one thing seemed certain. The number was bigger than the 8,000 or so fans who are able to crowd into City of Palms Park, and the Red Sox began looking for a bigger facility.

"Spring training is where you cleanse yourself of the sludge of winter and from the disappointment that twenty-nine out of thirty fan bases feel every year," says Steinberg. "What you don't want to do is deny me the opportunity to see it. I need it."

EIGHT

"Let The Tourists Put in Their Two Cents"

No student of baseball history would reasonably count the Houston Astros as part of the pantheon of the game's historic franchises. There's less history to the Astros than to other teams, of course; they were one of the original National League expansion franchises, coming into the league as the Houston Colt .45s in 1962. But with the Astros, it's less a matter of the depth of their history than it is its drabness. They've never been very good, and, unlike their fellow expansionists, the New York Mets, they've never been spectacularly bad either. For the better part of forty years they plodded along somewhere between the middle and the bottom of the National League standings, winning a couple of division titles before starting to win consistently in the twenty-first century, yet never making it to the World Series until 2005. Their Hall of Famers—infielder Joe Morgan and pitcher Nolan Ryan—wear the caps of other teams on their plaques in Cooperstown. The franchise's one great moment in the national spotlight came when it moved into the Astrodome in 1965. The "indoor baseball palace" was hailed in national magazines of the time as "the eighth wonder of the world." Today, it's seen instead as the park that ushered in a regrettable generation of bad baseball stadiums.

Kissimmee, Florida, the county seat of sprawling Osceola County, has had a similarly undistinguished history. In the list of Florida places whose names have rolled trippingly off the tongues of Americans through the years—Key West, Key Largo, Miami, Palm Beach, Daytona Beach, St. Augustine, St. Petersburg, Sarasota, Fort Myers, Naples—Kissimmee has always been absent. The Spanish had first explored the area in the 1500s, but quickly forgotten about it. Its name said it all: for much of its first two centuries, it was a part of the old Mosquito County.

In the 1880s, just before the state forged Osceola County out of parts of Orange (Mosquito County's new name) and Brevard counties, a Philadelphia saw maker by the name of Hamilton Disston bought up 4 million acres of state-owned land in the new county for twenty-five cents an acre. The purchase made him the largest private landowner in America, though most of his land was under water. Part of his deal with the state stipulated that he would drain the swamps covering much of the newly incorporated county by digging a series of canals that would not only drain the swampland but also serve to connect the Kissimmee River to a string of midstate lakes, eventually establishing a navigable waterway from Kissimmee all the way down to the massive Lake Okeechobee, and from there out to the Gulf of Mexico. Disston hoped the waterway might prove a spur to a hunting and fishing trade. But some Disston business reversals and a series of economic downturns ensured that Osceola County tourism never got off the ground, and the county instead became home to cattle ranches and citrus groves.

The Houston Astros and Osceola County. The anonymous team and the overlooked county: an unlikely pair to make any sort of baseball or political history. In the early 1980s, however, they came together in an innovative piece of politics and business that would change forever the way spring training was conducted. Contemporary spring training, the spring training of sprawling, built-to-order complexes, born of innovative financing and even more innovative politics, began in Kissimmee, Florida.

The story really begins, as do most modern stories of central Florida, with the arrival of The Mouse in 1971. Walt Disney World—forty-seven square miles, more than 30,000 acres, straddling the border between Orange and Osceola counties—transformed Osceola County's economy and its personality; and did it practically overnight. Citrus trees were felled to make way for hotels; rangeland was transformed into parking lots for fast-food restaurants and kitschy souvenir stands. Herds of cattle gave way to herds of tourists. Along the west end of U.S. 192, right out Disney's back door, hotel after hotel rose up out of the land. Best Western, Comfort Inn, Day's Inn, Econolodge, Hilton, Holiday Inn, Howard Johnson, Knight's Inn, Motel 6, Quality Inn, Radisson, Ramada, Rodeway Inn, Sheraton, Super 8, Travelodge, and dozens upon dozens of independent hotel operators rushed to provide shelter for the millions of Disney visitors. Kissimmee became Disney World's bedroom. By the mid-1980s, there were 113 hotels in Osceola County, with a total of 17,017 rooms. In the peak vacation months of February, March, and April, those rooms were more than 90 percent full.

In its 1977 session, the Florida legislature approved the Local Option Tourist Development Act, permitting counties statewide to levy a 1 or 2 percent tax on all transient lodging—hotels, campgrounds, condos, and the like—on all stays of less than six months. It became popularly known as the "bed tax," and Osceola County became the first county in the state to impose it. "Two Cents Makes Sense" and "Let the Tourists Put in Their Two Cents" were the campaign's rallying cries. On November 8, 1977, voters approved a 2 percent tax in a countywide referendum. The Osceola County Tourist Development Council, created along with the bed tax, estimated that the new revenue source could be worth $720,000 a year to the county. Its projections were a bit conservative. Within a year, the tax brought in more than $1.1 million; within five years, it was bringing in over $2 million a year; and within ten years, the take in Osceola County exceeded $4.5 million a year.

The tax's mandate stipulated that revenues be used to generate and support tourism. Osceola County built a permanent home for its Convention and Visitors Bureau. And it advertised—in newspapers and on radio and television stations across the Southeast, up and down the eastern seaboard, and into the Midwest. Major eastern newspapers, national magazines, even national television—nothing was beyond its budget. Ads touted Kissimmee's proximity to Disney World and all of central Florida's attractions. Travelers came from all over the world, but for most, Kissimmee and St. Cloud were never the destination. They never said they were going to Kissimmee. They were always going to Disney. "Where are you staying at Disney?" might have prompted an "Oh, someplace called Kissimmee," but that was it. Osceola County remained Disney's bedroom.

Officials and administrators had plenty of challenges as the county's economy and population exploded in the late seventies and early eighties. Among them was finding ways to stimulate growth while at the same time managing it. Another was trying to give Kissimmee and Osceola County an identity separate from that of Disney World.

A former Kissimmee city manager named Bud Parmer had an idea he thought might address both of those points. Since leaving the city manager's post in 1979, Parmer had been doing private consulting work for city and county governments in Florida. In 1983, he was a principal in a company called Tabcor, and he and his partner, Tom Brant, were brainstorming one day on how they might generate some business. They had talked off and on about the possibility of trying to bring a spring training team to Kissimmee. Parmer remembered an eighty-seven-acre piece of land near the rodeo grounds. The county, he said, didn't know "what the heck to do with it." So the two men drove down a dusty road behind the Osceola County Rodeo Grounds to look and were immediately energized by the notion of filling the land with spring training baseball.

County officials had actually explored the notion of using the land as some sort of sports complex as early as 1981. They had even explored the possibility of advertising for a marketing firm to help in the process. But the idea had never developed beyond conversation. Parmer and Brant were convinced it would work. Parmer decided it was time to take it to Larry Whaley, an old friend then serving on the county commission. Parmer found Whaley at a meeting of the Florida Association of County Commissions, told him that he and Brant had some contacts in the baseball world, and asked what he thought about bringing spring training to Osceola. Whaley thought it was a great idea and arranged for Parmer and Brant to meet with the full commission. "This is a no-lose deal for you," Brant told the commissioners. "If we don't perform, you don't pay us anything."

Tabcor's first meeting with the county was in January 1983. In August, it made its formal presentation. The company estimated the cost to build the complex at $3.3 million and projected that spring training would generate more than $4 million annually in direct and indirect economic impact for Kissimmee and Osceola County. And, as spring training proponents had been doing since the beginning of the century, the partners spoke to the intangible and incalculable benefits. "Baseball encourages and increases tourism whenever and wherever in the state it is played," wrote Brant and Parmer in their presentation:

> And the publicity generated by the press, radio and television
> newspeople, who keep a constant spring training vigil, is almost
> beyond calculation in terms of the number of column inches and
> minutes of radio and television exposure devoted to the baseball

heroes for consumption by an eager baseball audience back home in the cold North and Midwest. It is doubtful that a zillion postcards or 10,000 travel agents could do a better job for Florida tourism than major league baseball and its enormous contingent of traveling newspeople.

One provision of the contract called for Brant and Parmer to help the county find a way to pay for things. The county didn't have a lot of money in its general fund. While it had been collecting ever-increasing property taxes from all the new homes and businesses that had been added to the tax rolls during the boom years, it was spending that money as fast as it was collecting it on new schools, fire engines, fire fighters, police cruisers, police officers, roads, and other infrastructure, even a brand-new county prison (as sure a sign as any that Osceola County was now a thriving little corner of the world).

So the would-be stadium builders very quickly began eyeing the large pile of money that the tourist-development tax (TDT) was bringing in. In the six years since its inception in 1977, the bed tax had brought in $8.7 million. The 1983–1984 fiscal year promised to bring in another $2.5 million, with projections escalating from there. In early 1983, there was still more than $2 million sitting unspent in the county coffers. To Larry Whaley, it seemed a shame to waste all that money on advertising. "We wanted something in concrete," he said. "We wanted something here that would be permanent."

But could the county use that money for a bricks-and-mortar project like a baseball stadium? It had built the convention and visitors center with TDT money. Orange County, just to the north, had built and expanded its convention center with TDT money. Wasn't bringing spring training to the county the same as bringing a business convention? So wouldn't building a spring training complex be the same as building a convention center?

Today, the Florida statute governing how TDT money may be spent—a statute that's been revised several times since its original passage in 1977—makes explicit provisions for use of the money "to acquire, construct, extend, enlarge, remodel, repair, improve, maintain, operate or promote...publicly owned and operated sports stadiums [or] sports arenas." But no such provision existed in the statute in 1983, and nobody had yet thought of using the money in this way. Larry Whaley read the statute and felt that it would allow spending on a stadium. The county attorney, John Ritch, agreed but also sought the counsel of the Florida attorney general before signing off on the deal. "Sure, that's tourism" was Tallahassee's answer, and Osceola County had found a way to pay for spring training.

Not everyone in the county felt that just because they could buy baseball with their tourist tax money that they should. "The Tourist Development Council was against this," said Don Miers, who worked for the Houston Astros during the stadium's construction and today oversees the stadium for Osceola County as part of his responsibilities as director of the county's Event Facilities Department. "They felt that March was the wrong time of year to be bringing in tourists because we've already got them coming. All the snowbirds come down right after Christmas and stay through Easter." Whaley saw another reason behind the TDC's reluctance. "The Tourist Development Council were all hoteliers," he said. "And they wanted every penny spent on advertising."

Though the Tourist Development Council was an official county agency, mandated by the Florida statute creating the TDT and appointed by the county commissioners to administer the disbursement of the TDT money, the ultimate responsibility for how that money was spent remained with the county commission. The commission voted 5–0 to support the project, seeing it as creating an enduring community asset that would cost the community nothing and would, moreover, give some residents who'd never liked the tourists a reason now to appreciate their presence. "A lot of the old local residents were complaining about all the tourists being here," said Whaley, himself a third-generation Kissimmee resident, "and the stadium would enable us to say, 'well, we've got all these tourists here, but we also have a $7 million stadium and we've got professional baseball in Kissimmee now.' We've got something to show for that tourist tax money, something solid."

While all of this was going on at the county level, Tom Brant and Bud Parmer had a different priority: recruiting a team.

Before he'd come to Kissimmee in 1973, Parmer had been the assistant city manager in Clearwater. One of his duties had been negotiating the city's lease with the Phillies every year. He was hopeful that his old Phillies' contacts would pay off. His first call was to Dallas Green, then general manager of the Chicago Cubs. Green heard Parmer out but told him that the Cubs had just moved back to Mesa from Scottsdale a couple of years before and were quite happy in Arizona. Green suggested talking to the Brewers, who were getting restless in Sun City. Tom Brant then called Brewers general manager Harry Dalton. The conversation was cordial but distant enough to convince Brant that he and Parmer were going to have trouble landing a team on their own. "I said: 'You know what, Bud, we got a problem here, because we're calling these baseball people and they don't know who we are,'" said Brant. "And from what I know, following baseball kind of closely, this is kind of a closed circle."

So Brant and Parmer turned to Peter Bavasi, the former Dodgers, Padres, and Blue Jays executive, who was then working as a consultant with the city of St. Petersburg, trying to recruit a major league, regular season team to St. Petersburg's new domed stadium. He'd set up an office in Tampa, and Brant and Parmer went to meet him there. "We went through the thing in some detail and he said: 'Yeah, I'd be interested in helping you with this. I think I can get it done for you,'" said Brant. "And so I'm holding my breath and I'm thinking, I hope it isn't going to cost more than $15,000 because we're not going to make a lot of money on this thing anyway by the time we're done. And I said, 'OK. How much?' and he says, '$25,000' and I said, 'Fine.'"

Bavasi talked to the Mets and the Cardinals and to a couple of other teams. But the team he soon brought to the county was the Houston Astros.

The Astros were then training in Cocoa, Florida, in what was by common consent the worst spring training facility in all of baseball. It had been built for the Astros in 1964, to lure them east from Apache Junction, Arizona. Yet even when new, it was a bare-bones facility, built to the simple needs of the 1960s, and nothing had been done to dress it up as the years passed. "When we left in late March, we would close the door behind us and nobody would do a thing to that place until the next spring," said Barry Waters, a clubhouse assistant at Cocoa in the early eighties and today the Astros' traveling secretary.

"You know how we would clean that place when we arrived?" adds Dennis Liborio, Waters's boss back in 1980 and still the Astros' equipment manager. "We'd take a hose—Barry would take a hose—and wash the whole place down. There were cobwebs, animal droppings, everything in there, and we'd just wash it all out the door."

"I found a skunk living in there one year," said Waters. "I just opened the doors and waited until he left."

The locker room's bathroom stalls had no doors, like a World War II army barracks. Every player's most private moment was shared with forty other men. "Al Rosen came in [as general manager in 1980] and couldn't believe it," said Liborio. "He told me, 'Dennis, we gotta get some doors on these shitters.'"

The locker room was maybe 700 square feet, crammed with forty chicken-wire lockers; nonroster invitees, always a dozen or more strong, had to dress in the minor league locker room, another 700 square feet with maybe 100 lockers. "We had one washing machine and one dryer," said Liborio, "and they were going all day and all night long." The barracks were without heat or air conditioning, and if the players and team personnel staying there wanted television in their rooms, they needed to make arrangements with the local rent-a-center and pay for it out of their own pocket. The dirt parking lot was a quagmire, drainage was nonexistent, and every time it rained somebody's car got stuck. "One of the clubhouse assistants had a Jeep," said Waters, "and he was always pulling stuck cars out of the mud."

For all of the horrors of the locker room and barracks, the baseball facilities were worse. There was just the stadium field and one practice field, not unusual for facilities of that era. But the fields were unusable a lot of the time. The same poor drainage that plagued the parking lots plagued the outfields as well.

"Sometimes you couldn't get on the fields for days at a time," said Phil Garner, an Astros player from 1980 to 1987. "I remember once it got so bad we were taking grounders on this narrow strip of parking lot; it was the only spot in the whole place that was dry." Even when the fields were dry, they weren't very good. "Nobody wanted to play in Cocoa," said Jerry Remy, a second baseman for the Red Sox in the seventies and eighties and now the team's broadcaster. "Everybody wanted to skip those trips. That infield was the worst infield I ever played on. You were always afraid that a ground ball was going to bounce up and kill you."

It was not all misery and mud at Cocoa, of course. There was baseball, and one of Phil Garner's Cocoa memories is among the most vivid of his entire career: "Nolan Ryan was pitching and he was a notoriously slow starter in the spring," remembers Garner. "And one day he gives up this *bomb* of a home run. Now the field in Cocoa faced towards Cape Canaveral. And as you turned to watch this home run, here comes this rocket right over center field."

But the rocket's red glare was not enough to make anyone on the Astros want to stay in Cocoa. The deal that would bring them to Kissimmee was finalized in December 1983, and during spring training in 1984, a number of curious Astros players and team officials took the thirty-minute ride from Cocoa to get a look at their new home. They climbed over a barbed-wire gate at the end of the road behind the rodeo grounds and walked the land where the stadium, practice fields, and clubhouse were planned. There was no sign of the future that spring, only remnants of Osceola County's past—a couple of lonely head of cattle still grazing the land beyond the barbed wire. If seeing the stadium required a leap of faith, getting a feel for the neighborhood did not. The eastern end of U.S. 192 was still pretty lonesome, but you didn't have to drive far up the road to meet the civilization coming down from Disney. The entrance to the Florida Turnpike was right there. Out the back of the planned complex was the start of Boggy Creek Road, and fifteen minutes up Boggy Creek Road was the Orlando International Airport. Fifteen minutes up 192 was Walt Disney World. For a place that at first blush seemed in the middle of nowhere, the Astros' new home was certainly in the center of everything. On a Saturday morning in late February, more than 1,500 locals turned out for a ceremonial groundbreaking that featured Astros general manager Al Rosen, manager Bob Lillis, and players Joe Niekro, Alan Ashby, and Joe Sambito.

When Peter Bavasi brought the Astros and Osceola County together, it was like the heady first moments of teenage romance. Neither side could fully quite believe its good fortune in having found the other and in the other's seeming infatuation. The county asked the Astros what their ideal spring training facility would be. The team was taken aback a bit; they'd always been the beggars in these kinds of talks. "It was pretty much write your own ticket," said Miers, the county official who was then working for the Astros. "It was, like, wow! These guys will do anything for us."

The county was amenable in part because it was proud of its entry into the spring training world and wanted to do it up grand. "We wanted something that nobody else had," said Whaley. "We wanted a real state-of-the-art facility." But a good deal of the county's eagerness to please came from the awareness that it was playing with house money. Said Whaley, "When you don't have to dig into your own taxpayers' pockets, you can afford to do a first-class job."

So what do you want? asked the county. The Astros began tentatively, afraid of asking for too much. Well, how about four practice fields, they said. Done, said the county. What else? Well, a covered batting cage, big enough so we could use it to stretch or throw on days when it might rain.

Done, said the county. What else? We'd really like a clubhouse big enough for both our major and minor leaguers, so the minor league players could see the big leaguers and really feel like a part of the Houston Astros. Done, said the county. What else? Well, a dorm for our minor leaguers and some of our staff would be nice. This one gave the county pause. Uh, we make our money on our hotels, they told the Astros. Hotel money is building this place. Our hoteliers aren't going to like a dorm taking heads out of their beds. No dorm.

How big do you want the stadium? asked the county. We don't need a big one; 5,000 seats should be plenty, said the team. Are you sure? Yeah, 5,000 is good. We want to keep it cozy. Crowd out the foul territory, shorten the distance from home plate to the backstop by a couple of feet. Keep the fans right up close to the players.

The Osceola County spring training complex was forged out of three-way conversations among the county, the Astros, and the architects, a little-known, year-old firm out of Kansas City called Hellmuth, Obata and Kassabaum (HOK). Whaley wanted a room in the clubhouse that the county could use for meetings and functions. He wanted lights on the practice fields, so that county high schools might have use of them when the Astros were out of season. Rich DeFlon, the architect, suggested the architectural nuances. When the Astros said they'd like a hillside like the one they'd built in Cocoa for pitchers to run up and down, DeFlon suggested modeling the stadium after Holman Stadium at Dodgertown, where the stands were built into a berm. The berm would give the pitchers their running hill and give Osceola County a stadium evocative of one that was a big fan favorite. DeFlon positioned the concession stands between the entrance tunnels and the rest rooms, so that no fan could reach the restroom or return to his seat without passing a concession stand.

A signature feature of the complex became the cloverleaf of practice fields. Peter Bavasi first suggested it, and it was eagerly embraced by both the Astros and HOK. The idea was that the fields would fan out from the clubhouse, which was located in the center; all fields would thus be equally close to the locker room and trainer's room. The clubhouse would have a rooftop observation deck, in case any Astros manager wanted to play Bear Bryant and watch practice from the tower. The observation deck never caught on as a coaching tool, in part because the proximity of the fields made it easy for coaches and instructors to move from one to the other. The cloverleaf was a design that proved revolutionary in its efficiency, and it has become the industry standard, not just in spring training complexes, but in parks and recreation complexes around the country. Construction began in May 1984 and took just ten months. The complex, officially named Osceola County Stadium, was a hit with both tenant and landlord.

"I don't think there is another spring training facility comparable to ours," gushed general manager Al Rosen at the start of camp. Astros players immediately fell in love with their new home, and they found that their time on the practice field in Kissimmee was just half of what it had been in Cocoa. "Our workouts used to be four hours long," said Phil Garner, whose playing days with the Astros from 1980 to 1987 bridged the Cocoa-Kissimmee years. "It was only because we had just two practice fields over there. We'd be standing around for most of that four hours."

The team did nothing different in Kissimmee; players did the same drills in the same twenty-minute cycles they'd done over in Cocoa, drills that every other major league team was doing in its camp. Now, however, instead of finishing a drill and moving to the sidelines to sit and wait, players could move to the next field and their next drill. When it rained, they could still get their work done—throwing and hitting in the batting cages. Players were off the field and gone by lunch; off the first tee or making their first cast off the back of their bass boat in Lake Tohopekaliga by one o'clock.

The county, too, was all smiles during that first spring, in 1985. "I think we're still counting ticket stubs from the Yankees game that year," said Miers. The Astros had consistently been next to last in average Grapefruit League attendance in Cocoa; only the Texas Rangers down in Pompano had played before fewer fans during the last decade. The move to Kissimmee brought a 25 percent jump in per-game attendance, to an average of more than 3,600. That placed the Astros tenth among the eighteen Grapefruit League franchises. To Osceola County, it meant that people who had never come to the county now had a reason to do so. And people who had been visiting now had a reason to linger.

The most interested visitors to Osceola County Stadium in those first years were not fans, however, but representatives from other major league teams and from city and county governments across Florida and Arizona. The Twins, Mets, Reds, Royals, and Rangers, all of whom had quite a bit less in their spring homes than the Astros now had in theirs, came to look. Hillsborough County, Lee County, Charlotte County, Sarasota County, and St. Lucie County came sniffing around to see if they too might mine this gold brought in by sleepy tourists and become spring training landlords themselves. Within six years, all of those teams and all of those counties would be matched up in new facilities, some the equal of Osceola County's, some much better. And it would continue on into the twenty-first century. In 1985, Osceola County Stadium was the first new spring training facility built in nearly a decade, only the second built in the previous twenty years. Over the next twenty-five years, by contrast, Florida and Arizona would build nineteen new spring training complexes, rebuild four others virtually from the ground up, and make substantial improvements to five more. The Chicago White Sox alone would play in three brand-new facilities.

So swift was this change to the landscape, so rapid the escalation in the cost, amenities, and appointments of these new complexes that the revolutionary, state-of-the-art, one-of-a-kind facility built by Osceola County in 1985 was quickly obsolete. Ten years after moving in, the Astros were looking to move out. They'd lost any shyness they may have had back in 1984 about asking for what they wanted. They flirted with Arizona, listened to Las Vegas, were even involved in talks with some folks down in Texas about setting up a Mesquite League in the Brownsville–Corpus Christi area (the Rangers, Royals, and Reds would have completed that four-team league). Osceola County's spring training legacy was twofold: it showed cities and counties across Florida and Arizona that spring training could be the linchpin in building a small community's reputation and economy and that it could do it without disrupting the local tax structure. Kissimmee and Osceola County also taught major league baseball that no request was too outrageous when it came to looking for a new spring training home.

By the end of the 1990s, Osceola County seemed doomed to be devoured by the creature it had created.

It still had a lot to offer the Astros, however: proximity not only to Disney World and the airports and commerce of Orlando, but to spring training games in Lakeland, Winter Haven, Tampa, Viera, and Disney, all less than an hour away. But the offer that kept the Astros in Kissimmee had nothing to do with convenience and everything to do with cash. With money it received from the state in 2000, Osceola County rebuilt and expanded the Astros' stadium, adding 2,500 seats and replacing the bleacher-type seating with individual seats with backs. It razed the old clubhouse and built a new one, twice the size with twice the amenities. The Astros signed on for another fifteen years. And Kissimmee continued to revel in the association. "You look at what spring training does for this community," said Phil Garner, the Astros manager from 2004 to 2007. "Every story that comes out of our spring training mentions Kissimmee, Florida. You can't buy that kind of advertising. Well, you could, I guess, but it would cost you millions of dollars."

And nobody missed Cocoa. Well, almost nobody. "My wife missed Cocoa," said Garner. "She liked the beach."

NINE

Changing the Dynamic

Lee County and the Twins

Construction on Florida spring training parks in the seventies and eighties was rather akin to the construction on the condos that were exploding up and down the Florida coasts in those years. The condos of the seventies and eighties were simple dwellings—two bedrooms, two baths, 1,000 square feet built quickly and inexpensively, with an eye toward utility and not opulence. They were bought by people looking for a cheap investment, or as a maintenance-free vacation home to be used for only a few of the coldest weeks of the northern winter. No need to duplicate the amenities of home. The sunshine would provide all the comfort and luxury necessary.

So, too, with the new spring training ballparks. In St. Petersburg, Kissimmee, Port Charlotte, Plant City, and Sarasota, new parks went up that were the ballpark equivalent of two-bedroom, two-bath condos. Seats enough for the fans, clean showers for the players, practice fields and drill areas for the coaches. And if these ballparks lacked architectural distinction and character, what did it matter? The very presence of a spring training franchise in the community provided all of the signature and character a city needed.

But construction in Florida began to change in the late 1980s, reflecting America's widely growing belief that a home—even a second home—was an extension of the owner's identity, and no detail was too small or unimportant. Single-family homes replaced condos as the new standard.

One thousand square feet became 3,000, or 4,000, or 5,000. Linoleum and Formica were now marble and granite. Tiny patios and balconies were now terraced courtyards and columned lanais.

When Lee County—stung by the departure of its longtime spring training tenant and embarrassed that it had precipitated the departure—set out to build the first spring training complex of the 1990s, it was determined to create something that would not simply serve the baseball needs of its new tenants, but stand as an architectural centerpiece for the rapidly growing southwest Florida county and perhaps become an attraction beyond the few weeks each year it hosted spring training. The dreamers in Lee County succeeded beyond their wildest expectations. And in the process, they changed the way everyone—teams and host communities alike—looked at spring training. "The Twins changed the entire dynamic of spring training," said Rob Rabenecker, the general manager of Roger Dean Stadium in Jupiter, spring home to both the Cardinals and the Marlins, "because the Twins were the first team to show you could make money from spring training."

The story of Hammond Stadium and the Lee County Sports Complex is the story of an enduring, respectful, love-filled marriage between a sometimes-overlooked midwestern baseball franchise and a sometimes-overlooked southwest Florida city. It begins in the mid-1980s, with the end of an earlier, enduring, love-filled marriage. The Kansas City Royals had trained in Fort Myers since their inception in 1969. John Schuerholz, then the assistant general manager of the Royals, approached the Lee County commission on behalf of the team in 1985, looking for help in making some improvements to venerable Terry Park, the Royals' spring home and a spring training site since 1925. "The facility was old," said Schuerholz. "It presented itself decently but it was old and getting older and the accommodations to our fans were rather substandard." The Royals weren't asking for much. They wanted a new clubhouse and upgraded office facilities, both of which could easily be taken care of with one building. They also wanted upgrades to the main ticket office and were particularly insistent that the public restrooms—fetid, primitive, and few in number—be upgraded. The cost of the upgrades was pegged at $300,000. "They didn't want much," admitted John Yarbrough, the Lee County parks and recreation director. "Two years later we agreed to give the Twins ten times more than the Royals wanted to start with." But the Lee County commissioners were reluctant to give the Royals anything beyond the improvements they'd already made over the years. The county had spent $500,000 on improvements to Terry Park in the two years leading up to the 1985 requests; these new requests from the team were just too much for some on the commission. "All you teams want is more, more, more," complained one of the commissioners to the club.

The Royals saw it differently, feeling that they had given as much as they'd gotten from Fort Myers. They had been in the city for seventeen springs, during a time when Fort Myers was a lonely outpost of spring training. There were no other teams in southwest Florida; the Royals' shortest road trip was to Sarasota, some two hours away—on a good day. "Remember, when we trained in Fort Myers, I-75 hadn't been built," said Schuerholz. "So all our travel was on 41."

U.S. 41, the Tamiami Trail, the original north-south highway along Florida's Gulf Coast, is a fine road if you're looking for a Big Mac, groceries, a new bedspread, some plywood, a hotel room for under a hundred bucks a night, or a used Ford F-150. It is not a particularly good road if you are trying to get somewhere.

"We traveled for years as road warriors on [U.S.] 41," said Schuerholz, "made that sacrifice for years until I-75 started to become available in bits and pieces. We rode that out. We fought through that. We thought we were good partners."

The team was stunned that Fort Myers and Lee County were not only willing to let them go, but were indeed inviting them to go. "I'll never forget the response I got," said Schuerholz. "They [the county commissioners] quoted the then director of tourism: 'People don't come to Fort Myers for baseball,' he said. 'They come for shelling and golfing.'" So the Royals left— "forced to evacuate" is how Schuerholz put it—and traveled up the now fully open I-75 and across I-4 to Haines City and a new endeavor called Boardwalk and Baseball. The amusement park/baseball theme park would prove to be something less than the Xanadu it had seemed when it opened in 1988, but its troubles were all in the future when the Royals arrived, leaving Fort Myers to contemplate life without any baseball to complement its shelling and golfing. The new county commission—"All those county commissioners were voted out of office after they made the decision [to let the Royals go]," said Schuerholz with some satisfaction years later—seemed disinclined to test the theory of whether people didn't come to Fort Myers for baseball. They began efforts to secure another team almost immediately. The county found an interested party in the Minnesota Twins, then training in Orlando.

But bringing them south was not going to happen cheaply. "That seems to be the way things work in spring training," said Yarbrough. "You tend to take for granted what you have, and then they leave and you agree to more than what you would have to start with."

Aside from the decade during and after World War II, Fort Myers had never been without spring baseball. The history began in 1925, when Lee County was a sleepy little community of 6,700, best known to locals and outsiders alike as the winter residence of Henry Ford and Thomas Edison. When base-ball arrived, it was in the form of a third American icon, Philadelphia Athletics owner-manager Connie Mack. The proprietor of what was then perhaps baseball's signature franchise—the Athletics won eight pennants and five world championships under Mack—visited Fort Myers in 1923 at the behest of the president of the local Kiwanis Club. The county agreed to build a ball-park to Mack's specifications on fairground land just northeast of the Fort Myers city center, known even then as Terry Park. The Athletics arrived in 1925 and were an instant hit. Five thousand people—or approximately 75 percent of the entire county's population—turned out for the first game in March of that year, drawn mostly by the prospect of seeing Babe Ruth, who was on loan from the Yankees for the special day. Thomas Edison embraced the team. The seventy-nine-year-old inventor had a "tryout" with the team in 1926 and returned the following year to take batting practice and play a public game of pepper with Mack and Ty Cobb, who'd signed on with the Athletics to play out the string after his Hall of Fame career in Detroit. Babe Didrikson, the greatest female athlete of her day, pitched an inning in an exhibition game at Terry Park in 1934, giving up no hits and one walk.

The Fort Myers–Philadelphia marriage lasted a dozen years, during which the Athletics won three American League pennants and two world championships. But attendance at Terry Park took a big plunge during the Depression, and Mack, whose Athletics were always a lean operation, began exploring options where his costs might be lower. He found one in Mexico City and took the team there for one season in 1937, beginning a nomadic spring training existence for the final years of his fifty-year stewardship of the club.

The Cleveland Indians came to town for three years beginning in 1940, but the wartime travel restrictions soon took the Indians away. And a fire in the Terry Park grandstand shortly thereafter left Fort Myers without spring training until 1955. Then, the promise of a rebuilt Terry Park, with a 2,500-seat steel-truss-and-beam grandstand, brought the Pittsburgh Pirates to town. The Pirates were the doormats of the National League in 1955, and they too were spring nomads; they'd had six different spring training homes in the ten years since the end of the war. But Fort Myers embraced them—a city starved for spring training baseball embraced a team that was starved for affection of any sort. Connie Mack, ninety-two years old, was back to throw out the first pitch at the first Pirates game in Fort Myers. Roberto Clemente integrated the Pirates' first spring, though he was forced to endure the indignity of segregated housing and dining and seethed at the experience. Lights added to Terry Park made the first spring training night game possible in 1957. And when the Pirates won the World Series on Bill Mazeroski's game seven walk-off home run in 1960, Fort Myers celebrated with a fervor equal to Pittsburgh's. But the nature of spring training is impermanence, and in 1969, with the offer of a bigger stadium and a better deal, the Pirates headed north to Bradenton, and Fort Myers found a new tenant in the expansion Royals.

Perhaps burned by the spurning of their beloved Pirates, Fort Myers' citizens were slow to embrace the Royals. But when the Royals won the World Series in 1985, folks in Fort Myers began talking about the "pixie dust" in the dirt at Terry Park. First the Athletics, who'd won back-to-back world championships five years after coming to Fort Myers, then the Pirates and Bill Mazeroski and their triumph over Casey Stengel's mighty Yankees, and now the Royals, triumphant over the Cardinals. Fort Myers had matched St. Petersburg in having had three different teams win world championships after spring training in its city. But the pixie dust was not enough to keep the Royals from leaving. And it would not be pixie dust, but Lee County cash, that would bring in the Minnesota Twins to replace them and continue the tradition.

The Twins had quite a spring training history of their own when they began talking to Fort Myers in 1988. They'd been at Tinker Field in Orlando for more than a half-century, arriving in 1936 when they were still the Washington Senators. Tinker Field, too, had a history; it had been a spring training site since 1923, the Reds and the Dodgers having preceded the Senators in Orlando. And it was named for one of the legendary figures in early baseball: Chicago Cubs shortstop Joe Tinker, the "6" in the most famous 6-4-3 combination of all time, thanks to this immortal 1910 ditty by New York newspaperman Franklin P. Adams:

These are the saddest of possible words:
"Tinker to Evers to Chance."
Trio of bear cubs, and fleeter than birds,
Tinker and Evers and Chance.
Ruthlessly pricking our gonfalon bubble,
Making a Giant hit into a double.
Words that are heavy with nothing but trouble:
"Tinker to Evers to Chance."

Tinker Field itself was fine—clubhouse-challenged, restroom-challenged, and in need of updating to be sure—but still a functional facility, and Orlando had recently built the Twins a complex of four needed practice fields across the street. But what made the arrangement unworkable in the long term was the fact that there was no place for the Twins' minor leaguers there. They trained fifty miles away in Melbourne in a facility that was less than affectionately known as "the Rock." The Rock was literally attached to the Melbourne International Airport. Behind the baggage claim area was the parking lot of the Twins Airport Motel, a team-owned facility housing the minor league players during spring training and shuttered the rest of the year. Out the back door of the Twins Airport Motel was the Rock, also dormant the ten and a half months a year there was no spring training. The grass grew tall and the skin of the infield grew to weeds while the team was away. "It was a great training ground for groundskeepers," said Twins general manager Bill Smith, who joined the Twins' minor league operations in 1982, "because you basically had to start from scratch every year." This did not lend itself to producing the pristine conditions even minor leaguers had come to expect by the end of the 1980s. Conditions at the Rock were less frustrating, however, than having the two camps separated by so great a distance. "If you wanted to borrow players from the minor league camp to fill in during a spring training game, you couldn't do it," said Smith. "The manager and coaches couldn't see the minor league players play every day. It was a tough set-up."

The club's management looked at a number of sites throughout Florida. They were a little apprehensive about Fort Myers' distance from everybody else; whatever Tinker Field had working against it, Orlando was at least in the center of things. "We were concerned about that," said Twins president Dave St. Peter. "More concerned from a baseball standpoint, in terms of the travel. But it was our belief that we could mitigate that." On the business side of things, in abandoning Orlando, the Twins were abandoning a city that had become a vacation destination for tens of thousands of Americans every day; the Twins were the closest spring training to Walt Disney World. On the other hand, the relative remoteness of Fort Myers was offset by the fact that there was a considerable colony of Minnesotans and upper midwesterners living in Lee County, so there would likely still be a sizable population of potential ticket buyers. But what ultimately brought the Twins to Fort Myers was the enthusiasm of the Lee County people to bring them there.

"Lee County didn't just want spring training. They wanted to make this the best, the most modern, the most attractive facility ever built. Lee County realized that spring training can be a destination if you have the right facility," said Smith, who oversaw the team's interests in the construction of what would become the Lee County Sports Complex.

After looking at a half-dozen options, the county and the team jointly agreed on land located near the junction of Daniels Parkway and Six Mile Cypress, well removed from downtown and the population and commerce of Fort Myers, but on the road from the Fort Myers International Airport to Fort Myers Beach. "When you come to Fort Myers, what are you coming for?" asks Smith rhetorically. "You're probably coming for the beach. Everyone who goes from the airport to the beach has got to drive right past Twins spring training."

The fundamentals of the complex—stadium, clubhouses, major league practice field, half field, batting cages and pitching areas, and the now-standard cloverleaf of four practice fields—were agreed upon and sited in the plan very quickly. As to the details, the county listened to the Twins—as the county had listened to Connie Mack back in 1925—and functionality and fan accessibility were the team's mantras. The Twins, in turn, listened to the various departments throughout their organization. "The clubhouse staff and the players designed the clubhouse," said Smith. "The trainers designed the trainer's room. We even consulted the writers that covered the team on what they needed and would like to see in the press facilities."

The team and the county then spent a great deal of time and energy working on the nuances. The Twins wanted the place fan-friendly and accessible. The complex was designed so that when a player walks from the stadium field to the batting cages or to any of the major league practice fields, he must walk through the fans. When plans called for an eight-foot chain-link fence around the pitching practice area, the Twins insisted that it be lowered to four feet, to afford the fans not only a better view, but also a sense of intimacy impossible during the regular season. "We want to take down the barriers between the fans and the players," said Andy MacPhail, the team's general manager at the time.

It was a bold undertaking by both sides. They made a statement by building a ballpark with 7,500 seats, at a time when just about every other Florida spring training park had fewer than 5,000. And Lee County wanted a facility with style and flair. "They just didn't want a ballpark," said Smith. "They wanted to make [the whole complex] a showplace." A cascading fountain, centered around two sweeping stairways leading to the main concourse, is the ballpark's most striking exterior feature, but it is just one of many that set Lee County stadium apart from the more pedestrian spring training parks that had gone up in the preceding decade. Architects from Lesher and Mahoney, searching for something else that would bring character to the exterior, suggested a spire reminiscent of one on a recently razed county building to top the tower that holds the stairs and elevator leading to the offices, suites, and media facilities on the third and fourth levels of the stadium. Visible from both inside and outside the stadium, it's evoked Churchill Downs to some visitors, but it's become more commonly known as the "witch's hat." Finally, a wide, palm-lined promenade, some 100 yards long, leads off the main access road and frames the fountain and the front of the stadium. As the plans began to take shape, everyone involved grew ever more enthusiastic. Plans for the promenade called for some landscape flourish up the center of the concourse, and someone suggested four rectangular reflecting pools. The suggestion met with great initial enthusiasm until John Yarbrough injected a dose of reality. Never mind the temptation for beer- and sun-soaked fans to take a postgame dip. "Do you know what a maintenance problem you're talking about?" he asked. Four patches of grass went down instead, providing color and definition to the promenade with minimal maintenance. The complex went up in seventeen months between October 1989 and the beginning of spring training in February 1991. The final cost was $20 million. If success could be measured in popularity, they had a winner. "We opened and it was: stand back and don't get run over," said Smith about the Twins' first spring in Fort Myers. They sold out every game, unheard of in spring training in 1991. Andy MacPhail's accessibility brought fans to the ballpark early and in greater numbers than anywhere else, as they savored an experience that was quite unlike anywhere else. Fans stood as close as coaches to players in the batting cages and pitching areas, able to score autographs by the dozen from players making their way from area to area. The public face of the franchise, the enormously affable Kirby

Puckett, seemed to delight in signing autographs as much as the kids who pressed against him delighted in getting them. He would make his way through the throngs after a workout, spending an hour or more each day making eye contact and conversation as he signed his name. If a kid scored an autograph and then made his way down the line in the hopes of scoring a second, Puckett would often as not recognize the kid and give him a genial chewing out. "Hey, I just got you up, there," he'd say. "It's one per customer today." So great was the team's emphasis on providing access that they over-did it. Some two hours before the gates were scheduled to open for the first time, thousands of fans were already roaming the grounds, and Twins offi-cials found more than 100 fans walking around inside the stadium. "How'd you get in here?" they asked. "The stairway in left field," they were told. In a construction project where virtually no detail had been overlooked, no one had noticed that, in providing fans access to the practice field/batting cage/pitching area, they hadn't bothered to put up any kind of barrier between those areas and a walkway leading to the grandstand stairs.

Playing in front of a full house every day, the Twins set a major league baseball spring training attendance record—and a franchise record for spring training wins. And while preseason records are utterly meaningless and absolutely no harbinger of things to come, the Twins' spring success did continue into the regular season. They had finished last in the American League West in 1990, fourteen games below .500 and twenty-nine games behind the division-winning Athletics. They were not expected to fare much better in 1991, but they won the West by eight games, beat the Blue Jays four games to two in the American League championship series, and, with Jack Morris and Kirby Puckett cementing their places in October lore, beat the Braves in a stirring seven-game World Series. In the jubilant Twins locker room following their dramatic ten-inning game seven win, CBS commenta-tor and former Twins pitcher Jim Kaat asked manager Tom Kelly what the key to their dramatic turnaround had been. "It all started in our brand-new spring training facility in Lee County, Florida," Kelly told Kaat.

Back in Lee County, Florida, the proud residents nodded and said: We told you so.

"The locals told us: 'If you come here, you'll win,'" said Bill Smith. It was the pixie dust in the Fort Myers dirt, the locals said. First the Athletics, then the Pirates, then the Royals, now the Twins—world championships birthed and nurtured in the southwest Florida sun. The Twins have not revisited the World Series since their inaugural spring in Fort Myers. So they may be uncertain on the matter of pixie dust in the Fort Myers dirt. But as to gold dust—well now, that's an entirely different matter.

"There was never any discussion of: 'well, this is [how much money] we can make if we do this,'" said Bill Smith of the planning process. "It was rather: 'How can we make this place fan-friendly? How can we make it a great experience?' But there's no question [that] in making it a great experience, we also made it a great money maker." The commercial success of their new complex is something that took the Twins and Lee County by surprise. "I don't think anyone planned that we were going to change things," said Yarbrough. "But I think we were the first to understand that it's about more than just the game. It is about the experience."

The "experience" has proven to be spring training's most popular product. There had always been fans at preseason games, but they were for the most part locals, or vacationers who'd come to Florida to go to the beach or to visit retired friends and family and just happened to go to a ball game. The ball game was a sideshow. Spring training was largely a private affair. The Twins made it a public spectacle while maintaining the sense of intimacy so integral to the experience. It was grandeur on a human scale. "What I believe [the special character of Twins spring training] is, is the accessibility," said team president St. Peter. "We're from Minneapolis–St. Paul. We're not playing in Boston, New York, or L.A. We're proud of our on-field accomplishments, but the hype doesn't come along with the Twins year in and year out. With the Twins, it's more of a grassroots approach. We're more of a grassroots team. That's the overall marketing approach that we take. The character of this is that we try to get rid of all the hurdles and all the barriers of entry and allow fans to experience spring training with their team."

In 1990, the Twins had drawn just over 2,400 fans per game to their exhibitions at Tinker Field in Orlando. In Fort Myers, they averaged nearly 5,000 more fans per game, at $6 and $8 per ticket. Sellout crowds meant full parking lots, 2,000 cars at $5 per car. The fountain, the promenade, the easy navigation of the pristine grounds meant that the fans came even earlier to the games: the gates would open two and a half hours before the first pitch. They would walk about the practice fields, watching the minor leaguers. They would sit in the sun inside the stadium and watch batting practice. Longer stays at the ballpark meant more trips to the concession stands— keep the prices reasonable, keep the people coming back, never make them feel like they are being gouged. Give them every opportunity to dig into their pockets but make them eager to do it. Make the experience incomplete without a cap or a shirt that has both the Twins logo and a palm tree.

Success begat success. The demand for stadium billboards and program ads exploded, not only from local restaurants, bars, and amusements—the longtime staples of outfield signage—but now Minnesota businesses seeking to establish a Florida bond with their vacationing customers were looking for a piece of the action, and so were national advertisers like Coca-Cola and Budweiser. New and previously unimagined revenue streams presented themselves. Radio and TV wanted in on the party—in 2006, the team had twenty-five radio broadcasts and eight telecasts of spring games. That's led to home-plate signage, the revolving billboards aimed right at the center-field camera. In short, anything the Twins could sell back home in Minnesota, they could now sell in Fort Myers. It meant that, for the first time in 100 years of spring training, the trip to Florida showed up on the credit side of the team's year-end ledger. "I can flat out tell you [that] before we came to Fort Myers, [spring training] wasn't even close [to turning a profit]," said team president St. Peter. "Now we cash-flow spring training. Revenues continue to grow. The fan base continues to grow. Interest in spring training continues to grow. The overall exposure of spring training just continues to skyrocket."

And spring training continues to be good to the Minnesota Twins. They initially greeted the news that the Red Sox would be joining them in Fort Myers with some nervousness. Even in the early nineties, the Red Sox were an 800-pound gorilla of baseball, and the Twins worried that they'd be overlooked in the Red Sox hoopla. But Red Sox Nation descends upon Fort Myers in such numbers and so voracious for baseball that the spillover invariably makes its way to Twins games as well. "The Red Sox coming down has really reenergized the area," says St. Peter, "and brought baseball interest in this area to another level."

Nonetheless, the Twins' spring-training success is not dependent upon the Red Sox. A loyal corps of locals and vacationing Minnesotans keeps the turnstiles clicking. And the combination of Fort Myers and Hammond Stadium (in 1994, the stadium was named in honor of Bill Hammond, the Lee County administrator most responsible for bringing the Twins to Fort Myers) is enough of an attraction to bring fans of the visiting teams down I-75. St. Peter points out that the Twins rank in the bottom five teams in local revenues during the regular season. They rank among the top five in spring training revenues. He worries, however, that spring training may choke on its own success if teams are not careful. "We're very sensitive to ticket prices," he says. "At some point, I'm not sure you can push ticket prices beyond where they are right now for a spring training game that may feature three, four, or five of your regulars for three or four innings. At some point, you have to realize it is still spring training baseball. You know, where is that ceiling as it relates to those revenues?"

Feeding the revenue monster while also not compromising the special character that created the revenue monster is the challenge facing all clubs today. Business is great. Demand exceeds supply. But St. Peter, already gun-shy about raising ticket prices, is also wary of adding bunches of new seats or making other dramatic changes. "You lose the intimacy [when you grow]," he says. "It detracts from the overall fan's experience. We're not looking at anything that would detract from that." But that doesn't mean that the Twins aren't looking for opportunities to "generate incremental dollars." St. Peter summons a spring training–appropriate metaphor for what he and his brethren in major league baseball's front offices are looking to do. "Teams are pressed all the time to squeeze more juice out of the orange."

The Lee County Sports Complex has matured gracefully and remains what it was always intended to be: a pleasing venue that provides a fan with a feeling of access and privilege, and a fine place to ready a major league baseball team for the season ahead.

"There might be better stadiums with more bells and whistles and bigger scoreboards or this and that," said St. Peter. "But we know that there are many, many major league teams that would trade spring training facilities with the Twins in a New York minute. And I can tell you: we're not interested in trading."

TEN

Fields of Broken Dreams

Not all spring training stories work out as well as Lee County and the Twins.

This is a story of bad timing. It is the story of two of the most acclaimed, state-of-the-art, ahead-of-their-time spring training complexes ever built, and how both ultimately failed. At their spectacular christenings, both were places of beauty as well as functionality. Yet it did not take long for both to acquire a forlorn countenance. To visit either was to experience a sadness of possibilities unfulfilled.

They have nothing in common. And they have everything in common. Both were born of grand dreams and perhaps also of illogical hope. One was built with public funds, the other with corporate money. One was built off the grid, far from the rest of the spring training universe, and skeptics hollered from the start that its very isolation would be its doom. The other was built right on the bull's-eye of the spring training map, yet ultimately its location too would lead to its doom. Both owe their existence to men determined to make a dream a reality. One was a politician with astute business instincts, the other a corporate CEO with a sense of the romantic.

One complex was felled swiftly by natural disaster; the other suffered death by a thousand cuts.

One never hosted a major league spring training; its prospective tenant changed its mind and took its business elsewhere, despite otherworldly promises from an eager landlord desperate to get the team to come. The other hosted fifteen spring trainings, and its tenants never wanted to leave, but were told they must by a reluctant and accidental landlord eager to do something else with the land. The first still stands, in tattered and threadbare splendor; the second has vanished altogether.

The first is the Homestead Sports Complex, and the second is Baseball City.

The Homestead Sports Complex was to be down-and-out Homestead's deliverance. It was built in 1991 with $14 million of Miami–Dade County tourist-tax money. Homestead city manager Alex Muxo, the man who figured out the way to acquire the bed-tax money to build the facility, topped himself by persuading owner Dick Jacobs to move the Cleveland Indians from Tucson to out-of-the-way Homestead for spring training in 1993. The stadium was ready more than a year in advance. Six months before the Indians arrived, Hurricane Andrew arrived. Cleveland exercised the "act of God" clause in their contract, took their spring training to Winter Haven, and stayed there. Homestead has never been able to get another team to take so much as a second look at its impressive facility.

Baseball City was a victim of bad timing of an entirely different sort. It opened in 1988 as part of an ambitious, $80 million nostalgia-themed amusement park called Boardwalk and Baseball. It was the pet project of William Jovanovich, the president of Harcourt Brace Jovanovich, a company best known for its publishing branch, but at the time the nation's second largest amusement park operator as well. Jovanovich was a child of the twenties and thirties, and he envisioned an amusement park that would combine the boardwalk charms of Coney Island and Atlantic City during those years. Baseball would be as it was played in Jovanovich's youth—every day, by everyone, on every level. But no sooner had Boardwalk and Baseball opened—with Ted Williams breaking the ribbon with a swing of the bat—than Jovanovich's attentions were diverted by a hostile takeover attempt on Harcourt Brace by British media baron Robert Maxwell. Jovanovich successfully fought off the takeover, but the process left the company riddled with nearly $3 billion in new debt. To reduce the debt, Jovanovich reluctantly sold off the company's theme park division to Anheuser-Busch. The Budweiser people wanted Harcourt's Sea World brand. They had little interest in Boardwalk and Baseball and closed it two months after they bought it.

When you live in a duplex and your neighbors' half of the house is shuttered and their yard gone to weed, it is difficult for anyone to see the charms in your half. And so it went for the Royals, living next to a dead amusement park. Their fifteen-year lease in Baseball City had thirteen years to run when Boardwalk and Baseball went out of business. They played out the very long string amid dwindling crowds and gathering gloom.

And yet the legacies of these two star-crossed facilities involve more than just folly and failure. They have also provided catalysts for progress—albeit, once again, in strikingly different and wholly unexpected ways. In Baseball City's lame-duck years, after the closing of Boardwalk and Baseball and before the razing of the stadium and the rest of the spring training facility, the greatest theme park operator of them all seized upon Boardwalk and Baseball's idea of using baseball and spring training to complement roller coasters and fun houses. Disney's Wide World of Sports opened in 1998 to wild acclaim and standing-room-only crowds.

In Homestead, in the early nineties, after the construction of the stadium complex and its successful rebuilding after Andrew, the city leaders had the political wherewithal and the confidence to secure a financing package and proceed with the construction of the Homestead-Miami International Speedway. The speedway, which opened in 1995, has succeeded where the sports complex has failed. Today, it is the site of the season-ending NASCAR races as well as a springtime event on the Indy car circuit. One of the most successful race tracks in all of America, it would have never come to pass were it not for the baseball stadium that sits empty just up the road. These are certainly not the legacies anyone would have either imagined or hoped for. Nothing about these complexes has played out as imagined or hoped. And yet, in a sad, convoluted way, that is what makes their stories so compelling.

It glistens on the horizon, rising in the Florida sunshine in a splash of color, the coral and white stadium framed by the blue of the sky and the green of the palms. The archways and the wrought-iron gates bid welcome. But it glistens only from a distance.

Come closer and you can see that Homestead Stadium has lived a hard life; up close, the scars and flaws are all too apparent. The paint is peeling in places and stained in others. The locked wrought-iron gates are rusting. In the press box and luxury suites—where the tables and chairs are still painted and upholstered in the blue and red of the Cleveland Indians—buckets collect drips from a leaky roof. Hurricane Wilma blew through in 2005, and almost a year later, the roof still hadn't been repaired. There is an eerie and unnerving silence in this place that was never meant to be silent.

What a metaphor for Homestead's spring training dreams! From a distance, spring training glistened and beckoned to Homestead and seemed as perfect and as pleasing as a baseball park set against a cloudless blue sky. But as Homestead got closer to its spring training dreams, the blue sky and dreams turned into leaky roofs and locked gates and a silence that has lasted for more than fifteen years—and is likely to be endless.

In 1989, Homestead, Florida, was a working-class city thirty miles south of Miami and twenty-five miles north of Key Largo. It was a place that time had forgotten. Agriculture remained the heart of its economy, and 30 percent of the city's residents lived below the poverty line. Tourists stopped for gas and maybe a meal in Homestead as they traveled north to Miami or south to the Keys, but nobody ever gave a thought to vacationing there. The boom days of the 1910s and 1920s, when Henry Flagler's railroad came through on its way to Key West and Homestead was in the heart of south Florida's first big land boom, were long forgotten by the 1980s. The hurricane of 1926 destroyed the railroad and put Homestead into a malaise from which it had yet to recover as the twentieth century closed in on its final decade.

The city's quaint and genteel downtown survived from that era, in need of a little TLC perhaps, but rich in character and potential. Homestead was rich in natural assets as well, bordered by the Everglades to the west and Biscayne National Park to the east. It was close to Miami's international airport and had the same glorious weather that was attracting visitors and new residents to south Florida in droves. City leaders were looking for a way to burnish Homestead's image and make it a player in Florida's new economy. Elected officials and business leaders kicked around a number of ideas, but the one that seized their imagination was city manager Alex Muxo's suggestion that they explore the option of building a baseball stadium and bringing major league spring training to their city. Nothing would put Homestead on the national business and tourism radar faster than spring training. But how to pay for it?

The job of finding the money fell to Muxo. He knew he couldn't find it in the city's coffers; it would have to come from the county or the state. So he scoured documents that came out of the legislature and discovered some money in the county coffers, coming from a Miami Beach bed tax. He read further and discovered that it wasn't just Miami's money, it was county money. "It got a little negative, because people said Homestead was taking Miami Beach's money," said Muxo. "And it really wasn't. The tax was county-wide. It is just that Miami Beach was where all the hotels were located at the time, and it paid a larger share of the bed tax. Proportionately, we were getting a lot more than we were paying in. But it was perfectly legal."

This brought Homestead $15 million in early 1989, and the city, with no team as a partner, set out to build a facility that it hoped major league baseball would be unable to resist. Muxo and other city officials toured a number of existing sites and hired the Kansas City architectural firm HOK. HOK had designed what at the time were Florida's three newest spring training facilities—those in Kissimmee, Port St. Lucie, and Baseball City—and was establishing itself as the premier ballpark architect. (Indeed, Homestead and Baseball City would help to grow the firm's reputation. Baltimore's Camden Yards would cement it.) The complex contained minor league dorms and a dining hall in addition to the stadium, practice fields, batting cages, and major and minor league clubhouses.

As the stadium began to take shape and it was clear that it would out-class any facility currently in use, Homestead attracted a lot of curiosity. The Orioles, then training in Miami, looked at it. So did the Indians, committed to leaving Tucson and relocating somewhere in Florida. The Cubs, the Pirates, and representatives from major league baseball also took a quick look. Everyone's concern was Homestead's distance from the rest of the spring training world. Spring training had never been that far south. Could Homestead's new tenant interest anyone in coming there for games? How soon would the new tenants themselves tire of long rides up and down the Florida Turnpike?

Homestead was really not that far off the grid. The Orioles were forty-five minutes away in Miami; the Yankees were another half-hour beyond that in Fort Lauderdale. The Braves and Expos played in West Palm, two hours away. Homestead would not have even been the most isolated town in the Grapefruit League. Over on the west coast of the state, the Royals in Fort Myers were more than an hour from their closest road game in Sara-sota, though there the concentration of teams within an hour and a half was much greater than Homestead's. Still, Homestead's spot down there in spring training's lowest latitude was going to be a problem.

When the stadium was completed in the summer of 1991, the city still had not found a tenant, despite two years of looking. The complex was debt free and had cost the city nothing. Still, inevitably, people began calling the empty stadium "a pink elephant." The only serious prospects the city had were the Cleveland Indians, and they were far more interested in going to Inverness, which was even farther out in the spring training wilderness, up in Citrus County some sixty miles north of Tampa and sixty miles northwest of Orlando.

Nonetheless, Muxo kept throwing incentives at the Indians. The city would guarantee 5,000 tickets a game; it would agree to a short-term lease that paid the city less than its costs of operating the facility. Muxo introduced Indians owner Dick Jacobs to a Homestead developer who offered Jacobs some private-sector incentives, such as discounts on houses and golf memberships for the Indians' personnel. Muxo even had a plan for handling the most vexing challenge of them all. What if the city subsidized air travel for the Indians and for teams visiting Homestead? Muxo worked out a deal with the air force to allow the city to land commuter planes—fifty-seat turbo-prop charters run by Delta and American Airlines—at the Homestead air force base, a five-minute bus ride from Homestead Stadium. "What we said was—now I'm just making up numbers to make the point—what we said was if a team was going to spend $1,000 to travel by bus to Homestead and it was going to cost $5,000 to travel by plane, we'd subsidize the difference."

Citrus County and Inverness couldn't compete—wouldn't compete. The lead Citrus County negotiator, a former assistant city manager to Muxo in Homestead, accused his former boss of buying a team. Citrus County dropped out of the bidding in June 1991. In August, the Indians and Homestead reached agreement on a two-year deal, to begin in 1993, after the Indians' lease in Tucson expired.

The summer of 1992 was a time of tremendous anticipation in Homestead. "Spring Training Home of the Cleveland Indians" banners began going up all over the city. Muxo took to wearing an Indians cap everywhere he went. The stadium and dorm complex had its first tenant: the 1992 U.S. Olympic baseball team trained there prior to leaving for Barcelona in early August. The schedule for the following spring was announced. The first game would be March 6 against the expansion Florida Marlins. It would mark the first game anywhere for the Miami-based Marlins.

August 24, 1992, is a date forever seared into Homestead's memory. The devastation wrought in Homestead by Hurricane Andrew's 165-mile-per-hour winds was biblical—like San Francisco after its 1906 earthquake or New Orleans after Katrina. Ninety percent of the homes in Homestead were destroyed. These homes—many of them mobile homes or aging wood-frame cottages—were not just ruined, or damaged beyond repair, but left as piles of sticks or blown completely away, leaving only a debris-strewn concrete foundation slab. When the sun arrived that morning, so did the rats, the mosquitoes, and the looters. The police could not arrest the looters: the jails were full of evacuees. When the 70 percent of Homestead residents who'd evacuated the city began returning that afternoon, in some cases they could not even recognize their neighborhoods, much less their homes. How to begin to rebuild a city so completely destroyed? Where to begin?

Homestead resolved to begin with its new stadium. Andrew had blown down every foot of fence, toppled the scoreboard, filled the tunnels leading from the grandstand to the concourse with debris. The roof was peeled back, and damages were estimated at $7.5 million. Insurance covered the cost; and the city was more than willing to make the emotional investment in rebuilding. "The community needed something to rally behind," said Muxo. "You needed a phoenix. It was our consensus—the city council, the mayor, some of the community businesspeople—that we needed something to rally behind and give people hope. The worst thing in life is if you don't have hope."

Muxo became the face of south Florida's despair and its resolve to rebuild in the days after Andrew. He wept on CNN as he showed reporters the damage at the stadium in the days after the hurricane, wearing his Indians cap and a two-day growth of beard. The hat became a signature. He had it on for all of his television interviews, and the newspaper articles quoting him all invariably mentioned it. He was making a not-so-subliminal statement to the Indians. Homestead, even in its ruin, was committed to its affiliation with the Cleveland Indians and was hoping that the Indians would reciprocate.

Publicly, the Indians said and did all the right things. They called city officials as soon as telephone lines were back up and expressed their condolences and offered their support. They sent money and supplies to the relief fund. When team officials visited the city a month or so after Andrew, however, it was apparent that they could not bring their 1993 spring training there, rebuilt stadium or not. The rest of the city was still a pile of debris;

there were no restaurants, hotels, or anything else that players and their families either needed or had come to expect from a modern spring training. They made arrangements to use the complex the Red Sox had recently abandoned in Winter Haven. The Indians did agree to play their first two exhibition games in Homestead, and the stadium reopened on schedule on March 6, 1993, with that long-anticipated Indians-Marlins game. A sellout crowd of more than 8,000 fans and a national media contingent watched the Marlins beat the Indians. The game validated the city leaders' faith in rebuilding the complex. "It did what we had hoped it would do," said Muxo. "It gave the city hope." While the national news stories were a good part uplift, they also talked about the mountains of rubble piled about the city waiting to be carted away, the trailers that were serving as temporary homes and offices. "There used to be a city here," said the *Chicago Sun-Times.* "Now Homestead looks like a massive city dump." The Indians' refusal to make a commitment for 1994 made Homestead officials a little bit testy. "Our agreement was that they were going to Winter Haven on a one-year hiatus," Homestead mayor Tad DeMilly told the Cleveland *Plain Dealer.* "If they choose not to come back here it will be demoralizing." Choose not to come back, however, is exactly what the Indians did—announcing their decision in April 1993—and it has indeed been demoralizing, for more than fifteen years now.

Homestead did rebound from Andrew, and it is arguably in better shape than it had been before. The new homes are superior in size and quality to those Andrew destroyed. The Homestead-Miami Speedway—another public construction project put together by Muxo before he left the city for the private sector in 1994—has given Homestead the national identity it had hoped to get from baseball. And the city was swept along in the incredible Florida building tide. Businesses and national retailers moved to Homestead by the dozens. The city's population, which grew by less than 10 percent in the 1990s, grew by more than 20 percent in the first five years of the twenty-first century. But baseball has been notably resistant to Homestead's renaissance.

"Oh yeah, Homestead, isn't that down near Cuba?" quipped Chicago White Sox owner Jerry Reinsdorf to Homestead recreation director Alan Ricke at baseball's winter meetings one year in the late nineties. Ricke was trying to get Reinsdorf to consider Homestead when he was talking about taking the White Sox out of Sarasota. Ricke worked for six years at trying to find a major league tenant for the Homestead Sports Complex, and Reinsdorf's comment pretty much sums up the reaction he got.

The highwater mark was 1997. The Florida Marlins won the World Series that year, and Homestead citizens were not above rejoicing not only in the Marlins' triumph but also in the Cleveland Indians' defeat. And 1997 was also the year that baseball's two expansion franchises would decide upon their spring training home, and Homestead was hopeful of getting the Tampa Bay Devil Rays. The city was willing to offer the same package of incentives to the Devil Rays that it had given to the Indians back in '91. But spring training locations were growing closer together, and Homestead was getting farther away. Since the early nineties, the Orioles had left Miami, replacing the Yankees in Fort Lauderdale; the two-team complex in West Palm had migrated a few miles north to Jupiter. All this meant that there was now only one other preseason site within two hours of Homestead. "The city toyed with the idea of expanding the Homestead Sports Complex to be able to accommodate two teams," said Ricke. "This made sense as far as the teams were concerned; but Homestead was not in a financial position to justify the expense based on sheer speculation that not just one but *two* teams could be found to relocate."

The closest the city came to finding the major tenant it yearned for was in the 1998–1999 off-season, when the Florida State League's Daytona Cubs had reached an impasse in their negotiations with Daytona Beach and were looking for another option. They liked Homestead and were ready to commit but wanted a promise of support from the local business community before they did. Ricke arranged a meeting, at which the Cubs learned that the business community had already committed its promotional budgets to the big-time NASCAR events at the speedway and had no money and no interest in supporting minor league baseball. "This made it pretty clear to me that professional baseball of any kind in Homestead would never be more than a dream," said Ricke.

Homestead remains conflicted on what to do with its now aging and slowly decaying property. The city is not ready to let it go, however. One promoter with dreams of turning it into a soccer haven had a lease with an option to buy the place in 2004, but he ran into money troubles, and the city voided the deal and took back the property. The Homestead City Council then turned down a second company's bid to buy the property for $19 million and turn it into an entertainment complex that would have circuses, concerts, an IMAX theater, and the headquarters of the International Roller

Derby League. Plans for a regional park on the site have been proposed, and current Homestead recreation director Kirk Hearin feels that that remains the most likely scenario for the complex. With the stadium, in some form, still in place, he is sure. "There's no question that this place is still a great asset for the community," he said. Its value to the community may be more intangible and emotional than it is physical. Few communities have experienced a transformation the likes of which Homestead has seen before, because of and after Andrew. Homestead Stadium was there through it all—the dreams, the heartbreaks, the rebirth. It's an unlikely survivor, just like its city. Surely that has to count for something.

An act of God cost Homestead its chance at spring training. It would seem another act of God would be its only chance of getting it back. Should another category V hurricane strike elsewhere in Florida and flatten a facility, Homestead could prove a team's parachute. It stands ready to be used. The infield dirt has been replaced with grass for a soccer event, but that's an easy fix, and the fields have been otherwise maintained at a major league level. The dorm and the clubhouses simply need cleaning, and while it would take a bit of work to make repairs and to do the painting and polishing necessary to open the stadium gates to the public, Homestead did far more when it repaired the stadium in just five months after Andrew. Nobody in Homestead really wants to get spring training in that way; Andrew remains all too fresh in their minds, and they would not wish that sort of misery on anyone.

And yet…

"Baseball City" was once a real address. As late as 2002, the name appeared on Polk County documents and on signs directing travelers there from I-4. Newspaper stories carried "Baseball City, Fla." datelines, and television reporters signed off by saying: "Reporting from Baseball City, Florida, this is…" By 2006, you had to know where to look to find it, and then have faith you had, for there was no tangible evidence of its past. Traveling north on U.S. 27, some ten miles out of Haines City, it was the last right before the eastbound entrance ramp to I-4. The sign by the roadside read "Posner Park: Gateway to Polk County," and a half-mile paved road cleaved 350 acres of silent and dormant sand dunes. There was nothing there but the road, not any signs of what will likely come, a mix of residential, retail, and office buildings. There are certainly no indications that this was once one of the liveliest spots in central Florida. There is no sign of the Ferris wheel or the carousel or the mile-long, Australian jarrah-wood boardwalk. No sign of the eight giant, thirty-by-thirty-four-foot Norman Rockwell murals that covered the roof of the theater building, which could be seen by motorists passing on I-4. No sign of "A Taste of Cooperstown," the only permanent outside exhibit ever established by the Baseball Hall of Fame. No sign of the Hurricane, the ninety-five-foot-high wooden roller coaster that provided the backdrop for the two stadiums and five practice fields that comprised Baseball City, the spring training home of the Kansas City Royals from 1988 to 2002.

There is a puzzled wonder in the voices of those who once lived there. It seems unthinkable that something so elaborate and so busy could evaporate so thoroughly. "Do you know, it is completely gone now?" asks John Schuerholz, the general manager who brought the Royals there in 1988. "It is *completely* gone."

"It is just very sad to drive by it," said Kim Sams, who was the public relations director for Boardwalk and Baseball, "and to think of all that was there."

There was a bit of head scratching in early 1986, when Harcourt Brace Jovanovich president William Jovanovich proposed buying a moribund amusement park in the nethermost reaches of exurban Orlando and transforming it into something called Boardwalk and Baseball. It was something of an odd notion for an amusement park, but that wasn't what prompted the head scratching; the concept had a certain charm if not a definite logic. It certainly wasn't because the company lacked for resources or theme park wherewithal. It owned three wildly successful Sea World parks in Orlando, San Diego, and Cleveland and was building a fourth in Texas; it also owned venerable Cypress Gardens, Florida's original theme park in Winter Haven. What bothered the head scratchers was the park Harcourt Brace would be buying and where it was located. The park was called Circus World; it had been started in 1974 by Ringling Brothers, Barnum and Bailey, with financial backing from Mattel and had foundered under two owners in the dozen years it had been open. Pressed for a reason for this lackluster performance, most would have blamed its awkward location. The junction of I-4 and U.S. 27 was thirty miles from Orlando. It was only twelve miles from the ever-growing Walt Disney World, but they were dark and desolate miles in 1986, so it seemed much farther away. There was nothing between Disney and

Circus World on I-4, and precious little once you got there. "U.S. 27 was nothing but eighteen-wheelers and a few retirees" living in a nearby mobile home park, according to Floyd Perry, at the time a college baseball coach who would sign on as the director of baseball at the new park.

Nonetheless, with Disney set to open its third theme park, with Universal Studios ready to open, with Sea World, Busch Gardens, and Cypress Gardens all thriving, a new park seemed like a solid bet. Harcourt bought and closed Circus World in the spring of 1986 and set about getting ready to open it as Boardwalk and Baseball in the spring of 1987.

Spring training was booming, too, in the mid-1980s. Attendance records had been broken every year during the decade, and places like Plant City, Port Charlotte, and Port St. Lucie were transforming themselves from anonymous little dots on the map to boomtowns with national cachet by building stadiums and securing teams to play in them. There were a number of teams in play as possible tenants—nearing the end of their leases and/or playing in outdated facilities—when Boardwalk and Baseball was being planned in 1986. But the team the company wanted and the only team it negotiated with seriously was the Kansas City Royals. The Royals, in 1986, were a real trophy. They'd been a perennial playoff team for more than a decade; they were just one year removed from a world championship; and—conveniently for Harcourt Brace Jovanovich—they were in the throes of being rebuffed in their attempt to upgrade their spring training facilities in Fort Myers. "It didn't hurt at all that they had just won the World Series," said Roger Kurz, the director of marketing for Boardwalk and Baseball. "But really it was the team management, which had an excellent reputation in baseball."

The Royals' lead negotiator in the project was John Schuerholz. He met with Jovanovich and other top Harcourt officials several times in the summer of 1986 in the company's penthouse offices overlooking Sea World, and he quickly came to share Jovanovich's enthusiasm. "It was a unique and I thought phenomenal concept," said Schuerholz, "blending the entertainment world/amusement park world of Orlando/Central Florida with baseball." After the frustration of dealing with a county government in his unsuccessful effort to bring about improvements in Fort Myers, Schuerholz was delighted to be through with the angst of local politics: "We don't have the bureaucratic muddling, and now it is one business doing business with another business. Decisions can be made at the time."

In August 1986, it was announced that Kansas City would move its spring training to Baseball City once construction on a new stadium was complete in February 1988. HOK was brought in to design the 6,500-seat stadium. The firm's initial design evoked nineteenth-century parks, with spires and arches and flagpoles lining the roof. But it was ultimately decided that a more modern, angular line would flow more cleanly into the mile-long boardwalk that wound its way through the park and led to the stadium's main gate.

As part of the deal, Harcourt Brace also purchased the Single A, Florida State League Fort Myers Royals from the parent club; they, too, would move to Boardwalk and Baseball and begin playing as the Baseball City Royals in 1988. The rookie league Gulf Coast Royals played there, as did the Cleveland Indians' Gulf Coast League team. The announced intention was to play a baseball game every day of the year at Board-walk and Baseball, Christmas included. When none of the professional teams was scheduled, the park would bring in college and high school tournaments. And for those days when it was truly off-season for all of organized baseball, Boardwalk and Baseball hired some former college players and formed them into two teams, the Baseball City Grays and the Boardwalk and Baseball White Caps. Admission to any baseball game, save for Kansas City Royals spring training games, was free with a park admission.

Inside the amusement park, where the ride attendants were dressed in pink and gray baseball uniforms, there were nine batting cages; and fielding stations, where a machine would shoot a ground ball at a pay-ing patron, and allow for a throw to a first base target area, while a clock timed the speed of the pick-and-throw against the speed of an imaginary runner. There were pitching stations, including the usual arcade staple that clocked speed and one that allowed the patron to throw to a silhou-etted batter standing sixty-feet, six-inches away. For twenty-five cents a batter, you could throw until you either walked the silhouette or struck him out.

But what really set Boardwalk and Baseball apart from every other arcade in America was "A Taste of Cooperstown." A permanent exhibit of the Baseball Hall of Fame, the first outside Cooperstown in the hall's his-tory, the display was housed in a rehabilitated 1,200-square-foot building that had once stored the straw for Circus World's elephants. The project came about when Jovanovich called Hall of Fame president Ed Stack in late 1986 and inquired about a Hall of Fame exhibit at Boardwalk and Baseball. "It was very out of character for the Hall of Fame to do something like this off-site," said Ted Spencer, the curator who put the exhibit together. "Particularly a permanent exhibit." Nonetheless, Jovanovich's enthusiasm intrigued Stack, and the Hall's board of directors gave the project its blessing in early February. "I guess we saw it as a promotional opportunity," said Spencer. Nothing was taken off exhibit in Cooperstown; the satellite museum consisted entirely of duplicate items, which still made for a rich trove. There was a locker from Yankee Stadium with a Babe Ruth uniform, cap, and glove in it, as well as uniforms and equipment from more than a dozen Hall of Famers, including Ted Williams, Willie Mays, Lou Gehrig, and Henry Aaron.

Four Hall of Famers were there in the flesh for the park's grand opening in April 1987. In addition to Ted Williams breaking the ceremonial ribbon with his bat, Ernie Banks, Don Drysdale, and Frick Award winner Mel Allen were there as well. In baseball terms, Boardwalk and Baseball had an eight-run first inning. The notices in both the Florida and the national press were unfailingly positive. "Boardwalk and Baseball Yet Another Hit in Orlando" read the headline in dozens of Gannett newspapers. "If you're through shaking hands with Mickey Mouse at Disney World and feeding the dolphins at Sea World, then this amalgam of Americana is well worth exploring," wrote Richard Carpenter in the *Boston Globe*. Willard Scott and Mark McEwen—network morning show weathermen and barometers of the hot and trendy in popular culture—availed themselves of the park's satellite uplink and broadcast to the nation from inside Boardwalk and Baseball. ESPN signed on for a series called *Boardwalk and Baseball's Super Bowl of Sports Trivia*, and careful viewers of ESPN Classic can still see the program from time to time, hosted by a boyish and notably slimmer Chris Berman.

During that first year, fans watched the stadium rise from the tops of the Ferris wheel and the roller coaster, and when the Royals arrived in 1988, they were certain they'd found spring training nirvana. Diminished travel—there were five teams within thirty minutes, five more just over an hour out—meant less time on the bus and more time in the batting cages. The state-of-the-art training complex brought expected raves, but so too did the adjacent amusement park, especially the section known as Park Place, a quiet little arboretum in the center of the park.

"It was the most enjoyable blend, of not only an amusement park environment, but a pleasant sort of idyllic park-like setting that they created," remembered Schuerholz, "with walkways and trees and lamp posts and benches and reflecting ponds and bridges and music—classical music being pumped up through the shrubbery. I'd go there a couple [of] times a week just to refresh myself, just go and sit quietly and enjoy that environment, just to get away from the hubbub of [spring training]."

The Royals sold out nearly half their preseason games in 1988—this during a time when spring training sellouts were still exceedingly rare—and averaged more than 5,600 fans per game, setting a team record they would eclipse a year later and never approach again. Bo Jackson hit a 550-foot home run off Boston's Oil Can Boyd that added to his then exploding legend. Spirits were high; life was good. "I will always remember a moment from that year," said Dan Pearson, who handled all of the baseball public relations for Boardwalk and Baseball. "We played Boston. It was Easter weekend; it was spring break. We had 10 or 11,000 people in the park. At the same time, we were selling standing room only tickets and had 8,800 people in the stadium. And I said to myself, "This concept is going to work." It was the greatest day in park history, and it was never matched."

Even in its triumphant early days, however, Boardwalk and Baseball/ Baseball City was already suffering from the afflictions that would ultimately prove fatal. While the people who came to the park raved about it and loved it, not enough people came. "It was a tough sell," admitted Kim Sams, the park's public relations director. "You had Disney with three parks then, and you had Sea World. How many people on vacation had a fifth day for Boardwalk and Baseball?" They battled the notion in both Orlando and Tampa that Baseball City was just too far off the beaten path for the locals to bother with. Never mind how far it really was, or how long it really took to get there. Perception proved an impossible hurdle. "If people think you're way out there—you're way out there," as Pearson put it.

Meanwhile, the company debt incurred in fighting the 1987 takeover attempt forced Harcourt Brace Jovanovich to do some belt tightening. The company laid off 160 Boardwalk and Baseball employees in the summer of 1988, part of a larger layoff throughout its theme parks. And in 1989, after fighting it for more than a year, Jovanovich reluctantly put the company's theme park division up for sale. A lot of companies sniffed around; some smaller companies inquired about buying the two smaller parks, Cypress Gardens and Boardwalk and Baseball, separate from the Sea World parks. But Jovanovich insisted on selling everything together, and the only serious buyer to emerge was the Anheuser-Busch Company, proprietors of Busch Gardens in Tampa and Williamsburg, as well as a couple of smaller parks. It bought the six Harcourt Brace parks for $1.1 billion. Wall Street considered it a steal.

Anheuser-Busch insisted that it didn't buy Boardwalk and Baseball simply to close it; the facts make the claim rather difficult to believe. Anheuser-Busch took possession of the park in early November 1989. On January 17, 1990, barely two and a half months later, it closed the park in the middle of a Wednesday afternoon, announcing to the thousand or so people inside that the park was closing early and that people should head to the gates to collect a refund. The new owners then gathered the employees and told them the park was closing for good. Anheuser-Busch claimed that the park was hemorrhaging money and had no prospects for turning things around.

It was a particularly gloomy spring in Baseball City in 1990. Not only had Boardwalk and Baseball shut its doors, but spring training started a month late. In the absence of a labor agreement, owners imposed a thirty-two-day lockout on the players. Work stoppages are always dispiriting events; in Baseball City, it was particularly sad. The lockout and the locked gates next door combined to hold the Royals' per-game attendance average to just over half of what it had been in 1989.

Any hope employees had that Boardwalk and Baseball might be sold or might reopen were short-lived; the park began dismantling its rides and selling them off almost immediately. Anheuser-Busch announced that the land was for sale, though it also promised to honor the lease it had with the Royals, a lease that still had thirteen years to run. Because the Anheuser-Busch Company also owned the St. Louis Cardinals, there was some speculation that the Cardinals might move their spring training from St. Petersburg to Baseball City, but the company and the Cardinals made it clear that that was not, nor would it ever be, part of the plan. There was also some discussion of the propriety of one major league team owning the minor league affiliate of another; the Baseball City Royals, which had been owned by Harcourt Brace, were included in the sale to Anheuser-Busch. That never really became an issue anywhere but in a few early newspaper articles. "Baseball City was run by Anheuser-Busch's theme park division," said Pearson. "That division had nothing to do with the Cardinals, so it was never really a problem."

Pearson stayed on at Baseball City after the amusement park closed as the director of public relations and marketing. "My job was to find as many things as we could do that would help us lose as little money as possible," said Pearson. Baseball City was going to be a leaner operation than Boardwalk and Baseball had been—there would be no more promise of a baseball game every day—but the complex was still host to college tournaments and the Florida state high school tournament. The Baseball City Royals remained, playing their seventy games a year. But Florida State League baseball is a tough sell; the boom that has engulfed minor league baseball since the 1980s has largely eluded the Florida State League. Florida's midsummer twilights are sticky, buggy, and frequently rain-soaked; league-wide, attendance seldom cracks four figures, and the Baseball City Royals averaged fewer fans than most.* It all added up to a facility that was operated at what Pearson recalls as a substantial loss, and Anheuser-Busch continued to sell off pieces of the operation as it waited for a buyer to take the place off its hands. The Hurricane, the park's signature wooden roller coaster, was the last of the rides to go; it went to an amusement park in Arkansas in early 1992. And after the 1992 season, the Baseball City Royals were sold to a group from Daytona Beach, which moved them up to the eastern end of I-4 and into an affiliation with the Chicago Cubs.

And so Baseball City settled into the final full decade of its short life as a spring-training-only facility. In 1994, a grassroots movement to build better ties between the Royals and Polk County got under way. But the baseball strike of 1994–1995 stripped baseball of all of its goodwill, and the Royals' Baseball Advisory Committee died aborning. Still, aside from the sense of impermanence and uncertainty, Baseball City was a wholly satisfactory site for spring training. It remained a state-of-the-art facility, and Anheuser-Busch, for all its eagerness to sell the property, maintained it to the highest standard. Its location grew even more convenient; not only was it still at the geographic center of the spring training world, which meant shorter bus rides, but a number of high-end golf course communities—with restaurants, retail stores, and attendant amenities—sprouted just east

---

* In 1989, while Boardwalk and Baseball was thriving, a directive came down from the Florida State League to count attendance as the number of tickets sold, not the turnstile count, the thinking being that there were a lot of unused season tickets and the higher number would be a better attraction for advertisers. The Baseball City Royals' games were free to anyone with a Boardwalk and Baseball admission, so theoretically the Royals' attendance would include the 2,000–3,000 people in the park on any given day. But Pearson and the Baseball City Royals' general manager, Karl Rogozenski, took it one step further. Harcourt Brace sold season passes that were good for admission to all of its central Florida parks. There were approximately 77,000 of these passes sold, and that made their owners all de facto season ticket holders to the Baseball City Royals. So, for a couple of games, Pearson and Rogozenski announced the attendance at the Royals games at more than 77,000 until the Florida State League asked them to stop. Pearson telephone interview.

of Baseball City off I-4, providing pleasant housing options for the Royals' major leaguers and their families.

The weed-strewn, paint-peeling remains of Boardwalk and Baseball next door were a decided drag on the aesthetics of the place, however, and the Royals' tumble into baseball's competitive netherworld drove the fans away. From the late nineties forward, as the Royals were losing 100 regular season games a year, their spring training average attendance never topped 3,000, and most of those attending had come to see the visiting team. But the greatest pall over life at Baseball City in its final years was the sadness and frustration of living with a terminal illness and not knowing whether the end was months or years away. In telling the Royals that it would honor their lease, Anheuser-Busch made it clear that it would under no circumstances renew their lease, which was set to expire in 2002. Anheuser-Busch believed that the lease was what was preventing it from unloading the property. It told the Royals that they were welcome to leave whenever they'd like: there was no obligation or expectation for them to honor the lease. For the Royals, it was a best-of-times, worst-of-times situation. They had to get out, but they could shop around without having to buy until they found something they liked, so long as they had it in place by 2003. They listened on two occasions to pitches from Las Vegas, which was looking to acquire not so much a single team as a six- or eight-team league. In the fall of 2000, when voters in the Phoenix suburb of Surprise approved spending $45 million to build a two-team training complex in their community of 40,000, the Royals stopped looking. The Royals' leave-taking from Baseball City was greeted with indifference. There was no one to weep for the Royals. Their final game in Baseball City, on Good Friday 2002, came close to selling out, but the fans there—even some avowed Royals fans—were pretty sanguine about the team's departure, saying they'd get their baseball fix next year in Winter Haven or Lakeland or over at Disney where the Braves had set up shop.

Freed of the yoke of the Royals' lease, Anheuser-Busch was quickly, finally, able to sell the property. Three months after the Royals announced they were going to Surprise, Miami corporate raider and developer Victor Posner bought the land and everything on it for $13 million, $5 million less than Harcourt Brace Jovanovich had paid for Circus World sixteen years before, and $1 million less than it had cost to build the Baseball City portion of Boardwalk and Baseball. Posner's company announced plans for a community that would include residential, retail, hotels, and entertainment. The final event in the Baseball City stadium was the groundbreaking for Posner

Park in October 2003. Demolition of the stadium began a couple of months later. The land that was judged too far from everything when Boardwalk and Baseball was built in 1987 was described in news accounts of Posner Park as "one of Florida's hottest development corridors."

The story of Boardwalk and Baseball and Baseball City is one of what-ifs and if-onlys. If only the park had been next to Sea World, or someplace else on International Drive, inside what Pearson called the "tourist corridor," it would have likely been a phenomenal success. If only Jovanovich had not been forced to fight off a takeover attempt that prompted him to sell the company's theme parks. Certainly, he would have had more patience with the park than did Anheuser-Busch. And what if the park had been built a decade later, when the sprawl of Orlando and Tampa, growing together, turned the junction of U.S. 27 and I-4 into less of a remote outpost and more of a busy suburb? And, finally, what if Baseball City had had some residents who cared enough to keep the Royals where they were?

Had Baseball City been real, meaning, had it been supported by a local population and a local government and a local business community, spring training and the Royals might have had a chance. There would have almost certainly been someone in the community who would have seized the initiative and rallied troops to the cause. Baseball City and the Royals might have joined the class of 2000, the five local communities—Vero Beach, Kissimmee, Lakeland, Dunedin, and Clearwater—that received as much as $15 million in state funds to acquire or upgrade their existing spring training facilities and to keep their teams where they were.

But Baseball City hadn't been real. It was nothing more than a crossroads in an unincorporated part of Polk County. The county commission had officially designated the complex and the immediate surrounding area "Baseball City," just as it had designated the very same area "Barnum City" during the Circus World days a decade earlier. Calling it "Baseball City," however, couldn't make it a community. The nearest real community was Haines City, nine miles to the south on U.S. 27. A town of 13,000 people, Haines City had a cool relationship with Baseball City and Boardwalk and Baseball from the very beginning. It had good reason to feel slighted by its fancy new neighbor, for Boardwalk and Baseball had sought to distance itself from Haines City. The official address of Boardwalk and Baseball was a post office box in Orlando. It was Orlando the park wanted to be identified with, not Haines City. "Boardwalk and Baseball didn't want to associate with Haines City," said Pearson. "So Haines City never embraced the Royals the way we wanted them too."

The Posner Company—Victor Posner died shortly after buying the land in 2001—might have smiled kindly upon a spring training enterprise that was municipally owned and operated as a centerpiece of its planned community. It was, after all, a formula that had worked in Port St. Lucie, in Viera, and in Abacoa, the planned community that was privately developed around Roger Dean Stadium in Jupiter. But there was no one in Baseball City to care and to make things happen. Baseball City was like a highway rest stop—always crowded and bustling, but everyone there had merely stopped to use the facilities. They were all from someplace else and going someplace else. They might miss that little way station. But they very quickly adapted to life without it.

ELEVEN

Breathing Braves
Air

On John Schuerholz's desk at Disney's Wide World of Sports during his many years as Braves' general manager sat a copy of *Branch Rickey's Little Blue Book*, a posthumously published compendium of baseball thoughts, aphorisms, speeches, and essays that Rickey had accumulated during the half-century he was the boss of the Browns, Cardinals, Dodgers, and Pirates.

For all those who see baseball as a succor to the soul, a spirit that binds eras and generations, this is perfect. John Schuerholz, arguably the most important baseball executive of his generation, paying homage to and taking instruction from Branch Rickey, arguably the most important baseball executive of all time. "It's on my desk every day," said Schuerholz of the Rickey book, "at home and here."

On the fields beyond the walls of Schuerholz's Disney office is Branch Rickey's legacy.

Rickey did not invent spring training. With Dodgertown, however, he was the first to bring major and minor league players together in one camp, intending to use the six weeks to initiate the 600 Dodger farmhands into the Brooklyn way of playing and winning. Spring training became about getting in shape not just to play baseball, but to play Brooklyn Dodger baseball.

All of baseball has seen the wisdom of Rickey's way, though it took forty years for every organization to bring its minor league affiliates in from their separate and sometimes far-flung camps. This was mostly a function of the absence of space in the older spring training complexes; indeed, much of the city jumping since the mid-1980s stemmed from clubs wishing for more space in order to incorporate their minor leaguers into the major league site.

But while every organization today is trying to do what Rickey did sixty years ago, few have been able to do it as well. Only a handful of franchises have succeeded in instilling in eighteen-, nineteen-, and twenty-year-old kids the notion that they are a part of something bigger than themselves, certainly bigger than whatever farm team they might find themselves playing for that summer. Rickey successfully convinced his Dodgertown pupils that they were on a path that would bring them ultimately to Brooklyn, though no more than a few ever stood a real chance. But those few who climbed to the top of the Brooklyn pyramid stood upon the foundation of the many who did not, but shared their fierce pride in the organization.

The Dodgers have, for the most part, carried Rickey's guidon honorably and ably. The Dodgers' farm system has been historically strong and so, too, has the club's sense of pride. Under Paul Richards and Earl Weaver, the Orioles were the next club to do it well, during their glory years in the sixties and seventies. But it didn't last, and today the Orioles' minor leaguers are not even with the big club in Fort Lauderdale; they train across the state in Sarasota. Today, arguably, no team embodies the top-to-bottom ethos of organizational pride like the Atlanta Braves of John Schuerholz and Bobby Cox. And as it was with Rickey and Dodgertown, and with the Orioles and the "little field"—the half field in Miami where Richards and Weaver taught the Oriole way—Disney World is where it happens for the Braves. "This is where they learn the Braves way," Schuerholz said. "This is where they breathe Braves air."

Since their last-to-first turnaround in John Schuerholz's first year as general manager in 1991, no franchise in major league baseball has enjoyed more success than the Atlanta Braves. The Yankees have gotten to the World Series more often, and won it more often, but with the notable exceptions of Derek Jeter, Mariano Rivera, Andy Pettitte, and Jorge Posada, the players who won those championships for the Yankees were free-agent mercenaries bought at auction with truckloads of cash. The Atlanta Braves' fourteen consecutive divisional championships were won with a nucleus of men who came through the Braves' farm system. From Tom Glavine, David Justice, and Mark Lemke, through Chipper Jones, Andruw Jones, Jeff Francoeur, and Brian McCann, the great majority of fresh faces cycling through the Braves clubhouse each year during the team's great run are players who first learned the Braves way on the backfields at Disney and, before that, at their earlier spring home in West Palm. What is the Braves way? "It's not secret," said Paul Snyder, the Braves' director of baseball operations. "We don't reinvent the wheel here. We work on cutoffs and relays; we have bunting drills, base-running drills, sliding drills. That sort of thing." In other words, they do exactly the same things at the Braves' camp in Disney that they do over in Viera at the Nationals' camp, down in Fort Myers at the Twins' camp, or out in Tempe with the Angels. What the Braves have succeeded in achieving— and they are the envy of all of major league baseball for this—is coordinating the instruction *and* the attitude. That began with Schuerholz. "John has such great motivational skills and has such a great way with the English language," said Snyder. "He'll talk at our organizational meetings in January, and those scouts can't wait to get out of that room, and get their radar guns and get to work. I think the old schoolteacher comes out [in John] when he gets up on the dais."

Before beginning his baseball career in the Orioles' front office in 1966, Schuerholz taught eighth grade in Baltimore, and the schoolteacher does indeed live within the baseball executive. His start-of-camp talks to the Braves' uniformed staff—Bobby Cox and his major league coaches, the minor league managers and coaches—are peppered with references to George Bernard Shaw, Pablo Casals, and Miguel de Cervantes. Schuerholz concedes that there are sometimes "thirty question marks on the faces in the room" when he begins applying the verities from literature and music to baseball. But he perseveres. When Schuerholz arrived in 1991, the Braves were the worst team in baseball. He told the staff the story of Eliza Doolittle, the heroine of Shaw's *Pygmalion*. Eliza did not become a lady until she began believing she was a lady, Schuerholz said. No baseball team that does not believe in itself stands a chance, was the message. After the Braves had made it to the top, Schuerholz reminded them of the work required to stay there. "Only a mediocre team is always at its best," he says. He likes to tell the story of the reporter asking the immortal cellist Pablo Casals about his work ethic. "Mr. Casals, you are the greatest cellist who ever lived. You're ninety-five years old. Tell me, why do you practice your cello six hours a day?"

"Because," replied Casals, "I believe that I'm making progress."

For those who are perhaps wearying of all the highbrow metaphors, Schuerholz always concludes with the story of the lion and the gazelle. "Each morning, the gazelle awakens knowing that she must run faster than the fastest lion to survive that day," he says. "And the lion awakens that morning knowing that he must run faster than the slowest gazelle so as not to die from starvation. Both of them realize that, when the sun rises, they must be running for their lives."

Belief in oneself, a work ethic that trumps all others, an attitude that says no dream is impossible, and a vigilance that comes from knowing that, in the baseball jungle, every day is a fight for survival—these are the lessons. There may be some who miss a bit of the nuance, but Schuerholz's spring training talks are highlights, and the Braves' organization's belief in their general manager was absolute.

"He showed us how to win," said Snyder of Schuerholz. "We had good baseball people; but we didn't know how to win. You can have the greatest musicians in the world, but if they don't have a good conductor, it's not going to be as good as it could be."

There is something of a chicken-and-egg phenomenon at play here. Have the Braves been as good as they've been because of the talent and the coordination in their minor league system? Or have the scouts, coaches, and minor league players bought into the notion of a Braves way because it's easy to believe you've found the formula when the big club wins as much as it has?

However it happens, it does not, cannot, happen in a single spring, as the people responsible for making it happen will quickly remind you.

"The continuity is what's sustained us and made us what we are," said Snyder as he rattled off the names of men on the organization's coaching staff—Atlanta coach Brian Snitker, Myrtle Beach coach Rick Albert, Danville manager Paul Runge, Rome manager Randy Engle, among them—who signed with the Braves as players more than twenty-five years ago. "These are the people we lay the foundation with as players," said Snyder. "They learned the Braves way, and now they teach the Braves way."

For all of John Schuerholz's accomplishments with the Braves and for all that he is, together with Atlanta manager Bobby Cox, the personification of the Braves' enduring excellence, no one is more responsible for the team's sustained success since the mid-1980s than Paul Snyder. A genial grandfather, Snyder is one of those baseball lifers who's never drawn a paycheck outside the game. He tried to retire early in the twenty-first century, and the Braves named him to their Hall of Fame in 2005, only the third nonplayer (the others are former owners Bill Bartholomay and Ted Turner) to be so honored. But he was never fully retired, working part time as a special assistant to Schuerholz. A year after Snyder's induction, Schuerholz asked him to come back full time as the team's director of baseball operations. Snyder returned to full-time duties absent the cigar that had been his trademark, forsaken in deference to his health. But he retained his infectious zeal for the game and the people who play it. "Look at this," he says as he gestures to the pristine and empty fields at Disney World early on a perfect March morning, arriving, as usual, some minutes ahead of the players and coaches. "Is there anyplace else in the world you'd rather be?"

He's been a part of the Braves' organization for fifty years, signing with the team out of high school in 1957. A slow-footed outfielder-turned-first baseman who could hit for both power and average, Snyder was enjoying his best year in the minors in 1963, on his way to knocking in more than 100 runs, when Jack Tighe, his manager at Triple A Denver, abruptly told him that the front office in Milwaukee wanted him to stop playing and instead to take over as manager of the Braves' farm club in Greenville. Snyder was stunned; he was also hurt, insulted, and angry. "I didn't think I was quite through as a player," he said, but after he cooled down, he agreed to hear Tighe out. Over a late-night dinner, the two men talked about Snyder's fused back, the result of an injury three years earlier, and how it had robbed him of his already suspect speed and compromised what had always been average defense. By the time dinner was through, Snyder agreed to give managing a try. "He was honest with me," said Snyder of Tighe, "[told] me all I could do when I was healthy was hit," and while Tighe's honesty stung on that long-ago night, it also transformed Snyder's life. Managing proved but a way station on a journey to the front office. Joining the front office in the year the Braves moved to Atlanta, Snyder has held any number of titles over the years—scout, director of scouting, director of minor league operations, director of baseball operations, special assistant to two different general managers—but his duties have always been the same. He's been the Braves go-to guy when it comes to identifying, drafting, signing, and nurturing young talent. Snyder's mark on the Braves goes back to Dale Murphy and Bob Horner. Still, his real success did not begin until Ted Turner bought the team in the late seventies, hired Stan Kasten as president, and started spending some money. "We were drafting for so many years on signability instead of playing ability," said Snyder of his early days as scouting director. "We had such a meager amount of money, we tried to stretch it as far as we could. Luck doesn't shine on you too much that way. You can take a donkey and train it to run the Kentucky Derby. No matter how hard you train him, it doesn't work."

With Turner's money, Snyder drafted Tom Glavine in the second round in 1984 and signed him away from the Los Angeles Kings of the National Hockey League. He wanted to draft Deion Sanders, "the greatest athlete I ever scouted," he said. But manager Bobby Cox didn't like Sanders' attitude. "Bobby wants one rule for you and same rule for me," said Snyder. The Braves passed on the flamboyant outfielder/defensive back, though they would later acquire him in a trade with the Yankees. Snyder also made players like Chipper Jones, Kevin Brown, Kent Mercker, Jeff Blauser, and Steve Avery the team's first-round picks through the years; and he saw the makings of a major league star in Andruw Jones when Jones was a sixteen-year-old kid in Curaçao.

The man's eye for talent is envied and admired throughout the game, and his list of awards and honors pays tribute to his skill and success. In 2006, *Baseball America*, the weekly magazine of the minor leagues, named Snyder one of the twenty-five most influential men of the last twenty-five years; earlier, it had named the Braves' farm system the top organization of the past twenty years. Minor league baseball paid Snyder its ultimate tribute in 2006, when it named him the "King of Baseball." But what makes Paul Snyder perhaps the most beloved man in the Braves' organization is less his baseball savvy than his people skills. Paul Snyder is simply one flat-out nice guy. There were 127 ballplayers in the Braves' minor league spring camp in 2007. Snyder knew all of their names, knew their stories and their families, and was determined to know them better. "It's a big thing for me to come out here in the morning and see two or three moms and dads and maybe some grandmas and grandpas and just spend maybe five or ten minutes with each family," he said. "I think that makes them feel like a part of it."

Most of the families no doubt arrive already feeling "like a part of it." When the Atlanta Braves entered the lives of these players, it was at first in the person who scouted them. That scout, however, was followed very quickly by Paul Snyder. He's been in Central American homes with dirt floors and no plumbing; he's been in suburban mansions. He is the organization's closer, the guy brought in to seal the deal on the most difficult signings, and the most difficult signings have historically been the privileged kids, drafted out of high school. It's been a regular challenge during the Schuerholz years because the Braves' success has forced them to concentrate on high school players. "We have basically lived and died with the high school player," said

Snyder of the Braves and the draft. "Back where we've been drafting, we haven't been privy to the better college player." Snyder pointed to Charlie Morton, a twenty-three-year-old pitcher who was slated to play at Double A Mississippi in 2007, drafted out of Joel Barlow High School in Redding, Connecticut, in 2002. "His father's a lawyer and his mother's a doctor. When you have two very well-educated parents like that, it's difficult to sign a kid; they naturally want him to go to college."

Snyder's charming and persuasive way makes a gentle yet resonant argument: for any kid planning to go to college to major in baseball, the Braves' farm system is an Ivy League alternative.

Though it takes place within a few hundred yards of the bright lights and bustle of a major league spring training, minor league spring training is another world. It is something of a throwback to the old days, a mix of baseball drills and boarding school. The days begin early and end late, and baseball is but a part of the daily curriculum, though it is, quite obviously, the most elemental and essential part. Players, coaches, and staff arrive at the minor league locker room at the "Milk House," as the field house at Disney's Wide World of Sports is called, at 7:45 a.m. The coaches and staff have their daily meeting, and the players get ready to take the field at 8:30. "Early work" runs for forty-five minutes, from 8:30 to 9:15, and it concentrates mostly on individual skills. There is a wide range of baseball maturity and baseball skills at minor league spring training. The players all share the extraordinary athletic ability that got them signed to a professional baseball contract in the first place, but that ability can be at vastly different stages of development. At major league camp, players may be at different stages of their careers, but they are all at the same stage of their development—ready to play big league ball. In minor league camp, conversely, players are more or less at the same stage of their career—i.e., the beginning—but at different stages of their development.

"When we get a sixteen-year-old from the Dominican Republic, he is far different from a twenty-two-year-old college senior who graduated from, let's say, the University of Georgia," said Kurt Kemp, the Braves' director of player development. "There's a real wide spectrum there. It's very large physically; it's very wide maturity-wise. But they both present a given skill set of physical ability that we have to start with. We're trying to project what this sixteen-year-old will look like seven years from now as a twenty-two- or twenty-three-year-old." Every player in the organization has what Braves' shorthand refers to as the IDP, the individual development plan. The morning and evening staff meetings spend a lot of time talking about those IDPs. "What you're kinda doing is saying: 'Here's what this kid is and why we think he's a major leaguer prospect. And here's where he's not there yet,'" said Kemp. "And somehow, we have to bridge that gap."

At 9:15, the focus shifts to team drills. This involves the basics of getting players ready to play baseball—getting the pitchers' arms into game shape, getting the hitters live at-bats. But much more of this time is devoted to the nuances of the game. Here is the meat and potatoes of spring training, the reason that teams still spend six weeks together. Players will work on individual skills on their own: pitchers will throw, hitters will hit, infielders will take ground balls until their hands are too swollen to fit in their mitts. But no one works alone on bunt defense, or on cutoff plays and relays, or on what Kemp calls "pop-up priorities," knowing what your job is on a pop-up to the left side of the infield, knowing what your job is when there is nobody out and nobody on; knowing what it is with one out and runners on first and third. And so on. It's different in every instance, and the most intelligent baseball player who ever lived never got this part of the game purely by instinct. He got it by doing it over and over and over again, while the March sun darkened his neck and arms, until he grew so tired of the tedium of the same thing over and over again that he felt like screaming. But the smartest player, the player who gets it quickest, knows that the endless and boring repetition is the only way to make it seem like second nature in the eighth inning of a tie ball game in August.

Baseball wherewithal begins with God-given talent. You cannot successfully train a donkey to run the Kentucky Derby, as Snyder so beautifully puts it. But even these gifted thoroughbreds, the athletes who find their way into professional baseball, did not get there and will not stay there on natural talent alone. This takes a work ethic that is the equal of their talent. There is the individual work, and there is the synchronized work of nine athletes working as a team.

This is where the Braves way happens, under the tutelage of a full-time faculty—the twenty-five or so managers and coaches who comprise the uniformed staff of the six minor league teams plus the minor league roving instructors. This full-time faculty gets help, throughout the spring, from several dozen members of the minor league adjunct faculty. This cadre includes Hall of Famers like Henry Aaron and Phil Niekro, who spend a few days in uniform with the minor leaguers each spring; it includes staffers from the Braves' Dominican Republic academy. And it includes from time to time a number of the Braves' scouts. "When you're out there scouting, until you see what you have, it's hard to see what you're trying to get," said Kemp. "[We bring the scouts] here just to see what our talent level looks like, so that when they're out making a scouting judgment on a player, they're going to be able to say: 'Wow, this kid's better than anybody we have,' or 'We've got five kids that are better than this guy at this position.' It gives them a reference point."

Learning the Braves way, breathing that Braves air, is as much about attitude as it is about baseball. Thus, among the most important visits each spring is the one from Schuerholz, the master motivator. He tells the kids that they all count, that no one would be in that room if everyone in the organization didn't believe that they were *all* major league prospects. He reminds them that it was just a few springs ago that Jeff Francoeur and Brian McCann were sitting where they are now, listening to a variation on the same theme.

After the morning workouts come lunch and then the games. High school games draw a bigger crowd and generate more excitement than a minor league spring training game. On a Friday late in March, the Braves' two Class A teams played two Class A teams from the Tigers organization on adjacent fields at Disney. There were nineteen people watching one game, twenty-seven watching the other. A dozen of this number were Braves minor league pitchers not scheduled to pitch that day and thus allowed to watch the game in civilian clothes. (*Required* to watch the game would be more accurate; they must stay a minimum of five innings.) Most of the rest are girlfriends, parents, and grandparents. But occasionally a fan will choose the intimacy of the minor league game over the crowds and sensory assault of the major league game next door. For the baseball junkie—maybe not the *Baseball America*–reading, wish-I-worked-in-a-major-league-front-office zealot, but the fan who knows the game if not the players, and enjoys baseball for its own charms—it really doesn't get any better than minor league spring training games.

At the big league game, most fans see only what they are conditioned to look for. Edgar Renteria goes deep in the hole and makes a strong throw to first; well, Renteria has been one of the slickest gloves in the big leagues for more than a decade now. Watch a nineteen-year-old make the same play in a Class A game, and it brings a sense of discovery. That was a big league arm he showed right there, and you wait for the kid's next at-bat to see if he's got the stick to go with the glove. John Smoltz pitches out of a first-and-third, nobody-out jam, and raises nary an eyebrow nor a round of applause; it is something he's expected to do. But what of the kid just a year out of high school who does the same, showing what the scouts call "pitchability"? Fans unfamiliar with the term still recognize the quality. Minor league spring training gives the fan a chance to test his powers of observation against those of the big league scout. Who are the prospects here? Who's got the quick bat, the live arm, the impressive acceleration from first to second? Later, the fan might check: how do my observations compare to what *Baseball America* and the team's Web site say about the players I saw? Or maybe the names are committed to memory, and some years later, when the kid breaks in with the big club, the pleasure of discovery will return. *I knew it. Knew when he was nineteen that that kid had the goods and was going to make it.*

And then, as though to snap us out of our wistful reverie, comes a real mood spoiler—the autograph weenies. Autographs are the underbelly of spring training accessibility, and minor league camp is the home of the autograph futures market. The vultures are everywhere, men mostly, anywhere from eighteen to eighty years old, with matted hair and ill-fitting clothes. They carry duffle bags or drag rolling luggage filled with bats, balls, and loose-leaf binders, the binders stuffed with plastic sleeves filled with dozens, and sometimes hundreds, of baseball cards and eight-by-ten glossies.

There is nothing as soul stirring as the sight of a child getting an autograph from a professional baseball player. There is nothing as—what is it, exactly? unseemly? pathetic? both?—as an adult doing the same thing.

On a Sunday morning at Disney, as the Braves' Double and Triple A teams are getting set to play their counterparts from the Nationals, a boy with Down's syndrome offers a pen and a baseball indiscriminately to Nationals and Braves minor leaguers, who literally wait in line to sign the kid's ball. Not twenty feet away, a sixtyish man hands a Nationals farmhand multiple copies of his Single A card to sign, in the hopes that future big league success will turn the autographed cardboard into an eBay commodity. One scene is Rockwellian, the other Orwellian.

Yet even this skeevy underworld has not escaped the attention of those who would make a buck off spring training. There are not many ads on the outfield fences of the backfields at Disney, just two to four small pennants on each one. Most are big-time Disney corporate sponsors—companies like Hess that have a presence all over Disney World. But each of the backfields also has a banner for Sharpie, the pen of choice for autograph seekers and signers.

This baseball subspecies seems to materialize from the earth when the players are in transit and accessible—when they arrive in the early morning, break for and then return from lunch, or leave the field in the afternoon. The autograph creatures then crawl back under their rocks when the players take the field, and minor league spring training again gives the illusion that time has not simply stopped, but rewound, which puts the game back in a time when it was about conditioning and practice. On the backfields in spring training, it is not yet all about the commerce: it is still about the baseball.

When the games are over, the day is not. On at least five of the seven evenings during a typical spring training week, the minor league players have meetings that deal with everything from the mundane to the philosophical. There are meetings to cover the minor league insurance plan and organized baseball's drug and alcohol policy. But there are other programs that fall into the category of life skills, for example, English-language classes for the players from Latin America, or a program called Winning with Character, which acknowledges the fact that young men don't always make the best decisions. "We lose a lot more kids to drugs and alcohol and bad girlfriends than we do to lack of playing ability," said Snyder. Trying to prevent that makes the job of the minor league staff an around-the-clock affair.

"I don't feel like there's any way we feel our job ends here," said Kemp. "Part of the responsibility we have is to care for them off the field as well as on the field. Life happens to 160 kids. And it happens [in different ways]. We've got guys who are thirty-two years old and have three kids and are still playing professional baseball—guys who have been in the major leagues. And I've got sixteen-year-old kids from countries where they haven't even eaten right for all their lives. What kind of spectrum is that?"

Minor league camp does not limp to a close in the way major league camp does. By mid-March up in the big league camp, rosters and rotations are pretty well determined, and everyone is hoping just to get to opening day injury-free. But as the days wind down in minor league camp, the stakes go up. Most everyone in camp still has to prove himself in some way. A lot of these guys are quite literally fighting for their baseball lives.

Everyone in major league camp—generally fifty to sixty players at the beginning of camp in February—is effectively guaranteed a job come April 1. There will be the occasional player—generally a veteran, nonroster invitee—who might be given his outright release and is unable to catch on elsewhere. And there is sometimes a player or two—again, generally veterans of thirty or more, with professional careers of a decade or more—who finally see their major league dreams as beyond their reach and opt to retire rather than spend another year playing in Triple A. But the mightiest percentage of players in the major league spring training camps know they'll be playing baseball somewhere when the bell rings.

There is no such assurance in the minor leagues. In fact, the only guarantee is that come April 1, a bunch of careers are going to be over. The numbers tell the story. There were 127 players in the Braves' minor league camp in 2007. As camp unfolded, they were joined by 30–35 more players, cut from the big league camp. These 160 players were effectively competing for 98 roster spots in the Braves' minor league organization, 24 at Triple A Richmond, 24 at Double A Mississippi, and 25 each at Single A Myrtle Beach and Rome. The evaluation process goes on every evening. At the end of the day, Paul Snyder, the rest of the minor league administrative staff, and all the uniformed staff gather and go through the roster one by one and discuss every player and his progress, with particular emphasis on those on the bubble. "We were down last night for maybe three hours discussing four roster positions," said Snyder in late March 2007. "Every instructor that's here has a vote. If somebody says hold, we hold. It's early yet. We get down to the last couple of days, then we have to make an executive decision up here." For a humanist like Snyder, cutting a player is far and away the toughest part of the job. "I've sat there and released players and I've cried right with them," said Snyder. "Because you get close to them."

Some of those left off the full-season minor league teams at camp's end—roughly thirty-five or so—will be invited to extended spring training and will get the chance to compete for a spot on one of the two short-season rookie teams in the Appalachian and Gulf Coast leagues. They'll be joined in extended spring by another thirty or so players already under contract to the Braves organization who weren't invited to regular spring training because, in the estimation of the player development staff, they had no chance of making one of the full-season teams. These are perhaps from the Braves' Dominican program, or American high school and college players from the previous year's draft who may have signed late and not played in 2006. Or they could be young players coming off injuries that weren't going to leave them ready for April 1.

The final piece of extended spring training and the short-season roster equation will be the players signed from the June draft. The Braves will draft fifty players in June. They'll sign perhaps half of them. (The rest, "low rounders" for the most part, will opt to go to college, or if they're already college or junior college players, will opt to stay there and hope to be drafted in a higher round the next time around.) It is these 2007 signees who will leave no room for some of the old. "If you bring in twenty-five and release twenty and bring in twenty five and release twenty, all of a sudden you have too many players," said Kemp. "The simple math says if you bring twenty-five in, there's got to be some sort of attrition that goes on with twenty-five others." It is the way of the world, the old giving way to the young, fathers making room for sons, the baseball life equivalent of the Laura Nyro song: *And when I die / And when I'm gone / There'll be one child born / And a world to carry on.* Except when you're twenty-five years old and you've thought your whole life that baseball would end on your terms, perhaps in front of 45,000 cheering fans, rather than behind the closed door of Kurt Kemp's office in the spring, when the season is new, and every ballplayer believes his career year is just set to begin. For those cut from the Braves, it is a cruel irony that they reach the end of their baseball life—a fantasy life, they would all be quick to acknowledge—at Disney World. For Disney, as the marketing people have so effectively drummed into the American consciousness, is the place where dreams are supposed to come true.

"We try to do it with as much dignity as possible for the player," Kemp explained. "There was a time in days gone by when they just yelled it over a loudspeaker and they just said: 'Joe Smith, would you please report to the player development director's office,' and guys knew they were done—if they were calling you into the office, you were done. We try to do it in a way where we can pull the player aside, sit down individually, man-to-man, person-to-person, and explain to them our decision, of which I fully don't expect they are going to agree with, or like; but one I hope they respect, and understand that there has been a lot of forethought and work and time that has been put into that decision."

Twenty-five players. That's the over/under, the number that any Braves minor leaguer who can count has his eye on. Twenty-five professional baseball players are going to be *former* professional players before the beaches fill up for the summer. Maybe half those cuts will come at the end of regular spring training, and half at the end of extended spring. Part of the package of information Kemp provides to those he cuts is contact info for teams in the independent leagues. But it doesn't lessen the sting. "They signed with you to be a Brave," said Snyder. "Now [you've got] to tell them it's not going to happen."

So a lot happens in these anonymous and largely invisible minor league games on the backfields in the waning days of spring. The rosters throughout camp are fluid; no one is promised a spot at a particular level. Every player knows that a five-hit game could mean the difference between low A Rome and high A Myrtle Beach, or even a spot with Double A Mississippi. Every pitcher knows how slender the margin for error. Two scoreless innings in the middle of a close spring game can mean the difference between a bullpen spot in Mississippi and a bullpen spot with Triple A Richmond, where a call to the show can be just a sore arm away. Conversely, too many three-hit, two-walk innings in the spring can mean the difference between a spot in Double A and one of those closed-door conversations with Kurt Kemp. The few eyes that watch minor league spring games watch intently. For Snyder, Kemp, and the other talent evaluators who have to make the decisions, it is rather like working on a three-dimensional puzzle; they must balance the needs of the organization, the requirements of the various teams, and the best interests of the individual players.

"Ultimately one of the things that I have to do here is to try to place our kids at the right place for them to play," explained Kemp. "What I'm looking at is: I want the kid to play at the highest level he can that will challenge him, while not being at a place that will overwhelm him. We want them to have a chance to be successful there. But you get better by playing good people. You don't get a lot better if you're just way better than everyone else you're playing with.

"We want guys to experience success at a level before we move them up. Now what is success? It's not like there's a magic number; we want them to hit .270 or something like that. It's a feeling of their mental and physical readiness to be able to go to that next level. There's a right time. We can push guys too fast. [But] it's also not good if we don't move them when they're having a lot of success. We don't want them to be so overwhelming to the league and be so good that they now get stale. They need the next challenge for them to continue to grow as well. So it's a balance of both of those."

Sometimes a kid can be ready for that next level, but the next level just isn't ready for the kid. "Some of the decisions that are made are because of the people above you," added Kemp. "Let's say the guy above you is a prospect as well, and he's playing behind [a major league starter]. Well, I'm not going to get rid of either of you, but I can't move you; there's no place to go there. Sometimes, guys will have to play at one level for a little longer because of the people that are ahead of them."

The only *team* that ultimately matters in all of this is, of course, the Atlanta Braves, and every decision is made with an eye toward how it might best help the big club. The Braves own five of their six minor league clubs. While it is common for major league teams to own their rookie league clubs, the Braves are unique in owning their Double A and Triple A clubs, as well as two of their three A league teams. "We are totally different from any other organization," said Snyder. "We can play who we want to play, where we want to play them. We're not answering to somebody in a PDC predicament—a player development contract—that's interested in the turnstile. If we want to play a group that's maybe a tick behind where they should be, want to force our hand with two or three guys in Double A who maybe should be in Myrtle Beach, we can do that and that's our decision."

While that may have something of a liberating quality when it comes to personnel assignments, the reality is that each of the Braves' minor league teams must put nine players on the field every evening. Those nine players cannot all be shortstops; and while the Atlanta Braves are everyone's ultimate focus, there must be a plan in place for when Atlanta reaches down and snatches a player from Richmond, or when someone in Richmond gets hurt. "You need to at least have a plan in place for everything that might happen to you," said Kemp. "When I think, OK, this is the guy who's going to play shortstop for us, I have to think, if he gets hurt tonight, who plays short tomorrow night? It might be my second baseman. Plan A might be our second baseman can do it and our backup guy can play second, and then I've got to get a guy from Mississippi to Richmond. But I have a plan in my mind, for every guy, if he was to get hurt tonight, what am I doing to cover that? And secondly, how do I have to shift the organization in order to cover that guy?

"We've got to give ourselves enough flexibility. You have to protect your teams; you have to protect the levels of kids. I mean, you can't leave yourself exposed to where your only option is to bring a kid from the lower levels who's not ready to play there. If you're not covered with somebody who can handle himself there, then you end up pushing that man up, putting him in a position where maybe he can get some confidence knocked out of him because he's playing a little bit over his head. He's just not ready yet. He will be someday, but he's just not ready yet."

There is no workplace endeavor quite like it. Does a school system ever find itself with too many science teachers, as a ball club might have too many middle infielders? How many investment banks worry about the psyche of a young trader when they move him up a rung? What law firm returns from the Christmas holiday and forces its associates to demonstrate their legal skills publicly, knowing their coming year's assignments depend upon how well they perform in the audition? The excitement of spring training may be over in the major league camp. But the real spring training drama is found on the quiet backfields of minor league camp. "It's all cut and dried over there," said Snyder. "It's not cut and dried here."

TWELVE

The Chief Big Ho and Car Rentals

The Cactus League Comes of Age

The Cleveland Indians started the Cactus League in 1947. Forty-five years later, they left, and the announcement of their departure threw the Cactus League into a turmoil, with a lot of folks in Arizona and many more in the game questioning the league's continued viability. Instead, the Indians' leave-taking provided a call to action to the Arizona political and civic communities, and the result has turned Arizona into the 800-pound gorilla of spring training baseball.

Bill Veeck bought the Indians during the summer of 1946 and brought baseball to the desert the next spring, convincing New York Giants owner Horace Stoneham to come along with him. Veeck knew Arizona; during a year out of baseball in 1945, he'd run a dude ranch outside Tucson. You go to Phoenix and I'll go to Tucson, Veeck told Stoneham. The Indians and the Giants were barnstorming buddies; for years, they'd broken camp in Florida together and shared a Pullman north, playing for a week or so in the minor league parks of the midsized cities in Georgia, Tennessee, the Carolinas, and Virginia before the start of the regular season. Neither team ever had a long-term Florida base. The Giants trained in Miami in 1946 and for a couple of years before the war; they'd been in Winter Haven for two years in the early forties. The Indians, meanwhile, had spent one year before the war and one year after the war in Clearwater; before that, they'd spent two springs in Fort

Myers. Stoneham agreed to Veeck's proposal, and the two teams headed west in 1947. Stoneham was apparently the kind of man who was amenable to suggestions from his brother owners. In 1951, he agreed to trade training camps with the Yankees, the Giants going to St. Petersburg for a year and the Yankees heading to Phoenix. Yankees owner Del Webb was starting to build a new town he was calling Sun City just outside Phoenix, and this let him oversee both his construction and his baseball businesses at the same time. And Stoneham, of course, also let Walter O'Malley talk him into moving the regular season to California in 1958.

Veeck's reasons for moving to Arizona have become baseball legend. As in all baseball legends, there is a bit of myth and a bit of truth. Veeck wanted to take the Indians to Arizona, it is said, because he'd signed Larry Doby, the first black player in the American League, and he felt that Arizona would be more welcoming than segregated Florida. The problem with this is that Veeck did not sign Larry Doby until July 1947; he was not with the Indians during their first spring training in Tucson. But that does not mean that the story is not rooted in truth. Veeck had been looking to integrate baseball as early as 1943, when he owned the minor league Milwaukee Brewers and was recovering from wounds he received in the battle for Guadalcanal. He'd reached a deal to buy the bankrupt Philadelphia Phillies, with the intention of fielding a team stocked with Negro League stars beginning with the 1944 season. He made the mistake of alerting Judge Landis to his plans. Before Veeck knew what hit him, the commissioner had ordered the Phillies put under the control of the league, and National League president Ford Frick brokered a deal to sell the Phillies to someone less radical. But now, as the owner of the Indians, Veeck knew that, unless Jackie Robinson's debut was somehow an unmitigated disaster, Veeck would soon be following Branch Rickey's lead and integrating the American League.

Still, he was looking less to the future than to the past in electing to forsake Florida for Arizona. "I had moved our training quarters to Arizona, not so much in preparation for Doby as out of an unpleasant experience with the Milwaukee Brewers," wrote Veeck. The Brewers trained in Ocala, which, like all Florida parks, had a Jim Crow section of bleachers for the black fans. Veeck was sitting in the segregated stands one day, talking to the black fans, when the Ocala sheriff came up and told him he'd have to leave. Veeck, ever the provocateur, asked why.

"I'm not bothering them," he told the sheriff. "I'm enjoying our talk, and they don't seem to resent me too much. They won't mind if I stay here."

His refusal to leave brought the mayor, blustering about the violation of city ordinances. At that point, Veeck lost all of his feigned naiveté, threatening to take the Brewers out of Ocala that night and promising to tell the world why.

He would eventually tell the world that story in his rollicking autobiography. And he seized the next opportunity he had to take a team to spring training and brought it to Arizona. It was not all sweetness and tolerance in Tucson. The grandstand at City Ballpark was not segregated, but the hotel where the Indians had stayed in 1947 and were planning to stay again in 1948 was. Veeck agreed to find Larry Doby other lodgings, but only this once. "We did make it clear—and they agreed—that in the future they would take all of our players, regardless of race, creed or previous condition of servitude." But in reflecting upon that 1948 compromise in his autobiography, written fourteen years later, there is more than a hint of guilt in Veeck's voice: "It was easy enough for me to tell Larry that these things took time. It was true enough to say that we had, after all, broken through one color barrier even if he was going to have to wait a year. It was easy for me, because it was he who was being told to be patient and wait."

The Indians and Giants were alone in Arizona for five years, playing exhibitions against college and Triple A teams and shuttling back and forth between Tucson and Phoenix to play each other, before barnstorming east together at the beginning of April. But while Bill Veeck and Horace Stoneham first brought spring training to Arizona, the true father of the Cactus League was a man they called the Big Ho.

In spring training's first half-century, when camps had been held in nearly every corner of Florida, as well as all across Georgia, Alabama, Louisiana, Arkansas, Texas, California, and even in notably nontropical climes, such as French Lick, Indiana, and Atlantic City, New Jersey, only one major league team—and for only one season—trained in the perfect weather of Arizona. The Detroit Tigers spent the 1929 preseason in Phoenix. Arizona had never really sought spring training as Florida had, and its beginnings there were almost accidental. After the arrival of the Giants and Indians in 1947, the Cactus League's growth was partially by design but mostly by happenstance. The third team to come to Arizona was the Cubs, in 1952. Their arrival was one that came by design. It was due to the persistence and personality of a thirty-nine-year-old Mesa rancher and hotel owner by the name of Dwight

Patterson. Were it not for Patterson and the Cubs, who knows whether any-one else would have followed. Patterson had been a football and track star at Peoria High School in the valley during the 1920s and attended North-ern Arizona University, where his football skills earned him a place in the NAU Athletic Hall of Fame. He coached football at Northern Arizona for a couple of years before marrying into a wealthy Mesa family and returning to the valley to help make the family even wealthier. Patterson helped to expand the Dobson family's ranching and cattle business and added a hotel to the family's holdings. He also became involved in a wide assortment of civic activities—Little League baseball, school and hospital fundraising, and prominent roles in the Mesa Chamber of Commerce and the Jaycees. In 1951, this work would lead him to spring training and the Chicago Cubs.

The Cubs had trained on Catalina Island in California for thirty years; Cubs owner William Wrigley, of the chewing gum Wrigleys, had bought the entire twenty-one-mile-long island in 1919. He built the famed Atwater hotel, the Catalina Island Casino—which had no gambling but was instead a dance and concert hall—and virtually the entire town of Avalon, and he turned Catalina into one of the West Coast's most upscale vacation destina-tions during the thirties and forties. Few places on earth provided a more pleasant environment for spring training; the players hated to leave, even for the start of the regular season. "It's a long way back down to earth from there," said pitcher Bob Kelly, who first trained on Catalina in 1948. Located, however, some twenty-two miles off the coast of Los Angeles, Catalina was not terribly accessible. As exhibition games increasingly became an integral part of spring training—and not just a barnstorming appendage to the end of spring training—Catalina's isolation became more and more untenable. Phil Wrigley, William's son and now the president of the Cubs, knew this and knew as well that the team's days amid the bliss of Catalina were prob-ably numbered. Dwight Patterson knew it too, and he had a notion that, if the Cubs were going to leave their island retreat, it ought to be for Mesa. Patterson was part of a chamber of commerce group that had brought the Pacific Coast League's Oakland Oaks to Mesa in 1951. The minor league spring training was a money loser, and the chamber voted against making any future spring training investments. Patterson was not convinced that this was the right decision. Together with other like-minded members of the chamber and the Mesa Jaycees—"bankers, lawyers, journalists, farm-ers, ranchers, retailers, insurance salesmen, and at least one politician"—Patterson formed a civic group called the HoHoKams; its first and only mission, at the beginning, was bringing spring training to Mesa. The HoHoKams are one of Arizona's ubiquitous civic groups. They take their name from an ancient tribe that lived in the valley at the time of Christ. Little is known as to what became of their civilization; "Ho Ho Kam" means "those who vanished." Because they were an ad hoc group brought together for the purpose of bringing spring training to Mesa, the 1951 HoHoKams may have believed that they, too, might vanish once they got spring training up and running, retreating mysteriously into legend. They have done anything but vanish; they have been an integral part of Mesa spring training for more than fifty years.

In 1951, Patterson put the Cubs on Mesa's calendar and in turn put himself on Wrigley's calendar. When the Cubs visited the valley to play some exhibition games against the Yankees and the Indians, Patterson got them to stop in Mesa for a game against the Oaks. He set to work on Wrigley. He promised improvements to Mesa's Rendezvous Park. Wrigley asked for a dorm for the players; Patterson said no problem. By the time he returned to Catalina, Wrigley had a handshake deal with Patterson to bring the Cubs' spring training to Mesa in 1952. The Cubs would play in a city-owned facility, but it was the HoHoKams who negotiated and would manage the terms of the lease.

Mesa embraced Patterson's deal to bring baseball to the city, but only to a point. When the money put up jointly by the city and the Cubs to renovate Rendezvous Park came up $50,000 short, the city balked. The thirty-five original HoHoKam members each signed for a $3,000 personal loan to make up the shortfall. Mesa legend has it that most did so without telling their wives.

Patterson never asked any of his brethren to dig into their own pockets without first digging into his own. When an exhibition game was threatened by a wet field, Patterson ordered the grounds crew to soak the soggy dirt of the infield with gasoline and set it aflame. He then brought in helicopters to blow-dry the grass. He paid for it all himself. The HoHoKams elected Patterson their first chief, though they all took to calling him the Big Ho. Soon, it was part of his formal title; he was the Chief Big Ho, and when he stepped aside as Chief Big Ho, the HoHoKams retired the "chief." Subsequent leaders would be known formally as the Big Ho; Dwight Patterson would forever be the Chief Big Ho.

Patterson would serve on corporate boards and governors' commissions and would be an annual summertime guest at the Wrigley mansion in Chicago. He would also shuttle Cubs rookies, who lived in their dormitory underneath the grandstand at Rendezvous Park, to a local restaurant and buy them a steak; and at games at Rendezvous Field and, later, at HoHoKam Park, he was apt to be parking cars or taking tickets—just another HoHoKam volunteer in his cowboy hat and red shirt.

Patterson and the HoHoKams would provide a blueprint for Arizona spring training; there was not merely civic involvement, there was *citizen* involvement. The HoHoKams were men (and, ultimately, women) of influence and power in their community; they saw the success of spring training as a measure of personal and civic pride. Other groups—the Scottsdale Charros, the Tempe Diablos, the Chandler Compadres, and more—would play central roles in the spring training history of their towns as well. While their mission is public service, and they give millions to charitable endeavors each year, these are hardly egalitarian organizations. Many are as exclusive as the most private country club; membership is limited and by invitation only. They have a strong work ethic and a commitment to community; they also have access and connections, the means and the wherewithal to get things done. When the Cactus League was threatened in the early nineties, these were very handy people to have involved.

After the Cubs' arrival in Mesa, the Cactus League grew in fits and starts over the next two decades. The next team to arrive in Arizona was the Orioles, who trained in Yuma in 1954, their first year after moving to Baltimore from St. Louis. This gave Arizona four teams, apparently a critical mass; sportswriters began referring to Arizona exhibition games as the "Cactus League" for the first time. The Orioles stayed one year in Yuma, trained in Daytona Beach in 1955, and then returned to Arizona and trained in Scottsdale for two years. The Red Sox replaced the Orioles in Scottsdale in 1959, keeping the league at four teams until expansion in the early sixties. The Cactus League picked up the Los Angeles Angels in 1961, though the Angels played out in Palm Springs, California, where owner Gene Autry had a home. The National League's Houston Colt .45s grew the league to six teams when they arrived in Apache Junction in 1962. By the mid-sixties, however, the league was back down to four, as both Boston and Houston had decamped for Florida. Stability began to arrive by the end of the decade, though. Charley Finley brought the Athletics closer to their new Oakland home, moving from Bradenton to Mesa in 1968; and the expansion San Diego Padres and

Seattle Pilots both signed on a year later, the Padres training in Yuma, the Pilots in Tempe (keeping their spring training in Arizona after they moved to Milwaukee in 1970).

Eight years later, in 1977, the Cactus League steadied itself at eight members when the expansion Seattle Mariners set up in Tempe. Ensuing years saw a lot of movement, but mostly it was a game of in-state musical chairs; the Cubs moved from Mesa to Scottsdale in 1967; the A's moved from Mesa to Scottsdale in 1978 and were replaced in Mesa by the Cubs. The A's would then trade places with the Giants; the A's moving from Scottsdale to Phoenix, and the Giants moving the other way in 1983. The one team charting new waters was the Brewers, who moved from Tempe to Sun City to Chandler between 1972 and 1986.

This was old-time spring training: the parks were modest and small; the leases were short, most of them year to year, nothing over three to five years. Local parks and recreation departments ran the facilities, with parks-and-rec city budgets. There was not a lot of extra money, though that did not stop teams from asking their hosts to spruce things up. "Every winter, I'd get about a twenty-page letter from the Cubs' clubhouse manager," recalled Ron Pies, the parks and recreation director for the city of Scottsdale when the Cubs trained there (he would later move to city government in Tempe and oversee the spring trainings of the Pilots/Brewers, Mariners, and Angels in that city). "He'd make all these impossible demands for improvements. Once, he wanted the ceiling in the clubhouse raised up so he could hang uniforms. The clubhouse was under the grandstand; the ceiling was the underside of the stands."

Arizona watched with a mixture of envy and anxiety as Florida went on a building spree in the 1980s, with new parks going up in Kissimmee, Port Charlotte, Port St. Lucie, and Plant City. Arizona also watched Florida cannibalize itself and waited for the day when there'd be no more teams for other Florida cities to poach, and they'd come after Cactus League teams. Rumors rumbled throughout 1989 and 1990 that the Indians, Mariners, and Padres were all listening to what Florida cities had to say. By the time the Indians announced in early 1991 that they were close to a deal with Citrus County, Florida, north of Tampa, and that 1992 would be their last spring in Arizona, negotiations between the Mariners and Tempe for improvements to their facility there were at an impasse. The Angels and Athletics let it be known that they would be open to offers too. Even the Cubs took a look at the new complex going up in Homestead. Only the Giants and the Brewers publicly said they were committed to Arizona no matter what.

Some of the Arizona teams' interest in Florida was posturing, a ploy to get better leases and improvements to their existing facilities, and Arizona knew it. "They've got to talk that way," said Robert Brinton, the head of the Mesa Convention and Visitors Bureau. "You can't make someone jealous unless you're dating someone else." But that did not mean that Cactus League people made light of the threat. If only one of the lookers followed the Indians to Florida, the Cactus League could be down to six teams, and that could spell its doom. With only six or seven teams, there'd be too many split-squad games or exhibitions against Triple A or college teams. The managers, general managers, and scouts of the teams training in Arizona would see only a third of the other teams' players compared to their counterparts in Florida. However committed to Arizona individual franchises might be, it made no baseball sense to be a part of a small group. Most teams had leases that stipulated that, if the Cactus League got down to six teams, they could opt out. And there were any number of signs that that might happen. The Mariners seemed certain to be on their way out of Tempe; the Padres eschewed the chance to sign a long-term extension with their longtime home, Yuma, electing instead to extend their lease for just two years and give themselves a chance to see what would happen.

Arizona was also experiencing political troubles while all of this was festering. Governor Evan Mecham had been impeached and removed from office in 1988, accused of concealing a campaign loan and borrowing state money for his private business. Before he left office, and unrelated to the charges that got him impeached, Mecham had set off a national furor when he took Martin Luther King Day off the calendar as a state holiday. The state might have been able to survive the ensuing storm from that one, blaming it on the eccentric and politically disgraced Mecham. But a ballot initiative to reinstate the holiday was defeated by voters in 1990. The backlash caused the National Football League to move the 1992 Super Bowl out of Tempe; and while major league baseball issued no formal reaction to the voters' decision, back-channel communication soon made it clear that Phoenix had dropped off the list of prospective expansion cities for 1993. The Cactus League, founded on the belief that Arizona would be more racially tolerant than a segregated Florida, now had its very existence threatened by the perception of racial intolerance.

Spring training 1991 was not a happy time for the Cactus League. The prospect of its demise was palpable at every Cactus League game. The season began with a February 15 meeting between baseball commissioner Fay

Vincent and Arizona governor Rose Mofford. The governor had asked Vincent to intervene, to protect the Cactus League by preventing teams from leaving. Vincent told her point blank that major league baseball would not do that. "The Cactus League is very important to major league baseball," Vincent said after the meeting. "On the other hand we realize that each team has to make individual decisions with regard to finances and their conditions." That spring, newspaper articles in Arizona papers, in the hometown papers of the Cactus League teams, and in national papers such as the *New York Times* calculated the Cactus League's chances for survival, and the consensus was not optimistic. Florida officials quoted in those articles insisted that their aim was not to put the Cactus League out of business, but they also happily acknowledged that they had enough interested communities to absorb all of the Arizona teams, should that ultimately happen. There was an unmistakable smugness to some of the comments.

"No team plays in a desert climate, so why should any play in one during the spring?" asked Ron Safford, the director of sports development in Florida. "Game results miss media deadlines in the East. You can see twice as many players here as the Arizona league. Combine all that with sweetheart deals we can offer." The implication was clear. Florida might be insisting that it was not out to kill off the Cactus League, but it was nevertheless making it clear there was room for everyone in Florida.

While the gloom pervading the Cactus League was what made headlines in 1991, the bigger news, largely unreported, was the work that had been going on behind the scenes aimed at keeping the rest of the Cactus League teams right where they were. Rose Mofford, the new governor, was a baseball fan. As a young woman, the now sixty-eight-year-old Mofford had barnstormed with a national caliber women's softball team. One of her first acts after assuming office following Mecham's impeachment, when the rumors about the Indians and Mariners looking to go to Florida were first being heard, was to establish the Arizona Baseball Commission. The committee chair was Joe Garagiola, Jr., a well-connected Phoenix lawyer and the son of the former major league catcher and NBC broadcaster. The commission's charge was twofold: to pursue one of the major league expansion franchises promised for the early nineties and to find a way to keep any more spring training teams from leaving Arizona for Florida. To do this was going to take money, and Arizona didn't have any—in fact, there was a $140 million state budget shortfall. And the tourism and construction industries—the lifeblood of Arizona's economy—had taken a hit in the late eighties.

The first thing Garagiola did was to commission a study to determine how much money the Cactus League was worth to Arizona. The figure came back at $140 million a year. The number was such a surprise that it was greeted with some skepticism, even by Garagiola himself. "Even if they're wrong by half, that's still a major impact," Garagiola told the *San Francisco Chronicle* in 1991. "Those are pretty direct dollars, and they don't even take into account the number of players who live here in the off-season."

The commission succeeded in getting a bill before the legislature in 1990 that would allow Maricopa County to impose a 0.25 percent sales tax for stadium construction. Maricopa County is Phoenix and the surrounding communities, the part of the state the chamber of commerce and tourist brochures call the Valley of the Sun and the locals refer to simply as the valley. The bill did not pass. A year later, however, a measure passed the legislature creating the Maricopa County Stadium Authority; it was to be funded by a tax on rental cars, $2.50 per rental contract. The original bill had called for a $5.00 per-contract fee, but the legislature cut that in half. Some in the Cactus League worried that $2.50 would not be enough to do what needed to be done. Their fears were ill founded. Like Florida had some years earlier, Arizona had found a way to let the tourists pay for its baseball. The car-rental tax would save the Cactus League.

By the time the tax passed the legislature, the remote west valley town of Peoria was talking to the San Diego Padres about bringing their spring training from Yuma to the valley. Fifteen miles northwest of Phoenix, Peoria consisted of desert and farms, and it was at least a decade behind the valley's boomtowns in the development game. Peoria wanted some of the malls, restaurants, office parks, and housing stock that were blossoming all over the valley. It saw spring training as the spur to that development. "We got involved with the teams and spring training for a community resource," said J. P. de la Montaigne, the Cactus League Association's president who, as Peoria's community services director, oversaw the construction of the Peoria Sports Complex and oversees its operation today. "We didn't have any large parks at the time. But we really did it for economic development and for marketing. Having 'Peoria, Arizona' as a [dateline] in every newspaper in the country was quite a coup for us."

Fifteen years earlier, Peoria had bet that minor league spring training might be the catalyst for development; it had built a small minor league complex for the Brewers on land where it now wanted to build for the Padres. But commerce doesn't follow the minor leagues, and by the early nineties, the Peoria complex was still surrounded by vast tracts of flat earth, dotted by farm stands selling lettuce for fifty-nine cents a head. "You could come out here and look for two miles in any direction and not see anything," said de la Montaigne. "So you had to have some kind of vision about what this could bring to our community."

What it has brought to the lonesome tract of land near the intersection of Highway 101 and Bell Road is a boom that's stretched the limits of what the Peoria people dared to dream. There are condos, office buildings, two skating rinks (one ice, one roller), movie theaters, eight new hotels, and too many restaurants to count. Everything about the venture has exceeded expectations, beginning with the fact that Peoria snared not one spring training team, but two.

Peoria had talks with a number of clubs, including the expansion Rockies—who very quickly committed to Tucson—and two Florida clubs, the Orioles and the White Sox. The Padres' negotiations were the most encouraging. But talks stalled. The Padres were committed to Yuma until 1994, Yuma was making a pitch to keep them, and there was a strong preference among Padre fans for the team staying there. Yuma is only a three-hour drive from San Diego; a Padres fan could catch a spring training game in Yuma and be back in San Diego for the sunset.

In early 1992, the Peoria people began talking to the Seattle Mariners. At first, they weren't looking to get the Mariners to join the Padres; they were merely covering the bases in the event the Padres' talks fell apart. "After one meeting with the Mariners, we said: 'Why don't we try to do both of them?'" recalled de la Montaigne. "And we penciled it out and it actually made more sense to have two teams sharing one facility in terms of revenue. You double the revenue. But you don't double the expenses."

One of the greatest challenges in making its two-team complex a reality was quashing the notion that one of the teams would be the primary tenant and the other the stepchild. That had always been the case in shared facilities. The Braves and then the Cardinals played second fiddle to the Yankees in St. Petersburg through the years; the Cardinals dominated things when the Yankees left and the Mets arrived. In West Palm Beach, the Braves and the Expos shared a facility for years, but it was hardly a partnership. The Expos were effectively subleasing space from the Braves. The Expos resented their second-class status; the Braves resented the Expos' very presence. And in Peoria, de la Montaigne found teams initially hesitant about the idea of a dual complex. The city therefore designed identical facilities. The Padres' clubhouse and practice fields spread out beyond the left field fence, and the Mariners' did the same beyond right field. The contract called for everything to be shared equally: the home team gets 80 percent of the ticket revenues and the city gets 20 percent; all other revenue (from the concessions, novelties, advertising, parking) is split fifty-fifty. According to de la Montaigne, "So what we said was: 'you're both equal, you're both important to us. It's not that there's one A and one B [team], you're both A teams to us.'"

It's been a happy marriage. Each clubhouse and practice complex is out of sight of the other, and with separate parking facilities for players and team personnel, the only times the two teams need see one another are on the four days they play exhibitions against each other. And it's been a particularly satisfying investment for Peoria. Eleven years into the city's leases with the Padres and Mariners, a 2004 economic impact study conducted for the Cactus League Association showed that spring training had put $39 million into the Peoria economy that year. Sixty-nine percent of the fans at Mariners games and 55 percent of those at Padres games came to Peoria from out of state. Ninety-nine percent of those fans said that spring training was a factor in their decision to visit, and nearly two-thirds of them claimed it was the primary factor in their decision to visit.

Peoria changed the business model. Of all the new spring training complexes built since Peoria—meaning, new complexes in new cities, not refurbished or even new complexes in existing cities—only two were built as one-team facilities. The others all serve two teams. When Goodyear, Arizona, broke ground on its complex for the Cleveland Indians, it planned a stadium that could accommodate two primary tenants, leaving enough land beyond the clubhouse and practice fields to build another complete set, should the need one day arise, as it did when the Reds committed to joining the Indians beginning in 2010.

Not everyone championed the Peoria model, however. Ron Pies, the parks and recreation director for the city of Tempe, whose Cactus League involvement went back to the 1960s when he'd been Scottsdale's parks and rec director, was particularly vocal in his opposition to using tax dollars to entice teams. Pies was a member of the governor's commission that helped to secure the rental car money; he was a member of the advisory board to the Maricopa County Stadium District, the entity created to manage the rental-car money. Few in the Cactus League command as much respect. Pies was losing the Mariners to Peoria, but he was already in talks with Gene Autry to bring the Angels from Palm Springs to replace them. He was more concerned about Yuma losing the Padres and the precedent it would set. "I just went ballistic," he said. "Yuma was a neat town; they did everything the Padres wanted. And I said: 'We're not getting into this game I've seen in Florida; we're not getting into this game of using taxpayer dollars in Arizona to steal teams from other Arizona cities.'" But Pies' arguments fell upon deaf ears. The Padres might have gotten from Yuma all they got from Peoria, had they asked. But Yuma would still be a three-hour bus ride to exhibition games in the valley, and the Padres were through with those. Pies was also concerned about the cost to Peoria; the sticker price was a whopping $32 million. The other early car-rental tax projects—upgrades to Tempe Diablo Stadium and to Phoenix Municipal, where the Athletics trained—were decidedly less grand, each around $5 million. Both were paid for with money collected from the early years of the car-rental tax. In Peoria, on the other hand, the state would be spending money that it would take years to recoup.

Once you buy on credit, it's easy to buy more. The Cactus League went on a spending spree. Arizona tourism was on the rebound, the car-rental money was rolling in, and it promised to do so forever. Cities issued bonds for their matching funds against the prospects of an increased tax base from the development that would surround the new and updated facilities. Mesa leveled Hohokam Park in 1996 and built, by spring training '97, a brand new Hohokam in its footprint, a jumbo-sized spring training park, with seats and berm space for 12,500 fans. It cost $18 million.

Next came a new home for the Brewers, who had jumped around more than any other team since arriving in Arizona twenty-nine years before. Since 1986, they'd been training in Chandler, in a low-end facility built privately but subsequently taken over by the Maricopa County Stadium District, which found itself in a protracted struggle with the city of Chandler over the maintenance costs for the complex. When a developer offered to donate fifty-five acres of private land in the west Phoenix neighborhood of Maryvale for a new spring training complex, the Brewers, who had hoped to stay in Chandler, headed there.

They weren't happy about it. Maryvale was a woebegone section of town, marked by gang violence, shuttered storefronts, tumbling housing prices, and an elevated incidence of childhood leukemia, attributed to the discovery of an industrial cleaning solvent in neighborhood wells some fifteen years before. Maryvale Baseball Park was going to be the linchpin in a hoped-for gentrification. It cost $18 million, and while spring training has worked no miracles in the neighborhood, Maryvale has shown decided progress in the decade since the Brewers arrived. There's still little by way of upscale commerce, but there are fewer shuttered businesses. New fast-food restaurants stand neat sentry on the busy street corners, and they've been joined by a couple of new hotels (though the Brewers' official team hotel is out in Mesa, more than twenty miles from the stadium). The housing stock in Maryvale will never be confused with Scottsdale's, but the rusted cars and graffiti are gone, and there is a decided pride of ownership in most of the lower-middle-class homes along 51st Avenue. The most impressive part of the neighborhood remains Maryvale Baseball Park. Now ten years old, it remains pristine, picturesque, and perfect. But of all the spring training leases in major league baseball, the Brewers' lease in Maryvale is the shortest, set to expire in 2012. And for cities in both Florida and Arizona with designs on spring training riches and fame, that makes the Milwaukee Brewers suddenly the most popular girl at the dance.

The Brewers' arrival in Maryvale in 1998 coincided with the arrival of regular season baseball in the valley in the form of the Arizona Diamondbacks. This was far and away the biggest baseball news. But even spring training stories shunted Maryvale to the lower paragraphs. The Diamondbacks would take their camp in Tucson, their choice of sites prompted by a wish to expand their fan base beyond the valley, to become truly the *Arizona* Diamondbacks and not just the Phoenix Diamondbacks. And they were going to share a brand-new facility in Tucson with the Chicago White Sox, the first team to leave Florida and come to Arizona since the Athletics thirty years before. Things were looking good for the Cactus League in 1998. Just seven short years after fearing it would soon be writing its epitaph, the Cactus League had built four new stadiums and refurbished two others, had grown from seven teams to ten and locked in a rosy future.

But good is not perfect. By the spring of 1999, the biggest story was about the one that got away.

THIRTEEN

How the Dodgers Almost Left Vero Beach the First Time

"Can you imagine giving all this up?" asked the Dodgers' longtime traveling secretary, Bill DeLury, during the spring of 2005, as he looked out at the palm-lined courtyard between the new office building/clubhouse and Holman Stadium in Dodgertown. To baseball purists and Dodgers traditionalists, the idea was unthinkable—as unthinkable as, well, as the idea that the Dodgers would ever leave Brooklyn.

But it has happened, leaving some wondering how and others wondering how it could have taken so long. After a half-century of rock-solid unity between the sleepy upscale coastal community and one of baseball's most tradition-bound franchises, the Dodgers and Vero Beach endured an emotionally tumultuous decade trying to make it last. First came the Dodgers' threat to leave, then the community's cries of anguish, followed immediately by the effective marshaling of political forces to keep them. The Keep Our Dodgers campaign looked like a success, with a new deal and a twenty-year commitment signed in 2000. But it wasn't the same somehow. Vero Beach saw its Dodgers differently now. And Dodgertown, which traded some of its old charm for modern amenities, no longer had the same emotional leverage on the new owners that it had had on the old. Six years into their new twenty-year agreement, the Dodgers started talking about moving again. This time, there would be no community rally to save them.

In the year they celebrated their fiftieth anniversary in Vero Beach, 1998, the Dodgers first started talking about leaving. In the middle of that fiftieth anniversary spring training, the O'Malley family, after a forty-seven-year stewardship of the team, passed title of the team and all of its holdings to media baron Rupert Murdoch and his Fox Corporation for a then-record price of $311 million. "Family ownership is probably a dying breed," said Dodger president Peter O'Malley as he put the team up for sale the year before. "[Owning a team is] as high risk as the oil business. You need a broader base than a family." There was more than a little unease at the announcement. The O'Malleys were the last of the great baseball families to sell out to corporate America, and there were equal parts irony and melancholy to that. The O'Malleys, of course—at least patriarch Walter O'Malley—were among the first to demonstrate beyond measure that sentiment was no match for the dollar when they took the Dodgers from Brooklyn to Los Angeles. But now, a generation later, the O'Malley family (Peter O'Malley owned the team together with his sister, Terry Seidler) was the standard-bearer for tradition and continuity in a baseball world gone mad with the bottom line. Peter O'Malley's departure threatened to leave a void in the game as vast as the one his father had left in Brooklyn exactly forty years before.

Moreover, there was a great deal of consternation about the man to whom O'Malley had chosen to sell. Murdoch and Fox had a reputation for bringing tremendous upheaval to the many and varied businesses they seemed to acquire on almost a monthly basis. Murdoch was seen as "an aggressive, continent-hopping dealmaker with no sentimental or historical attachment to the country's most tradition-bound sport." His future brethren in the owners' fraternity worried that his bottomless pockets— his assets were estimated at nearly $4 billion—would allow him to spend with impunity, further upsetting the already unbalanced salary structure in major league baseball. Fans, meanwhile, worried that he wouldn't spend any money at all on the team, that his real objective in acquiring the Dodgers was to enhance the value of Fox Sports West, the cable channel that televised Dodgers games—and to use his status as a baseball insider to solidify the $500 million in contracts that regional Fox Sports channels held with twenty-three other major league clubs, as well as the national contract the Fox broadcast network had for the playoffs and World Series. Baseball seemed to hold both its nose and its breath in approving the sale to Murdoch.

What this meant for Dodgertown and Vero Beach became evident soon enough. After announcing that it did not intend to run the Dodgers as a money-losing operation, Fox put everything in play. If there was a nickel more to be made anywhere in the organization, Fox wanted to make it. In the summer of 1998, Craig Callan, the Dodgers' vice president in charge of Dodgertown, together with the team's general counsel, Sam Fernandez, and Fox executive Gary Erlich were tasked with exploring whether or not Vero Beach remained the best option for Dodgers spring training. Dodgertown had history and charm in abundance, but its facilities—clubhouses, trainers' rooms, weight rooms, executive offices, and the villas where the team's executives stayed—all dated from the 1970s and were looking a little tired. They lagged behind the facilities other teams enjoyed in both Florida and Arizona. But should the Dodgers have to spend their own money on upgrading them, when nobody else in baseball did? asked the owners. Why were the Dodgers in the Florida real estate business at all? Why should the Los Angeles Dodgers be the only team in major league baseball to own its spring training facilities—paying not only staff salaries and maintenance costs but more than $320,000 a year in property taxes—when every other team trained in sparkling new, municipally owned facilities for practically nothing? "We were to take a look and see: is it possible to put us on a level playing field with all the other teams in baseball?" said Callan of his committee's charge. "The only way to do that would be for the city/county to purchase the facility, reimburse us for improvements, and then treat us like every other spring training site does with their teams." And if Vero Beach wasn't interested in playing by the Dodgers' new rules, other places would be.

Near the close of the 1998 baseball season, a handful of Dodgers executives were invited to the Fort McDowell Indian Reservation, northeast of Scottsdale. There, in a conference room at the casino, in a majestic setting at the base of the Four Peaks, leaders of the Yavapai Apache tribe showed them drawings and models for a Dodgertown in the desert. The plans were for a complex that was lavish in every detail. It included six full-sized practice fields (one more than Dodgertown), two half fields (one more than Dodgertown), a 12,500-seat stadium (roughly twice the size of Holman), a conference center, dining hall, and accommodations for 250 (roughly equal to what Dodgertown had but all brand-spanking new), golf courses, and other recreational opportunities. The Yavapai were also offering some instant Dodgers tradition. The drawings shown to the Dodgers featured Chavez Ravine Drive, Lasorda Loop, Vin Scully Way, the Walter O'Malley Clubhouse, and the Sandy Koufax Field. The $30 million complex would be built at no cost to the Dodgers, with revenues from the Fort McDowell casino and the state of Arizona. The Dodgers would get a thirty-year lease at $1 per year.

While optimists in Arizona and fatalists in Florida began assuming that the Dodgers' departure was a fait accompli as soon as the Yavapai plans became public in the fall of 1998, the Dodgers moved very cautiously. For all of the grandeur of the Fort McDowell plans, they were still but a promise on paper. In the best of scenarios, the complex couldn't be ready before spring training 2001, and some Dodgers officials were skeptical that it could ever be built, thinking that the cost for what they'd been shown was probably closer to $50 million than $30 million. Dodgertown didn't have to be built. Moreover, a deal with Vero Beach to stay at Dodgertown could help to deflect some of the public relations battering the Fox Dodgers were taking over what many saw as a callous stewardship of the team's heritage.

"Our first intent was to stay in Vero Beach," said Callan. "We wanted to stay." Talks to keep the Dodgers in Vero Beach were cordial and orderly. The city and county had known for a year that they might face a decision on whether or not to become a spring training landlord. Peter O'Malley had requested a meeting with city and county officials in 1997, shortly after announcing that the team was for sale. He told the mayor, the city manager, and the county administrator then that new owners were certain to reexamine their spring training options, and a likely scenario involved a new owner wishing to sell Dodgertown to the local government and then to lease it back. By the summer of 1998, talks among Craig Callan, Indian River County administrator James Chandler, and Vero Beach city manager Rex Taylor had gotten into specifics, and in the fall the Vero Beach City Council and the Indian River County Commission both voted to pursue options for keeping the Dodgers. The city and county appealed to the Florida legislature. They were looking to tweak some Florida statutes that would provide state money to help in the purchase of Dodgertown. Spring training 1999 began with a rush of sentimental newspaper articles lamenting the Dodgers' possible departure from Vero Beach. In Tallahassee, meanwhile, the Florida legislature prepared to debate legislation that would prevent that from happening.

Representative Charles Sembler of Vero Beach, together with Senator Patsy Kurth of Palm Bay, the two Vero Beach representatives in the Florida legislature, filed a bill during the 1999 session that would provide $7.5 million in state funds toward the acquisition of Dodgertown by the city and county. The money was to be matched by $7.5 million in local funds (it would eventually become $11.5 million in local funds). The local money would come from bonds, to be repaid with money that would be raised with a 1 percent increase in the local bed tax.

The bill faced the usual doubts from the fiscal watchdogs—including those who felt that billionaire Rupert Murdoch shouldn't be on the public dole. "What is the compelling state interest in taking $7.5 million of hard-earned taxpayer dollars away from educating our schoolchildren, public health, the safety of our citizens and other critical functions of state government?" asked the head of a group called Florida TaxWatch. The naysayers' sound bites were countered by an aggressive behind-the-scenes lobbying effort funded by the Dodgers and by Tommy Lasorda, who spoke in favor of the bill before a legislative committee and afterward playfully threatened Governor Jeb Bush. "You better sign this bill," he told him. "Because I know where the power is in your family and if you don't sign it I'm calling your mother." One Dodgers front office executive watched Bush's reaction to Lasorda's quip and thought to himself: *he didn't like that*. Bush had threatened throughout the legislative session to veto all "turkeys," as he called them, bills he considered to be the singular interests of individual legislators— any legislation, in other words, that he saw benefiting special interests and not the welfare of all Floridians. But while this appropriations bill had been written specifically with Vero Beach, Rupert Murdoch, and Dodgertown in mind, Bush wasn't convinced it was one of his turkeys. "The problem is, it is precedent-setting," said Cory Tilley, Governor Bush's spokesperson. "The question is, 'Can we do this for every team and is it an appropriate use of state funds?' If one team leaves, it could start a trend and we don't want that either. It's a tough call."

Vero Beach remained hopeful throughout the process, but it dared not get cocky. The bill had a couple of rocky moments in the legislature. The Fiscal Policy Committee in the senate removed the appropriation, then restored it a day later. Governor Bush's office remained in contact with the Dodgers throughout, and when the legislation successfully passed both houses and landed on Bush's desk at the end of the legislative session in May, there seemed to be cause for relief if not outright celebration. Bush then stunned the Dodgers, and broke a lot of hearts in Vero Beach, by vetoing the bill.

When life's verities are shattered, it is sometimes hard to know how to react. Few of Vero Beach's 18,000 citizens predated the arrival of the Dodgers. For permanent residents, the Dodgers had always been a part of the city's economy, personality, and identity. For the winter residents and the retirees, spring training and the Dodgers might well have been a deciding factor in choosing Vero Beach over St. Augustine or Hobe Sound. "Dodger baseball and Dodger spring training are [the Vero Beach] community brand," said Penny Chandler, the executive director of the Indian River Chamber of Commerce. "Spring training brings a lot of attention to Vero Beach and to Indian River County." Now, in the summer of 1999, the brand seemed doomed; the Dodgers seemed certain to be going elsewhere. The realization that Vero Beach might soon be without its community signature numbed the city. And it brought reflection—not only on a half-century's memories, but also on exactly what Vero Beach would be losing when the Dodgers departed. The decision to fight for the Dodgers was not a sentimental one; it was business.

The first attempt to demonstrate what the Dodgers meant to Vero Beach financially came in 1952, when the Dodgers' first lease was nearing its end and some members of the city council were balking at renewal. Dodgers general manager Buzzie Bavasi sent traveling secretary Lee Scott to the Hialeah Racetrack with a certified check for $40,000. Scott brought back 20,000 two-dollar bills. Bavasi, Scott, and some deputies then spent the better part of two days stamping the back of each bill with the words "Brooklyn Dodgers." In anticipation of a Monday city council meeting, Bavasi gathered the Dodgers players—all 600 of them—on a Friday afternoon and told them that the cafeteria was out of order and would be for the weekend. He then disbursed the marked bills and sent the players out into the local economy. With Bavasi's planted bills fresh in everyone's memory and the promise of a new stadium forthcoming, Walter O'Malley had little trouble negotiating the Dodgers' second lease.

Financial impact studies have grown vastly more sophisticated since then, but they remain an essential ingredient—perhaps *the* essential ingredient—in all talks on whether or not state and local governments ought to be in the spring training business. When the Dodgers storm broke in the summer of 1998, and in the two years thereafter, the figure on the team's financial impact on Indian River County, which was quoted in every newspaper story and in every public hearing, was $30 million. The number derived from a series of economic impact studies generated by the Indian River Chamber of Commerce and by the Indian River County Community Development

Cap Anson, who was not the first to take a team south for spring training, but who got credit for being the first for more than a half-century. (National Baseball Hall of Fame Library)

Ned Hanlon, manager of the 1890s Baltimore Orioles, who changed spring training from fat farm to baseball camp that taught skills and team tactics. (National Baseball Hall of Fame Library)

Early spring trainings were only part baseball. Here, in a postcard from the 1910s, John McGraw takes the Giants on one of their seven-mile morning hikes in Marlin, Tex. (National Baseball Hall of Fame Library)

Waterfront Park in St. Petersburg, 1920s. Spring training baseball was played on the site from 1922–2008. (City of St. Petersburg)

From the beginning, press coverage of spring training generated interest and ticket sales well in advance of the start of the regular season. Here, France Laux, (L), radio voice of the St. Louis Cardinals during the 1930s, interviews, (L to R) Dizzy Dean, Lefty Gomez and Pepper Martin, St. Petersburg, Fla., 1936. (National Baseball Hall of Fame Library)

John Wright (L) and Jackie Robinson at baseball's first integrated spring training, Daytona Beach, Fla., 1946. (National Baseball Hall of Fame Library)

Wendell Smith of the *Pittsburgh Courier* and *Chicago's American*. (National Baseball Hall of Fame Library)

Segregated seating at Al Lang Field.
(Copyright *St. Petersburg Times*. Reprinted with permission.)

Two future Dodger presidents at spring training in Daytona Beach, 1946. Walter (L) and son Peter O'OMalley. (Courtesy walteromalley.com)

In 1948, Branch Rickey brought the Brooklyn Dodgers to a former World War II air base in Vero Beach, Fla. Dodgertown would remain the team's spring home for 61 seasons. (Courtesy walteromalley.com)

Newspaper photographers from the 1920s–1950s loved to send back an opening-day photo of the team taking the field en masse for the first time each spring. Here the Pittsburgh Pirates take the field in Fort Myers, late 1950s. (National Baseball Hall of Fame Library)

Al Lang (R) with Connie Mark, at the dedication of Al Lang field in 1947. (National Baseball Hall of Fame Library)

Casey Stengel reviews the balk rule with Yankees pitchers and catchers, St. Petersburg, 1952. (AP Worldwide)

Walter and Kay O'Malley were a constant presence at Dodgertown. Here they are shown (seated in stands) with Pee Wee Reese (left) and Carl Erskine in 1975. (Courtesy walteromalley.com)

Dwight Patterson, father of the Cactus League. (Courtesy Mesa Historical Museum)

Spring training hosts built national reputations and tourism business off their associations with major league baseball. (Courtesy walteromalley.com)

Department. The studies showed the direct economic impact at $15–17 million. Direct impact includes salaries paid to Dodgertown employees, taxes, utilities, donations to local charities, purchases of local goods and services by Dodgertown, and money spent in the community by Dodgers-generated tourism. Indirect impact estimates, using various multiplier factors, increased the total impact estimates to $29 million, $31 million, and $36 million in three different studies done during the 1998–1999 period.

The Jeb Bush veto of state aid for Dodgertown in May 1999 galvanized the Vero Beach business community. A good portion of that $15–17 million in direct impact and virtually all of the $15–20 million in indirect impact were destined for their pockets, after all. Yet there was also much civic pride in the group that mobilized to save the Dodgers; they were the spiritual heirs of Bud Holman. "The committee started as kind of a chamber thing, and then it spun off and involved more and more community leaders," according to Tony Donadio, who chaired the Keep Our Dodgers committee during 1998–2000. "As we kept on going we brought in more people that were interested—board of realtors people, attorneys, radio people, bankers. People who had a stake in the community and understood the value of the Dodgers to our community and what it really meant if they were to leave. Because of the fifty-year tradition, it involved the whole community; it was a community concern. And a lot of people didn't realize that."

The Keep Our Dodgers committee was the work of William Curtis, president of the First National Bank in Vero Beach and at the time the president of the Indian River Chamber of Commerce. The committee numbered more than two dozen, a veritable who's who of the Vero Beach power structure: city and county officials, the chief of police, lawyers, architects, real estate developers, the doyens of the Vero Beach philanthropic community, and even Dodgers executive Craig Callan. They met actively for a period of nearly two years. Curtis recruited Donadio, a local architect who was new to the chamber, to serve as the committee's chair. "We saw our role as: we gather the facts and we disseminate the information," said Penny Chandler of the chamber, who served on the committee. Task one was gathering the information, particularly the economic information. Wayne Kleinstiver, whose day job was in commercial and industrial real estate, worked with economists from the University of Florida in putting together the chamber of commerce's economic impact study, the one that came in with a bottom line of $31 million. Kleinstiver also made his own appraisal of the various parcels of Dodgertown real estate, and concluded both privately and publicly that the city would be getting more than fair value on the land and buildings alone at the prices being discussed.

Dissemination of the information gathered by the committee was made on two levels. The first was an enthusiastic, tub-thumping public campaign. It sold Keep Our Dodgers T-shirts and blanketed the town with Keep Our Dodgers posters. It set up an information booth at Downtown Fridays, a monthly street fair in Vero's downtown shopping district. Committee members wrote letters to the editor and sent faxes to Governor Bush and the legislature when the state aid bill came up for reconsideration. They also lobbied privately with local and state officials—ultimately to win votes, but mostly to keep the issue fresh and alive. "We pretty much felt that the important thing was to educate the public and educate the [county] commission," said Donadio. "There were a lot of people out there who felt that we [didn't] need to be buying this facility from the Dodgers when the Dodgers were a multimillion-dollar corporation. I don't think people saw what they would lose compared to what they were paying to buy the facility. All people were seeing was that bottom $19 million they had to spend. They weren't seeing the $30–36 million they'd lose."

While Craig Callan's place on the Keep Our Dodgers committee—he was officially listed as an ex officio member—testified to the Dodgers' continued, good-faith interest in Vero Beach, the team also pursued alternatives. The early offer of the Yavapai tribe, which had seemed almost too good to be true when it was first floated the year before, indeed turned out to be too good to be true. The Dodgers' fears of the actual cost of the project were right—much closer to $50 million than the $30 million originally estimated. And it turned out that there would be no state money available for a long time. Anticipated proceeds from the car-rental tax through the year 2017 had already been spent. When tribal leaders met with the Dodgers in mid-June, they presented a scaled-back plan, absent the housing that had been a part of the original proposal. The cost was still at $40 million, even with the cutbacks, and there was still hope that some of it would be coming from state coffers that were barren. It was pretty clear to the Dodgers at that point that Fort McDowell was going to be a nonstarter. "That was just never going to come to fruition," said Callan. "We never really came close to something." So the Dodgers began serious discussions about a plan that would remake the spring training map as radically as Walter O'Malley had remade baseball's map when he fled Brooklyn for California.

"The real direction that we were going was to Las Vegas," said Callan. "Probably to do it, you would have to have six teams, total, to move to Vegas. In spring training, you want ease of travel, and if we had just [gone] alone, we'd be tied up traveling every day to Arizona, and we'd have the fact that other teams wouldn't want to lose the practice time [traveling to Las Vegas]. So the only way to do it was to start your own league, just like the Cactus League or the Grapefruit League."

The Dodgers had little trouble finding five other teams interested in at least talking to Las Vegas. The Royals needed to get out of Baseball City. The Orioles and Rangers, looking for better than what they had in Fort Lauderdale and Port Charlotte, were interested. And the Astros and Blue Jays, nearing the end of their leases in Kissimmee and Dunedin and looking for upgrades from the local governments that owned their complexes, also took part in the Las Vegas discussions.

These were serious and earnest talks, which would become ever more so in the months ahead, and the ramifications were not lost on Tallahassee. Jeb Bush may have judged that the political fallout from the Dodgers' leaving for Arizona, when weighed against the political fallout of giving $7 million in public money to Rupert Murdoch, was a wash. But six teams packing up and leaving for Las Vegas was certain to be an economic calamity and a political disaster. Six teams represented nearly a third of the teams then training in Florida—and who was to guarantee that the six wouldn't be joined by more when the Las Vegas project became viable? A Florida Sports Foundation economic impact study of spring training, conducted in 2000, showed a statewide impact of $450 million. Should six teams leave and take their proportional one-third of the estimated spring training revenue with them, it would mean roughly a $150 million hit to the Florida economy. This was no longer a single-community issue, a turkey for Vero Beach. "Governor Bush was aware of [the discussions with Las Vegas]," said Callan, "and when he heard that six teams could be leaving the Grapefruit League, discussions started about a statewide initiative—so it's not just Dodgertown site-specific—to help fund existing facilities and help retain major league baseball teams."

In the wake of his veto, Bush began hearing from across the state that this was a *Florida* issue; the Grapefruit League community was in a state of near alarm. "I like to use the analogy, what if Silicon Valley all of a sudden began losing its software industry or computer industry?" said Dunedin city manager John Lawrence, who was worried about keeping the Blue Jays.

"The whole philosophy is to show the governor [that] spring training is a statewide industry." A study by the Tampa Bay Regional Planning Council was released in November that claimed spring training brought $195 million to west central Florida alone. Ad hoc committees formed across the state to lobby Tallahassee into putting up money to help local communities keep their spring training teams. "The governor's veto of Dodgertown did wake up everyone," said David Cardwell, executive director of the Grapefruit League Association, an organization of host cities put together at the time to lobby Tallahassee. "It was the veto of the money that got everyone saying we need[ed] to do a better job of saying this is not just a local activity."

Once again, as with the Yavapai proposal the year before, the fact that Las Vegas was a promise and Dodgertown was real bought Vero Beach more time. The Dodgers announced in the late summer that they would return for another spring training in 2000, and make no decision on their long-term future until after the Florida legislature had another chance to consider state aid to Vero during its session in the spring of 2000. They continued to talk with Las Vegas.

The 2000 version of the state aid bill—which easily passed both houses and was quickly signed by Governor Bush on June 1—was not limited to Dodgertown and Vero Beach. It made state money—up to $500,000 per year for a maximum of 30 years—to any local government "to pay the cost of or debt-service financing the acquisition, construction or renovation of a 'facility for a retained spring training franchise.'" "Facility for a retained spring training franchise" was lawyer-speak for any major league spring training complex built prior to 1990. Provisions of the law called for local governments to put up at least 50 percent of the cost of any project, and it required a current lease of at least fifteen years. It gave priority to clubs that had been in the same location the longest.

The legislation brought money to Osceola County, which upgraded the Astros' clubhouse and stadium; to Lakeland, which rebuilt Joker Marchant Stadium; to Dunedin, which revamped the Blue Jays' stadium; and to Clearwater, which raised the bar by building in partnership with the Phillies, who contributed $14 million of their own money to help make the brand-new Bright House Networks Field a showplace on a par with the ballpark at Disney's Wide World of Sports.

Vero Beach and the Dodgers were a lock for getting state money under this bill, though one potentially sticky provision of the bill stipulated an October 1, 2000, deadline for applications. Indian River County and the Dodgers had no deal in place. This meant that negotiations that had been going on in a desultory and mostly abstract manner for more than three years now needed to be completed and an incredibly complex financial deal executed in less than four months. The two sides had to first reach an agreement on a price. Only 65 of Dodgertown's 450 acres were in play. The Dodger Pines property across the street—the eighteen-hole golf course and clubhouse—was to be sold to a developer in an entirely separate transaction. The 50 acres or so that comprised the nine-hole Dodgertown Golf Club were to be designated "collateral development" and were actually a part of the agreement between the county and the Dodgers. The plan was for a mixed residential/retail community, privately developed but subject to the approval of both the Dodgers and the county, given the community's proximity to the soon-to-be-county-owned and Dodgers-operated baseball complex. What the county was buying was the 65 acres it had originally leased to the Dodgers in 1948, the land with the housing, conference center, practice fields, and Holman Stadium. Both sides hired their own appraisers to value the property; from those appraisals, they agreed on a price of $10 million for the land and its buildings. Additionally, the county agreed to pay $7 million into a construction fund for the building of a new major league clubhouse and office building and for rehabbing the practice fields and villas. Finally, $2 million went into a capital reserve account, to be put into escrow to pay for capital repairs and upgrades down the road. The construction fund was to be controlled by the county, the escrow account by the Dodgers. The state would provide $7.5 million of the total price—the state's payments to the county would eventually total $15 million, including interest—the city of Vero Beach, $1.4 million; and Indian River County, the balance of the $19 million total. The county's share would be financed by bonds, which would be repaid from a 1 percent increase in the county's tourism tax. The $19 million essentially ended the county's financial obligations to the partnership. The Dodgers would be responsible for all operating and maintenance costs; they would pay any overage costs from the construction fund of $7 million.

The Dodgers would sign a twenty-year lease at $1 per year. They would also hold options for four five-year renewals of the lease at the same $1 per year. Neither side could assign the terms of the lease to a third party. If the Dodgers were to terminate the lease prior to the end of the twenty-year term—or were to effectively terminate it by simply failing to show up in Vero Beach one spring—they would be obligated to retire the debt incurred by the county in the issuance of the bonds that covered the purchase price.

If the county wished to sell the land prior to the end of the agreement, the Dodgers would have the first option to purchase at then-market value as determined by an independent appraiser.

The memorandum of understanding (MOU) was signed on July 24, 2000. It had been a remarkably tranquil negotiation. While some of the public saw the deal as the Dodgers holding a gun to the community's head, the city and county really saw the Dodgers more as partners than adversaries. "I never, ever felt that the community was being held hostage," said Penny Chandler of the chamber of commerce.

"The negotiations went on for two, two and a half years," said Joe Baird, the county administrator for Indian River County, who as assistant county administrator handled much of the negotiation on the memorandum of understanding. "They stuck with us. They really wanted to be here."

Despite the harmony between the Dodgers and county officials, and the delight of the Vero Beach business community, the MOU still needed to be approved by both the Indian River County Commission and the Vero Beach City Council. And as with any public expenditure, that gave the whatever-it-is-I'm-against-it faction the chance to have their voices heard. "You always have the very few die-hards that believe that something like this is beyond the scope of government," said Baird. "[These people believe] government should be staying with the basics. They should do public safety, transportation, general government—no economic development." Most of the specific concerns voiced at two public hearings centered on whether the MOU contained sufficient protection against the Dodgers' breaking the lease. Lesser concerns were whether the Dodgers would keep their minor league team in Vero Beach.

In the end, the county commission and city council ultimately found the concerns wanting; both bodies voted their approval on July 27, 2000. "This was an economic development deal, not unlike another industry, so you have to look at it from that perspective," said Chandler. "This is about the economics of your community, and who provides jobs. It was a good solid business transaction."

"One of the things I keep telling the community is, we have not been able to attract an employer of 200 people in the last twenty years that I've been here, so why would we lose one, with a payroll of $4.5 million," said Baird.

There were no grand civic celebrations when the deal was done. The Vero Beach High School band didn't play. The Dodgers were going to be around for at least the next twenty and, likely, the next forty years to come; but spring training in 2001 began without anyone taking notice that Dodgertown was now open under new ownership.

It turned out to be a false spring. There was just never any buzz in the new Dodgertown. Crowds at Holman Stadium were disappointing. The only time the old place came alive now was when the Mets or the Cardinals or the Red Sox came to town. When word broke in early 2006 that the Dodgers were talking to Glendale, Arizona, about moving spring training there, it was received with disappointment, but little shock; resignation, but little anger. Civic rallies were pointless. Vero Beach wanted a spring training partner, not a hostage. By the time things became official in November 2006, the attitude was goodbye and good luck, Dodgers. *Now, who do we get to replace 'em?*

FOURTEEN

The Oasis League

Las Vegas Ups the Ante

The Cactus League had loved the Los Angeles Dodgers from afar beginning the moment they became the Los Angeles Dodgers. But it was an unrequited love, and the Cactus League understood that that was how it must be. Geographically, it made all the sense in the world that the Dodgers train in Arizona, a one-hour flight or a half-day's drive from their home in Los Angeles. This wasn't about what made sense, however; this was about the O'Malley family's love of Dodgertown and Vero Beach. The team might have come to Arizona in the early sixties, in that window of time before Walter O'Malley purchased the Dodgertown property and when Vero Beach needed a better deal out of its lease. Once O'Malley took title to the land, however, the Dodgers were permanently out of play.

Now, the O'Malleys were gone, and not only were the Dodgers dating again, but they had eyes for Arizona. After years of pining, Arizona seemingly had only to ask and the Dodgers would say yes. Fort McDowell pursued the Dodgers, believing that the money that had built Peoria, Maryvale, and the new HoHoKam would be there for it as well. But it wasn't. Car-rental money had been promised through the year 2017. Still, the Yavapai Nation was interested in moving ahead anyway. "I sat in on meetings when they were trying to get the Dodgers, and anybody who was anybody was behind it," said Ron Pies, a Cactus League official and Governor's Commission on

Baseball member. "And the Indians said: 'We'll do it. We just need infrastructure.' And the state said: 'We can't help you.'"

Public spending for private gain is always a dicey matter for elected officials. It didn't matter that the money was coming from a tax on visitors, not residents; nor that the legislature could have implemented an increase in the car-rental tax or another tariff that would have targeted the visitor, not the resident; nor that the economic impact studies showed that the money would come back as much as ten times over in jobs, taxes, and money spent in the local economy. The fact remained that Arizona had already spent nearly $100 million of public money on spring training in the previous five years alone. The self-preservation antennae in the state capitol building must have told the legislators that it was enough for now. If voter perception was that the pols in Phoenix were giving away too much public money, it only followed that the voters would soon be looking to throw the profligate scoundrels out. So the state did nothing, even though it meant losing out on something it had wanted so badly for so long. Arizona's window to grab the Dodgers was small, open for just a few short months in 1998–1999. The team's energies thereafter were concentrated on working out a deal to remain in Vero Beach. Their backup plan was Las Vegas, and the better part of a decade would pass before the Dodgers would talk to Arizona again.

To lose the Dodgers because there was suddenly no money—having had money enough to do whatever it had wanted for so long—galvanized the Cactus League. Clearly, there was still work to be done to ensure continued fiscal viability. Arizona didn't want to lose out on another opportunity like this, and it certainly did not want to be vulnerable to losing existing teams. Officials had to find a way to keep the coffers full. For the Cactus League, if the months after the Dodgers–Fort McDowell courtship fell apart had been a movie scene, it would have been Scarlett O'Hara grabbing the earth at Tara and promising the heavens that she would never go hungry again.

Competition from longtime rival Florida didn't faze Arizona now. That challenge had been successfully met. "Quite frankly, we were most concerned about Vegas, not Florida," said Ted Ferris, the president and CEO of the Arizona Sports and Tourism Authority. "Las Vegas scared us, because they've got a budget that nobody can match up there. With the gaming revenue as a funding stream, once they apply that stream of revenue to chase professional sports, it's going to be strong competition. It's really been the fear of mixing gambling and the sports book with professional franchises that's allowed us to keep them at bay, but whenever that's overcome, they will be a formidable threat. Because they don't need to necessarily go out and raise a tax, they just need to apply some of their gaming revenues and argue that 'We'll get additional gaming revenues to replace that from the people we bring into Vegas to follow sports.'"

The Las Vegas flirtation with spring training was born out of the 1995 baseball players strike, some foot-dragging by the Tucson city government, and arguably even by a decision by Frontier Airlines to cancel nonstop daily service between Denver and Tucson. Frontier did not go so far as to blame the baseball strike for the cancellation of its Denver-to-Tucson route, but it did acknowledge counting on a busy March, flying Rockies fans down to see the team in spring training, and it was instead filling only 30 percent of its seats. Coincidentally, the airline announced at the same time that it would be doubling its Denver–Las Vegas flights to meet a growing demand.

The Rockies, meanwhile, were having trouble getting Tucson to live up to its promises to make major improvements to venerable Hi Corbett Field, the Indians' former training site, which the Rockies had taken over in 1993. Hi Corbett was the oldest stadium in all of spring training—its construction in 1928 predated the Indians' arrival by nearly twenty years—and it was showing its age. In the early years of the Cactus League's resurgence in the 1990s, the Colorado Rockies and Hi Corbett were the forgotten players. The car-rental tax that pumped cash into Cactus League facilities was a Maricopa County–only tax; no money flowed south to Pima County and Tucson. The Rockies were suffering from a bad case of facilities envy. They'd also been lonesome road warriors, off by themselves down in Tucson, for their first two spring trainings, and now they were starting to feel abandoned by their hosts as well.

The problem for Tucson was one of logistics. Its promise to the Rockies when persuading them to move in and replace the Indians was twofold: the city would provide upgraded facilities by 1996, and it would work to attract an additional team or teams to Tucson to give the Rockies some playmates and limit the time they would have to spend on I-10 bus rides. In the spring of 1995, Tucson was negotiating with the Diamondbacks and discussing building a new, two-team facility. The Rockies were given a choice: join the Diamondbacks in the new facility or commit to a refurbished Hi Corbett and allow Tucson to continue searching for a Florida team to join the Diamondbacks in the new complex. A number of Florida teams seemed to be in play. Most frequently mentioned were the Reds, nearing the end of their lease in Plant City and tired of the isolated location; the Royals, who needed to get out of Baseball City no later than the end of their lease in 2002; and the White Sox, who liked Arizona because owner Jerry Reinsdorf had a home there. The Rockies leaned toward staying at Hi Corbett in exchange for what in effect meant another three local road games every spring. Three fewer round trips to Phoenix—twelve hours they wouldn't have to spend on a bus.

But all of this was still theory. Even after the Diamondbacks committed to Tucson in the spring of '95, there was still no movement on a third team and, more important, no movement on financing either the new complex or the Hi Corbett refurbishment. So when the Rockies' general manager, Bob Gephard, got a call from the Las Vegas Visitors and Convention Authority in the summer of 1995, he took the call and listened with interest.

Las Vegas, as Ted Ferris pointed out, could afford anything it wanted. Its March weather is a little chillier and breezier than Arizona's, but it is still temperate, generally rain-free, and wholly baseball appropriate. Attract enough teams, and it might offer the same ease of travel that the Phoenix area does. But Vegas didn't have those teams, nor the prospect of getting them, when it was talking to the Rockies. Las Vegas is 300 miles from Phoenix. The Rockies would have been three times as far from spring training games if they were in Vegas as they were now in Tucson. And they'd still be off by themselves. The talks, as a result, didn't get very far. The Rockies used Vegas to hasten the progress of talks and commitment back in Tucson.

But if the Rockies soon forgot about Las Vegas, Las Vegas didn't soon forget about spring training, which seemed the perfect way for the city to get into the professional sports game. The aversion that sports leagues, and particularly baseball, had always had to Las Vegas as a site was proximity to the sports book in Vegas and the temptation, or at the very least the appearance of temptation, that would inevitably accompany that proximity. But spring training didn't present that problem. The games are far too random; only a lunatic would attempt to wager money on the outcome of any one game, or even on the outcome of any one season. And while, on any given day, Vegas could no doubt easily produce a critical mass of overserved, sleep-starved gamblers looking to get even however they can before their flight leaves for home, no book would ever accept a bet on a spring training game. It seemed the perfect way to get the camel's nose inside the tent of professional sport.

But to do so, Vegas couldn't pluck just a single team; it would have to harvest an entire crop. The late nineties seemed to be the perfect time to do so. A number of teams in Florida were coming to the end of their leases: the Reds, the Rangers, the Astros, the Royals, the Orioles, the Blue Jays, and finally, after the sale of the team from the O'Malley family to the Fox Corporation, the Dodgers. Las Vegas was looking to field a four- or six-team league. It proposed to build one *über*-complex, with two 10,000-seat stadiums and individual clubhouses and practice complexes for all the teams. One stadium would be located near the Strip, with the teams rotating through it. The cost was pegged—in 1996 dollars—at $50 million.

Talks between the city and various teams began in 1996, died out for a time, and then resumed in earnest in late 1999 after Jeb Bush vetoed the first spring training funding bill passed by the legislature, and Arizona determined that its car-rental money was exhausted. The closest the Oasis League came to becoming reality was on March 27, 2000, when after a summit among seven Florida teams—the Dodgers, Royals, Rangers, Astros, Blue Jays, Orioles, and Devil Rays—and Las Vegas, the city offered the teams what was called a "nonfinancial conceptual plan." The teams toured the proposed site near the airport. However tantalizing Las Vegas may have been, the clubs decided for the moment to remain right where they were; the conceptual plan never moved beyond concept.

Nonetheless, this is the meeting that caught the attention of the Florida legislature and Governor Bush. Had Florida not passed its legislation in 2000, it would have almost certainly lost six teams. The Oasis League was not then targeting Cactus League teams, though the Cactus League knew it would likely be only a matter of time before it did. This possibility brought back the insecurities of the early 1990s, and that was not a place Cactus League officials wished to revisit. They determined that the best defense was a good offense.

Professional football helped to get the Cactus League a new pot of money. Or perhaps it was the reverse: the Cactus League helped the NFL's Cardinals get a new $455 million stadium in the west valley town of Glendale. In either case, the story has its genesis in the fall of 1999, when fears were growing that both the Cardinals and the Fiesta Bowl had outgrown Arizona State's Sun Devil Stadium. The Cardinals would flee Arizona; the Fiesta Bowl would inevitably lose its prestige and sink to second-tier bowl status. Governor

Jane Hull established a commission called the Plan B Task Force to explore funding for a new football stadium. Its principal charge was to find a way to fund it without also increasing the state's income or sales taxes. It was a project without a lot of initial support. The Cardinals were not a popular cause. They had been playing abysmally since arriving from St. Louis in 1988, and in recent years they'd routinely played in a half-empty stadium. Cardinals owner Bill Bidwell was widely viewed as a cheapskate, reluctant to spend money to put a good team on the field. Even before the task force began its work, the political pollsters had determined that an expensive public give-away to the Cardinals would be a nonstarter with Arizona voters. So the task force began looking for ways to broaden its charge and thus to increase its chances for success. "They knew if it was just a Cardinals football stadium, it wasn't going to pass," said Ron Pies. So the task force reached out to the baseball community through the Governor's Commission on Baseball and the Cactus League Association.

"When we started out, we did not have the Cactus League as a part of our plans," said Ferris, a member of the task force. "Then, when we started hearings and took testimony, we learned of this Las Vegas threat." The northwest valley town of Surprise was already in negotiations with a number of teams. But it needed money to build. The Cactus League also sensed that its existing teams—West Coast teams, mostly—would likely be most susceptible to entreaties from Las Vegas should the Oasis League ever become a reality. Arizona needed money not simply to attract new Cactus League teams, but to keep its current teams happy when their leases came up for renewal. So the Cactus League became a part of what would ultimately come out of the Arizona legislature and be put before voters as Proposition 302.

Adding the Cactus League still left a bill that essentially did little but give millions in public money to billionaires. It still left the bill in trouble. Before it went before the voters, there would be two more components. One was tourism promotion. Prop 302 would initiate a 0.5 percent bed tax, and it would institute a 3.5 percent car-rental tax, on top of the $2.50-per-car-rental-contract tax that Maricopa County had had since '93. Under this new legislation, it was going to cost more to vacation or travel on business in Arizona. "The thought was that we had to promote tourism to offset the negative impacts of higher taxes," said Ferris. "That's something the tourism industry demanded in order to give their support on the higher taxes on their own industry." The fourth piece of the Prop 302 puzzle was the funding of youth sports facilities, starting at $1 million per year and increasing by $100,000 per year, every year for the thirty-year life of the legislation.

Still, Prop 302 was a bill in trouble, not just with the voters, but with many of the people for whom it might have provided tourism, Cactus League, and youth sports money. "We started out as a statewide bill," said Ferris. "It started out with all fifteen counties statewide, and the other fourteen counties [aside from Maricopa] said: 'We don't want to be a part of your bill. We don't want taxes leveled in our county just to create assets for Maricopa County.'"

So, by the time it came out of the legislature, Prop 302 was a Maricopa County–only bill. Maricopa County would pay all the taxes; Maricopa County would reap all the benefits. The vote became a Maricopa County–only vote. That saved the bill; statewide, it would have never stood a chance of passing.

Even within Maricopa County, it faced resistance. Two weeks before the election, polls showed the referendum losing by ten points. An advertising campaign waged throughout the summer and fall emphasized spring training and youth sports development—particularly, youth sports. These were small pieces of the bill, to be sure, but much easier to sell to undecided voters. "What was interesting about those polls, that showed two-to-one against, was that there was 40 percent of the electorate that was undecided," said Mark Coronado, who was then working to put together a spring training deal for Surprise and joined the fight to get 302 passed. "In my experiences in running campaigns, the undecided voter doesn't have a reason to vote no yet, they just don't know why they should vote yes."

On the Sunday before the election, the woebegone Cardinals pulled off a stunning upset of the Washington Redskins; and two days later, Prop 302 pulled off an upset of its own, winning 52–48 percent. The bill also created the Arizona Sports and Tourism Authority (AZSTA)—something of a misnomer because it concerns only Maricopa County—to distribute the money that the new taxes would generate.

The big trophy for the Cactus League was the new stadium in Surprise, a rapidly growing community in the northwest corner of Maricopa County, just west of Peoria on Bell Road. The town was first laid out and settled in 1938 and named after Surprise, Nebraska, the hometown of its founder. It remained so remote from the rest of the valley for so long that one local legend claimed that the founders called it Surprise because they thought it would be a surprise if it ever came to anything. A second legend said that the town took its name from the fact that travelers were surprised to find anything resembling civilization so far removed from the rest of civilization.

The completion of the Highway 101 loop around the northern end of Phoenix in the early nineties, however, sucked Surprise right into the vortex of the valley's building frenzy. Just one square mile in size when it was incorporated in 1960, Surprise was sixty square miles in 2000, on its way to being more than seventy-five square miles, as the city council regularly annexed vast tracts of unincorporated county land through the years and brought them within the city limits. Surprise's population had grown 333 percent during the nineties, to more than 30,000. It would grow another 140 percent in the first half of the 2000s, to just under 75,000. By the middle of the first decade of the twenty-first century, it was estimated that construction on a new home in Surprise was being completed almost every hour.

In January 2000, the city started thinking about spring training. Surprise's new director of parks and recreation, Mark Coronado, had a background in both politics and spring training. He'd served as a legislative aide early in his career and was following with interest the progress of a bill in the Arizona senate that would ultimately become Proposition 302. As a recreation supervisor in Peoria when that complex opened in 1993, part of his duties involved working with the Padres and Mariners during the spring training season; he was also following with interest the unrest in the Grapefruit League. In January 2000, just one month into his new job in Surprise, Coronado told acting city manager Al Deshazo that the stars were aligned for Surprise to make a run at spring training. "You know, we've thought about spring training," replied Deshazo.

"A lot of people think about it, Al," said Coronado, "but it's all about timing and funding." And Coronado went on to talk about the spring training component of what was then known as Senate Bill 1220—the eventual Prop 302—and about how the timing might never be better, with as many as six or seven Grapefruit League teams at or near the end of their Florida leases. "If you like, I'd like to take this to the next level," said Coronado.

"Go ahead," said his boss. "But don't spend any money."

By spring training 2000, with Las Vegas holding its very public meeting with seven Florida teams and Florida scrambling to pass legislation that would keep those teams right where they were, Coronado had private talks with the Cleveland Indians, the Texas Rangers, and the Houston Astros. Very soon, the Baltimore Orioles and Kansas City Royals joined the conversation. The Rangers more or less gave Coronado a verbal commitment early in the process—sort of a you-put-this-together-the-way-you're-saying-and-we're-on-board kind of promise—and Coronado started working hard on the Houston Astros. This was Surprise's dream marriage: one American League team, one National, and both from Texas, an easy trip to Surprise for the teams' fans.

Houston, however, was more interested in staying in Kissimmee in the new facility they would get with the money the Florida legislature had appropriated, and they declined the Surprise overtures. Enter the Royals, lame-duck tenants at the doomed Baseball City complex, starved for affection after years of being told by their Anheuser-Busch landlords that they weren't wanted. The new facility was nice. The love of the people in Surprise was even nicer. "They are people who really wanted to have us," said Royals president Herk Robinson. By mid-June, with Prop 302 trailing in the polls by that two-to-one margin, the Rangers and Royals signed a memorandum of understanding that bound them to Surprise, with the understanding that the deal would be contingent on Prop 302 passing. The Rangers, the Royals, and the city of Surprise joined the fight to get the proposition passed—some ads featured Nolan Ryan and George Brett—and Surprise moved ahead with architectural plans and construction bids. In January 2001, just two months after Prop 302 had passed, Surprise broke ground on its new $48 million complex. It all happened so fast that the AZSTA wasn't ready for it. It had made provisions for revenue collections and payouts for the Cardinals' stadium, but plans for funding spring training had lagged behind. "They never anticipated someone would build a two-team facility so quickly," said Coronado. So AZSTA's promise to Surprise was to provide $26 million, $6 million less than the two-thirds the legislation provided for.

As the bulldozers pushed the earth around for Surprise's new complex, getting even that money suddenly seemed problematic. No sooner had Surprise begun construction than a Phoenix developer filed suit against the state, challenging the constitutionality of Prop 302 and the Arizona Sports and Tourism Authority it had created. John F. Long was the man who had donated the land and fronted the construction costs for the Brewers' Maryvale complex, but his suit challenging 302 had nothing to do with spring training. It was all about the location of the Cardinals' stadium. It provided some anxious months in Surprise, for during the nearly two years the suit was pending, the AZSTA money was frozen. It meant that Surprise was going to have to front the entire $48 million, which might not ever get reimbursed should Long's suit ultimately be successful. Nonetheless, the city never considered suspending or abandoning its project. "The city council and the mayor felt we had a moral and a professional obligation to the Royals and the Rangers to bring them here in 2003—as we had signed contracts for," said Coronado. "There was never any hesitation on our part, but there was a lot of concern about when we'd get paid, and if we got paid, how much would that be."

The city essentially borrowed the money from itself to pay for the spring training construction. It had just issued $60 million in municipal property corporation bonds to fund the building of a new public safety building, new water and sewer infrastructure, and new parks and recreation facilities. The parks-and-rec piece of the pie came to $23 million. That was the money Surprise was going to use to pay its portion of the complex's costs. It was more than enough if AZSTA came through with the full $32 million; just enough if AZSTA paid the promised $26 million; and quite a bit less than enough if the lawsuit put AZSTA out of business. Still, the city had $60 million in the bank, and it took the money earmarked for water and sewer improvements and a public safety building to build the baseball complex, confident that it would ultimately be reimbursed.

"What gave the city some certainty and some assurance was that we had a signed contract with a state government body," said Coronado. "We were pretty confident that the state of Arizona wasn't going to steer us wrong. Baseball and spring training is such a big economic force and such a big tourist attraction that it was in the best interests of the state to build this facility and relocate two teams from the Grapefruit League."

The lawsuit ultimately worked to Surprise's financial advantage. By the time the suit was resolved in the state's favor in 2003, AZSTA's revenues were running ahead of projections, and it was able to reimburse Surprise $32 million, a full two-thirds of the $48 million cost.

Back in Florida, meanwhile, Surprise Stadium—or the Surprise Recreation Campus, as the city calls it—disabused Grapefruit League people of any notion they may have harbored that the $75 million the Florida legislature had appropriated in 2000 would arrest the shift in the balance of power from the Grapefruit to the Cactus League. From Tallahassee down the Gulf Coast, across Alligator Alley to Fort Lauderdale, up I-95 to Viera, and across the center of the state to Lakeland, they looked on slack-jawed as Arizona built a $48 million showpiece and stole two Grapefruit League teams. How do they do it? Florida wondered. Hadn't they declared their coffers dry just five years before? Now, there seemed to be no bottom to the Arizona money pot. Surprise Stadium was where the torch was passed, where Florida figuratively raised its arms over its head and bowed down in we-are-unworthy homage to Arizona and what it had done with and for the Cactus League.

And Arizona wasn't finished. After Surprise, the newest of the Cactus League cities, AZSTA next funded improvements for the oldest and most tradition-bound of the Cactus League cities. Between 2004 and 2006, Arizona spent $6 million in sprucing up Phoenix Municipal for the Athletics, $20 million in new practice fields and a stadium overhaul for Tempe Diablo Stadium and the Angels, and $23 million on venerable Scottsdale Stadium.

Scottsdale is the valley's It town. It has the richest history, the liveliest arts scene, the priciest real estate, the most chic shops, the toniest restaurants, the most famous golf courses, the most beautiful people.

And right in the center of it, and very much a part of it, is Scottsdale Stadium and San Francisco Giants spring training. Scottsdale and the Giants rival Mesa and the Cubs for the largest crowds in the Cactus League. They win hands down for the best-dressed crowd. While most of the 10,000 in Scottsdale Stadium on any given day are dressed exactly like everybody else at a spring training game—in shorts, sandals or sneakers, and a team hat and T-shirt—there is a critical mass of fans in Scottsdale dressed as though they are going clubbing; but then, that is sort of what they're doing. The party pavilion in right field and the berm running from center to left are filled with twenty-somethings: young men in unbuttoned Hawaiian shirts, the waistbands of their boxers showing above shorts that ride low on the hips, and young women in summer dresses and high wedge heels—sexy but stable, no risk of digging a thin heel into the grass and causing an ungainly tumble. The air beyond the outfield is rich with the smell of Budweiser and Coppertone. Scottsdale Stadium is just three blocks from Old Town Scottsdale, home to bars and restaurants, including the Pink Pony and Don and Charlie's, the bars where the players used to drink before spring training's popularity made them hostages in their rented mansions. But baseball talk still fills the air in the Pink Pony, Don and Charlie's, and the other Scottsdale bars during March, and on game days, Scottsdale Stadium becomes an extension of the downtown bar scene. One flows seamlessly into the other. It is difficult to imagine downtown Scottsdale without Scottsdale Stadium, and equally difficult to imagine Cactus League baseball without a Scottsdale presence.

Yet Scottsdale Stadium was the very last Cactus League facility to get modern upgrades. Scottsdale always wanted to keep spring training and the Giants. The Giants wanted to stay in Scottsdale. The Scottsdale Charros, the aggressive and influential civic group that had been sponsoring spring training on behalf of the city for forty-five years—and gave somewhere in the neighborhood of a half-million dollars to Scottsdale charities every year from the money it raised on spring training—certainly wanted the Giants to stay. The business community, which realized an estimated $20 million from spring training tourism every year, wanted the Giants to stay. Certainly, the cash-laden spring training pilgrims spending that $20 million did not want to see Scottsdale fall off the Cactus League itinerary. The elements and attitudes were all in place for an easy deal. Still, making it happen was tougher than anyone expected. It took the better part of two years to work out a deal, and while things never got so bad that the Giants actually started talking to other towns, they did make it clear to Scottsdale that they would leave at the end of their lease in 2007 if the facilities were not modernized.

The problems, as always, were political and financial. At first, the city proposed building a new minor league complex on the city-owned but privately operated Coronado Golf Course. The affordable public course—$25 greens fees in a town where the average greens fee was north of $150—may not have had a well-connected constituency, but it had a noisy one. It also had strong allies in the neighborhood surrounding it. It's never good politics to big-foot the little guy to help the plutocrats, and the city backed off from that one, but not before its eye was blackened, and the whole process slowed so as to avoid a second misstep. The other tension injector was uncertainty about funding; when talks began in 2003, the AZSTA money was still frozen by the lawsuit challenging the authority's constitutionality.

Finally, things were worked out, and Scottsdale got its new facility in time for the World Baseball Classic spring training of 2006. The cost of the improvements was $23 million, nearly three times what it had cost the city to raze the original stadium in 1991 and build the stadium that was now being upgraded. Some of the money went for two new practice fields beyond the right field fence; some went for improving the drainage on the minor league fields at Indian School Park. Some went for unseen changes in the stadium itself, including press box and clubhouse expansion. The most notable changes came in the outfield, where the berm was doubled in height and a private party function area built and controlled by the Charros rose beyond the right field fence. The Charro Lodge and Pavilion is the center of the outfield party scene. On days when it's not rented to private functions, the average fan can pay $75–125 for access that includes a free buffet and open bar, the chance to see and be seen, and, for a few years anyway, the opportunity to be in the very best place, just beyond the right field fence, to catch a Barry Bonds home run.

Ah yes, the right field fence. To accommodate the Charro Lodge and the new Giants bullpen, the right field fence was moved in ten feet compared to the old Scottsdale Stadium. Not exactly the House That Ruth Built, but certainly the Fence That Barry Influenced.

As toxic a thought as Barry Bonds was to so much of baseball as he neared Henry Aaron's home run record, he was also the single most electrifying presence in the game. Even spring training games paused to take notice when Bonds came to bat. And even the most rabid Bonds-hater, the fan so outwardly delighted at a Bonds strikeout or warning-track fly ball, the one who booed so lustily when Bonds was introduced, who openly wished for some form of career-ending injury to befall Bonds before he reached 755—even that fan felt somehow cheated by a game in which Bonds failed to hit a home run. When the Giants elected not to re-sign Bonds after the 2007 season, a bit of the energy went out of Scottsdale Stadium on game days.

With the completion of the improvements to Tempe Diablo and Scottsdale stadiums, the Cactus League now has a full collection of parks that are all as bright as the desert sun. New stadiums don't stay new forever, of course, and it is in providing for future needs that the Cactus League has its biggest advantage over the Grapefruit League. Five and six years away from the expiration of its next leases, the AZSTA already has $40 million in place to provide whatever repairs and upgrades the teams may want come renewal time. It is even planning for and setting aside money for the end of the Rangers/Royals lease in Surprise in 2022. This money, like all grants from AZSTA, must be matched by local funds. Host communities like Peoria have therefore started similar savings plans in their capital improvement budgets, to ensure that they'll qualify for the state money when the time comes. "These are all modern facilities that really don't lack for anything," said Ferris of the current stadium inventory. "They've got six full practice fields, they've got a couple half fields. They've got large clubhouses for both major and minor leagues. So it's not like it was in both Scottsdale and Tempe where they were lacking facilities and we had to bring them up to a standard.

With these, it's going to be more [like] put in some seats, put some paint on, put some carpet in, dress up way-finding signage, just stuff like that."

The model that the Cactus League is using for these future repairs is the $5 million dressing-up it gave to Phoenix Municipal Stadium, spring home of the Athletics, in 2004. "So what we did is, we took Phoenix Muni and we grew it by inflation—construction inflation, 5 percent a year—and brought it out to those years, '12, '14, '16, when the leases were coming up, so we would adjust for [the] higher costs of construction," explained Ferris. "And then, if it was a two-team facility, we bumped it by another 50 percent. So for Peoria and Surprise, whatever that Muni amount was, we bumped it another 50 percent, plus grew it by 5 percent a year." In 2005 dollars, that comes to about $5 million per single-team facility, $8 million per two-team facility.

"We knew we had to do this," said Ferris. "Because we're making commitments to Goodyear and Glendale, and these other communities are going to be howling if they think we're taking all the money off the table, so when they come in to get a lease extension with their teams, you know, there's nothing there. So we have reserved what we hope is sufficient monies to get twenty-year extensions with each one of those teams. So we kinda [feel] like our future is assured for quite a period of time here, the next couple of decades."

There is nothing like it in Florida, and this has caused a great deal of hand-wringing in the Grapefruit League. "We've got a lot of our leases coming up between 2015 and 2020," said Jeff Mielke of the Lee County Sports Authority in Fort Myers. "Ten years isn't very far down the road. And if we're going to set money aside to help teams maintain the facilities, refurbish the facilities, you need to start talking about that now." As of now, there is no sign that Tallahassee shares Mielke's concern. The system that has been in place since 2000 seems to be the system that Florida is left with: only when crisis looms is the state likely to consider appropriating any funds.

In just fifteen years, the natural order of the spring training world reversed itself. The Grapefruit League is now in the defensive posture, worried about whether there will be any more state funding as well as, for the first time, about those long bus rides up and down I-75 and I-95. The Cactus League is mature, solvent, well run, with a high degree of coordination and cooperation among the state, the host cities, and the various civic groups, like the Charros and the HoHoKams. If not exactly cocky—that is decidedly not the way they feel—Cactus League officials have at least reached a comfort level sufficient to give back a bit of the needling that Florida gave to Arizona during the Cactus League's troubled years. Remember the Florida official who opined in those pre-Diamondback days, "no one plays in a desert climate; why would anyone want to train in a desert climate"? Here's Ted Ferris on Florida's weather, "I think hurricanes will be a factor [in teams' decisions]," he said. "They've had that recent flurry of hurricanes. Hurricanes come through and they knock down light standards and you get damages, and you have to determine: is insurance covering it, and do you have to get money from local government or the state? After a time, I think the inclement weather and the unpredictability of the weather in Florida is in our favor as well."

But if the Cactus League's future is assured vis-à-vis the fears it once had regarding the Grapefruit League, its confidence in the future takes on a bit of whistling-past-the-graveyard when it comes to Las Vegas. "You don't ever want to get cocky to the point where you let down your guard," said Ferris. "I think we feel good about the future because the funding is assured; the teams are locked up into long-term deals. We know the teams like it. They're making money. We've got great weather, and there are a lot of economic reasons why teams that are here aren't going to see a better situation. Unless it was Vegas. Vegas is always going to be out there and always something we're going to have to keep an eye on, because of their gaming revenues, because of their climate, and the fact that some of the advantages we have could be replicated there."

In the spring training jungle, the line between predator and prey is thin and ever shifting.

FIFTEEN

A Tale of Three Cities

In the spring of 2006, right before the start of spring training, the banners flapping on the light poles along Route 17, leading from Chain of Lakes Park to downtown Winter Haven, read, "Winter Haven Welcomes Our Indians." They may as well have read, "Don't Let the Door Hit You in the Ass on Your Way Out." On the square behind city hall, fronting Winter Haven's Central Park, street signs bore the symbols of two of the city's signature institutions. The north-south streets carried the image of a Cypress Gardens water skier; the east-west streets showed the image of Chief Wahoo, the Cleveland Indians' controversial, albeit enduring mascot. The director of the Winter Haven Chamber of Commerce speculated that the Chief Wahoo signs would soon be for sale on eBay.

The fourteen-year marriage between the Cleveland Indians and the city of Winter Haven was in trouble in early 2006. No one had yet filed for divorce, but the signs were not good. The Indians lamented that the city had not understood their needs; the city saw the Indians as philanderers, incapable of either emotional or financial commitment. The couple would try counseling, as it were, talking to one another throughout the spring and summer, but both had mentally moved on, and the talks were futile. The Indians were seeing other cities—lots of other cities. Winter Haven was not seeing other teams but was talking bravely about life after spring training. The Indians felt they could do better than Winter Haven. The city felt it didn't need the Indians—or any other baseball team—because it had enough other things going for it. In the fall, the Indians finally, officially, announced that they had decided to leave. Few people wept; fewer still were surprised.

It had always been a marriage more of convenience than of love. Winter Haven married the Indians on the rebound, still carrying a torch for its true love, the recently departed Red Sox. The Indians were recent widowers of a sort when they came to Winter Haven; the sparkling new facility down in Homestead that had brought them east from Tucson had been ruined in Hurricane Andrew, and they didn't have a lot of options for their 1993 spring training. But the city and the team grew close that first spring, the bond forged by nearly incomprehensible tragedy. Two Indians pitchers, Steve Olin and Tim Crews, were killed and teammate Bobby Ojeda was seriously injured in a boating accident on Little Lake Nellie during the Indians' first spring in Winter Haven. It was shortly after dark, and the three men were on the lake following a day-long picnic during a spring training off-day. Crews, who had just bought a ranch on the shores of the lake, had his 150-horsepower, open bass boat at full throttle and did not see the wooden pier stretching out nearly 200 feet from shore. Police reports said the boat slammed into the pier at eye level at a speed of sixty miles per hour.

The Indians' pain became Winter Haven's pain. "The community, I think, buffered the team, and allowed them to grieve," said Bob Gernert, the executive director of the Winter Haven Chamber of Commerce. Community reaction to the tragedy was cited as a factor when the team announced at the end of spring training that it would not be going to Homestead after all, but instead would sign a long-term lease with Winter Haven. Over the next half-dozen years, as the Indians emerged as one of the best teams in baseball, Winter Haven's citizens flocked to Chain of Lakes Park and embraced the Indians as their own. Thirteen years later, however, comforting memories were no match for the cold realities of baseball economics. They never are. The story of the Indians' search for a spring training home in 2006 is the story of spring training in the twenty-first century.

Chain of Lakes Park is old-time baseball. It is the Rexall Drug Store with a soda fountain in an age of CVS and Walgreen's. Built in the 1960s in a style popular in the WPA parks of the 1930s, its sixteen columns support the roof of a grandstand that runs from shallowest left field around to shallowest right. The box seats sit open to the sun in front of the grandstand. The core of the park is timeless and classic. The wings of the ballpark, the additions, are anything but. Down the left and right field lines and in the bleachers in left field, the mood is spoiled by three sets of aluminum bleachers, of the sort found in high school football stadiums, added in the eighties to accommodate the ever-swelling throngs of Red Sox pilgrims. The years have also been cruel to the view beyond the outfield fence. What had once been orange groves, the very symbol of old Florida, have morphed over time into condos, the very symbol of the new Florida.

The press box at Chain of Lakes Park is the most dangerous in the Grapefruit League. Foul balls hit straight back at a certain angle ricochet off the underside of the roof and crash among the writers. No evidence suggests that the Red Sox, whose prickly relationship with the press is one of the undying constants of its century-long history, actually planned it that way. Still, writers had better be vigilant. The press box at Chain of Lakes has its charms as well. Writers sit in the open air, surrounded by the sounds and smells of the game. Writers and fans may or may not miss Winter Haven when it gets dropped off the Grapefruit League itinerary. But writers and fans with a feel for the game's timeless charms are going to miss Chain of Lakes Park when it's gone.

Anyone with any feel for either baseball or modern urban politics can see why Chain of Lakes is doomed. The charming 5,000-seat ballpark has been made into an awkward, jury-rigged 7,500-seat ballpark, which would need a major rebuild to bring it up to contemporary standards, with contemporary services and amenities. The Indians' clubhouse, down the right field line, is likewise showing its age and lacks the square footage for modern needs like weight rooms and fully equipped trainers' rooms. Office space is cramped. Together with the Orioles' complex in Fort Lauderdale, Chain of Lakes—for all of its aesthetic charm—is the most antiquated complex in all of spring training.

The stadium's location is convenient and appealing, sitting right at the junction of Cypress Gardens Boulevard and U.S. 17, not much more than a mile from downtown, in the heart of commercial Winter Haven. And it sits right on the shores of Lake Lulu. It is a most pleasing parcel of real estate. A perfect spot for a baseball field. The problem is, it's also a perfect spot for other things as well, things that, from a community standpoint, can generate more money and sustained energy than spring training.

And, indeed, Winter Haven wants the land for other uses. Where there are now practice fields, community leaders see upscale shopping, restaurants, and hotels. Where there are now Grapefruit League parking lots, they see a modern city center, with offices and residences. Where Chain of Lakes Park now sits, they see more shops and restaurants and open green space, all connected by a promenade along the shores of the lake.

"We had it appraised maybe two and a half, three years ago, and the value of the Chain of Lakes property—the land value alone—was in the $12 million range," said Winter Haven city manager David Greene in early 2006. "So if you visualize land value at approximately $12 million—and that's certainly an old number compared to what land prices in Florida have done over the last couple of years—it's not unreasonable to think that you could see perhaps a couple of hundred million dollars' worth of taxable value on that sixty-acre site. The Chain of Lakes property is much more valuable to the community than present usage would indicate."

The city first broached the matter of a new facility for the Indians in 2000, when the state of Florida first made funds available to local communities to upgrade or rebuild their spring training complexes. The Indians told the city at the time that they weren't willing to commit to a fifteen-year lease, one of the conditions for applying for the state money. That started the clock ticking on the Indians' departure, but the two sides continued to talk in a desultory manner over the next five years. The city and everyone else in the Grapefruit League universe were acutely aware that in 2002 the Phillies had changed the rules in Florida spring training construction by contributing $14 million of their own money to get their ideal new stadium in Clearwater. As Florida moved toward another round of state funding in 2006, the Phillies and Clearwater had become the new paradigm. Winter Haven's position with the Indians was clear; it was no longer looking at the team as guests or simple tenants, it was looking at them as partners. "First, the city will not pay the full cost of a new facility for any ball team, end of discussion," said Greene. "It's a fair-share issue. These dollars that we're talking about here are relatively miniscule on the grand scheme of the cash flow, year in and year out, of a major league baseball team. The average [professional athlete] who's nothing special makes $5 million a year. That would certainly cover the team's share of the principal and interest on a new facility."

But the Indians soon balked at their role in the partnership. "They had a handful of options that were out there. And they said to us, 'it's just not in our business plan right now to continue [discussing the four-way partnership—city, county, state, and team],'" said Michael Stavres, the city's director of Leisure and Environmental Services.

That was in early 2006, and unlike fourteen years before, when the Red Sox announced that they were moving to Fort Myers after a quarter-century in Winter Haven, there was remarkably little consternation over the prospect of the Indians following them out of town. "We've not seen any public reaction like there was when the Red Sox left," said the chamber's Gernert. "The longer the Indians' looking has gone on, the less people here seem to care." He traced the community's apathy back to 2000 and the Indians' refusal to sign a fifteen-year lease. "We were shocked at that," he said. "We weren't sure we were wanted." While the Indians began a tour that would take them all across Florida and ultimately to Arizona in search of a new home, the city of Winter Haven contemplated life without spring training after forty years—and found itself remarkably sanguine.

"I'll be honest with you," said Greene. "It doesn't matter to me whether they stay or go. It really doesn't matter. I have any number of really neat things that are going on in this city that are a much more productive way to spend my time than worrying over the Cleveland Indians, or any baseball team for that matter."

The Indians and spring training, according to Greene, were no longer vital to the psyche or the identity of the city of Winter Haven. "Not in the slightest," he said. "I would submit to you that Cypress Gardens as well as our own label of Winter Haven as 'The Chain of Lakes City' has a much greater standing nationally as compared to major league baseball playing fifteen or sixteen games a year here."

What Winter Haven was seeing as the Indians made ready to leave was what the Indians were costing it in terms of lost opportunity. The city was going to get a big cash-flow shot in the arm when the Indians left town. The lease with the team called for the city to receive a percentage of ticket sales, parking, and concessions. The Indians also paid rent on their office space. This meant income of $300,000–350,000 per year. The city's annual cost to maintain Chain of Lakes to the major league standard was somewhere around $1.2–1.3 million, leaving an annual shortfall of right around $1 million.

On the financial returns side of the equation, according to Greene, things are amorphous. "I think it's safe to say that there is a degree of benefit that occurs within the community for the purposes of restaurants, lodging facilities, and those kinds of things. But I don't think we have, or any community has, a clear, true handle on what that benefit really is."

"The [nonlocal fan] may be just coming to Winter Haven for the day," adds Stavres, "and the economic value comes from maybe buying fuel here, maybe eating at a restaurant or stopping and getting souvenirs, those kinds of things. But the likelihood of their staying the night or staying a week here is not that great."

While no one's suggesting that it will be easy to say goodbye to spring training after more than forty years, the people who tend the municipal purse strings in Winter Haven are looking at what $1 million will buy them. "I grew up here; this is where my family is," said Stavres. "I grew up in that ballpark with the Red Sox. But I'm on a different side of it now because I get to see the other priorities that we have with our community. If I had the million dollars that we put into Chain of Lakes Park annually, and could put it into programs for the youth of our community, or into our senior population, or into our adult recreation, I could go a long way in meeting our needs. Yeah, it's great to have spring training. It's great for our ego; we're the smallest town with spring training. But at the end of the day, we have to ask: What are our priorities? What do we really need?"

The Indians' eagerness to pursue options outside of Winter Haven made them the most visible and viable free agent on the 2006 spring training market. Cities across Florida chased the Indians like major league teams chase a twenty-eight-year-old, top-of-the-rotation, free-agent pitcher. The Indians were the starlet in the gossip columns. Who were they seen with? Who was likely to be their new significant other?

Between December 2005 and September 2006, the Indians had conversations with Cape Coral, down in Lee County across the river from Fort Myers. They visited Apopka, up in Orange County north of Orlando. They talked with Charlotte County about upgrading the Rangers' old facility in Port Charlotte. They had talks with Bonita Springs, also located in Lee County, halfway between Fort Myers and Naples. They considered an intriguing plan from Florida Atlantic University that involved building a spring training complex on campus in a public/private partnership among FAU, the city of Boca Raton, and Palm Beach County. They explored another public/private partnership between Osceola County and Disney World. All of this was on top of conversations the Indians had had earlier in the decade with Fort Myers about sharing City of Palms Park with the Red Sox. They did not, this time, talk with either Homestead or Inverness, the Hernando County city north of Tampa where they once thought they'd had a deal back in the days before they'd even left Tucson. Yet there lingered a possibility of reconciliation with Winter Haven, with

Polk County money being the driving force in those talks. Then, rather late in the summer, they began quietly having earnest talks with Goodyear, Arizona.

Throughout the spring and summer of 2006, all signs pointed to the Indians landing somewhere in Florida. This is where our fan base is, they said. This is where we want to stay. Time was on the Indians' side. Their current lease in Winter Haven expired after spring training 2008, but they held three five-year options for renewal. As anxious as they were to get out of Winter Haven and into a new facility, they didn't have to jump at just anything. Theoretically, if they exercised all of their options, they had until 2023. But while the Indians didn't need to rush into anything, there was some urgency on the part of the local communities. There was an October 1 deadline for making application to the Florida Sports Foundation for the state funds that had been approved by the legislature in May. A fully executed lease needed to be a part of any city or county application for state money.

The deal that came the closest to keeping the Indians in Florida would have brought the Indians to Disney World, to share the stadium at Disney's Wide World of Sports with the Atlanta Braves. The Braves initially had a ten-year exclusive on the Wide World of Sports complex. This was up after the 2007 spring training, and they had agreed to allow Disney to seek another team to share the stadium. Disney's proposal to Osceola was that it would donate land to the county, and the county would build the practice facility. The estimated cost was $25 million, as much as $15 million of which was expected to come in matching funds from the state. That still left a big nut for the county to swallow, in addition to an estimated $1.3 million in yearly maintenance costs. The county had limited interest in that deal and asked Disney for a counterproposal. Disney offered to give the county a dollar from every ticket sold and offered the county $975,000 each year to cover maintenance costs or debt service. That still left $475,000 coming out of the county's coffers every year. They passed on the deal.

It is likely that even had Disney and Osceola County been able to come to terms, the project would have been a nonstarter. "We would have had some problems with that application," said Larry Pendleton, the executive director of the Florida Sports Foundation, the state agency responsible for reviewing applications and disbursing the state's spring training funds. "If Osceola was going to be the applicant, yet the games were going to be played in a private facility, we were going to have a tough time working our way through that scenario—practice publicly, play privately—when in the past all our certifications were public/public. I wish we could have kept Cleveland, but for us,

I'm just as glad we didn't have to [make a decision] on that application. We were going to have a problem with it."

Some Florida talks progressed further than others. Cape Coral was the first city to talk to the Indians. Though the relationship never really evolved beyond the flirtation stage, they flirted with one another for a long time. The first conversations came in December 2005; it was August 2006 before the two sides admitted it wasn't going to work and stopped seeing one another. The story of Cape Coral is the story of the problems and possibilities that attend a community's association with spring training. It also offers a mirror to that of Goodyear, Arizona, the city that finally landed the Indians.

Cape Coral is one of Florida's original buy-a-piece-of-paradise cities. Two entrepreneurial brothers from Maryland coaxed it out of 2,000 acres of Lee County wilderness and marshland in the late 1950s. Jack and Leonard Rosen bought up the peninsula then known as Redfish Point, across the Caloosahatchee River from Fort Myers, and renamed it Cape Coral in 1957. Over the next decade, they elevated and filled five miles of the land's marshy riverfront; dredged 400 miles of interconnected, navigable canals; and platted a community with 138,000 80-by-125-foot lots. Their Gulf American Corporation marketed the city in magazines and newspapers, advertising a "Waterfront Wonderland." They flew prospective buyers over the lots in small planes, six planes making five flights an hour, six days a week, giving 500 people a day an aerial view of thousands of waterfront home sites. People from all over the world paid $900 for a landlocked building lot or $1,900 for a canal-front lot, many without ever setting foot upon the land they were buying.

But while sales were brisk, development was not. The first residents of Cape Coral lived liked frontiersmen. There were no schools or stores or doctors, and the closest bridge to the mainland was located thirty minutes north of their settlement at the southern tip of the peninsula. When Cape Coral was finally incorporated as a city in 1970, its land mass made it the third largest city in the state geographically, yet it had but 11,000 residents.

The boom the Rosen brothers planned for finally emerged at the end of the twentieth century and the start of the twenty-first. By then, two new bridges to the mainland had made Cape Coral a bustling bedroom community to Fort Myers. Its population passed 100,000 in the 2000 census, and by 2006 had grown to 160,000. And yet, fewer than half of the original 138,000 lots have been developed. City planners expect a build-out population of more than 400,000 by 2030. Should this happen, it will make Cape Coral's population larger than Miami's.

But as city planners in the early twenty-first century sought to attract the jobs and services these residents will demand, they found themselves facing an identity crisis. Nobody knew where Cape Coral was. The city was constantly being confused with Coral Springs or Coral Gables, both on the east coast near Miami. Then, the thought of spring training came in. "We're on our way to being the second largest city in the state of Florida," said Eric Feichthaler, Cape Coral's mayor and the man responsible for putting baseball on the public agenda in Cape Coral. "And I think we should be recognized for that. Having a spring training baseball team puts you on the map as a legitimate city."

Feichthaler was a thirty-three-year old tax attorney with no prior political experience when he ousted an incumbent old enough to be his grandfather in the 2005 city election. During the campaign, he talked about bringing a stadium to Cape Coral, a stadium that would house major league spring training during February and March and host concerts, youth sports, and amateur tournaments during the balance of the year. "Practically everybody I talked to said: 'Yes, that's great. We should be doing that. Even if it costs a little bit of money,'" he said. Feichthaler even had a site picked out for the stadium—a city-owned, 200-acre tract of land in the northernmost reaches of town called Festival Park.

Feichthaler saw spring training as the spur that would bring much-needed infrastructure to that largely undeveloped corner of the city. He envisioned a highway dotted with new hotels and restaurants and other businesses leading into the stadium. While he talked of this as a long-term vision for the city, in December 2005, it moved to the political front burner. The Grapefruit League Association's executive director, David Cardwell, arranged a meeting between Cape Coral and the Cleveland Indians. Feichthaler showed the Festival Park site to Indians president Paul Dolan and others. But the courtship stalled there. Both left the meeting with the sense that the ball was in the other's court. "What I would like is for the team to have a proposal," said Feichthaler two months after the Indians' visit to Cape Coral. "And that's just not happening. They want *us* to have a proposal. And we can't do that until we have a better sense of the numbers."

Feichthaler's enthusiasm for spring training resonated with voters and the Cape Coral business community. But when he brought his plan to pursue the Indians back to city hall, he found it did not have the same impact on his fellow city councilors. (Cape Coral operates with a weak-mayor, manager-council form of government.) "Half our city doesn't have infrastructure," said councilor Tim Day, one of four members of the eight-member council to stridently criticize the notion of bringing spring training to Cape Coral. "We don't have city water, we don't have city sewers. We even have crappy roads. So what is your first priority as government? To give people roads and water and sewer, or invest in a multimillion-dollar major league baseball complex out in the middle of nowhere that's going to be used for six weeks a year?

"It's a money loser. You lose money on the maintenance end, you lose money on the utility end, you lose money on the infrastructure. I can't find anything good about it. And what's it going to cost—$40 million? I can build a high school, a *really nice* high school, for $40 million."

Feichthaler and Day represented two sides of an argument that went back a century. What is this going to do for our community versus what is this going to cost our community? The money will come back to us in many ways and many times over versus the money is better spent elsewhere. Both arguments have merit; both are reasonable; both have always had support. "There's a huge body of information out there, with conflicting perspectives about the economics of baseball," said Mike Jackson, the economic development director for Cape Coral. Jackson was quick to point out that he did not have a dog in the fight, that he was a staffperson, not a politician, and the politicians would be the ones making the decisions. His job was to provide analysis. His thoughtful assessment would provide fodder for both sides. "There are two or three parameters that I have to look at to determine whether it's a good or bad deal financially—*financially*—for this city," he said. "Will it spur investment in taxable real property; will it spur investment in hotels and offices and restaurants? What kinds of jobs are being created as a consequence of that activity? And, from a local perspective, are there other opportunities that are forgone as a consequence of this investment? Is it good for a community to have spring training? My view is that it probably is. I think that there is a psychological, sociological benefit for a community. From my perspective, putting Cape Coral on the map—and this is a big part of economic development, people need to know where they're going—then it might be beneficial.

"From an economic perspective, I think it's very hard to say it will pay for itself. Because the numbers aren't there. You can do the math, and it doesn't work. But that leads to the next question: is that all bad?

"The cities of the nation routinely make investments in non-revenue-generating facilities that are used by the citizens of the community, whether it's baseball fields or swimming pools or boat docks or boat launching facilities. Those are not routinely designed to be revenue centers or pay for themselves. The history of government in the United States is that we routinely spend money so that our citizens will have benefit. That's something we all accept. The question I would ask the politicians, who have to make the decisions, is: 'is this the kind of benefit that you want for the citizens of Cape Coral?'"

Mayor Feichthaler clearly believed it was. "Whatever can make us proud to be Cape Coral," he said, "I want to foster that kind of thing." He was still trying in August. After the Florida legislature passed its spring training bill, which would make up to $15 million available to Cape Coral if it could reach a deal with the Indians, Feichthaler wrote to Paul Dolan, asking him for an outline of the team's needs in a new spring facility. Dolan declined, saying they were deeply involved at the time in discussions with one city in Florida and another in Arizona, and that it was not in the team's best interests to open another door. Feichthaler's hopes of Cape Coral spring training were finally dashed. In truth, they had probably been doomed from the start. Securing a franchise is a difficult and chancy proposition even when everyone in the community is enthused and committed. It is quite impossible when there is doubt. And from the beginning, Cape Coral had doubt. "The lack of political will saps the energy out of you," admitted Feichthaler in the spring of 2006, as it was becoming apparent that not everyone in Cape Coral shared his dream.

Goodyear, Arizona, had all the political will that Cape Coral lacked. The politicians there had more than consensus; they had a mandate. The citizens of Goodyear had passed a bond issue in 2004, approving $10 million in public money toward the development of a spring training complex. "We are the only city that's ever asked their public: do you want spring training or not?" said Brian Dalke, Goodyear's deputy city manager, who put together the city's deal with the Cleveland Indians. The citizens of Goodyear said yes resoundingly to spending their money on spring training: the measure passed by a two-to-one margin.

The bond issue capped a decade-long curiosity on the city's part when it came to spring training. Its first contact was in 1995, when Houston Astros owner Drayton McLane, also the owner of McLane Sunwest, a grocery distributor that employed 500 people in Goodyear, made some inquiries about bringing the Astros out from Florida. City leaders passed on the opportunity, realizing that, with a population of only 9,000 people, the city wasn't ready. Goodyear also determined that it wasn't ready in 1999–2000, when the Dodgers briefly came into play. City officials again talked about spring training among themselves, but again they made no attempt to pursue it. But in 2003, when Arte Moreno bought the Angels and began looking at the team's spring training situation, he also came to Goodyear. Moreno owned 20,000 acres there, and expressed an interest in moving the Angels' camp across the valley from Tempe. "We took a look at it," said Dalke, "took a look at the numbers and said: 'We're ready.'" While Goodyear may have been ready for spring training baseball in 2003–2004, as it turned out, Moreno wasn't ready to move his Angels; they elected to stay in an upgraded facility in Tempe. But the attention from the Angels and the public mandate galvanized political support for spring training at Goodyear's city hall. "There was a real commitment by the mayor and council," said Dalke. "They said: 'Let's not only keep this on our radar screen. Let's make it a priority.'"

By the 2004 vote on spring training, Goodyear was poised for an explosion in its population, city infrastructure, and, it hoped, amenities and quality of life as well. The town of 9,000 had grown to a city of almost 50,000. Its population continues to grow at a rate of 16 percent of year and is projected to peak at between 350,000 and 400,000 by the year 2030. But, like its west valley neighbors, Peoria and Surprise, Goodyear had been something of a Rodney Dangerfield, don't-get-no-respect kind of town. Few beyond the immediate environs of the valley knew where or what it was.

The town has its roots in the Goodyear Tire and Rubber Company. In 1917, the company bought 16,000 remote, unincorporated desert acres twenty miles west of Phoenix to grow cotton for use in the company's tires. The settlement that grew up on and around the land Goodyear used to grow cotton quite naturally took the company's name. It was incorporated as a town in 1946, by which time the town's economy had shifted from cotton farming to aircraft manufacture. The Goodyear blimps that first began flying over American sporting events in 1960 were manufactured in Goodyear, Arizona.

Now, the city that bore the blimp's name was seeking a ground-level connection with professional sport. Its spring training recruitment efforts took on greater purpose and urgency in early 2006, following an announcement by the Arizona Sports and Tourism Authority that it had enough money to fund just one more spring training facility before the expiration of its legislative authorization in 2031. Goodyear was determined to be that facility. It needed a site and a funding plan, and most of all, it needed a major league team—or teams, as the hope was always to build a two-team facility. As Cape Coral and the other Florida cities might have told Goodyear, getting a team was going to be easier with a site and especially with a funding plan already in place.

Land was not likely to be a problem. More than 85 percent of Goodyear's 115 square miles had yet to be developed. The city settled on a 200-acre tract on Estrella Parkway, just north of a planned city center to be completed sometime in 2009–2010. The landowners agreed to sell the property to the city for thirty-three cents on the dollar, the benefit to the landowners coming in the development and revenue potential in the land they would retain adjacent to what the city planners were calling Ballpark Village. The 8,000-seat stadium would be integrated into a downtown area of parks, shops, and office space. The practice facility would be two blocks north on Estrella. "Goodyear's spring training facility will be unlike any other spring training facility in the valley," said Eric Judson of JMI Sports, the company that developed a city center around Petco Park in San Diego and was now being hired to do the same in Goodyear. "For the first time, a spring training facility will be part of a larger master plan that will act as a catalyst for significant economic development."

The costs of land acquisition and construction of a one-team facility were pegged at roughly $74 million. Infrastructure and other costs would push the total price tag to more than $85 million. The city would receive $37 million from AZSTA—once it secured a team and its plan was approved. The city's share of the cost would come from the issuance of public improvement corporation and general obligation bonds. The city's operation, maintenance, and debt service expenses would be budgeted at $6 million annually.

In April 2006, Brian Dalke sent letters to thirteen of the eighteen Grapefruit League teams, inviting them to consider Goodyear as a location for spring training. We have the funding; we have the site; and we have a development team and plan in place, he explained. "Now we are making our final push to make the vision become a reality by securing two major league baseball teams that desire to make Goodyear their spring training home. To accomplish this last and most important goal, we need you!" Dalke heard from the five Grapefruit League teams that were nearing the end of their leases and that would be expecting new facilities or substantial upgrades to what they now had. The Cleveland Indians were, of course, one of those five. They listened, initially in need of a lot of convincing. "They were very upfront throughout the whole process. They told us: 'We're planning to stay in Florida,'" said Dalke. But the more the Indians listened, the more receptive they became.

Goodyear mayor Jim Cavanaugh, Dalke, consultant Eric Judson, and a core of staffers made their pitch to Paul Dolan and members of his staff during a meeting in Cleveland in August. "I think it was truly a Wow! factor," said Dalke. "They saw the interest of the community and the developers. We knew they were still talking to cities in Florida. They felt that there was so much more support here from this community [than there was in Florida]."

If it was the Wow! factor that got the Indians to seriously consider Goodyear, it was the $$$! factor that sealed the deal. Florida cities were still looking for a cash contribution from the club; they wanted a spring training partner. The Indians' signature on the lease was all the partnership that Goodyear was asking. While talks continued between the Indians and Bonita Springs, and continued more earnestly between the Indians and Disney/Osceola County, by the time the Indians' chief financial officer, Ken Stefanov, came to Goodyear in early September, the conversation was on deal points and on the structure and viability of the city's financing package. By the end of the month, they had the language on a memorandum of understanding finalized. Goodyear would build a $77 million stadium and training complex from city and AZSTA funds and would absorb all operation and maintenance costs. The Indians would pay $100,000 per year—to be later adjusted for inflation—for a period of twenty years. The two parties would share the revenues from tickets, concessions, parking, novelty sales, and stadium advertising. The city would keep all revenues from premium seating and stadium naming rights.

With Indians president Paul Dolan appearing via teleconference, the Goodyear city council approved the MOU on September 26, 2007. The document was executed a day later. On November 1, Dolan toured the site of the Indians' new spring home. "This location is superb," he said, "the development vision is extraordinary, and the city's team of professionals is second to none."

Nine days later, however, Goodyear's euphoria turned into anxiety.

On November 10, the neighboring city of Glendale announced that it had finalized a memorandum of understanding with the Chicago White Sox and the Los Angeles Dodgers to build a two-team facility in Glendale, opening in 2009. From the beginning of the process, both cities—Glendale and Goodyear—had operated on the premise that AZSTA had enough funds for one more facility. Not only did they need to put together a package satisfactory to their teams, they needed to put together a package that would trump the other when it came before the AZSTA board. The board had long expressed its preference for funding two-team facilities and reiterated that position in the wake of the two MOUs.

But there was another wrinkle. Glendale's two teams included another Cactus League team, one with six years remaining on its lease down in Tucson. Even though the Arizona Sports and Tourism Authority was a Maricopa County–only entity, it still bore the name of the entire state, and the perception that public money might be used to aid one Arizona community in poaching from another was something AZSTA was quite sensitive to. Before any decision had been rendered, AZSTA representatives told the White Sox that, if Glendale received approval, the White Sox would not be allowed to leave Tucson before their lease ended in 2012, unless they found a team to replace them.

So, the White Sox went after the Indians. Getting the Indians to backfill the final five years of their lease in Tucson would solve two problems for the White Sox. It would free them to move to the valley immediately, and it would remove the Goodyear proposal from the competition for AZSTA funds, virtually assuring approval of the Glendale plan. The White Sox had first approached the Indians about taking over their lease in Tucson back in 2003. Indians officials toured Tucson Electric Park and talked about the move internally before declining. Despite their forty-five-year history in Tucson, the Indians had decided that the travel to the valley made it a less-than-ideal site in the here and now; and the lack of direct flights from Cleveland to Tucson was by itself a deal breaker.

The White Sox had repeated their offer to the Indians when their deal in Glendale began to gel. Again, the Indians had declined. Now, they tried again; again, the Indians declined. The Indians could afford at this point to wait out the process. They still had options for another fifteen years in Winter Haven if they had to return there. Should AZSTA choose Glendale over Goodyear, the offer to go to Tucson could probably be revisited then; there was no one else on the radar looking to take over the White Sox's lease.

And there was always the chance that, because of the complications with the White Sox, AZSTA would choose the Goodyear proposal to fund.

Or AZSTA could find a way to fund both.

Wanting to find a way to do exactly that, AZSTA went looking under the sofa cushions for money—and found an additional $32 million. The money came not from the AZSTA revenue streams, but from the pot of money that had saved the Cactus League in the first place, the $2.50-per-car-rental-contract tax that Maricopa County had passed back in 1991. After AZSTA had come into existence in 2002, it had entered into an intergovernmental agreement with the Maricopa County Stadium District (MCSD). The agreement called for MCSD, after servicing its bonds, to turn over all funds to AZSTA. "They agreed that, whatever revenue they had left over, they would flow to us, so long as we combine it with our own monies and use it for Cactus League purposes," said Ted Ferris, the executive director of AZSTA. "In effect, it's trying to create one-stop shopping." When the MCSD check came to AZSTA in the fall of 2006, it was heavy by $1.1 million. Maricopa County car rentals were running ahead of projections. AZSTA "reforecast" its projected revenue and determined that it could afford both Glendale and Goodyear, if both parties were willing to delay the reimbursement schedule for ten years, until 2017. Both agreed. Goodyear will get one-half of its actual construction costs, somewhere between $34 million and $37 million. Glendale will get two-thirds of its cost, up to $54 million. AZSTA made it one giant Christmas gift to Goodyear, Glendale, and the Cactus League, announcing its intention to fund both proposals on December 21.

"We're tapped out," said Larry Landry, the AZSTA board chair, after the announcement.

"Yeah, we've heard that before," replied Nick Gandy of the Florida Sports Foundation.

In the spring of 2008, Goodyear landed the second team it had coveted, signing an agreement with the Cincinnati Reds to share the facility beginning in 2010. In the full flush of anticipation, Goodyear could not wait for the visibility that spring training would bring to its growing community and the vitality it would bring to its new downtown when March 2009 arrives. The city is enormously proud that it has done what a dozen or so others across Arizona and Florida could not. However, some of those cities—Chandler, Yuma, Vero Beach, Winter Haven—could well warn Goodyear that, while twenty years might seem like forever, it is really but an eye blink. And whether it be twenty years, forty years, or sixty years, the nature of spring training is impermanence; teams eventually move on. Sooner than it can imagine or believe, Goodyear might find itself looking at the end of spring training.

No one is yet willing to bring that particular skunk into the city's garden party. And while Goodyear knows that it's a possibility that spring training will not be forever, it is confident that, whatever happens beyond life with the Indians, it has made the right investment in its future.

"We do know we have a twenty-year commitment," said Dalke. "If [the teams] were to ever move away from that, could we adjust? Can we take a public asset in the middle of an urban village and work with it? Absolutely. Absolutely."

SIXTEEN

St. Pete Bids Spring Training Adieu

What would Al Lang be thinking? Here was a major league baseball team looking to pack up and take spring training away from St. Petersburg forever, and the city's mayor—a populist like Al Lang, a baseball fan like Al Lang—was allowing it to happen. In fact, not only was he not lying down in front of the moving van to stop it, he was helping to load the truck! Spring training, it seemed, was not that important to St. Petersburg any more.

"We're now a major league city," explained Mayor Rick Baker. "The most important thing once you become a major league city is that your major league team succeeds. If having them train in Charlotte County helps them develop a support base in southwest Florida, that helps them succeed during the regular season, then that's good for the city."

It's easy to overlook the fact that Tropicana Field, the Rays' regular season home, is in St. Petersburg and to assume the team plays in Tampa because of its name. But they are really the St. Petersburg Rays. St. Petersburg has been the team's spring training home, too, and that's been a problem for both team and city. Regular season trumps spring training, any baseball person will tell you. With both in the same city, the spring games don't create much of a buzz. Rays fans never stormed the gates at Al Lang Stadium; why not wait a month and see a real game at the Trop? Little interest in spring training translates into little anticipation for the regular season, and the real cash value in spring training—as it has been since the days of John McGraw—is in generating that anticipation.

Hosting the Rays in the spring means virtually no financial impact for St. Petersburg. In years past, fans from New York and St. Louis came to St. Pete to watch the Yankees, Cardinals, and Mets, and filled the city's hotels and restaurants. The Rays bring nobody to the city. Fans who go to Al Lang Stadium for a game go home to have dinner and sleep. St. Petersburg's hotels get some room nights from the Rays' minor leaguers, but an out-of-town team would take over virtually an entire hotel for six weeks for its spring training headquarters. Rays executives live at home and work out of their regular season offices.

Now, the Rays are leaving for Port Charlotte in the spring of 2009. Not because there's anything lacking in the St. Petersburg baseball facilities, but because the business opportunities are constricted. "This is about expanding our business and expanding our fan base," said Michael Kalt, the Rays' vice president for development. When, in 2006, the Rays first approached the city about taking the preseason elsewhere, they were surprised to find the suggestion met with great enthusiasm. The city and team anticipate that the move south will help trade spring training dollars for regular season dollars, building anticipation in St. Petersburg at the same time they're expanding their fan base into Charlotte County.

There was another reason that city officials welcomed the Rays' leaving: Al Lang Stadium and the downtown waterfront land on which it sits would now be available for other uses. Al Lang Stadium—with its backdrop of sailboats beyond the outfield—is inarguably a perfect place to watch a springtime baseball game. But even baseball fans distressed at the prospect of losing one of the game's treasured venues concede that fifteen games a year is a gross underuse of such a spectacular property. St. Petersburg waterfront is all public space; any development must be for public use and must pass a referendum. Everyone in St. Petersburg already has an idea about how that land might be used. But the most talked-about suggestion thus far? A new, open-air, retractable-roof regular season stadium for the Rays.

And the future of spring training in St. Petersburg? That seems doomed. "I'm not pursuing it," said Baker. "You would have to spend an awful lot of money to build a new facility, and at the end of the day you'd now have a competitor to your major league baseball team. So I don't see it happening."

And what would Al Lang think? "I would promise you that Al Lang—in a millisecond—would trade the two spring training teams that he had for a major league baseball team in St. Petersburg," avows Baker.

If St. Petersburg is content—happy even—to see spring training go away; Port Charlotte is thrilled to have it come back. Charlotte County—halfway between Fort Myers and the Tampa/St. Pete/Sarasota metro area—had been home to Texas Rangers spring training from 1987 to 2002. The years after the Rangers left have not been easy ones for the county. In 2004, Hurricane Charley—with 145-mile-per-hour winds—hit Charlotte County head-on. Charley destroyed 10,000 homes, damaged 16,000 others, and temporarily closed 3,500 businesses. The damages totaled $11 billion.

The storm largely spared Charlotte County Stadium; but with the county in ruins around it, the stadium was nobody's priority. As the county recovered, however, it began to pay attention to the long-neglected facility. While the Rangers were in Port Charlotte, they had an exclusive lease on the property; there were only two or three days available every year for county activities. Now, with the Rangers gone and the county confronted with the decision to either use the facility or raze it, it suddenly became a pretty busy place. It was rechristened Charlotte Sports Park and became the centerpiece of the county parks system. The biggest of the many events held there—in both size and community impact—was the Charlotte County Invitational, a college baseball tournament held every March for five years, which made Port Charlotte one of the busiest places on the Gulf Coast.

"That tournament did more to show people the economic impact of sports than whatever I could share verbally," said Laura Kleiss Hoeft, the county's director of parks, recreation, and cultural services. Ninety of the tournament's ninety-eight teams stayed in Charlotte County, and they kept the restaurants so full that locals had a difficult time getting a table.

The county does not expect to get rich on spring training. The Rays will not be bringing flocks of fans to the hotels of Charlotte County; most of the Rays' fans in Charlotte Sports Park's stadium will be locals or day-trippers from St. Petersburg. "We understand there isn't a humongous economic benefit to this. It has a civic benefit, and I think that we're looking at this as the anchor, but [spring training] is not the total," said Kleiss Hoeft.

This is a different sort of spring training partnership. The county will retain its access to the facility for all but the six weeks of spring training. The team and the county will share the cost of operating the facility, currently budgeted at $950,000. Every dollar the county brings in from concerts, tournaments, and other activities will be applied toward operating costs, so there is a financial incentive for the Rays for the county to do well with its other activities. But the team sees another, more important benefit to community access. They want Charlotte County's citizens to feel a sense of belonging in Charlotte Sports Park, whether they're there for a concert or a Rays game. And they want to transfer that sense of belonging to the Rays' regular season, to shorten the road between Port Charlotte and St. Petersburg.

The Rays understand that they are never going to generate the kind of preseason revenue that the Red Sox or Yankees do; their proximity precludes that. But they feel that they've found a niche with this cozy little partnership with a county that is just close enough, and just far enough away.

In its 2006 session, the Florida legislature passed a $75 million appropriations bill that made up to $15 million available to up to five local governments—cities and counties—for the purpose of maintaining and upgrading spring training facilities, to keep their major league tenants satisfied and in place. The legislation was written with no specific community or situation in mind, but it was born of the knowledge that five communities had leases nearing their end and facilities in need of upgrades or replacement: Fort Lauderdale and the Orioles; Bradenton and the Pirates; Sarasota and the Reds; St. Petersburg and the Rays; and Winter Haven and the Indians. The bill was modeled on the successful 2000 legislation, with one major adjustment. The 2000 legislation was limited to communities with existing leases with major league teams. With the Indians likely leaving Winter Haven and the Rays beginning to show interest in exploring opportunities outside St. Petersburg, the 2006 bill made other Florida communities eligible for the funds, provided that a team's current city signed a document acknowledging its willingness to let the team go.

The bill's sponsors and supporters expected the legislation to bring some stability to the Grapefruit League, to stop the flight to Arizona, and to fix the spring training map for at least the next decade or more. It did not work out that way. No city in Florida could put a lease together with the Indians. And while three of the five awards are proceeding smoothly—Port Charlotte is refurbishing Charlotte Sports Park for the Rays; Bradenton is making some improvements to McKechnie Field and building minor league dorms for the Pirates; and St. Lucie County has been reimbursed for some past improvements to the Mets complex—two others, in Fort Lauderdale and in Sarasota, blew up.

Sarasota has a spring training heritage that goes back to the 1920s, and the collapse of its deal with the Reds was a shocker. The deal was grounded in a mutual admiration between community and team and had seemed solid in every respect. The plan was ambitious; Sarasota would build a stadium on a par with Tampa, Clearwater, or Disney, a real Grapefruit League showplace. It was going to cost $40 million, $10 million of which would have come from the Reds, who liked it in Sarasota. The team seemed willing to make the contribution. When quizzed early in the process about the team's commitment to Sarasota—were they willing to sign a twenty-year lease?— Reds owner Robert Castellini told the Sarasota County Commission: "I'll sign a *thirty*-year lease and I'll sign it right now."

Financial times were good in 2006; the city and county commissions voted unanimously to support the project, and the state readily approved its $15 million share. However, when the project was launched in 2007, the real cost to build the facility was pegged at $54 million, not $40 million. The city and county came up with a $44 million budget but could not bridge the final $10 million gap, and the grand plan was quickly scaled back. By the summer of 2007, the city and team proposed a plan to instead renovate and improve Ed Smith Stadium. Even this decidedly less-ambitious project was still going to cost $41 million.

Meanwhile, tumbling real estate prices had given the Florida economy a real battering. In these suddenly changed financial times, the Sarasota City Commission decided to put its share of the project—roughly $16 million, to come from property taxes—before the voters. The November referendum would be defeated by 200 votes, but by November, the matter was pretty much moot. In July, the Sarasota County Commission had failed to approve the use of county tourist-tax money for the project. Some of the county commissioners favored using the tourist-tax dollars for beach cleanup, which was presently being funded out of the county's unexpectedly strapped property tax revenues. Without the county money, it didn't matter what the city's voters said; the project was finished.

The Reds then called Vero Beach and were told by Indian River County administrator Joseph Baird that the county had just entered into an exclusive negotiating agreement with another major league team. Next, the Reds called Goodyear, which desperately wanted a second team to go with the Indians; but Goodyear had already spent all of its money and so, too, had the state authority that was funding half of the complex for the Indians. Goodyear promised to try to find the money somewhere. The Reds spent the fall of 2007 in limbo, waiting to see what would happen.

Goodyear quickly found the money by determining that it could bond out the $32 million it would cost to build the Reds' portion—practice fields and a clubhouse—of the shared facility. It also exacted a promise from the Arizona Sports and Tourism Authority that if AZSTA's revenues—already spent through the next ten years—ran ahead of expectation, then Goodyear would get any extra, up to two-thirds of the full cost of the two-team facility, now totaling $108 million. The two parties signed a ninety-day exclusive negotiating contract in January 2008. By April, they had a deal. The news didn't please a lot of Reds fans. Sarasota is only 600 miles from Cincinnati—fans could drive down in a day—Goodyear is three times that far.

In February, meanwhile, one of the Sarasota County commissioners who had previously voted against funding the county's share of the project reversed her vote. The county, too late, was on board for keeping the Reds.

Little time was spent mourning the Reds, however. Two weeks after they announced they were leaving, word leaked out that Sarasota was talking to the Red Sox.

A midsummer headline in the *Sarasota Herald-Tribune* read, "Red Sox Have Hearts Aflutter." County commissioner Jon Thaxton, the most intransigent opponent of funding the stadium for the Reds, felt the Red Sox would be "a great addition" to the local economy. An online petition that opposed spending public money to attract the Red Sox collected only 300 signatures. An online petition supporting the move pulled together more than 2,200 signatures during the same time span.

Talks moved at the speed of first love. The two sides first spoke in late April 2008. By mid-July, the city was showing the Red Sox an array of stadium plans and asking them to indicate their preference. (They chose a 10,000-seat replica of Fenway Park.) The projected cost of the new facility for the Red Sox was north of $80 million, almost twice what the city and county had refused to spend on the Reds. This time, however, few blinked. A quickly prepared economic impact study claimed that the Red Sox would bring $47 million to the Sarasota economy, and that figure was also nearly twice the $24 million impact claimed for the Reds the year before. The fairgrounds, rejected by the county as a site for the Reds, was back as an option for the Red Sox. The city bought two parcels of land adjacent to Payne Park—where spring training baseball had been played from the twenties through the eighties—in case it wanted to put the new stadium there. Sarasota realtors claimed that second-home buyers from Boston would energize the stagnant housing market.

The Red Sox's lease in Fort Myers runs until 2019, but there are buyout options each year beginning in 2009. When Sarasota called the team right after the Reds announced they were going to Goodyear, the Red Sox thought it an opportune time to listen. City of Palms Park is bursting at its seams, with no room left to grow. "We can't accommodate the demand for tickets," said chief operating officer Mike Dee. The Sarasota overture lit a fire under Lee County. While there had been abstract talks about a new complex for some time, those talks got more specific; county parks officials took Mike Dee on a helicopter tour of some prospective sites in Fort Myers and neighboring Estero in early July. But Lee County was caught by surprise at the speed and intensity of the talks in Sarasota. "We're playing catch-up down here," a county official admitted in midsummer.

By summer's end, everyone in Sarasota, from downtown waitresses to county commissioners, was convinced that the deal was doable. Part of the giddiness stemmed from the allure of the Red Sox; much of it came from a sense of relief at being given a second chance after letting the Reds slip away.

All that really needed to be resolved, it seemed, was the prickly issue of the money. The working number was $80 million. It might be less if some of the existing facilities at Ed Smith Stadium could be used; it might be much more if the fairgrounds was the final site and a new fairgrounds needed to be built elsewhere. How could a city and county that felt they couldn't afford $41 million less than a year before now talk about spending $80 million, in an economy that had notably worsened in that year? The difference, city and county officials believed, was the enthusiasm of the business community for a deal with the Red Sox—an enthusiasm that was markedly missing during the talks with the Reds. The belief was that private money would complement public money in a deal with the Red Sox. Though how much private funding was available, no one was willing—or able—to estimate.

One financial point did seem clear. If Sarasota made a deal with the Red Sox, it would have to do so without the $15 million in state money that had been given to the city to support its deal with the Reds. That money had been paid to the city monthly, beginning in January 2007, and was collecting in a trust fund. But the city would not be able to draw on it to build for the Red Sox. There were at least two legal issues. First, the money was awarded based on a contract with the Reds, and that contract was not the one being executed. Second, there is a provision in the statute calling for any city attracting a team from another city to secure the blessing of the original city. Sarasota seemed very unlikely to get such a letter from Fort Myers. Lee County was more apt to take up arms to keep the Red Sox than it was to wish them bon voyage to Sarasota.

Tallahassee watched the Sarasota goings-on with a degree of distress. "I think it opens up a big can of worms where you've got communities trying to steal other communities' teams, and using state money to do it," said Larry Pendleton of the Florida Sports Foundation. It's been Pendleton's job to get that state money from the state legislature. It hasn't been easy thus far, and he worries it will be impossible in the future if legislators see themselves as funding an intra-Florida turf war. If Sarasota County taxpayers wish to build for the Red Sox, they'll have to do it without state help.

One additional question still remained to be answered at the end of the summer of 2008: did the Red Sox even want to come? In addition to the promised grand facility they were being offered, tugging the Red Sox toward Sarasota was its location seventy-five miles north of Fort Myers. It is that much closer to the spring training away games in Bradenton, Tampa, Clearwater, and Dunedin.

The ties that bound in Fort Myers included the team's long and warm relationship with Lee County and the extraordinary financial success of its spring trainings there. Perhaps even more important was the Red Sox's keen sensitivity to their fans and the awareness that hundreds of Red Sox fans have chosen to buy vacation or retirement homes in the Naples–Fort Myers area, based largely on the Red Sox's presence there. If the team leaves, how betrayed will these fans feel? The ownership group has made few public relations missteps in its years in charge. It was not likely to make a decision of this size without playing out every variable.

Also collecting state spring training money throughout 2007–2008, and leaving it unspent in a trust fund, was Broward County and the city of Fort Lauderdale. Government concerns about money killed the deal there too, but it wasn't local or state government. It was federal.

In the summer of 2006, the Orioles and Fort Lauderdale reached agreement on a deal that would renovate aging Fort Lauderdale Stadium—built for the Yankees in 1962—and create fields on adjacent land for the Orioles' minor leaguers, who'd been training across the state in Sarasota. Though the plan necessitated razing a high school football stadium, which met with some local resistance, what really prevented the project from getting under way was a review by the Federal Aviation Administration. Orioles spring training sat next to Fort Lauderdale Executive Airport, on land deeded to the city but controlled by the FAA; it had approval over any development plan. The FAA asked for an appraisal of the land from the city based on its highest-value use. City officials demurred, saying the land was being used as parkland and to appraise it as though it were commercial property would be to engage in hypotheticals. The FAA insisted. Only with such an appraisal could the FAA determine if the terms of the lease with the Orioles were fair, it said, and only then would it grant approval. The back-and-forth continued for eighteen long months.

Finally, in June 2008, the FAA ruled that the roughly $100,000 rent the Orioles were paying was grossly inadequate. The fair market value of such a lease, it ruled, was $1.3 million, and unless the lease were rewritten using that number, the FAA would not approve the deal. The city and county were stunned and asked the FAA to reconsider. It agreed to reconsider, but did not change the ruling.

A 1,000 percent rent increase was not to the Orioles' liking, of course. But by the time the FAA finally issued its ruling, the Orioles had long since turned their attentions to Vero Beach. They'd called Indian River County in the summer of 2007, and county administrator Joe Baird informed the county commission that he was "in serious negotiations with a major league baseball franchise" to take over the Dodgers' lease. At the request of the team, Baird declined to reveal their identity, but promised that the picture would become more clear by early fall.

Now, Indian River County's spring training future depended on getting the Dodgers gone. The team that had broken so many hearts with their decision to move was now clogging the doorway. The team had always planned that the 2008 spring season would be their last in Vero Beach, but that schedule was predicated on a September 1, 2007, groundbreaking for their new facility in Glendale. When that groundbreaking was delayed, so too was the notification of their date of departure from Vero Beach. It might be 2008, they said, but it might be 2009. The dithering frustrated county officials, who nonetheless continued negotiations with the Orioles.

They talked about $14 million in improvements to Holman Stadium, and they talked with Ripken Baseball—the youth baseball organization overseen by Orioles Hall of Famer Cal Ripken, Jr.—about establishing a Ripken Baseball Academy on the grounds of the dormant nine-hole Dodgertown golf course, now owned by the city of Vero Beach. When the Dodgers finally notified the county in July 2008 that they would not be back in 2009, the path seemed clear for the county and the Orioles. Still, there was no announcement.

Throughout the spring and summer of 2008, the Orioles seemed reluctant to pull the trigger on their Vero Beach deal, much to the consternation of some in Vero Beach. A number of target dates came and went. Not only was there no deal, there was still not even any formal acknowledgment by either party that the Orioles were indeed the unnamed team in the negotiations. The Orioles were in no rush; rushing only served to close out other options. They had committed to going back to Fort Lauderdale in 2009, and there was no one competing with them for the Dodgertown facilities. It was also to their advantage to wait and see how things played out with the Red Sox and Sarasota. Sarasota had contacted the Orioles at the same time it had reached out to the Red Sox. Because of the minor league association, as well as the troubles in Fort Lauderdale, Sarasota had thought originally that the Orioles might be its best bet to replace the Reds. Should the Red Sox deal not materialize, Sarasota would become an option for the Orioles. Should the Red Sox and Sarasota come to a deal, then the Red Sox's old complex in Fort Myers might be a good fit for the Orioles. And, unlikely though it seemed, if Fort Lauderdale somehow convinced the FAA to change its mind, the Orioles could still choose to go back there.

Though Vero Beach seemed by far the most likely destination for the Orioles, no deal's ever done until the contract is signed and the money's in place. And even then, as Sarasota and Fort Lauderdale can testify, it's still sometimes not a deal. Only one thing is certain in this expensive game of musical chairs. When the music stops in 2010, the Grapefruit League map is going to look mighty strange, because it will be without at least three, and maybe four, of its most historic cities.

What at first blush seemed to be a time of great chaos—four cities chasing two teams; any number of possible outcomes; not enough money here, unused money there; deals finalized and then abandoned—is actually a perfect example of spring training normalcy. Spring training's most permanent quality is its impermanence. Since 1902, nine of the thirty major league teams have moved their permanent, regular season homes from one city to another. Eight of those moves came between 1953 and 1973; most came because the team was going broke where it was. Spring training moves over that period are in the hundreds; there have been eleven moves since the mid-1990s alone. Most of those shifts came for reasons far more capricious. We need desperate times or extraordinary opportunities to leave our homes. But to change our vacation plans?

Major league baseball teams are always going to be outnumbered by the cities and towns that are interested in hosting their spring trainings. Thus, they will continue to be tempting attractions and the objects of spirited competition. In the beginning, investing in spring training was betting at the $2 window, and the lines at the window were relatively short. The ante is considerably higher now, and you must jockey for position just to play. But the money is, in the grand scheme of baseball, still relatively small. You can build a palace of a spring training facility for $75–80 million. By contrast, the new regular season stadiums for the Mets and Yankees cost $1 billion each.

If you're a town interested in spring training, there's always going to be a team available—if not now, then in a year or two. And those teams are always going to be willing to listen. The partnerships between host cities and their teams seem inevitably to reach a level of exhaustion, whether it comes after fifteen years, as it did with the Rangers and Port Charlotte, or after sixty, as it did with the Dodgers and Vero Beach.

This past-as-prologue will give hope to community officials interested in spring training, particularly those from towns that are still relatively new, with identities to build and reputations to make—and there's no shortage of those kind of towns in the places where spring training baseball is played. Across Florida and Arizona, scarcely a month passes without someone—in local government or perhaps from the chamber of commerce—floating the idea of bringing spring training on board. Or back on board: how long before Winter Haven develops a case of seller's remorse? Most of the suggestions will never leave the room where they are made. Others will make it into the community, into a newspaper story maybe, or onto the agenda of a city council or county commission meeting. Maybe a dozen will reach the point where a community official actually talks to a team official, shows him an empty piece of land, and asks him to imagine hotels and shops and restaurants and a ballpark that's prettier than any ever built. Half of those might see some money invested in the notion—an architect hired perhaps, or a financial impact plan developed. And maybe one of those will actually come to fruition, find that happy confluence of an available team, a public willing to spend money, and a place and a time that are perfect.

Which will leave an empty stadium and a community suddenly without spring training someplace else. And that will start the cycle again.

SEVENTEEN

Camelback Ranch

Everything the spring training story has been about comes together in Glendale: big money; big-spectacle spring training; baseball teams as opportunists; an aggressive city on the uptick, looking to grow its profile even more and willing to spend whatever it takes to do so; and a spring training complex that will, in size and opulence and cost, dwarf everything that has come before it—the biggest, dressiest, sexiest spring training experience of all.

Glendale, a city of 240,000 people on Phoenix's western edge, is grabbing at professional sports the way a glutton goes for the drumstick. It already has the National Football League's Cardinals, the National Hockey League's Coyotes, and the splendidly appointed, publicly built stadium and arena to house them. It has had Super Bowls and BCS (Bowl Championship Series) title games and expects one day soon to host an NCAA Final Four. The city sees spending another $81 million in public funds—city and state—to add spring training as an investment that is a logical expansion of its sports brand. But it is not about the sports, officials insist. It's about everything that sports will bring in its wake. "Destination-point opportunities," the city manager calls them.

Glendale is getting a lot of baseball history and tradition for its $81 million, for it has secured two of baseball's tradition-steeped original franchises. The baseball teams stand to make millions from their new spring

Xanadu. This, the critics and the shunted cities say, is a deal that is about money and nothing else. Not so, say the teams. We are merely bringing our spring training to where our fans already are.

To come to this desert baseball resort, the Los Angeles Dodgers will leave not only a complex that has been their home for sixty years but, more significantly, a facility that went through a major upgrade, at taxpayers' expense, less than a decade ago. The Chicago White Sox, meanwhile, are leaving a state-of-the-art facility that was built to their specifications in 1998. Both teams are leaving in the midst of valid leases. They are leaving because they believe there is more money to be made in Glendale than in Vero Beach and Tucson. And they are leaving because they can. There is nothing immoral or unethical, and certainly nothing unusual, about what White Sox owner Jerry Reinsdorf and Dodgers owner Frank McCourt are doing. Yes, they are breaking leases, but in corporate America a lease is a business asset; most have provisions for renegotiating the terms, and they are renegotiated all the time. However, they are almost always renegotiated out of sight of a public that has limited interest in the assets of an ordinary business, but a real proprietary interest in everything concerning the professional sports teams they root for. "I can understand why they're doing this," said Joe Baird, the county administrator in Indian River County, Florida, and its representative in its dealings with the Dodgers. "It's business." Baird acknowledges that things have changed since 2000, when the Dodgers' current twenty-year lease was signed. "And, hey," he added, "we're almost halfway through that lease. In this day and age, that's pretty good."

Tucson Electric Park, built in 1998 to welcome the Arizona Diamondbacks to major league baseball and to lure the White Sox west from Sarasota, remains a perfect spring training facility. While a bit removed from downtown, the location is accessible and convenient for the fans who arrive by car—two minutes and two easy turns off I-10, with ample parking and convenient postgame egress. While the stadium's architecture is angular and perhaps a bit sterile, it is nonetheless a very comfortable place to watch a baseball game. There are 8,000 close-to-the-action seats, a 360-degree boulevard of a concourse that is within constant sight of the playing field and the Santa Catalina Mountains on the horizon. There is a right field party pavilion and the requisite outfield berm, which seats another 3,000 or so. The White Sox operate out of a 40,000-square-foot clubhouse, with six practice fields, locker room space for major and minor leaguers, state-of-the-art weight and trainers' rooms, and enough office space to serve a small government agency.

But they have been playing their Cactus League games at Tucson Electric Park in front of too-few fans. Since arriving in Tucson in 1998, they've averaged fewer than 6,000 fans per game. That puts them well behind the Cubs, Giants, Mariners, and Angels, and much closer to the bottom of the Cactus League attendance standings than they are to the top. White Sox fans have not come in large numbers to Tucson; it baffles White Sox officials a bit. Tucson residents don't come in droves either, though the White Sox think they have a handle on that one: Tucsonans find the location, out in a light industrial section in the southeast corner of the town near I-10, inconvenient and unappealing, too far removed from where people live, up in the foothills or near the center of the city.

But in the valley? There are White Sox fans all over the valley; the White Sox draw better on the road when they travel up I-10 to play the Giants and the Angels, and especially the Cubs, than they do at home in Tucson. There are lots of Chicagoans in the valley. An Arizona State University study in 2000 showed that Cook and DuPage counties in Illinois—greater Chicago—both ranked among the top counties-of-origin for new Phoenix residents during the 1990s. Cook County was second. All of the other leading counties came from nearby states—California, Nevada, and Utah. White Sox officials quote figures that claim one in every seven valley residents can trace his or her roots back to Chicago. One in seven. In a metro area of almost 4.4 million people, that would be 625,000 Chicagoans. Take away the Cubs fans and that still leaves more than 300,000 White Sox fans already living in the valley. You'd only need 3 percent of them to sell out a spring training game.

And the Dodgers? Same thing. Not enough fans in Vero Beach—not enough Dodgers fans anyway. "By the second year [of our ownership] it just felt odd to me to be in this great setting, going to games in Dodgertown and hearing the loudest cheers when the other team did something positive," said Dodgers owner Frank McCourt. "Every other team we were playing was an East Coast team. The fans for that team would be there in significantly greater numbers. There was something very jarring to me in that."

And in the Valley of the Sun? The same Arizona State study that showed Cook County as the second-greatest source of new valley residents showed Los Angeles County as the number one source.

One of the Chicagoans with a home in the valley is White Sox owner Jerry Reinsdorf, and he has long wanted to move his spring training there.

The Sox were involved in discussions for the Maryvale project in the late nineties but stepped aside for the Brewers and instead made the best of it in Tucson. But Reinsdorf was restless there, and the half-full houses at Tucson Electric Park didn't help, and in 2005 he set the wheels in motion to move up to the valley, where his heart had been all along.

John Kaites is the guy to whom Reinsdorf turned to put it together. Kaites is a Phoenix lawyer and lobbyist, well connected politically after serving three terms in the Arizona state senate, more visible in the community than most perhaps, from his prepolitical days as a TV weatherman on Channel 12 in Phoenix. His career, he eagerly explains, has benefited greatly from the help of two important mentors. Politically, it was Senator John McCain, who met Kaites while he was a state legislator and backed him in an unsuccessful run for Arizona attorney general in 1998. In business, it was Jerry Reinsdorf.

Kaites met Reinsdorf while serving as a state legislator. Long an admirer of the White Sox's owner, he asked if he could buy Reinsdorf dinner and pick his brain. "I'm buying him dinner," said Kaites, seemingly more struck by the audacity of his having asked than by the irony of the young public servant picking up the millionaire's dinner check. A friendship developed: Kaites played a small role in the White Sox's move from Florida to Tucson in 1998, and when Reinsdorf determined the time was right for a move to the valley from Tucson, he hired Kaites to make it happen. Quietly. "You don't want to do anything to offend your host city until you're ready to move, and then you want them to be a partner in that transition." Working through the Arizona Baseball Commission, Kaites sent out a request for information (RFI) to valley communities in early 2005, asking which might be interested in building a new spring training facility for the White Sox, though the White Sox were referred to only as an unidentified major league team. He was looking for more than interest in sending out the RFI; he was looking for suitability on a number of different fronts. "You have to find the right location, the right city, a city that has the economic capability to pull it together," he said, "in a location that's not too close to the other parks so you're not drawing fans away, but yet close enough to other parks so you're not driving too far. And at the same time balancing the politics of southern Arizona with the politics of central Arizona."

Goodyear, Queen Creek, Gilbert, and Casa Grande all responded to the RFI. Glendale did not, at least not at first. Casa Grande was some distance south on I-10, down in Pinal County. If Casa Grande were going to get spring training, it was going to have to pay for it without state money, which was limited to Maricopa County. City officials made what Kaites thought was an impressive proposal, and he thought they could probably pull it off with local money. But it was simply too far away, an hour or so from the west valley towns. Casa Grande, the White Sox felt, wasn't going to get them into the valley, just closer to it.

The team soon fixed on Goodyear. The White Sox signed an exclusive agreement with the city in the fall of 2005, each party agreeing to negotiate with nobody but the other for a period of ninety days. But the White Sox quickly came to have doubts about a marriage to Goodyear. Kaites explained that they were afraid that the city would have to spend too much of its future revenue to make this happen. "We were concerned that we would cripple that city by bringing the White Sox there," he said, "that they wouldn't be building city halls or fire houses or anything else. And if the regional mall didn't come in on time and if the sales tax dollars didn't come in, the project would have to be trimmed back at a time when you're already fully committed to the project.

"Jerry taught me that no deal's a good deal unless everyone wins out of it. And when we went forward to look for a city, we didn't see how—short term—Goodyear would have won. Because, short term, we would have put that city under so much financial stress."

So the White Sox let their negotiating period with Goodyear expire without a deal. That was at the end of 2005. During all this time, the Dodgers were what Kaites called an "interested participant" in the conversation, but they were not yet ready to make the leap. Goodyear knew that there was the possibility of a second team during the negotiating period. It did not know it was the Dodgers.

The Dodgers had been down this road before. Since Peter O'Malley sold the team to the Fox company in 1998, taking spring training to Arizona had been more or less a permanent agenda item around Dodger Stadium. There was always a lot of sentiment for it among the baseball people, who would have minor league and rehab facilities much closer to home, and among the staffers, who never liked being a continent away from their families and lives every February and March. There was never any one thunderbolt in the Dodgers' offices that marked the moment of decision; it came after a long, protracted, evolutionary process over a period of years, starting even before Frank McCourt's purchase of the team in 2004.

By the time Reinsdorf talked to McCourt about a spring training partnership in late 2005, the Dodgers had reached the point where they were kicking the tires on a plan to move to Arizona. "We were not going to go into the Cactus League just for the sake of it," said McCourt. "We felt we owed it to our fans to have a facility as good, if not better, than what we had at Dodgertown—I'm talking about fan amenities, the accessibility, and the charm of the whole environment. So it wasn't just a let's-move-at-all-costs kind of thing. It never got to that point. It was, hey, if we can get closer to our fan base and do that in the Phoenix area, great, so long as we have something that's special. Because we had something very very special at Dodgertown.

"It wasn't like we were rushing to get out of Vero Beach. We were very comfortable there, very very mindful of the long-term nature of the relationship, and the history and the tradition and so forth, which was very comfortable for us. It was something that, if the right opportunity presented itself, we'd consider it, and if it took another five years or ten years, so be it."

In early 2006, finally, the Dodgers felt that the White Sox had brought them the right opportunity. And there was hardly any anguish over leaving Vero Beach. "This wasn't a close call," admitted McCourt.

Though not a part of the original group responding to John Kaites's RFI, Glendale belatedly submitted a proposal for a two-team facility, with a private, ancillary development piece that could ultimately provide more than $300 million worth of shopping, hotels, restaurants, and golf courses. "We were blown away by Glendale," said Kaites, referring not just to its spring training proposal, but to what it had already done with the two much larger professional sports facilities it already had. "They are a city with five to seven times the economy of Goodyear. There's a great synergy with the freeways, and they had a blank canvas in terms of farmland."

Kaites and Reinsdorf were particularly impressed with the structure of the ancillary development piece. "They deferred the risk off on the developer for the revenue stream [to pay for this]," said Kaites. "The developer has taken most of the risk in raising the sales tax revenue to pay for the stadium. The taxpayers of Glendale put no real new money into this. They are financing off of future money from the facility, and the developer takes the risk on that." The deal was structured so that the developer, Rightpath Limited, would buy the land surrounding the complex from the city at a discount in return for a promise to develop by a certain date. If the developer does not meet the deadline, the land reverts back to the city.

The Dodgers joined the discussion in early 2006. For Jerry Reinsdorf and the White Sox, a partnership with the popular and long-sought-after Dodgers brought more than simply the potential for greater spring training earnings. In the short term, it would help to mute much of the criticism of his jumping from Tucson to the valley. There had long been a lot of concern in Arizona about using state money to deprive one Arizona town of a valued asset and give it to another. But if that were the price necessary to lure the Dodgers west?

For Frank McCourt and the Dodgers, Glendale presented the right opportunity—a city willing to listen to what the Dodgers wanted, which was essentially a transfer of the theme-park feeling of Dodgertown. The complex will include an 11,000-seat stadium with luxury boxes and other premier-seating areas, 40,000-square-foot clubhouses, and six and a half practice fields for each team, all of it dressed and appointed to the nines.

McCourt grows very animated in describing what the Dodgers are already referring to as Camelback Ranch—the name comes from the local name for the part of town where this is being built—which he knows will be a piece of his legacy, the mark he leaves on the franchise.

"The design of the facility, with the stadium on one end, and eventually the conference center on the other end, and the lake that connects the two with a beautiful park, and walking trails and bike trails and so forth going through—that sort of acts as the spine of this great facility and this great setting. And at the same time, it acts in a much more subtle way as a means to separate the two complexes, so that the White Sox can have their complex just the way they want it, with the personality and characteristics just the way they want, and we can do the same.

"It's going to be a great, great facility, physically, in terms of its amenities and its layout, but especially in the character of the place, the attention to detail, the landscaping, and of course we're still going to have that intimacy and that accessibility."

Sitting in Walter O'Malley's old office in Dodger Stadium, talking about the first mark *he* will make on Dodgers history, Frank McCourt has just described Walter O'Malley's Dodgertown.

But Walter O'Malley's Dodgertown is not today's Dodgertown. The golf courses are gone, sold and gone to weed. The upscale housing development planned for the eighteen-hole course stalled early on and has been dormant for years. A mini-town development, the mixed-use residential, commercial, and office complex that was to arise on the nine-hole Dodgertown course, also never came to fruition, and after two false starts the land reverted to the Dodgers, who eventually sold it to the city, which has been slow in finding a use for it. It has become something of an eyesore beyond the outfield fence.

Holman Stadium, meanwhile, has unbounded charm but only marginal creature comforts. Dodgertown still looks great. But it has looked better.

Dodgertown's greatest shortcoming from a modern, big-business spring training point of view is its remoteness—not so much its distance from Los Angeles, though that is a factor, but its distance from the population numbers that a modern spring training seems to need. Vero Beach is a city of fewer than 20,000 people; Indian River County has just 120,000. That is one-fortieth the population of metro Phoenix.

Dodgertown gives one the feeling of having gotten away from it all. Camelback Ranch will give one the feeling of being in the middle of it all.

John Kaites expects that, within five years, a commercial strip around the new White Sox/Dodgers complex will rival any in America:

"You will see," he said, "from 107th and Camelback, which is where our facility is, up to 99th Avenue and Northern"—Kaites is talking about a two- to three-mile, right-angle stretch of road running from the new spring training complex, past the University of Phoenix Stadium, and up to the clubs and restaurants that surround the Jobing.com Arena—"probably the greatest entertainment corridor in the world. Because of all the things that are going to pop up on what was once farmland selling at $25,000 an acre five years ago. It could become the most expensive real estate in Arizona in fifteen years. It's just that tremendous synergy as each one of these facilities builds off the other. We'll have national championship basketball games, and Fiesta Bowls, and Super Bowls and baseball and hockey and concerts, plus resorts and golf courses, retail and restaurants. The developer has this great canvas on which to paint an incredible project."

The development piece of this project is not unique. In the late 1980s, Thomas A. White built all of St. Lucie West, including an exit off I-95, around the new spring training complex for the Mets, which had been built by St. Lucie County on land donated by White. The stadium went up first, and the "Port St. Lucie" datelines in New York papers gave the project instant viability. Five years later, and seventy miles up I-95 on the outskirts of Melbourne, the agribusiness A. Duda & Sons transformed some of its farmland into the city of Viera, now the county seat of Brevard County. Like White, the Duda company started by donating land to the county, on which the county built a spring training complex for the Florida Marlins, later used by the Expos (and now by the Washington Nationals).

Both of these communities would appear to be unbridled successes. The jury is still out, however, on Abacoa, a self-contained village in the northwest corner of Jupiter, Florida, which was built around Roger Dean Stadium, the spring training home of the Cardinals and Marlins. As with St. Lucie West and Viera, baseball came first and was the catalyst for what followed. Abacoa is a planned, "new urban" community, a movie-set downtown radiating out into schools, homes, and parks. The residential piece of Abacoa has sold out as quickly as the homes have been built, with 4,000 of a proposed 6,000 homes built. The community has attracted a satellite campus of Florida Atlantic University and a major research institute that will ultimately employ 1,000 people. But downtown Abacoa—the town center—has remained a problem. A movie theater right across the street from the ballpark closed, and roughly a third of the town's forty-one storefronts were empty in the fall of 2007, seven years after the downtown opened. The original developer defaulted on his loan, and the town center has gone through three owners, including the bank, since. Moreover, the few businesses that have flourished have been bars, and this has not pleased Abacoa's wealthy residents. "If you died and went to hell, this is what you would experience," said one at a public forum in 2007 about the fights, public drunkenness, and loud music.

Residents and town officials still talk about "finding the right mix" for downtown, and they believe that Abacoa will ultimately fulfill the developer's vision of "a wonderful place where people come together." But it has not been without growing pains. Perfect spring training complexes do not always give birth to perfect communities around them, at least not right away.

Glendale foresees no such trouble. Abacoa, Glendale city manager Ed Beasley would tell you, is an example of what can happen when you don't anticipate most contingencies, as he believes Glendale has, by putting the risk on the developer. "I think what happens a lot of times is that people get tied up into the glory of the team or the sport or the opportunity, and all of a sudden they say, well, there's nothing developing around it. Well, yeah, what did you expect if you put it out there and didn't have any developer lined up?" The way Glendale has planned it, according to Beasley, is that the spring training development will complete the city's sports and entertainment district. There is nightlife by the Jobing.com Arena; hotels and office space by University of Phoenix Stadium; and the development around the ballpark will comprise what he calls a "family entertainment" district, with resorts and recreation opportunities. The city expects to realize $1 billion in direct and indirect revenue from the sports and entertainment district in the first two years following the White Sox's and Dodgers' arrival.

But if the stadium, practice fields, and clubhouses are the only things ever to rise from the Camelback Ranch soil, the White Sox and Dodgers still stand to win big. Ticket sales alone will see to that. The White Sox have averaged around 6,000 fans per game in Tucson in recent years; the Dodgers fewer than that in Vero Beach. If they both sell out in Glendale—which is particularly likely for the Dodgers, who played before sellout crowds every day during a one-week barnstorm through the Cactus League in 2008—ticket revenues alone will add more than $1 million a season to their top line. If you apply the fan cost index, a formula developed by the research group Team Marketing Report, which calculates what a family of four will spend at a ball game—including food, parking, and souvenirs—and adjust for spring training prices, it adds a minimum of $2.5 million to each team's top line. Marketing, advertising, and stadium-naming rights will all also be better for the White Sox, and markedly better for the Dodgers, in Glendale than they are in Tucson and Vero Beach. But don't suggest to Frank McCourt that this move is about money.

"I actually ran into people when I was at Dodgertown early in spring training, and people would stop me and say, 'we understand why you're going, it makes total business sense,' and after I'd heard that three or four times, I found myself actually responding: 'No, it's not a business decision. This is a decision that is in the best interests of our fans.'

"It just seemed to me that our fans were missing out on a very big part of the baseball experience. There's something very romantic and charming and hopeful about spring training, and our fans were missing it."

It is very clear that the Dodgers' talking point on the move to Glendale was that this was a move for the fans. In announcing the move to Glendale in November 2006, McCourt said it was being done "in order to bring this wonderful tradition closer to our legions of West Coast fans," and the drumbeat of this-is-for-the-fans has continued, throughout the organization, ever since.

In a one-hour conversation about the move from Vero Beach to Glendale, McCourt used a variation on the phrase "we're doing it for our fans" thirty-five times. Vero Beach was "really a challenging venue for our fans"; "our fans...were not participating in spring training"; "from the vantage point of the fan experience"; "providing our fans with the best experience in baseball"; "fans were...asking, 'are we thinking of going to the Phoenix area?'" "quite clear from the fan experience point of view"; "fans wanted spring training closer to home"; "what our fans wanted"; "owed it to our fans"; "give your fans a chance to see the big league talent"; "decision in the best interest of our fans"; "it's really all about the fans"; "get spring training closer to the fans"; "do what's right for the fans"; "ended up in a place that is perfect for our fans."

The hard sell became oversell, which meant that not everyone was buying it. "It's an economic decision, and to spin it that it's a convenience to the people in L.A., I can't agree with that," said longtime Dodgers owner Peter O'Malley. "And I'm not taking a shot at Frank McCourt here. He did it for his own good business reasons; and economically it makes all the sense in the world for Frank to go to Arizona. It's a smart economic decision that will be a big plus to the Dodgers' bottom line."

Both men, as contradictory as it may seem, are right. The move is about the fans and about the business—if you remember that another word for "fan" is "customer."

McCourt concedes that there is gold to be mined from the Arizona desert. "I'm confident it'll be great for business," he said. "But my—our—philosophy is, if we do what's best for the fans, it's good for business."

O'Malley concedes that nothing is forever, and that Dodgers tradition won't end just because Dodgertown is no more. "It was an era," he said. "Dodgertown was an era. When we owned the ball club, it was an era. That era has ended. And new eras begin. And don't say that 'oh, it's not the same,' or 'it's not as good,' or 'it will never be the same.' That's not the way to look at it. Dodgertown was a special place and a special period of time. But [there will] be others. Arizona will be great. It will be different. It will be sizzling, and all that. And it will be great."

But O'Malley is one Dodgers fan for whom the move will forever be bittersweet.

"This would never have happened on my watch," he said. "I would have found another way to make the money. I would have never left Vero Beach."

EIGHTEEN

Bottom of the Ninth in Vero Beach

The day Vero Beach believed could never arrive came on St. Patrick's Day, the day Walter O'Malley had made into a spring training national holiday. For a half-century, St. Patrick's Day had been a day of great celebration in Dodgertown; it now seemed the entirely appropriate day for an Irish wake.

That the final game should fall on the day that was most associated with the man most associated with Dodgertown was completely coincidental. This final season for the Dodgers and Vero Beach had looked star-crossed from the moment the schedule came out in the fall—doomed, it seemed, to be anticlimactic. The Dodgers in 2007 had said yes to major league baseball's invitation to travel to China in mid-March to play a pair of exhibition games against the San Diego Padres in Beijing. Fans in Florida moaned. Even though major league baseball promised that a split squad would remain behind and play games in Vero Beach, the China trip meant there would still be a hole in the middle of the spring—half the Dodger players, and probably most of the stars, would be absent for more than a week. Then the news got even worse. The original expectation was that the players and staff who'd traveled to China would return to Vero Beach to complete the spring when their midmonth trip was finished; major league baseball had drawn up a schedule with games set through the end of March. But the Major League Baseball Players' Association didn't think the China players should be asked to fly all the way back to Florida if there were major league options in Arizona, which it so happened there were; as the Dodgers would be returning from China, the Oakland Athletics would be vacating Phoenix Municipal Stadium to cross the Pacific to begin the regular season in Japan against the Red Sox. So the China Dodgers would fly from Beijing to Phoenix and the stay-behind Dodgers would leave Vero Beach on the eighteenth to join them, and the reunited team would play its last week of exhibitions as a part of the Cactus League.

It was a plan that engendered grumbling all around. Fans and city officials in Vero Beach, already feeling abandoned, were now feeling a little cheated as well. And the players' union did its members no real favors, for they, too, were inconvenienced. Major league players are used to hunkering down, generally with their families, in rented homes for the six weeks of spring training. Now, they were forced to make a series of annoying little midspring moves, a bigger inconvenience by far than simply spending a few more hours in the first-class seat of a chartered jet.

But what looked at first blush to be a lost moment turned out instead to be the perfect time to say goodbye. St. Patrick's Day is still the heart of spring training; the focus is still on the spring games. By month's end, players and fans have already mentally turned the page to the regular season. Anticipation is much too powerful a foe of reflection; looking back is too great a distraction when opening day is close enough to touch. And the Dodgers' leave-taking from Vero Beach was entitled to some reflection.

With the Dodgers' departure from Vero Beach, baseball was losing something. No sport has such a palpable connection to its past, and Dodgertown is a living part of baseball's past. Given the forthcoming closing of Yankee Stadium, there would be only three places in all of America where major league baseball has been played for longer than it had been played at Holman Stadium: Fenway Park, Wrigley Field, and Hi Corbett Field in Tucson.* The spring training complex at Vero Beach will continue to function, and baseball will still be played at Holman Stadium. But it won't be Dodgertown. When a new team arrives, the clock will begin afresh. Rickey

---

* While the Tigers have trained in Lakeland since 1934 (with only a brief break during World War II) and the Phillies in Clearwater since 1947, they've moved around within those cities and now play their exhibition games in stadiums that date to 1966 and 2004, respectively.

and O'Malley and Robinson and all the rest will forever be a part of Vero Beach's history, Dodgers' history, and baseball's history, but it will be living history no longer.

If Vero Beach and baseball lose something with the Dodgers' move to Glendale, the Dodgers lose more. Dodgertown was a tangible link to Brooklyn. "When this ends today, that all goes away," said Bill DeLury, a Brooklynite who first came to Dodgertown in 1951 to run the mail room and has been with the team ever since, most notably as the team's traveling secretary in the seventies and eighties. The Brooklyn Dodgers' history will always be Dodgers' history, but there will be a disconnect to that history now.

Dodgertown's final game was a time for tradition as well as reflection, and here again serendipity came into play. Or maybe it was Tommy Lasorda's "Big Dodger in the Sky" orchestrating a day that would give players, fans, and writers a memory and a story-telling opportunity that would prove a worthy finish to the Dodgers' six-decade run in Vero Beach.

It started with the China roster. While bringing baseball to China may have presented a lucrative marketing opportunity for major league baseball, for the 2008 Dodgers it was a major intrusion on their preparation for their season. So when the Dodgers left for China on March 13, they took manager Joe Torre, outfielders Andruw Jones and Matt Kemp, and a bunch of kids who would be spending the summer playing for Triple A Las Vegas and Double A Jacksonville. The rest of the starters, including virtually all of the pitching staff, would remain behind in Vero Beach. Vero Beach got much the better of the divided squad, after all. And it got something more. Frank McCourt, who'll never be voted man of the year in Vero Beach, gave the forsaken fans in the Dodgers' longtime spring home one final, special gift. He asked Tommy Lasorda to manage the team that would play the final games at Dodgertown. *Tommy Lasorda.* A man who reeked of baseball history and dripped of baseball sentimentality, center stage at a historic and sentimental moment. Were it not for China, were it not for the players' union vetoing a return to Florida, this could have never happened. And yet it was perfect. What an inspired choice. It would never have been the same if Joe Torre had returned to Vero Beach and retaken the reins. Joe Torre's Dodgertown lineage went back to when he'd arrived at camp just a month before. Tommy Lasorda's went back to the days of Branch Rickey.

Lasorda's role was largely ceremonial. Bench coach Bob Schaefer, pitching coach Rick Honeycutt, and third-base coach Larry Bowa would be making all the baseball decisions in Vero Beach. But for the fans who crowded into Holman Stadium during the Dodgers' final week, that mattered little. Lasorda's walk in from the right-field clubhouse to the Dodgers' bench was a Hollywood star's walk down the red carpet, cameras firing and declarations of love cascading down the foul line as he made his way to the Dodgers' bench along the third-base line. Since his retirement as manager in 1996, Lasorda had remained a Dodgertown fan favorite; in his role as special assistant to the chair, his popularity still eclipsed that of any Dodgers player.

Lasorda was a man conflicted during this final spring. From the moment the Dodgers had announced their impending move to Arizona in November 2006, Lasorda had faithfully espoused the company line: this move is good; this move is all about the fans. He was still working the practiced riff into every interview during the final week. "We're not leaving because we don't like it here," said Lasorda on the day before the final game in Vero Beach. "We're leaving because our fans can't get here. We've got the greatest fans in baseball. We had 3.8 million of 'em come to our ballpark last year. This move is going to give a lot of those fans a chance to see spring training. *That's* why he [Frank McCourt] is doing it. He's doing it for the *fans.*"

And yet nobody was more distressed about the Dodgers leaving Vero Beach than Tommy Lasorda. "My father taught me that one door will close on you and another one will open," he said. "If you're so concerned with the one that closes on you, you'll never find the one that's open." But at age eighty, Lasorda knew that there were few doors ahead, and behind this particular closing door were the memories, events, and friends from more than three-quarters of his life.

On the morning of the final game, Lasorda woke at four o'clock in Dodgertown Villa 112, the two-room suite that has been his spring home since he was first named the Dodgers' manager in 1977. He started packing, and let the memories and the thoughts wash over him. He thought of arriving at Dodgertown for the first time in 1948, a scared twenty-one-year-old pitcher who wanted to go home, intimidated even by the chow line, which stretched outside the dining hall and around the corner of the building—600 players long and him at the very end of it. He remembered watching Jackie Robinson and Duke Snider and Pee Wee Reese play pool in the Dodgertown rec room, and not quite believing his good fortune at being in the same room with these men. And being eighty years old and having been asked to manage the Dodgers one final time, he couldn't quite believe that good fortune either. And Walter O'Malley and the St. Patrick's Day parties that had lasted long into the morning—*those were some swell parties we had*. And the memorial mass the day before, another Dodgertown tradition, started by Kay O'Malley in the mid-sixties to remember those members of the Dodgers family who had died during the preceding year. And of St. Helen's Church, where he'd attended mass during all those spring trainings, and all of the friends—*all these wonderful friends of mine*—that he'd made at St. Helen's. Would he ever see these people again? Would he ever again have cause or occasion to return to Vero Beach? Would he ever again see Dodgertown after tomorrow? He was doubtful. *I'll probably never come back here.* He thought about tomorrow, and how he was going to feel when the bus pulled away from Dodgertown for the final time. If he was this blue today, how was he going to handle tomorrow?

"I wasn't tired, but I felt like I was tired, because of what I was going to go through," he later said of his early morning mood.

Tommy Lasorda never once said he'd rather stay in Vero Beach than move to Glendale. He would never so betray the organization. And he didn't need to say it. His feelings were quite clear in the things he did say. "Let's hope that I get the same feeling out of Arizona that I have here," he said just before walking onto the Holman Stadium field for the final time.

The Dodgers' final spring game at Holman Stadium drew more fans than had the Brooklyn Dodgers' final game at Ebbets Field: 7,327 to 6,673. Fans started arriving before eight in the morning, ahead of the players, at about the same time that National Public Radio's *Morning Edition* was running its homage to Dodgertown. A columnist for the Vero Beach newspaper counted license plates from thirty-five states, the District of Columbia, and three Canadian provinces. The fans bought green St. Patrick's Day hats and jerseys and T-shirts with the Dodgertown 60th Anniversary logo. They searched in vain for merchandise that marked Dodgertown's final season, or Holman Stadium's final Dodgers game, for there was none. With the Glendale complex still nothing more than graded earth with some surveyors' stakes in the ground when this spring training began, there was still the chance that the Dodgers could return in 2009. It would be an awkward and anticlimactic return; and should it happen, having final-season merchandise from the next-to-final season would only compound the embarrassment. In this case at least, it was better to leave a few dollars on the table.

Most fans seemed to want a picture of themselves in front of one of the many Dodgertown signs, or in the stands behind home plate, with Holman Stadium's field in the background. There will never be another spring training complex like this, they seemed to feel. Some fans apparently contemplated taking a piece of Dodgertown home with them. One asked some groundskeepers if he could borrow a wrench. Stadium security spent the final innings scanning the crowd like Secret Service agents, looking for potential looters. On Sunday, 150 baseballs had been stolen from a minor league equipment shed.

Reporters from across the land descended upon the final-day fans, coaxing quotation pearls from white-haired men and women with Brooklyn roots; from lifelong Vero Beach residents who remembered missing school as a kid to watch the Dodgers; and even from pilgrims from California who'd felt a need to see Dodgertown before its end. All expressed regret at Dodgertown's passing; some expressed understanding at why it must be; a few vowed to follow the Dodgers to Glendale, at least in the first year, at least for a game or two. The Dodgers wore their green hats and brought out the green bases in honor of St. Patrick's Day. After the game, there was a reception on the pool terrace for the Dodgers family and for city and county officials. Nothing like the old days, but still, a nod to tradition.

Perhaps the most poignant detail of the entire day was the presence of Carl Erskine. Brooklyn's steadiest pitcher during their final, halcyon days, Erskine won 122 games in his thirteen-year Dodgers career. He was also the dedication-day pitcher at Holman Stadium on March 11, 1953, when the Dodgers christened their new spring stadium by beating the Philadelphia Athletics, 4–2. He has home movies of that day. He remembered the overflow, exuberant crowd, just as on this final day; he remembered the pregame ceremony and the plaque dedicating the stadium to Bud Holman. He remembered getting a base hit, a single up the middle. Pitchers always remember their base hits. And he remembers A's owner Connie Mack, who'd just turned ninety, and though no longer the Athletics' manager, still sitting on the open-air, unprotected bench. Few members of the Dodgers family have laid their head down upon a Dodgertown pillow for more nights than Carl Erskine. "I'm wed to Dodgertown," he said. For the last twenty-five years, he'd been a regular at the Dodgers' fantasy camp, and at the camp-ending players-coaches game in Holman Stadium, Erskine had always played the national anthem on his harmonica, and Nancy Gollnick, who ran the fantasy camps, asked him to do the same for the final game. Erskine's national anthem was as polished and as poised as his performances on the mound had been fifty-five years earlier.

Erskine's link to the beginnings of Dodgertown was lost on few of the fans at Holman Stadium that day. What most of those fans could not have realized was that his presence actually brought them back much, much further. Erskine connected everyone there to Holman's first day. Through Erskine, everyone there was also connected to Connie Mack, who had not only been at Vero Beach on Holman's first day, but was there in March 1888, when Ted Sullivan brought major league spring training to Florida for the first time.

Game time temperature was seventy-six degrees with a few puffy white clouds and a twenty-five-mile-per-hour wind blowing from home plate out toward left. A day for home runs; there would be eight of them before the day was through. Lasorda addressed the crowd before the start of the game, and if it wasn't exactly Lou Gehrig telling the Yankee Stadium fans that he was the luckiest man on the face of the earth, it nonetheless had emotion and charm. "You're going to make me cry," said Lasorda, trying to quiet the crowd following a thirty-second standing ovation.

Early in the game, the fans behind the first-base dugout began a familiar rhythmic ballpark chant, with a final-day twist.

"Don't go, Dodgers!"

Thump. Thump. Thump thump thump.

"Don't go, Dodgers!"

Thump. Thump. Thump thump thump.

The cheer elicited some boos from fans who misinterpreted the cheerers' intent, thinking they were wishing the Dodgers ill instead of exhorting them not to go to Arizona. Explanations were rendered and accepted, and the chastened boo-ers joined in. But a cheer that has to be explained cannot be good, and everyone soon lost interest. There was exhaustion in the crowd on this afternoon, a disconnect between game and emotion. As the Dodgers' time in Vero Beach grew shorter, the skies grew darker. By the close of the sixth inning, the skies were completely overcast and the Dodgers trailed the Houston Astros 10–5. Then, the breeze blew the clouds out as quickly as it had blown them in, and by the eighth inning the skies were sunny again. The

Dodgers had started to rally. The Dodger players had never given up on this game. They were sharing the bench this day with a Hall of Fame manager and a Brooklyn Dodgers legacy who went back to Dodgertown's beginnings. And even though these Dodgers had only a limited connection to that history themselves—nobody on the current Dodgers roster had more than five springs at Dodgertown—they understood that this was a spring training game set apart. So, the Dodgers' starters stuck around, a half-dozen of them either in the lineup or on the bench when the ninth inning began—unheard of in a midmonth spring game.

The Dodgers came to bat in the bottom of the ninth trailing 12–9, but the park was alive with possibility. The fans were no longer mourners at a wake; they were once again baseball fans, willing their team to rally.

"Let's go, Dodgers!"

Thump. Thump. Thump thump thump.

Prospects Delwyn Young and Blake Dewitt opened the inning with walks off journeyman major leaguer Stephen Randolph, raising the energy level noticeably in Holman Stadium. Astros manager Cecil Cooper yanked Randolph and brought in Triple A prospect Carlos Hines. First up against Hines was pinch hitter Russell Martin, the Dodgers' young all-star catcher, the emerging team leader, who was not scheduled to play this day but was one of those Dodger regulars who'd felt compelled to stay on the bench all game. Alas, Martin would strike out, and pinch hitter Anthony Raglani, who'd played in Double A Jacksonville in the previous year, would then fly to center. Two down.

That brought up Preston Mattingly, the son of former Yankee great and current Dodger coach Don Mattingly. The inning before, in his first at-bat with the big club this spring, Mattingly had homered. This time, he sent Hines's 1–2 pitch sharply back up the middle. The ball hopped over shortstop Edwin Maysonet's glove into left center, scoring Young, sending Dewitt to second, and making it 12–10 Astros. There was a bit of discussion in the press box on whether to score the ball a hit or an error. The call went E-6.

Hit or error? Didn't matter in the stands. Few likely even noticed when the scoreboard flashed the error signal. Holman was filled with noise now. Old-fashioned, soul-warming, rally-soundtrack noise. What is that wonderful Roger Angell quote about baseball and time? "Since baseball time is measured only in outs, all you have to do is succeed utterly; keep hitting, keep the rally alive, and you have defeated time." Keep the rally alive, and Dodgers spring training will live. For one batter more, for one inning more.

"Let's go, Dodgers!"

Thump. Thump. Thump thump thump.

James Tomlin, pinch hitting for pitcher Mike Myers, was next. Hines's first two pitches were low, 2–0, and catcher Josh Johnson went to visit his pitcher on the mound. The next pitch was also low, ball three; the one after that was outside, and the bases were loaded.

Now, it seemed inevitable. The Dodgers were going to win this final game, send Tommy Lasorda out a winner, send the Dodgers fans in Vero Beach home with one final memory. What a sweet way to go. And look who was up. Rafael Furcal. Another all-star who was still there in the ninth inning. Furcal, who'd tripled twice and homered already today. Surely, this moment was the reason he had stayed in the game. So that he could finish off an offensive day that would never count but would also never be forgotten.

Hines's first pitch was a strike on the outside corner, followed by a ball high and away. Seven thousand fans urged Furcal on to final-day destiny. Whatever was about to happen, Holman Stadium was going out noisy and full of life. In its final moments, it was what it had always been in its best moments. No museum, no shrine. This was a ballpark.

Furcal grounded the 1–1 pitch to second. Astros second baseman Danny Klassen picked it up, threw to first, and just like that, it was over. And the air went out of Holman Stadium. After sixty years, it ends with a grounder to second? This can't be right. History, destiny, not to mention 7,000 fans, demanded that this final rally succeed. Surely, something so protracted and so grand had not ended this suddenly and this ingloriously?

But it had, and it was right. For this was not a happy day, and there should not be any happy events intruding upon the melancholy.

"Go Team, Go!"

Spring training is tastiest in small portions. The writers who wax most rhapsodic about the spiritual and rejuvenating powers of spring training are the columnists and magazine writers who come in for a week or so at a time, absorb just the right quotient of sunshine, and then retreat to worship from afar. The beat writers, who are in that sun every day for a month and a half, harbor no such illusions. They X out the days on the calendar like a prisoner awaiting parole.

The vacationers, down for a week—time enough for a half-dozen games—return home with tans and stories enough to make them the center of conversations all year long. The team employees, away from home and family for six long weeks, and the local stadium staff, working an unbroken string of seven-day weeks, grow weary of the monotony and yearn for the start of the regular season for reasons that have little to do with baseball.

For fans, the six weeks of spring training are one big movable and continuing feast. For the players, baseball staffers, and writers, spring training is broken into three parts. The most enjoyable time comes before the exhibition games start—a week for the position players and two weeks for pitchers and catchers. The players' days are short, the season is new, and there is little to complain about. The scouts, coaches, general managers, and the baseball operations staff simply watch and absorb. There are no decisions to be made yet on who stays with the big club, who goes to Triple A, or who gets placed on waivers. At the beginning of camp, all the holes—theoretically, at least—are filled. The roster—carefully built over the winter—is perfect right now. Now is the time to watch with fresh eyes and enjoy, storing everything for future discussions. For the writers, so early in camp, every story is fresh and new. The arrival of another regular in camp—almost a daily occurrence—is another feature story. The manager's daily press scrums are relevant, because his first impressions of new players are news.

The second phase of spring training comes when the exhibition games begin. For the veteran players, the early games are a time of getting one's baseball legs again, a time to settle into the day-in, day-out rhythm of the baseball life. For a pitcher, it's a time for "just getting his work in." Long ago, managers selected the opening day starting pitcher based on spring training performance. No more. The opening day starter is most likely determined before camp begins; managers and pitching coaches don't want starting pitchers trying to prove anything in spring training; they want simply to get them on a schedule that will gradually build up their pitch count and arm strength. By the start of the exhibition season, pitchers are working on regular rotation, every five days for the starters, and if there's a rainout or an off-day, they'll throw a simulated game in the cage or pitch in a minor league, or even an intersquad, game. During these early games, a pitcher's job might actually be less about getting opposing hitters out than about working on something specific—maybe throwing the change-up in a fastball count, throwing that new pitch in a game situation often enough to develop confidence in it—getting his work in.

For the baseball operations staff, these early games are a time to look critically at what's working and what's not, and to begin talking in general terms about the decisions that will have to be made in a couple of weeks. Not a lot of pressure yet, but the mood is no longer what anyone would call relaxed. The writers begin struggling to find story angles that are fresh, but the start of games at least allows for observation and reporting on performance, not merely promise.

St. Patrick's Day is a line of demarcation. Presidents' Day comes near the beginning of spring training, and Easter sometimes comes near the end, but St. Patrick's Day is spring training's big holiday. Walter O'Malley of the Dodgers saw it as a way to celebrate both his Irish heritage and the midway point in spring training, and St. Patrick's Day parties at Dodgertown became legendary. But it is actually the Cincinnati Reds who came to define the

St. Patrick's Day spring training celebration. In 1978, the Reds took to the field on March 17 with green on their uniforms wherever there was supposed to be red—caps, stockings, numbers, the chest logo with the word "Reds" inside the big C. It was a sensation; the actual uniforms were auctioned for charity and have now become an expensive baseball collectible; one was on display in the Hall of Fame for years. It did not take long for major league baseball teams to realize there was commercial potential here. Now, almost every team wears a green hat or a green uniform jersey on St. Patrick's Day, and so, too, do a lot of the fans. St. Patrick's Day jerseys and caps are among the spring training souvenir stands' biggest sellers.

In the business office, St. Patrick's Day—the midpoint of the exhibition games—is the time to begin tallying the ledgers. By this point in the preseason, there should be a good sense of what the profits will be. "You do 40 percent of your attendance [in] the first two weeks of games," said Robert Brinton of the Mesa Convention and Visitors Bureau and the Mesa HoHoKams, "60 percent over the last two weeks." Counting the money may take more time these days than it ever did before—most teams will net $1 million or more—but it is hardly a new spring training phenomenon. In fact, it sometimes took on great urgency in the past. As late as the 1970s, White Sox general manager Roland Hemond was selling players to other teams at the end of the preseason in order to pay the spring training bills.

St. Patrick's Day is also an important benchmark from a baseball standpoint. Historically, March 17 was the halfway point of the preseason. Now, with opening day pushed up from mid-April to early April, St. Patrick's Day marks the start of crunch time. Two weeks to go. The fans' excitement quickens, for the starters start to stretch it out a bit. You may see a starting pitcher go six or seven innings and a position player get four at-bats. The anonymity of the lineups lessens as you get deeper into March.

The last two weeks of spring training are the busiest and most important time of the entire year for the baseball operations staff, for this is when the team is actually formed. The late March days stretch deep into the evening for the baseball ops people; the roster must be cut from the fifty or sixty players who started camp down to the twenty-five who will comprise the team on opening day. The days are filled with questions that must have answers. Who gets that last spot on the bench? How many pitchers do we need for our April schedule? ten? eleven? twelve? What players have minor league options left that will give us flexibility in the fluid early weeks of the season? Who goes on the disabled list? Who's on the waiver wire that might help? Which of our veterans can we use at Triple A, and which ones should we maybe look to place on waivers?

For the players on the bubble, the last two weeks are a time of great anxiety. Nothing moves more slowly in spring training than a player who's just been cut and must leave the major league locker room, with its major league spreads and major league per diem, and move his person and his stuff to the minor league locker room—a move that is sometimes just across the hall, sometimes across the camp, sometimes across town, and sometimes, as in the case of the Baltimore Orioles since the 1990s, all the way across the state, from Fort Lauderdale to Sarasota.

For the veteran players assured of their places on the team and for the writers, St. Patrick's Day is when the ennui settles in. Make no mistake: for the players those baseball ops people are talking about in late March—the pitchers fighting for the last two spots in the bullpen, the utility guys looking to score that last spot on the bench—the last two weeks of camp are everything. But these players number no more than a half-dozen in any camp, and they are fighting for generally no more than two or three unclaimed roster spots. For the rest of the players, the final two weeks are spent marking time and hoping that this still rather long stretch of meaningless games won't bring injury. Let's be careful out there. Don't wanna get hit by any kid pitcher's ninety-seven-mile-per-hour, directionally challenged fastball. Don't do anything stupid. Remember Billy Martin back in '52? Joe DiMaggio was down at the Yankees' camp in St. Pete doing some television work and asked Billy to slide into second for the cameras. Head first or feet first, Billy asked, eager to please. Don't matter, said Joe. So Billy went running into second, unsure of what would look better on camera, still unsure when he slid awkwardly and snapped his ankle. Missed half a season.

The games—for players, uniformed staff, and writers—take on a deadening absence of purpose. "I am so sick of these games," complained a veteran baseball writer late one spring training, knowing that he'd already written everything there was to be written from this particular camp, but knowing he still had to file another 1,500 words of copy that night, and for another seven or eight nights more before the regular season began.

"Who are we playing tomorrow?" Red Sox manager Terry Francona asked reporters in late spring 2008. It didn't matter. Home game or bus ride; that's all anyone needs to know about the spring training schedule.

To hear players talk, you would think the buses had racks and thumb screws instead of reclining seats and on-board movies. Bus rides are the bane of the spring training player. Lost time, players and coaches will tell you. Could be back at camp, taking batting practice, or working in the weight room. Perhaps they are so hated because bus rides take a big leaguer back to his minor league days—a place no big leaguer ever wants to go. Perhaps there are no hidden reasons at all. The bus rides are disliked because they are long and they are boring, and they take place, on average, every other day.

For the Red Sox, the Twins, and the Orioles, down in the Grapefruit League's lowest latitudes, the bus ride for a 1 p.m. game can begin as early as 7:30 in the morning; the ride home might not end until twelve hours later. And virtually every game is a day trip. Sometimes, a team shifting coasts in Florida, or traveling from Tucson to Phoenix, might spend one night away. The Red Sox's chief operating officer, Mike Dee, talks about a coming day when there might be spring training road trips. The Red Sox, he says, could bus up to Orlando and stay for three days, playing the Braves, the Astros, and the Tigers, and get three road games out of the way with one bus ride. But that plan is not without its problems. It commits a player to playing three straight preseason games, which regulars rarely do, and keeps him from doing any additional work back at camp. So for now, it's on the bus in the morning, back on the bus in the afternoon.

And the view out the window is as drab as it is familiar. The interstates connecting many spring training cities in Florida are almost always choked with traffic, major league traffic—New York, D.C., Chicago, L.A. kind of traffic. And while they run parallel to some of the most beautiful real estate in America, the Atlantic Ocean and the Gulf of Mexico never come into view. Instead, there are jumbles of big-box stores and fast food restaurants clustered around each exit, with vast tracts of scrub palm and empty land in between.

The center of the state below I-4 is a Florida few tourists see, home to the sprawling phosphate mines near Bartow and nearly 10 million acres of fruit and vegetable farms and cattle ranches. Who knew that Florida, the land of beaches and beachfront condos, theme parks and retirement communities, is still one of America's top agricultural producers and is ranked in the top ten in beef production? Do the players, within the cocoon of their bus, and within the inner cocoons of their iPods, Wiis, cell phones, and laptops, even notice? And what is any of it to a twenty-year-old pitcher traveling from Fort Myers to Port St. Lucie to pitch in his very first major league spring training game?

In Arizona, too, where the distances between stadiums are much shorter, travel is still a nuisance, for I-10 and the loop roads around Phoenix can be numbingly choked with traffic even during a midmorning ride to the game; they are virtually certain to be traffic clogged on the rush-hour ride home. The view from the road between Tucson and the valley, meanwhile, is stunning in its beauty, the desert vista largely unsullied by development, the distinctive outline of Picacho Peak—a landmark for desert explorers centuries ago—dominating the horizon for the first half of the ride, both coming and going. But what is it to gaze upon land that is unchanged from the time when ancient tribes gazed upon it centuries ago if you're hitting just .190 and there is only a week of spring left?

Few lament the end of spring training. There is little like it in the American experience, something whose beginning is awaited impatiently and greeted eagerly each year, yet whose demise is met with indifference, relief, even glee. Any baseball player or fan will tell you: as good as spring training is, it's easily trumped by opening day. "The funny thing about spring training, I find, is that starting the day after the season, spring training is the most important thing in the world," said Charles Steinberg, the Dodgers' vice president of marketing and public relations and a man who can sell the romance of baseball as effectively as anyone who ever lived. "You count the days, you literally count the days, until pitchers and catchers report. Invariably, on the last day of the season, we put up on the scoreboard how many days until spring training starts. Also invariably, in my experience, the day after spring training, you don't think of it again until the end of the season."

The last day of spring training looks a bit like a refugee camp, if refugees traveled first class. A mountain of luggage gets lined up outside the clubhouse—equipment trunks, player duffels, and front office files, but also cribs, strollers, golf clubs, and bicycles—as baseball makes ready to go home. On the final day of the 2006 spring training season, Jeff Maultsby, a bearish, gregarious man, and at the time the Cincinnati Reds' director of Florida operations, greeted everyone he bumped into with a boisterous "Go team, go!" It was a good-natured double entendre: good luck on the championship quest ahead, and goodbye for another year; it'll be nice to get our lives back to normal around here.

"Spring training is what we work for most of the year," he said. "It is the time of year we look forward to the most. But at the end, you have mixed emotions. There's a bit of sadness, in the sense that your friends in the organization are leaving you for another year. But it's certainly an opportunity for us to kind of catch our breaths collectively and say, whew, we got through it. It's seven days a week and it's a lot of hours per day. But it's what we signed up for; it's what we love.

"We love it. But we like getting through it too."

After the teams leave, spring training cities take on the feel of college campuses in the summertime, and it is a long, hot summer in Florida and Arizona. They each have their own professional teams now, of course. Yet while there is comfort in that, it is different. It is reality, the day-to-day ebb and flow of life, where things like bills and appointments and the some-times-cruel accounting of won-lost records cannot be ignored. It is different in the spring, a time of hope and the suspension of care, a holiday celebra-tion, when company's come to call. And when it's over, while there may be relief and the wish to take a nap, there is an emptiness as well, a sense that something special has gone and will not return for some time. But it will return.

Pitchers and catchers report in just 320 days.

APPENDIX

Major League Baseball Spring Training Sites, 1901–Present

National League

Arizona Diamondbacks

1998–	Tucson, Ariz.

Atlanta Braves (includes Boston 1901–1952
and Milwaukee 1953–1965)

1901	Norfolk, Va.
1902–1904	Thomasville, Ga.
1905	Charleston, S.C.
1906	Jacksonville, Fla.
1907	Thomasville, Ga.
1908–1912	Augusta, Ga.
1913	Athens, Ga.

Appendix source: mlb.com/pressbox/events/spring_training (accessed August 10, 2008)

1914–1915	Macon, Ga.
1916–1918	Miami, Fla.
1919–1920	Columbus, Ga.
1921	Galveston, Tex.
1922–1937	St. Petersburg, Fla.
1938–1940	Bradenton, Fla.
1941	San Antonio, Tex.
1942	Sanford, Fla.
1943–1944	Wallingford, Conn.
1945	Washington, D.C.
1946–1947	Ft. Lauderdale, Fla.
1948–1962	Bradenton, Fla.
1963–1997	West Palm Beach, Fla.
1998–	Lake Buena Vista, Fla.

Chicago Cubs

1901–1902	Champaign, Ill.
1903–1904	Los Angeles, Calif.
1905	Santa Monica, Calif.
1906	Champaign, Ill.
1907	New Orleans, La.
1908	Vicksburg, Miss.
1909–1910	Hot Springs, Ark.
1911–1912	New Orleans, La.
1913–1916	Tampa, Fla.
1917–1921	Pasadena, Calif.
1922–1942	Catalina Island, Calif.
1943–1945	French Lick, Ind.
1946–1947	Catalina Island, Calif.
1948–1949	Los Angeles, Calif.
1950–1951	Catalina Island, Calif.
1952–1965	Mesa, Ariz.
1966	Long Beach, Calif.
1967–1978	Scottsdale, Ariz.
1979–	Mesa, Ariz.

Cincinnati Reds

1901–1902	Cincinnati, Ohio
1903	Augusta, Ga.
1904	Dallas, Tex.

1905	Jacksonville, Fla.
1906	San Antonio, Tex.
1907	Marlin Springs, Tex.
1908	St. Augustine, Tex.
1909	Atlanta, Ga.
1910–1911	Hot Springs, Ark.
1912	Columbus, Ga.
1913	Mobile, Ala.
1914–1915	Alexandria, La.
1916–1917	Shreveport, La.
1918	Montgomery, Ala.
1919	Waxahachie, Tex.
1920	Miami, Fla.
1921	Cisco, Tex.
1922	Mineral Wells, Tex.
1923–1930	Orlando, Fla.
1931–1942	Tampa, Fla.
1943–1945	Bloomington, Ind.
1946–1987	Tampa, Fla.
1988–1997	Plant City, Fla.
1998–	Sarasota, Fla.

Colorado Rockies

1993–	Tucson, Ariz.

Florida Marlins

1993–2002	Viera, Fla.
2003–	Jupiter, Fla.

Houston Astros

1962–1963	Apache Junction, Ariz.
1964–1984	Cocoa Beach, Fla.
1985–	Kissimmee, Fla.

Los Angeles Dodgers (includes Brooklyn 1901–1957)

1901	Charlotte, N.C.
1902–1906	Columbia, S.C.
1907–1909	Jacksonville, Fla.
1910–1912	Hot Springs, Ark.

1913–1914	Augusta, Ga.
1915–1916	Daytona Beach, Fla.
1917–1918	Hot Springs, Ark.
1919–1920	Jacksonville, Fla.
1921	New Orleans, La.
1922	Jacksonville, Fla.
1923–1932	Clearwater, Fla.
1933	Miami, Fla.
1934–1935	Orlando, Fla.
1936–1940	Clearwater, Fla.
1941–1942	Havana, Cuba
1943–1945	Bear Mountain, N.Y.
1946	Daytona Beach, Fla.
1947	Havana, Cuba
1948	Ciudad Trujillo, D.R.
1949–2008	Vero Beach, Fla.
2009–	Glendale, Ariz.

Milwaukee Brewers (includes Seattle Pilots 1969)

1969–1972	Tempe, Ariz.
1973–1985	Sun City, Ariz.
1986–1997	Chandler, Ariz.
1998–	Maryvale, Ariz.

New York Mets

| 1962–1987 | St. Petersburg, Fla. |
| 1988– | Port St. Lucie, Fla. |

Philadelphia Phillies

1901	Philadelphia, Pa.
1902	Washington, N.C.
1903	Richmond, Va.
1904	Savannah, Ga.
1905	Augusta, Ga.
1906–1908	Savannah, Ga.
1909–1910	Southern Pines, N.C.
1911	Birmingham, Ala.
1912	Hot Springs, Ark.
1913	Southern Pines, N.C.

1914	Wilmington, N.C.
1915–1918	St. Petersburg, Fla.
1919	Charlotte, N.C.
1920	Birmingham, Ala.
1921	Gainesville, Fla.
1922–1924	Leesburg, Fla.
1925–1927	Bradenton, Fla.
1928–1937	Winter Haven, Fla.
1938	Biloxi, Miss.
1939	New Braunfels, Tex.
1940–1942	Miami Beach, Fla.
1943	Hershey, Pa.
1944–1945	Wilmington, Del.
1946	Miami Beach, Fla.
1947–	Clearwater, Fla.

Pittsburgh Pirates

1901–1916	Hot Springs, Ark.
1917	Columbus, Ga.
1918	Jacksonville, Fla.
1919	Birmingham, Ala.
1920–1923	Hot Springs, Ark.
1924–1934	Paso Robles, Calif.
1935	San Bernardino, Calif.
1936	San Antonio, Tex.
1937–1942	San Bernardino, Calif.
1943–1945	Muncie, Ind.
1946	San Bernardino, Calif.
1947	Miami Beach, Fla.
1948	Hollywood, Calif.
1949–1952	San Bernardino, Calif.
1953	Havana, Cuba
1954	Fort Pierce, Fla.
1955–1968	Fort Myers, Fla.
1969–	Bradenton, Fla.

St. Louis Cardinals

1901–1902	St. Louis, Mo.
1903	Dallas, Tex.
1904	Houston, Tex.

1905	Marlin Springs, Tex.
1906–1908	Houston, Tex.
1909–1910	Little Rock, Ark.
1911	West Baden, Ind.
1912	Jackson, Miss.
1913	Columbus, Ga.
1914	St. Augustine, Fla.
1915–1917	Hot Wells, Tex.
1918	San Antonio, Tex.
1919	St. Louis, Mo.
1920	Brownsville, Tex.
1921–1922	Orange, Tex.
1923–1924	Bradenton, Fla.
1925	Stockton, Calif.
1926	San Antonio, Tex.
1927–1929	Avon Park, Fla.
1930–1936	Bradenton, Fla.
1937	Daytona Beach, Fla.
1938–1942	St. Petersburg, Fla.
1943–1945	Cairo, Ill.
1946–1997	St. Petersburg, Fla.
1998–	Jupiter, Fla.

San Diego Padres

1969–1993	Yuma, Ariz.
1994–	Peoria, Ariz.

San Francisco Giants (includes New York 1901–1957)

1901–1902	New York, N.Y.
1903–1905	Savannah, Ga.
1906	Memphis, Tenn.
1907	Los Angeles, Calif.
1908–1918	Marlin Springs, Tex.
1919	Gainesville, Fla.
1920–1923	San Antonio, Tex.
1924–1927	Sarasota, Fla.
1928	Augusta, Ga.
1929–1931	San Antonio, Tex.
1932–1933	Los Angeles, Calif.

1934–1935	Miami Beach, Fla.
1936	Pensacola, Fla.
1937	Havana, Cuba
1938–1939	Baton Rouge, La.
1940	Winter Haven, Fla.
1941–1942	Miami, Fla.
1943–1945	Lakewood, N.J.
1946	Miami, Fla.
1947–1950	Phoenix, Ariz.
1951	St. Petersburg, Fla.
1952–1983	Phoenix, Ariz.
1984–	Scottsdale, Ariz.

Washington Nationals (includes Montreal Expos 1969–2004)

1969–1972	West Palm Beach, Fla.
1973–1980	Daytona Beach, Fla.
1981–1997	West Palm Beach, Fla.
1998–2002	Jupiter, Fla.
2003–	Viera, Fla.

American League

Baltimore Orioles (includes St. Louis Browns 1901–1954)

1901	St. Louis, Mo.
1902	French Lick, Ind.
1903	Baton Rouge, La.
1904	Corsicana, Tex.
1905–1906	Dallas, Tex.
1907	San Antonio, Tex.
1908	Shreveport, La.
1909–1910	Houston, Tex.
1911	Hot Springs, Ark.
1912	Montgomery, Ala.
1913	Waco, Tex.
1914	St. Petersburg, Fla.
1915	Houston, Tex.
1916–1917	Palestine, Tex.
1918	Shreveport, La.
1919	San Antonio, Tex.

1920	Taylor, Ala.
1921	Bogalusa, Ala.
1922–1924	Mobile, Ala.
1925–1927	Tarpon Springs, Fla.
1928–1936	West Palm Beach, Fla.
1937–1941	San Antonio, Tex.
1942	Deland, Fla.
1943–1945	Cape Girardeau, Mo.
1946	Anaheim, Calif.
1947	Miami, Fla.
1948	San Bernardino, Calif.
1949–1952	Burbank, Calif.
1953	San Bernardino, Calif.
1954	Yuma, Ariz.
1955	Daytona Beach, Fla.
1956–1958	Scottsdale, Ariz.
1959–1988	Miami, Fla.
1989–1990	Miami/Sarasota, Fla.
1991	Sarasota, Fla.
1992–1995	St. Petersburg, Fla.
1996–	Ft. Lauderdale, Fla.

Boston Red Sox

1901	Charlottesville, Va.
1902	Augusta, Ga.
1903–1906	Macon, Ga.
1907–1908	Little Rock, Ark.
1909–1910	Hot Springs, Ark.
1911	Redondo Beach, Calif.
1912–1918	Hot Springs, Ark.
1919	Tampa, Fla.
1920–1923	Hot Springs, Ark.
1924	San Antonio, Tex.
1925–1927	New Orleans, La.
1928–1929	Bradenton, Fla.
1930–1931	Pensacola, Fla.
1932	Savannah, Ga.
1933–1942	Sarasota, Fla.
1943–1944	Medford, Mass.
1945	Atlantic City, N.J.

1946–1958	Sarasota, Fla.
1959–1965	Scottsdale, Ariz.
1966–1992	Winter Haven, Fla.
1993–	Fort Myers, Fla.

Chicago White Sox

1901–1902	Excelsior Springs, Mo.
1903	Mobile, Ala.
1904	Marlin Springs, Tex.
1905–1906	New Orleans, La.
1907	Mexico City, Mexico
1908	Los Angeles, Calif.
1909–1910	San Francisco, Calif.
1911	Mineral Wells, Tex.
1912	Waco, Tex.
1913–1915	Paso Robles, Calif.
1916–1919	Mineral Wells, Tex.
1920	Waco, Tex.
1921	Waxahachie, Tex.
1922–1923	Seguin, Tex.
1924	Winter Haven, Fla.
1925–1928	Shreveport, La.
1929	Dallas, Tex.
1930–1932	San Antonio, Tex.
1933–1942	Pasadena, Calif.
1943–1944	French Lick, Ind.
1945	Terre Haute, Ind.
1946–1950	Pasadena, Calif.
1951	Palm Springs, Calif.
1952–1953	El Centro, Calif.
1954–1959	Tampa, Fla.
1960–1997	Sarasota, Fla.
1998–	Tucson, Ariz.

Cleveland Indians

1901	Cleveland, Ohio
1902–1903	New Orleans, La.
1904	San Antonio, Tex.

1905–1906	Atlanta, Ga.
1907–1908	Macon, Ga.
1909	Mobile, Ala.
1910–1911	Alexandria, La.
1912	Mobile, Ala.
1913	Pensacola, Fla.
1914	Athens, Ga.
1915	San Antonio, Tex.
1916–1920	New Orleans, La.
1921–1922	Dallas, Tex.
1923–1927	Lakeland, Fla.
1928–1939	New Orleans, La.
1940–1941	Fort Myers, Fla.
1942	Clearwater, Fla.
1943–1945	Lafayette, Ind.
1946	Clearwater, Fla.
1947–1992	Tucson, Ariz.
1993–2008	Winter Haven, Fla.
2009–	Goodyear, Ariz.

Detroit Tigers

1901	Detroit, Mich.
1902	Ypsilanti, Mich.
1903–1904	Shreveport, La.
1905–1907	Augusta, Ga.
1908	Hot Springs, Ark.
1909–1910	San Antonio, Tex.
1911–1912	Monroe, La.
1913–1915	Gulfport, Miss.
1916–1918	Waxahachie, Tex.
1919–1920	Macon, Ga.
1921	San Antonio, Tex.
1922–1926	Augusta, Ga.
1927–1928	San Antonio, Tex.
1929	Phoenix, Ariz.
1930	Tampa, Fla.
1931	Sacramento, Calif.
1932	Palo Alto, Calif.
1933	San Antonio, Tex.

1934–1942	Lakeland, Fla.
1943–1945	Evansville, Ind.
1946–	Lakeland, Fla.

Kansas City Royals

1969–1987	Fort Myers, Fla.
1988–2002	Baseball City, Fla.
2003–	Surprise, Ariz.

Los Angeles Angels

| 1961–1992 | Palm Springs, Calif. |
| 1993– | Tempe, Ariz. |

Minnesota Twins (includes Washington Senators 1901–1960)

1901	Phoebus, Va.
1902–1904	Washington, D.C.
1905	Hampton, Va.
1906	Charlottesville, Va.
1907–1909	Galveston, Tex.
1910	Norfolk, Va.
1911	Atlanta, Ga.
1912–1916	Charlottesville, Va.
1917	Atlanta, Ga.
1918–1919	Augusta, Ga.
1920–1929	Tampa, Fla.
1930–1935	Biloxi, Miss.
1936–1942	Orlando, Fla.
1943–1945	College Park, Md.
1946–1990	Orlando, Fla.
1991–	Fort Myers, Fla.

New York Yankees

1901	Baltimore, Md.
1902	Savannah, Ga.
1903–1904	Atlanta, Ga.
1905	Montgomery, Ala.
1906	Birmingham, Ala.

1907–1908	Atlanta, Ga.
1909	Macon, Ga.
1910–1911	Athens, Ga.
1912	Atlanta, Ga.
1913	Hamilton, Bermuda
1914	Houston, Tex.
1915	Savannah, Ga.
1916–1918	Macon, Ga.
1919–1920	Jacksonville, Fla.
1921	Shreveport, La.
1922–1924	New Orleans, La.
1925–1942	St. Petersburg, Fla.
1943	Asbury Park, N.J.
1944–1945	Atlantic City, N.J.
1946–1950	St. Petersburg, Fla.
1951	Phoenix, Ariz.
1952–1961	St. Petersburg, Fla.
1962–1995	Ft. Lauderdale, Fla.
1996–	Tampa, Fla.

Oakland Athletics (includes Philadelphia 1901–1954 and Kansas City 1955–1967)

1901	Philadelphia, Pa.
1902	Charlotte, N.C.
1903	Jacksonville, Fla.
1904	Spartanburg, S.C.
1905	Shreveport, La.
1906	Montgomery, Ala.
1907	Dallas, Tex.
1908–1909	New Orleans, La.
1910	Atlanta, Ga.
1912–1913	San Antonio, Tex.
1914–1918	Jacksonville, Fla.
1919	Philadelphia, Pa.
1920–1921	Lake Charles, La.
1922	Eagle Pass, Tex.
1923–1924	Montgomery, Ala.
1925–1936	Fort Myers, Fla.
1937	Mexico City, Mexico
1938–1939	Lake Charles, La.

1940–1942	Anaheim, Calif.
1943	Wilmington, Del.
1944–1945	Frederick, Md.
1946–1962	West Palm Beach, Fla.
1963–1968	Bradenton, Fla.
1969–1978	Mesa, Ariz.
1979–1983	Scottsdale, Ariz.
1984–	Phoenix, Ariz.

Seattle Mariners

| 1977–1992 | Tempe, Ariz. |
| 1993– | Peoria, Ariz. |

Tampa Bay Devil Rays

| 1998–2008 | St. Petersburg, Fla. |
| 2009– | Port Charlotte, Fla. |

Texas Rangers (includes Washington Senators 1961–1971)

1961–1986	Pompano Beach, Fla.
1987–2002	Port Charlotte, Fla.
2003–	Surprise, Ariz.

Toronto Blue Jays

| 1977– | Dunedin, Fla. |

Acknowledgments

This is not a book about Dodgertown or the Los Angeles Dodgers. It is quite impossible to write a history of spring training, however, without a long look at the history the Dodgers made in over sixty years in Vero Beach, and the history they made in leaving for Glendale. And it would have been quite impossible to write that history without the cooperation of many in the Dodgers organization. My reporting began in Vero Beach in 2006 and ended in Los Angeles in 2008, and I am deeply grateful to the people who extended their kindness along the way. The Dodgers' owner and chair, Frank McCourt, was generous with his time, as was general counsel Sam Fernandez and executive vice president Charles Steinberg. (When the eloquent Dr. Charles writes his book on baseball, I intend to be the first to order a copy.) In Vero Beach, Dodgertown director Craig Callan suffered through my questions and requests for more than two years, offering his insight and assistance with patience and courtesy.

I am likewise indebted to former Dodgers owner Peter O'Malley for his willingness to share his memories and his family's love of Dodgertown. Thanks too to Brent Shyer and Robert Schweppe of Mr. O'Malley's staff, who provided photographs and encouragement. Before I even met Shyer and Schweppe, I was in their debt, for they are also the men responsible for www.walteromalley.com, a Web site chronicling the life and career of the longtime Dodgers owner. Of all the baseball history sites on the Web, few are as rich in original documents, photos, stories, and memories. Peter O'Malley, Shyer, and Schweppe have given a wonderful gift not only to Peter's father's memory, but also to all lovers of baseball history.

Virtually all of the material in chapter 1 and much of the background elsewhere in the book came from material in the archives of the National Baseball Library at the Hall of Fame in Cooperstown. Librarian Jim Gates, research director Tim Wiles, and their staff always make the normally delightful experience of visiting Cooperstown all the better.

I have had the privilege of speaking twice on spring training at the Cooperstown Symposium on Baseball and American Culture, which is jointly sponsored each year by the Hall of Fame and the State University of New York at Oneonta. I am grateful to Jim Gates, Bill Simons of SUNY, and their committee for giving me that chance. An early version of the Dodgers' negotiations to sell Dodgertown to Indian River County appeared in the proceedings of that conference in 2006.

The following people contributed in ways large and small to the completion of this book. What they have in common is that they all helped more than they probably realize: Jay Alves, Larry Babcock, Joseph A. Baird, Rick Baker, Ed Beasley, John Blake, Tom Brant, Robert Brinton, Brian Britten, Lori Burns, Rob Butcher, Pat Calhoon, David Cardwell, Penny Chandler, Peter Chase, Emily Christie, Mark Coronado, William Curtis, Brian Dalke, Tim Day, Mike Dee, J. P. de la Montaigne, Bill DeLury, Anthony Donadio, Woody Duxler, Carl Erskine, Eric Feichthaler, Ted Ferris, John Fineran, Darrell Fry, Nick Gandy, Glenn Geffner, Bob Gernert, Nancy Golnick, David L. Greene, Brad Hanje, Kirk Hearin, Steve Henson, Mike Herrman, Mike Jackson, Tony Jackson, Joe Jareck, Judy John, Camille Johnston, Eric Judson, John Kaites, Michael Kalt, Kurt Kemp, Laura Kleiss Hoeft, Jeff Kuenzli, Tommy Lasorda, Dennis Liborio, Grady Little, Tony Masserotti, Jeff Maultsby, Jeff Mielke, Don Miers, Tom Moulton, Rick Mussett, Alex Muxo, Rick Nafe, Peter O'Malley, Bud Parmer, Dan Pearson, Larry Pendleton, Floyd Perry, Bret Picciolo, Ron Pies, Phillip Porter, Rob Rabenecker, Josh Rawitch, Scott Reifert, Blake Rhodes, Alan Ricke, Mark Rogoff, Kim Sams, John Schuerholz, Dan Shaughnessy, Larry Shenk, Katie Siegfried, Alex Slemc, Bill Smith, Paul Snyder, Ted Spencer, Dave St. Peter, Jimmy Stanton, Michael Stavres, Charles Steinberg, John Steinmiller, Terry Stewart, Bart Swain, Mike Swanson, John Timberlake, Rick Vaughn, Kathy Wall, Barry Waters, Larry Whaley, Ann Louise Wikoff, Reggie Williams, Maury Wills, John Yarbrough, and John F. Zipp.

I am also grateful to the assistants and colleagues who facilitated my conversations with these people. And I want to thank the dozens of major and minor league baseball players, managers, and coaches who allowed me to listen in on pre- and postgame press scrums or gave me a brief moment of their time on fields and in locker rooms across Florida and Arizona over three springs.

Of all the fortunate things that have happened in my professional life, one of the best has been meeting Tim Bent of Oxford University Press. As is always the case with a skilled editor, this book bears his profound mark in ways unseen by anybody but me, and I am most grateful. Likewise, my debt to his assistant, Dayne Poshusta, increases with each passing week. Merryl Sloane's precise and thorough copyediting brightened the manuscript considerably, and I thank her for the care she took with my work. Twenty-five years ago, Charles Everitt was the editor who bought my first book. Working now as a literary agent, he helped to make my relationship with Oxford happen.

At Northeastern University, my colleagues in the School of Journalism suffered my distractions during the writing of this book and picked up a share of my workload so that I might complete it. I want to particularly thank director Steve Burgard and colleagues Bill Kirtz and Link McKie. The university provost's office gave me a grant to help offset the cost of travel for this book. I must note, however, that I received very little understanding from my colleagues or my students whenever I was leaving Boston in February and March for reporting trips to Florida and Arizona.

My friend Victor Merina read portions of the manuscript and buoyed my confidence with his kind words.

No one has contributed more to this book, or to my life, than my wife, Cathy.

Charles Fountain
Duxbury, Massachusetts
August 19, 2008

Selected
Bibliography

Aaron, Hank, with Lonnie Wheeler. *I Had a Hammer: The Hank Aaron Story*. New York: HarperCollins, 1991.

Arsenault, Raymond. *St. Petersburg and the Florida Dream, 1888–1950*. Gainesville: University Press of Florida, 1996.

Ashe, Arthur R. *A Hard Road to Glory: A History of the African-American Athlete, 1619–1918*. New York: Warner, 1988.

Barber, Red. *1947: When All Hell Broke Loose in Baseball*. New York: Da Capo, 1982.

The Baseball Encyclopedia, 8th ed. New York: Macmillan, 1990.

Bavasi, Buzzie, with John Strege. *Off the Record*. Chicago: Contemporary, 1987.

Beauchamp, Catherine W. *Look What Happened in Osceola County*. Kissimmee, Fla.: Osceola County Historical Society, n.d.

Cody, Aldus M., and Robert S. Cody. *Osceola County: The First 100 Years*. Kissimmee, Fla.: Osceola County Historical Society, 1987.

Creamer, Robert W. *Babe: The Legend Comes to Life*. New York: Simon and Schuster, 1974.

Duxler, Woody, and Fred Boher. *Hi Corbett Field: Tucson's Field of Dreams*. Tucson: Privately published, 2006.

Gibson, Bob, with Lonnie Wheeler. *Stranger to the Game: The Autobiography of Bob Gibson*. New York: Viking, 1994.

Gilbert, Bill. *They Also Served: Baseball and the Home Front, 1941–1945*. New York: Crown, 1992.

Golenbock, Peter. *Fenway: An Unexpurgated History of the Boston Red Sox*. New York: Putnam, 1992.

Hartzell, Scott Taylor. *St. Petersburg: An Oral History*. Charleston, S.C.: Arcadia, 2002.

Harwell, Ernie, and Tom Keegan. *My 60 Years in Baseball*. Chicago: Triumph, 2002.

Johnson, Rody. *The Rise and Fall of Dodgertown*. Gainesville: University Press of Florida, 2008.

Kahn, Roger. *The Boys of Summer*. New York: Harper and Row, 1972.

———. *Beyond the Boys of Summer*, edited by Rob Miraldi. New York: McGraw-Hill, 2005.

Lacy, Sam, with Moses J. Newson. *Fighting for Fairness: The Life Story of Hall of Fame Sportswriter Sam Lacy*. Centerville, Md.: Tidewater, 1998.

LaHurd, Jeff. *Spring Training in Sarasota, 1924–1960*. Charleston, S.C.: History Press, 2006.

Lamb, Chris. *Blackout: The Untold Story of Jackie Robinson's First Spring Training*. Lincoln: University of Nebraska Press, 2004.

Langill, Mark. *Dodgertown*. Charleston, S.C.: Arcadia, 2004.

Leavy, Jane. *Sandy Koufax: A Lefty's Legacy*. New York: HarperCollins, 2002.

Mack, Connie. *My 66 Years in the Big Leagues*. Mattituck, N.Y.: Amereon House, 1950.

Maraniss, David. *Clemente: The Passion and Grace of Baseball's Last Hero*. New York: Simon and Schuster, 2006.

McCarthy, Kevin M. *Baseball in Florida*. Sarasota, Fla.: Pineapple, 1998.

Mead, William B. *Even the Browns: The Zany True Story of Baseball in the Early Forties*. Chicago: Contemporary, 1978.

Monteleone, John J., ed. *Branch Rickey's Little Blue Book: Wit and Strategy from Baseball's Last Wise Man*. New York: Macmillan, 1995.

Montville, Leigh. *The Big Bam: The Life and Times of Babe Ruth*. Garden City, N.Y.: Doubleday, 2006.

Noll, Roger, and Andrew Zimbalist, eds. *Sports, Jobs and Taxes: The Economic Impact of Sports Teams and Stadiums*. Washington, D.C.: Brookings Institution Press, 1997.

Okkonen, Marc. *Baseball Uniforms of the 20th Century*. New York: Sterling, 1991.

Okrent, Daniel, and Harris Lewine, eds. *The Ultimate Baseball Book*. Boston: Houghton Mifflin, 1979.

Osceola County, Florida. *Osceola County Centennial: 1887–1987*. Kissimmee, Fla.: Privately published, 1987.

Rampersad, Arnold. *Jackie Robinson: A Biography*. New York: Knopf, 1997.

Richards, J. Noble. *Florida's Hibiscus City: Vero Beach*. Melbourne, Fla.: Brevard
  Graphics, 1968.
Robinson, Frank, with Al Silverman. *My Life in Baseball*. Garden City, N.Y.:
  Doubleday, 1968.
Robinson, Jackie, as told to Alfred Duckett. *I Never Had It Made*. New York:
  Putnam, 1972.
Schuerholz, John, with Larry Guest. *Built to Win*. New York: Warner Books,
  2006.
Seymour, Harold. *Baseball: The Early Years*. New York: Oxford University Press,
  1960.
——. *Baseball: The Golden Age*. New York: Oxford University Press, 1971.
Shanks, Bill. *Scouts Honor: The Bravest Way to Build a Winning Team*. New York:
  Sterling and Ross, 2005.
Shaughnessy, Dan, and Stan Grossfeld. *Spring Training: Baseball's Early Season*.
  Boston: Houghton Mifflin, 2003.
Simons, William M., ed. *The Cooperstown Symposium on Baseball and American
  Culture, 2001*. Jefferson, N.C.: McFarland, 2002.
Snyder, Brad. *A Well-Paid Slave*. New York: Viking, 2006.
Stout, Glenn, and Richard A. Johnson. *Red Sox Century*. Boston: Houghton
  Mifflin, 2000.
Tygiel, Jules. *Baseball's Great Experiment: Jackie Robinson and His Legacy*. New
  York: Oxford University Press, 1983.
Veeck, Bill, with Ed Linn. *Veeck—as in Wreck*. New York: Putnam, 1962.
Vitti, Jim. *The Cubs on Catalina: A Scrapbookful of Memories about a 30-Year
  Love Affair between One of Baseball's Classic Teams and California's Most
  Fanciful Isle*. Bay City, Calif.: Settefrati, 2003.
Zinsser, William. *Spring Training*. Pittsburgh, Pa.: University of Pittsburgh Press,
  2003.

Source Notes

Abbreviations

NBL	National Baseball Library, Cooperstown, N.Y.
SN	*Sporting News*
SPMHA	St. Petersburg Museum of History Archives
SPT	*St. Petersburg Times*
STNBL	Spring training file, National Baseball Library
WSP	Wendell Smith Papers, National Baseball Library

Prologue

p. 1 Lasorda at Dodgertown—author observation, Vero Beach, Fla., Feb. 19, 2005.

p. 1 Caro quote—conversation with author, Vero Beach, Fla., Mar. 2, 2005.

p. 1 Bisher quote—*SN*, Mar. 7, 1981, STNBL.

p. 3 Angell quote—Roger Angell, *Late Innings: A Baseball Companion* (Simon and Schuster, 1982), p. 67.

p. 3 game of catch and Navarro autographs—author observations, St. Petersburg and Vero Beach, Fla., Feb.–Mar. 2006.

p. 3 Steinberg quote—interview, Dr. Charles Steinberg, Fort Myers, Fla., Feb. 23, 2006.

p. 4 Pesky quote—Dan Shaughnessy and Stan Grossfeld, *Spring Training: Baseball's Early Season* (Houghton Mifflin, 2003), p. 185.

p. 5 fan memories—conversations overheard by and with author, various spring training sites, 2006–2008.

p. 5 Manny Mota—author observation, various dates, 2005–2008.

p. 5 Johan Santana and Carlos Silva—interview, Bill Smith, Fort Myers, Fla., Mar. 23, 2006.

p. 5 bicycle-built-for-two—author observation, Tucson, Ariz., Mar. 8, 2007.

p. 6 "essence of baseball's core" and all subsequent Steinberg quotes—Steinberg interview.

p. 8 attendance figures—Web sites of the Arizona Sports and Tourism Authority (az-sta.com/cactusleague) and the Florida Grapefruit League Association (floridagrapefruitleague.com).

p. 8 Tom Grieve quote—Richard Justice, "A New Florida Has Spring in Its Step," *Washington Post*, Mar. 21, 1989.

Chapter 1

p. 10 "name was better known"—Harold Seymour, *Baseball: The Early Years* (Oxford University Press, 1960), p. 173.

p. 10 Anson and integration—Seymour, *Baseball: The Early Years*, pp. 334–335; also see David L. Porter, Cap Anson entry in *Biographical Dictionary of American Sports*, STNBL, and Arthur R. Ashe, *A Hard Road to Glory: A History of the African-American Athlete, 1619–1918* (Warner, 1988), p. 74.

p. 12 Spalding quote—Howard W. Rosenberg, "Spring Training Didn't Start in Florida," *Orlando Sentinel*, Mar. 7, 2004, STNBL.

p. 14 Bad Bill Dahlen—Lowell Reidenbaugh, "Where Are Pranks of Yesteryear," *SN*, Mar. 8, 1980, STNBL.

p. 15 "looking like aldermen"—Seymour, *Baseball: The Early Years*, p. 182.

p. 15 "Men Are All Overweight"—*Brooklyn Eagle*, Mar. 15, 1896.

p. 15 Tris Speaker—Jim Nasium, "Spring Training Fancies and Fallacies," *SN*, Jan. 21, 1932, STNBL.

p. 15 1892 spring trip costs—Stan Isle, "$469 Spring Tab in 1892—Now It's $150,000," *SN*, Mar. 6, 1971, STNBL.

p. 16 Brooklyn's late plans—"Baseball News and Gossip," *Brooklyn Eagle*, Mar. 4, 1900.

p. 16 Hanlon background; McGraw quote—Robert Creamer, "Team: The Old Orioles," in Daniel Okrent and Harris Lewine, eds., *The Ultimate Baseball Book* (Houghton Mifflin, 1979).

p. 17 Orioles-Giants series—Barry Gottehrer, "The Funny Side of Spring Training," *American Legion Magazine*, Mar. 1963, STNBL.

p. 18 embroidered horse blankets—Harry Cronin, "Go South, Young Man" (city unknown), *Sunday News*, Mar. 5, 1961, STNBL.

p. 18 "can't expect a man…with his nose in his coat collar"—Marshall Smith, "Gone Are Rowdy, Roughing It Days," unidentified clipping, Mar. 29, 1963, STNBL.

p. 20 Marquard and Schreck stories—Gottehrer, "The Funny Side of Spring Training."

Chapter 2

p. 22 Al Lang's background—Karl Grismer, *The Story of St. Petersburg* (St. Petersburg, 1948), pp. 313–314.

p. 22 St. Petersburg's history—Raymond Arsenault, *St. Petersburg and the Florida Dream, 1888–1950* (University Press of Florida, 1996), chaps. 3–5.

p. 23 "Your Al will never amount to anything"—Scott Taylor Hartzell, "Al Lang's Life Began When It Was Almost Over," *SPT*, July 14, 1999.

p. 23 Dreyfuss quote—Kevin M. McCarthy, *Baseball in Florida* (Pineapple, 1998), p. 143.

p. 24 lost $1,000—Grismer, *Story of St. Petersburg*, p. 236.

p. 25 "Famous Philadelphia sporting writers"—*Everybody's Magazine*, c. 1926, untitled, uncredited partial clipping, Baseball folder, SPMHA.

p. 25 "owes more to Al Lang"—*St. Petersburg Evening Independent*, Feb. 28, 1960.

p. 26 "other bowery aspects"—Gay Blair White, "Al Lang: St. Petersburg's Ambassador to Major League Baseball," Program for the Dedication of Al Lang Field, Mar. 1947, Baseball folder, SPMHA.

p. 26 condition of waterfront—Gay Blair White, "Goodbye Waterfront Park," Program for the Dedication of Al Lang Field, Mar. 1947, Baseball folder, SPMHA.

p. 27 meeting the trains—*SPT*, Feb. 28, 1960.

p. 27 Lang's networking; Landis quote—*Everybody's Magazine*, c. 1926, SPMHA.

p. 28 details on Waterfront Park—Robert Carroll, "Boston Braves Coming March 5th," undated clipping, SPMHA.

p. 29 Lang's baseball dinners—Pat Donahue, "St. Pete—Spring Baseball's Capital," *Tourist News*, Festival of State Edition, 1926.

p. 30 Huggins quote—Frank Graham, "A Name Is Changed," undated column, c. 1962, SPMHA.

p. 31 Montville quote—Leigh Montville, *The Big Bam: The Life and Times of Babe Ruth* (Doubleday, 2006), pp. 159–160.

p. 31 "What was more important"—Montville, *The Big Bam*, p. 167.

p. 31 alligators—Montville, *The Big Bam*, p. 198.

p. 32 1939 discussions and plans for new ballpark—"Controversial Ballparks," uncredited, undated clipping, files of Rick Mussett, St. Petersburg City Hall.

p. 34 "I know they're the Yankees"—Bob Boyson, "Yankee Move Would Be a Mistake," St. Petersburg *Sunday Independent*, Feb. 19, 1961, SPMHA.

p. 34 Robison report to chamber of commerce—J. Roy Stockton, "Spring Training in Florida," *Florida Historical Quarterly*, Jan. 1961, STNBL.

Chapter 3

p. 35 "orange and grapefruit league"—*Syracuse Herald*, Mar. 15, 1923, cited on www.barrypopik.com/index.php/florida/entry/grapefruit_league_grapefruit_circuit_grapefruit_loop.

p. 37 Landis-Roosevelt letters—James A. Percoco, "Baseball and World War II: A Study of the Landis-Roosevelt Correspondence," *Organization of American Historians Magazine of History*, Summer 1992, online at www.oah.org/pubs/magazine/sport/percoco.html.

p. 38 Roosevelt and Griffith—Bill Gilbert, *They Also Served: Baseball and the Home Front, 1941–1945* (Crown, 1992), p. 42.

p. 38 soldiers following pennant races—Gilbert, *They Also Served*, p. 43.

p. 38 61 players in military by 1942—Gilbert, *They Also Served*.

p. 38 219 players—William Mead, *Even the Browns: The Zany True Story of Baseball in the Early Forties* (Contemporary, 1978), p. 99.

p. 39 Arthur Daley quote—Mead, *Even the Browns*, p. 74.

p. 40 Dodgers throwing snowballs for camera—Mark Langill, *Dodgertown* (Arcadia, 2004), p. 11.

p. 40 Southworth and McCarthy quotes—Mead, *Even the Browns*, pp. 75–76.

p. 40 Hubbell and ping-pong—Mead, *Even the Browns*, p. 76.

p. 41 Lakeland history—public library page, City of Lakeland Web site, www.lakelandgov.net/library/oldspeccoll/home/lakeland_history.htm.

p. 41 Clare Henley background—"The Great Floridians Program," MyFlorida.com Web site, www.flheritage.com/services/sites/floridians/?section=1.

p. 41 "only places open...were the phone booths"—Joe Falls, "Memories of the Old Lakeland," *SN*, Mar. 11, 1972, STNBL.

p. 42 Willie Horton barbeques—Joe Falls, "Bugs, Barbecues and the Friday Fights," *SN*, Feb. 28, 1983, STNBL.

p. 42 Joker Marchant background—"Parks and Recreation," City of Lakeland Web site, www.lakelandgov.net/parkrec/facilities/JokerMarchantStadium.html.

p. 43 "Y'all put the peanut shells"—See www.lakelandgov.net/parkrec/facilities/JokerMarchantStadium.html.

p. 43 "most fan friendly" park—John Henderson, "Vero Beach May Lose Its Famous Dodgers," *Denver Post*, Mar. 28, 1999.

p. 43 "We have a college campus atmosphere"—interview, Maury Wills, Vero Beach, Fla., Feb. 20, 2005.

p. 44 Robinson in Daytona Beach—Arnold Rampersad, *Jackie Robinson: A Biography* (Knopf, 1997), pp. 140–148.

p. 44 Bud Holman calls Rickey—Brent Shyer, "Holman Approaches Rickey," online at www.walteromalley.com/hist_dtown. All subsequent Shyer references and citations come from the www.walteromalley.com Web site.

p. 44 Bud Holman background—J. Noble Richards, *Florida's Hibiscus City: Vero Beach* (Brevard Graphics, 1968), pp. 302–303.

p. 45 Vero Beach in 1947—Richards, *Florida's Hibiscus City*, p. 198.

p. 45 Bavasi's meeting with Holman—Shyer, "Holman Approaches Rickey."

p. 45 "Rickey University"—Rampersad, *Jackie Robinson*, p. 140.

p. 45 "Men can imitate"—John J. Monteleone, ed., *Branch Rickey's Little Blue Book: Wit and Strategy from Baseball's Last Wise Man* (Macmillan, 1995), p. 66.

p. 46 Jimmy Powers quote—Shyer, "Jackie Robinson Emerges."

p. 46 Rickey and the strings—Monteleone, *Branch Rickey's Little Blue Book*, p. 68.

p. 46 carrying bats to beat off snakes—Langill, *Dodgertown*, p. 10.

p. 47 blow a whistle each morning at six—Shyer, "Vero's First Exhibition."

p. 47 Holman builds swimming pool—Shyer, "Jackie Robinson Emerges."

p. 47 "Take All You Want"—Langill, *Dodgertown*, pp. 12–23.

p. 47 big league barracks; "just keep bustin' your ass"—Wills interview.

p. 48 Robinson and "colored cab"—Jackie Robinson, as told to Alfred Duckett, *I Never Had It Made* (Putnam, 1972), pp. 103–104.

p. 48 black players and haircuts—Wills interview.

Chapter 4

p. 49 Wendell Smith biography—Wendell Smith, undated interview with Jerome Holtzman, Typescript in WSP.

p. 51 *Courier* paid expenses—Rampersad, *Jackie Robinson*, p. 119.

p. 52 "premature leak could destroy"—Rampersad, *Jackie Robinson*, p. 167.

p. 52 "I understand . . . he is a much better ball player"—Wendell Smith to Branch Rickey, Dec. 19, 1945, WSP.

p. 53 "don't want to find ourselves embarrassed"—Rickey to Smith, Jan. 8, 1946, WSP.

p. 53 "most happy to feel . . . you are relying on . . . me"—Smith to Rickey, Jan. 14, 1946, WSP.

p. 54 Smith meeting Robinson at bus station—Rampersad, *Jackie Robinson*, p. 139.

p. 54 "Negro mayor of Daytona Beach"—Chris Lamb, *Blackout: The Untold Story of Jackie Robinson's First Spring Training* (University of Nebraska Press, 2004), p. 90.

p. 54 "get the niggers out of town"—Lamb, *Blackout*, p. 88.

p. 54 "city officials...regard them as two more ballplayers"—Jules Tygiel, *Baseball's Great Experiment: Jackie Robinson and His Legacy* (Oxford University Press, 1983), p. 105.

p. 54 second-class versus third-class—Lamb, *Blackout*, p. 91.

p. 55 epistle to black fans—Wendell Smith, "A Special Note to the Fans," *Pittsburgh Courier*, Apr. 20, 1946, WSP.

p. 55 *Pittsburgh Courier* circulation—Jonathan Eig, *Opening Day: The Story of Jackie Robinson's First Season* (Simon and Schuster, 2007), p. 131.

p. 55 "Press Box, Yankee Stadium"—Wendell Smith, "Robbie Bats .296, Fields Brilliantly," *Pittsburgh Courier*, Oct. 11, 1947, WSP.

p. 56 paid $50 a week by Rickey—Jerome Holtzman interview of Smith, WSP.

p. 56 Smith and Robinson growing apart—Rampersad, *Jackie Robinson*, p. 207.

p. 57 Curt Flood in Tampa—Brad Snyder, *A Well-Paid Slave* (Viking, 2006), p. 42.

p. 57 "ground rule conditions that are not pleasant"—Sam Lacy, with Moses Newson, *Fighting for Fairness: The Life Story of Hall of Fame Sportswriter Sam Lacy* (Tidewater, 1998), p. 89.

p. 58 hole in the fence in West Palm Beach—Tygiel, *Baseball's Great Experiment*, p. 318.

p. 58 "not about being an Uncle Tom"—Snyder, *Well-Paid Slave*, p. 42.

p. 58 "baseball...hasn't done all it can"—Tygiel, *Baseball's Great Experiment*, p. 318.

p. 58 "I liked it better"—Tygiel, *Baseball's Great Experiment*, p. 316.

p. 59 "degrading as hell"—Tygiel, *Baseball's Great Experiment.*, p. 318.

p. 59 Sam Lacy and Elston Howard—Lacy with Newson, *Fighting for Fairness*, pp. 87–88.

p. 59 "I regret...I can't be more active"—Frank Robinson, with Al Silverman, *My Life in Baseball* (Doubleday, 1968), p. 18.

p. 59 Vic Power—Tygiel, *Baseball's Great Experiment*, p. 317.

p. 59 "Spring Training Woes"—Wendell Smith, *Chicago's American*, Jan. 23, 1961, WSP.

p. 60 "If you are Minoso, Smith or Pizarro"—Wendell Smith, *Pittsburgh Courier*, Mar. 26, 1961. Quoted in David Maraniss, *Clemente: The Passion and Grace of Baseball's Last Hero* (Simon and Schuster, 2006), pp. 145–146.

p. 61 St. Petersburg NAACP press conference—David K. Rogers, "The Spring Home of Segregation," *SPT*, May 12, 1996.

p. 61 NAACP letter to every major league team—Jack E. Davis, "Baseball's Reluctant Challenge: Desegregating Major League Spring Training Sites, 1961–64," *Journal of Sport History*, Summer 1992, p. 152.

p. 61 Topping statement—Davis, "Baseball's Reluctant Challenge," p. 154.

p. 61 Yankees' search for new hotel—Rogers, "Spring Home of Segregation."

p. 62 Cardinals' reaction; Bob Gibson quote—Bob Gibson, with Lonnie Wheeler, *Stranger to the Game: The Autobiography of Bob Gibson* (Viking, 1994), p. 58.

p. 62 Smith updates on progress—Smith, "Negro Players Gain in Quality Bid," *Chicago's American*, Feb. 6, 1961, WSP.

p. 63 "have to subscribe to what has been done in the past"—Smith, "Negro Players Gain in Quality Bid."

p. 63 "Hell, no, I'm not happy"—Hank Aaron, with Lonnie Wheeler, *I Had a Hammer: The Hank Aaron Story* (HarperCollins, 1991), p. 212.

p. 63 "only room for four men"—Smith, "Negro Players Gain in Quality Bid."

p. 63 St. Petersburg Yacht Club episode—Snyder, *Well-Paid Slave*, pp. 56–58.

p. 64 "our own little civil rights movement"—Gibson with Wheeler, *Stranger to the Game*, p. 59.

p. 64 DeSoto motel—Smith, "Integrates Motel—Periled," *Chicago's American*, undated clipping, [Spring 1961?], WSP.

p. 64 "clients…would reject my business, I believe"—Smith, "What a Negro Ballplayer Faces Today in Training," *Chicago's American*, Apr. 3, 1961, WSP.

p. 65 "Fat Cats" and "Uncle Toms"—Snyder, *Well-Paid Slave*, p. 59.

p. 65 "[Didn't he] realize"—Smith, "What a Difference a Name Makes," *Pittsburgh Courier*, June 3, 1961, WSP.

p. 65 "My position...is the same as Bill Veeck's"—Smith, "End Spring Degradation, Negroes Ask," *Chicago's American*, July 30, 1961, WSP.

p. 66 Banks, Doby, and Smith quotes on getting credit for the story—Smith, "Negro Players Gain in Quality Bid."

Chapter 5

p. 67 building of Holman Stadium—Brent Shyer, "21-Year Lease Signed," "O'Malley Proposes Stadium," both at www.walteromalley.com. All subsequent Shyer references are from www.walteromalley.com.

p. 68 "sand, marl and muck"—Shyer, "Emil Praeger Design."

p. 68 cost of Holman Stadium—Shyer, "Emil Praeger Design," "Holman Stadium Dedication."

p. 68 heart-shaped pond—Langill, *Dodgertown*, p. 31.

p. 68 palm trees ringing outfield—Langill, *Dodgertown*, p. 27.

p. 68 Dick Allen crashing into palm—Langill, *Dodgertown*, p. 65.

p. 68 stadium named in honor of Bud Holman—Shyer, "Holman Stadium Dedication."

p. 68 first to arrive and last to leave—interview, Peter O'Malley, Los Angeles, Calif., May 15, 2008.

p. 69 "How are you? How's your family?"—interview, Jaime Jarrin, Vero Beach, Fla., Feb. 28, 2005.

p. 69 "Call me Walter"; "never the same after Vero Beach"—Rody Johnson, *The Rise and Fall of Dodgertown* (University Press of Florida, 2008), p. 37.

p. 69 cocktail parties for press—Jarrin interview.

p. 69 "O'Malley's warmth was mostly external"—Roger Kahn, *The Boys of Summer* (Harper and Row, 1972), p. 424.

p. 69 "wonderful man"—"Dodgertown Memories, Manny Mota," www.walteromalley.com.

p. 69 "Kay and Walter were just wonderful"—"Dodgertown Memories, Lee Lacy," www.walteromalley.com.

p. 69 "always very proud of this place—Jarrin interview.

p. 70 "Dad was a planter"—O'Malley interview.

p. 70 details of the controversy over the Vero Beach airport and the Dodgers' purchase of Dodgertown—Johnson, *Rise and Fall of Dodgertown*, pp. 77–78, 81–88, 90–93.

p. 71 "dollar a year … really wasn't fair"—O'Malley interview.

p. 71 "Our roots were so deep"—O'Malley interview.

p. 72 three appraisals—O'Malley interview.

p. 72 building of Dodgertown golf course—Shyer, "Golf Courses Privately Built."

p. 72 "When they put that golf course up there"—"Dodgertown Memories, Lou Johnson," www.walteromalley.com.

p. 72 O'Malley and the bunkers—Shyer, "Golf Courses Privately Built."

p. 72 eighteen-hole course—O'Malley interview.

p. 72 property eventually totaled 465 acres—interview, Craig Callan, Vero Beach, Fla., Feb. 26, 2005.

p. 73 "city didn't have the money"—O'Malley interview.

p. 73 barracks pranks and high jinks—Langill, *Dodgertown*, p. 114.

p. 74 Vin Scully quote—"Dodgertown Memories, Vin Scully," www.walteromalley .com.

p. 74 inviting Cubs to share Dodgertown—"Dodgertown Memories, Vin Scully," p. 26.

p. 74 off-season activities—Shyer, "O'Malley's Dodgertown Vision."

p. 74 "marriage … produced its first baby"—Langill, *Dodgertown*, p. 89.

p. 74 homemade street signs—Shyer, "Jackie Robinson Emerges."

p. 74 formal street signs—Langill, *Dodgertown*, p. 71.

p. 74 "baseball … facility disguised as an arboretum"—Tom Verducci, "Play Ball," *Sports Illustrated*, Feb. 23, 2004.

p. 75 "only two people, father and son"—O'Malley interview.

Chapter 6

p. 79 1890s costs—Stan Isle, "$469 Spring Tab in 1892—Now It's $150,000," *SN*, Mar. 6, 1971, STNBL.

p. 79 1913 costs and owners' calls for cutbacks—J. J. Ward, "The Folly of Spring Training," *Baseball Magazine*, Apr. 1913, STNBL.

p. 79 1930s costs—Dan Daniel, untitled clipping, *SN*, Feb. 6, 1936, STNBL.

p. 79 1960 costs—J. Roy Stockton, "Spring Training in Florida," *Florida Historical Quarterly*, Jan. 1961, STNBL.

p. 79 1970s costs—Isle, "$469 Spring Tab in 1892."

p. 79 late eighties costs—Ross Newhan, "Spring Training Still One of the Great American Traditions," *Los Angeles Times*, Mar. 1, 1987, STNBL.

p. 79 "100 percent commercial"—Dan Daniel, "Is Spring Training Really Necessary," *Sport*, Mar. 1947, STNBL.

p. 79 "unbelievable"—quoted in Bruce Lowitt, "Bidding for Baseball," *SPT*, Feb. 28, 1988.

p. 79 200 meals a night—Joseph Durso, "Spring Training: Place in the Sun for Old-Timers and Big Business," *New York Times*, Apr. 1, 1974, STNBL.

p. 79 Cincinnati travel agency—Mark Albright, "The Boys (and Fans) of Spring," *SPT*, Mar. 16, 1987.

p. 79 $3 million per team spent by tourists—Albright, "The Boys (and Fans) of Spring."

p. 79 $54 million on up; Martinez quote—Albright, "The Boys (and Fans) of Spring."

p. 80 $295 million impact—Diane Steinle, "Phillies Request Astroturf in Talks with Clearwater," *SPT*, Oct. 1, 1987.

p. 80 Red Sox most popular—Nick Carfardo, "Minor Triumphs and Major Fiasco," *Boston Globe*, Mar. 18, 1990.

p. 80 sending $1 to Dunedin—Carfardo, "Minor Triumphs and Major Fiasco."

p. 80 attendance figures—mlb.com/pressbox/events/spring_training.jsp?content= st_ attendance.

p. 81 "Politicians are making these claims" and all subsequent Porter quotes—interview, Phillip Porter, Tampa, Fla., Aug. 20, 2007.

p. 82 "disagree...100 percent"—interview, Jeff Mielke, Fort Myers, Fla., Feb. 28, 2006.

p. 83 Zipp research—John F. Zipp, "Spring Training," in *Sports, Jobs and Taxes: The Economic Impact of Sports Teams and Stadiums*, edited by Roger Noll and Andrew Zimbalist (Brookings Institution Press, 1997), p. 446.

p. 84 "the money...was going to filter"—interview, Larry Pendleton, Tallahassee, Fla., Feb. 21, 2007.

p. 85 "libertarian gene kicks in"—Jerome Stockfisch and Josh Poltilove, "Two States Vie over Spring Training Baseball," *Tampa Tribune*, Apr. 13, 2006.

p. 85 lease terms—author interviews with various community officials throughout Florida and Arizona, 2005–2008.

p. 86 "Kissimmee, Florida...Where's that?"—interview, Larry Whaley, Kissimmee, Fla., Jan. 19, 2007.

p. 86 "this stadium loses a million and a half"—interview, Robert Brinton, Mesa, Ariz., Mar. 6, 2007.

p. 86 "half the teams commute and go home"—interview, Don Miers, Kissimmee, Fla., Jan. 25, 2007.

p. 87 Cocoa Expo—Ed Pierce, "The History of the Cocoa Expo," www.cocoaexpo. com/05FacilityGuide.

p. 87 Roy Hobbs tournament; 10,000 room nights—Mielke interview.

p. 87 United States Specialty Sports Association—Miers interview.

p. 88 Disney's Wide World of Sports facts—www.disneyworldsports.disney.go.com.

p. 88 "two main pillars" and subsequent Williams quotes—interview, Reggie Williams, Lake Buena Vista, Fla., Jan. 18, 2007.

Chapter 7

p. 91 "give it to you in some verse of poetry" and all subsequent Steinberg quotes—interview, Charles Steinberg, Fort Myers, Fla., Feb. 23, 2006.

p. 92 Red Sox Nation background—interview, Dan Shaughnessy, Fort Myers, Fla., Mar. 16, 2006.

p. 92 citizenship in Red Sox Nation—www.redsox.com/nation.

p. 92 Red Sox Nation statistics—www.boston.redsox.mlb.com/bos/fan_forum/rsn_map.jsp.

p. 92 "less comfortable with it"—Shaughnessy interview.

p. 93 Stahl suicide—"Drained Bottle of Carbolic Acid," *Cincinnati Enquirer*, Mar. 29, 1907. Also see "Worried to Death," *SN*, Apr. 6, 1907. Both articles in Chick Stahl file, NBL.

p. 94 blackmail and syphilis; deaths of Julia Stahl and Fred O'Connell—Glenn Stout and Richard A. Johnson, *Red Sox Century* (Houghton Mifflin, 2000), pp. 66–67. Also see Peter Golenbock, *Fenway: An Unexpurgated History of the Boston Red Sox* (Putnam, 1992), pp. 26–28.

p. 95 "When I first learned I'd been sold to Boston"—Ed Linn, *Hitter: The Life and Turmoils of Ted Williams* (Harcourt, Brace, 1993), p. 80.

p. 95 "Wait until you see Foxx hit"—Linn, *Hitter*, pp. 81–82.

p. 95 players falling off elephants and horses—Tim Horgan, "Spring Training Kindles Strange Memories," *Boston Herald*, Feb. 27, 1975, STNBL.

p. 95 "lay-up drills on an eight-foot rim"—Dan Shaughnessy, "Ace's Breaking Pitch Appears to Be Outside," *Boston Globe*, Feb. 23, 2007.

p. 95 Pumpsie Green—Golenbock, *Fenway*, p. 226.

p. 95 "money, guns and lawyers"—Dan Shaughnessy, "It Was Spring Haven for Fans and Follies," *Boston Globe*, Apr. 4, 1992.

p. 95 Earl Wilson—Golenbock, *Fenway*, pp. 229–230.

p. 96 Tommy Harper—Steve Fainaru, "In Racism's Shadow," *Boston Globe*, Aug. 4, 1991.

p. 96 Rice and Crowley—Larry Whiteside, "Rice, Crowley in Tiff," *Boston Globe*, Mar. 13, 1981.

p. 96 Boggs on TV—"Boggs Will Tell His Side on 20/20," *USA Today*, Mar. 20, 1989.

p. 97 2005 ticket prices—*MLB Spring Training Media Guide, 2005*.

p. 97 "Naked greed"—Mel Antonen, "Red Sox Raise Prices, Still Sell Out," *USA Today*, Jan. 20, 2005.

p. 98 "humble and grateful"—Antonen, "Red Sox Raise Prices."

p. 98 average sale is $200—Sasha Talcott, "Where Spring Training Counts: Fans' Enthusiasm Translates into Profits for Red Sox Operations in Florida," *Boston Globe*, Mar. 10, 2005.

p. 98 Steinberg quote and all subsequent Steinberg quotes—interview, Charles Steinberg, Fort Myers, Fla., Feb. 23, 2006.

p. 99 "ownership that embraces the fans"—Shaughnessy interview.

p. 99 Mike Dee quote and all subsequent Dee quotes—interview, Mike Dee, Fort Myers, Fla., Feb. 23, 2006.

p. 100 "take fifteen Red Sox games"—interview, Craig Callan, Vero Beach, Fla., Aug. 2005.

p. 100 Red Sox Grapefruit League crowds—floridagrapefruitleague.com/ attendance.

Chapter 8

p. 103 Kissimmee history—Aldus M. Cody and Robert S. Cody, *Osceola County: The First 100 Years* (Osceola County Historical Society, 1987), pp. 6–41.

p. 104 Osceola County hotel statistics and bed-tax revenues—Osceola County, Florida, *Osceola County Centennial, 1887–1987* (Privately published, 1987), pp. 474–480.

p. 105 Parmer-Brant partnership—interviews, E. A. "Bud" Parmer, Tallahassee, Fla., Feb. 21, 2007; and Thomas A. Brant, Winter Park, Fla., Mar. 24, 2007. All subsequent Brant quotes from same interview.

p. 105 county explored sports complex in 1981—Minutes, Osceola County Board of County Commissioners, May 11, 1981; Nov. 16, 1981.

p. 105 "Baseball encourages and increases tourism"—"Economic and Non-Economic Impact and Pro-Forma Revenue Statement: Osceola County Major League Baseball Spring Training Project," prepared by Tabcor, Inc., Orlando, Fla., Aug. 15, 1983, private files of Thomas A. Brant.

p. 106 Larry Whaley quote and all subsequent Whaley quotes—interview, Larry Whaley, Kissimmee, Fla., Jan. 19, 2007.

p. 106 "to acquire, construct, extend, enlarge"—2006 Florida Statutes, Title XI, Chapter 125.0104, Tourist Development Tax, procedure for levying; authorized uses; referendum, enforcement, paragraph (5)(a)1.

p. 106 Larry Whaley's and John Ritch's positions on using TDT money—Whaley and Brant interviews.

p. 107 "Sure, that's tourism"—Richard Justice, "A New Florida Has Spring in Its Step," *Washington Post*, Mar. 21, 1989.

p. 107 "Tourist Development Council was against this"—interview, Don Miers, Kissimmee, Fla., Jan. 25, 2007.

p. 108 Brant and Parmer hire Peter Bavasi—Brant interview.

p. 108 Cocoa background and all quotes—interviews, Barry Waters, Dennis Liborio, and Phil Garner, Kissimmee Fla., Feb. 20, 2007.

p. 109 Jerry Remy quote on Cocoa—Remy's remarks were made during the telecast of a Boston Red Sox game on the New England Sports Network (NESN) in the summer of 2005.

p. 110 Astros visiting site—Liborio interview.

p. 110 description of stadium site in 1983—Liborio, Brant, and Parmer interviews.

p. 110 ceremonial groundbreaking—Osceola County *News & Gazette*, Feb. 23, 1984.

p. 110 descriptions of talks among county, team, and architect—Brant, Miers, Parmer, and Whaley interviews; Justice, "A New Florida Has Spring in Its Step."

p. 111 cloverleaf of practice fields—Miers and Brant interviews.

p. 112 "don't think…another spring training facility comparable"—"New Spring Complex a Smash Hit," *SN*, Feb. 28, 1985, STNBL

p. 112 "workouts used to be four hours long" and all subsequent Garner quotes—Garner interview.

p. 112 Astros spring training attendance—mlb.com/pressbox/events/spring_ training_ attendance.

Chapter 9

p. 116 "changed the entire dynamic of spring training—interview, Rob Rabenecker, Jupiter, Fla., Feb. 4, 2006.

p. 116 Schuerholz approached Lee County—interview, John Schuerholz, Lake Buena Vista, Fla., Mar. 17, 2006.

p. 116 "The facility was old" and all subsequent Schuerholz quotes—Schuerholz interview.

p. 116 "They didn't want much" and all subsequent Yarbrough quotes—interview, John Yarbrough, Fort Myers, Fla., Mar. 1, 2006.

p. 117 "All you teams want is more, more, more"—Schuerholz interview.

p. 118 Athletics, Indians, and Pirates history in Fort Myers—television documentary, *Untold Stories: The First Pitch*, WGCU-TV, Fort Myers, Fla., 2005.

p. 119 Roberto Clemente integrated—Maraniss, *Clemente*, pp. 67–71.

p. 120 Twins facilities in Orlando and Melbourne—interview, Bill Smith, Fort Myers, Fla., Mar. 23, 2006.

p. 120 "great training ground for groundskeepers" and all subsequent Smith quotes—Smith interview.

p. 120 "We were concerned about that" and all subsequent St. Peter quotes—interview, Dave St. Peter, Fort Myers, Fla., Mar. 1, 2006.

p. 121 details on planning and construction; Andy MacPhail quotes—Smith and St. Peter interviews.

p. 122 witch's hat—Smith interview.

p. 123 Kirby Puckett signing autographs—Smith interview.

p. 123 fans in stadium on opening day—Smith interview.

p. 123 "started in our brand-new spring training facility"—Smith interview.

p. 125 details on revenue streams—St. Peter interview.

Chapter 10

p. 128 general background of Homestead and of Baseball City—various clippings, Jan. 1988–Apr. 1990.

p. 130 job of finding the money fell to Muxo—telephone interview, Alex Muxo, May 25, 2006.

p. 131 Miami Beach and bed tax—Muxo telephone interview.

p. 132 "pink elephant"—Bud Shaw, "Homestead Has to Face Hard Facts," Cleveland *Plain Dealer*, Apr. 17, 1993.

p. 132 Muxo introduces Jacobs to Homestead developer—Victoria White, "Details Emerge of Bid to Attract Indians," *SPT*, June 18, 1991.

p. 132 "if a team was going to spend $1,000"—Muxo telephone interview.

p. 132 Citrus County dropped out—White, "Details Emerge of Bid to Attract Indians."

p. 133 "needed something to rally behind—Muxo telephone interview.

p. 133 Indians sent money and supplies—Muxo telephone interview.

p. 134 "gave the city hope"—Muxo telephone interview.

p. 134 "used to be a city here"—Dave Van Dyck, "Building Hope in Homestead with Baseball," *Chicago Sun-Times*, Mar. 8, 1993.

p. 134 "If they choose not to come back"—Bud Shaw, "Homestead's Dream Comes True," Cleveland *Plain Dealer*, Mar. 7, 1993.

p. 134 "isn't that down near Cuba"—Alan Ricke, e-mail to author, May 25, 2006.

p. 135 "city toyed with the idea of expanding"—Ricke, e-mail to author.

p. 135 "professional baseball…would never be more than a dream"—Ricke, e-mail to author.

p. 135 IMAX theater and roller derby—Forest Norman, "Strike Three, You're Out," *Miami New Times*, Feb. 3, 2005.

p. 136 "this place is still a great asset"—interview, Kirk Hearin, Homestead, Fla., May 17, 2006.

p. 137 "completely gone now"—interview, John Schuerholz, Lake Buena Vista, Fla., Mar. 17, 2006.

p. 137 "very sad to drive by"—interview, Kim Sams, Lake Buena Vista, Fla., May 22, 2006.

p. 138 "nothing but eighteen-wheelers and…retirees"—interview, Floyd Perry, Lakeland, Fla., May 21, 2006.

p. 138 attendance records had been broken—Bruce Lowenstein, "Baseball Teams Field Lavish Offers for Spring-Training Sites in Florida," *Wall Street Journal*, Apr. 8, 1987.

p. 138 "I thought phenomenal concept"—Schuerholz interview.

p. 138 "one business doing business with another"—Pulliam, "88 Spring Home of Royals."

p. 139 original design evoked nineteenth century—Perry interview.

p. 139 game every day—Perry interview.

p. 139 amusement park details—Boardwalk and Baseball press release, "Putting the Baseball in Boardwalk and Baseball," Mar. 1987, Boardwalk and Baseball file, NBL.

p. 139 Hall of Fame exhibit; Ted Spencer quotes—interview, Ted Spencer, Cooperstown, N.Y., May 10, 2006.

p. 140 uniforms and equipment from Hall of Famers—National Baseball Hall of Fame press release, "Baseball Hall of Fame Exhibit Announced for Boardwalk and Baseball," Feb. 4, 1987, Boardwalk and Baseball file, NBL.

p. 140 Hall of Famers at park opening—"Boardwalk and Baseball Grand Opening Plans," notebook containing memos, photos, and clippings in the collection of Kim Sams.

p. 140 press reviews of park opening—clippings in Boardwalk and Baseball file, NBL.

p. 140 "pleasant sort of idyllic park-like setting"—Schuerholz interview.

p. 141 Royals attendance figures—www.mlb.com/mlb/pressbox/events/spring_training.

p. 141 "greatest day in park history"—telephone interview, Dan Pearson, June 1, 2006.

p. 141 "It was a tough sell"—Sams interview.

p. 141 "If people think you're way out there"—Pearson telephone interview.

p. 141 layoffs—"Harcourt Sets Layoff of 750 at Theme Parks," *New York Times*, Aug. 25, 1988.

p. 141 Anheuser-Busch buys parks—"Selling Parks Won't Save Harcourt Brace," *SPT*, Sept. 30, 1989.

p. 142 closing of park—Carl Chambers, "Boardwalk and Baseball: A Brief History," online at www.dizzyrambler.com/index.html.legends/themeparks.

p. 142 park was hemorrhaging money—Helen Huntley, "Boardwalk and Baseball Closes Its Gates for Good," *SPT*, Jan. 18, 1990.

p. 142 "Baseball City was run by...theme park division"—Pearson telephone interview.

p. 142 Pearson on running Baseball City—Pearson telephone interview.

p. 143 Royals and Polk County—Tom Ford, "Despite Strike, County Continues 'Royal' Treatment," *Tampa Tribune*, Nov. 30, 1994.

p. 143 remained a state-of-the-art facility—Pearson telephone interview.

p. 144 average attendance never topped 3,000—www.mlb.com/mlb/pressbox/events/spring_training.

p. 144 lease prevented selling property—Steve Newborn, "Royals, Rangers Might Move Spring Training to Arizona," *Tampa Tribune*, Nov. 1, 2000.

p. 144 listened to Las Vegas—Dave Nicholson, "Las Vegas Wants Royals, Reds for Spring Training," *Tampa Tribune*, May 4, 1996. Also interview, Craig Callan, Vero Beach, Fla., Feb. 26, 2005.

p. 144 final-day crowd—Michael Egger and Bill Heery, "Polk Faithful Give Baseball Royal Send-Off," *Tampa Tribune*, Mar. 30, 2002.

p. 144 Posner bought property—Ted Jackovics, "Posner Buys Polk Property," *Tampa Tribune*, Jan. 23, 2001.

p. 144 final event in stadium—Bill Heery, "Huge Polk Project Underway," *Tampa Tribune*, Oct. 17, 2003.

p. 145 "one of Florida's hottest development corridors"—Jackovics, "Posner Buys Polk Property."

p. 145 Haines City population—U.S. Census, 2000.

p. 146 "didn't want to associate with Haines City"—Pearson telephone interview.

Chapter 11

p. 147 Rickey's book on Schuerholz's desk—author observation, Mar. 17, 2006.

p. 148 "Braves way"—Schuerholz interview, Lake Buena Vista, Fla., Mar. 17, 2006.

p. 149 Snyder quotes—unless otherwise indicated, all Paul Snyder quotes come from a series of interviews and conversations with the author, Lake Buena Vista, Fla., Mar. 22–24, 2007.

p. 149 Schuerholz speeches at spring training—Snyder interviews. Also see John Schuerholz, with Larry Guest, *Built to Win: Inside Stories and Leadership Strategies from Baseball's Winningest GM* (Warner Books, 2006), pp. 136–143.

p. 151 late-night dinner—Snyder interviews. Also see Thomas Stinson, "On Path to Hall, Snyder Saw It All," *Atlanta Journal-Constitution*, Aug. 19, 2005.

p. 151 "He was honest with me"—Snyder interviews.

p. 153 Kemp quotes—unless otherwise indicated, all Kurt Kemp quotes come from author interview, Lake Buena Vista, Fla., Mar. 23, 2007.

p. 156 "pitchability"—Snyder interviews.

p. 156 autographs—author observation, various sites, 2006–2007 spring training. Also author observation at Walt Disney World, Mar. 22–24, 2007.

p. 157 off-field programs—Kemp interview.

p. 158 extended spring training particulars—Snyder and Kemp interviews.

Chapter 12

p. 164 Veeck and Philadelphia Phillies—Bill Veeck, with Ed Linn, *Veeck—as in Wreck: The Chaotic Career of Baseball's Incorrigible Maverick* (Putnam, 1962), pp. 171–172.

p. 164 Veeck and Ocala; bringing Indians to Tucson—Veeck with Linn, *Veeck—as in Wreck*, pp. 177–179.

p. 166 Dwight Patterson background—Graciela Sevilla, "Cactus League's Patterson Dies, Helped State Get Pro Baseball," *Arizona Republic*, Oct. 11, 1999.

p. 166 Cubs history on Catalina; Bob Kelly quote—Jim Vitti, *The Cubs on Catalina: A Scrapbookful of Memories about a 30-Year Love Affair between One of Baseball's Classic Teams & California's Most Fanciful Isle* (Settefrati, 2003), pp. 1–12.

p. 167 HoHoKams history—www.mesahohokams.com.

p. 167 signed for loans without telling wives—interview, Robert Brinton, Mesa, Ariz., Mar. 6, 2007.

p. 167 Patterson taking rookies to dinner and ripping tickets—John MacDonald, "Dwight Patterson: A True Favorite Son," *Arizona Republic*, Oct. 13, 1999.

p. 169 "I'd get a twenty-page letter"—Interview Ron Pies, Tempe, Ariz. Mar. 7, 2007.

p. 171 Vincent-Mofford meeting and Vincent quote—Scott Bordown, "Cleveland's Defection May Start a Trend," (Toronto) *Globe and Mail*, Feb. 28, 1991.

p. 171 "No team plays in a desert climate"—quoted in Bob Sherwin, "Razing Arizona: Cactus League in Jeopardy if Florida Entices One More Ballclub Away from the Southwest," *Seattle Times*, Feb. 17, 1991.

p. 172 $140 million; Garagiola quote—Tim Keown, "Cactus League Slide," *San Francisco Chronicle*, Mar. 11, 1991.

p. 172 Peoria background; de la Montaigne quotes—interview, J. P. de la Montaigne, Peoria, Ariz., Mar. 2, 2007.

p. 174 Peoria economic impact—appendix to "Cactus League Baseball Attendee Tracking Survey," FMR Associates, Tucson, Ariz., 2003–2004.

p. 175 Pies quotes—interview, Ron Pies, Tempe, Ariz., Mar. 7, 2007.

p. 175 Maryvale in 1998—Drew Olson, "1998 Home Has Its Drawbacks: Brewers Unhappy with Park's Location," *Milwaukee Journal Sentinel*, Mar. 11, 1997. Also see Tom Haudricourt, "Brewers Set Up Camp in New Digs; Team Isn't Worried about Area's Negative Image," *Milwaukee Journal Sentinel*, Feb. 14, 1998.

p. 176 Maryvale today—author observation, Mar. 2–4, 2007.

Chapter 13

p. 177 "Can you imagine giving all this up?"—conversation with Bill DeLury, Vero Beach, Fla., Feb. 21, 2005.

p. 178 sale of Dodgers to Fox—Mark Maske, "Baseball Owners Buy into Murdoch's Deal for Dodgers," *Washington Post*, Mar. 20, 1998.

p. 178 O'Malley quote—Dave Anderson, "Brooklyn Has a Reason to Smirk," *New York Times*, Jan. 7, 1997.

p. 178 "aggressive continent-hopping dealmaker"—Richard Sandomir, "Warily, Baseball Prepares to Make Murdoch Owner of the Dodgers," *New York Times*, Mar. 8, 1998.

p. 178 assets estimated at $4 billion—Ken Daley, "Owners Undecided on Whether Murdoch Would Be Good for Game," *Dallas Morning News*, Jan. 25, 1998.

p. 179 forming committee on spring training—interview, Craig Callan, Vero Beach, Fla., Feb. 26, 2005.

p. 179 $320,000 a year in property taxes—Indian River County, Fla., "Application for Certification of Retained Spring Training Facility to the State of

Florida Office of Tourism, Trade and Economic Development, Submitted by Indian River County, Florida, Regarding the Acquisition and Improvements to Dodgertown," Sept. 19, 2000, section 14 (hereinafter referred to as Indian River County, "Application for Certification").

p. 179 "We were to take a look and see" and all subsequent Callan quotes—Callan interview.

p. 179 Fort McDowell plans—interview, Sam Fernandez, Los Angeles, Calif., May 14, 2008. Also see John Henderson, "Vero Beach May Lose Its Famous Dodgers," *Denver Post*, Mar. 28, 1999.

p. 180 tweak some Florida statutes—James Chandler and Rex Taylor, "Staff Report to the Indian River Board of County Commissioners and Vero Beach City Council on Los Angeles Dodgers Spring Training," Oct. 28, 1998.

p. 180 bill filed in legislature—Jo Becker, "Effort to Keep Dodgers Seeks State Funding," *SPT*, Apr. 21 1999.

p. 181 Florida TaxWatch—quoted in Becker, "Effort to Keep Dodgers."

p. 181 behind-the-scenes lobbying—Deborah O'Neil, "Law May Help Cities Keep Their Ball Clubs," *SPT*, May 1, 1999.

p. 181 "I'm calling your mother"—"Dodgers Considering Arizona for Spring Home," *Tampa Tribune*, May 28, 1999. Also interview, Joseph Baird, Vero Beach, Fla., Mar. 2, 2005.

p. 181 *he didn't like that*—Fernandez interview.

p. 181 "it is precedent-setting"—quoted in O'Neil, "Law May Help Cities Keep Their Ball Clubs."

p. 182 "community brand" and all subsequent Chandler quotes—interview, Penny Chandler, Vero Beach, Fla., Mar. 1, 2005.

p. 182 two-dollar bills—Langill, *Dodgertown*, p. 8.

p. 183 financial impact studies—Indian River County, "Application for Certification," section 14.

p. 183 "committee started as...a chamber thing" and all subsequent Donadio quotes—interview, Anthony Donadio, Vero Beach, Fla., Mar. 3, 2005.

p. 183 Keep Our Dodgers committee—interview, William Curtis, Vero Beach, Fla., Mar. 3, 2005.

p. 183 committee members—Keep Our Dodgers committee roster, July 2000. Private papers of William Curtis.

p. 183 Kleinstiver appraisal—Wayne Kleinstiver, "The Dodgers Issues," June 5, 2000. Private papers of William Curtis.

p. 184 Yavapai tribe's scaled-back proposal—Michael Kaiser, "Tribe Trims Offer to Dodgers," Vero Beach *Press Journal*, July 3, 1999.

p. 184 "what if Silicon Valley…began losing its software industry"—quoted in Deborah O'Neil, "Cities Team to Keep Baseball," *SPT*, Nov. 8, 1999.

p. 186 Tampa Bay Regional Planning Council study—Steve Newborn, "Baseball Has Big Impact on County, Report Says," *Tampa Tribune*, Nov. 20, 1999.

p. 186 David Cardwell quote—O'Neil, "Cities Team to Keep Baseball."

p. 186 Dodgers return for 2000—"Dodgers Stay at Vero Beach," *New York Times*, Aug. 5, 1999.

p. 186 details on state aid bill—Laws of Florida, Chapter 2000-186, "Florida Spring Training Facilities Legislation."

p. 187 details on Dodgertown purchase—Callan interview. Also see Memorandum of Understanding between Indian River County, City of Vero Beach, and the Los Angeles Dodgers, July 24, 2000, p. 4.

p. 187 terms of lease—Memorandum of Understanding, pp. 2–5.

p. 188 "They really wanted to be here" and subsequent Baird quotes—interview, Joseph Baird, Vero Beach, Fla., Mar. 2, 2005.

Chapter 14

p. 190 Pies quote on Fort McDowell and all subsequent Pies quotes—interview, Ron Pies, Tempe, Ariz., Mar. 7, 2007.

p. 191 Ferris quote on Las Vegas and all subsequent Ferris quotes—interview, Ted Ferris, Glendale, Ariz., Mar. 5, 2007.

p. 192 Frontier cancels flights—Jeffrey Lieb, "Frontier Abandons Service to Tucson," *Denver Post*, Mar. 11, 1995.

p. 192 Rockies talks with Vegas—"Rockies May Set Up Camp in Las Vegas," *SPT*, Nov. 19, 1995.

p. 192 Rockies' preference for Hi Corbett Field—Irv Moss, "Hi Corbett Has Its Advantages," *Denver Post*, June 30, 1995.

p. 193 Las Vegas plans—Dave Nicholson, "Reds Training in Vegas? Say It Ain't So," *Tampa Tribune*, May 3, 1996.

p. 194 "nonfinancial conceptual plan"—Marc Topkin, "Rays Listen to Vegas Make Spring Pitch," *SPT*, Mar. 28, 2000.

p. 194 undecided voters and all subsequent Coronado quotes—telephone interview, Mark Coronado, May 23, 2007.

p. 197 Surprise census data—www.idcide.com/citydata/az/surprise.htm.

p. 197 one new home every hour—Mayor's Welcome Message, www.surpriseaz.com.

p. 197 Coronado-Deshazo conversation—Coronado telephone interview.

p. 198 Herk Robinson quote—Steve Newborn, "Royals, Rangers Might Move Spring Training to Arizona," *Tampa Tribune*, Nov. 1, 2000.

p. 200 Scottsdale scene—author observation, Mar. 4 and 9, 2007.

p. 201 $20 million in economic impact—Spring Training 2004 Economic Impact Study. Cactus League Association Files.

p. 201 proposal to build on golf course—Lesley Wright, "Giants Will Stay in Scottsdale," *Arizona Republic*, Mar. 12, 2005.

p. 201 Scottsdale Charros—interviews, Mark Stanton, Ed Reading, and Mike Turner, Scottsdale, Ariz., Mar. 9, 2007.

Chapter 15

p. 205 Winter Haven signs—author observation, Feb. 9, 2006.

p. 205 for sale on eBay and all subsequent Gernert quotes—interview, Bob Gernert, Winter Haven, Fla., Feb. 9, 2006.

p. 208 David Greene quote and all subsequent Greene quotes—interview, David Greene, Winter Haven, Fla., Feb. 9, 2006.

p. 208 wouldn't commit to fifteen-year lease—Greene interview.

p. 208 Stavres quote and all subsequent Stavres quotes—interview, T. Michael Stavres, Winter Haven, Fla., Feb. 9, 2006.

p. 209 Indians lease details and city's maintenance costs—Stavres interview.

p. 211 Disney/Osceola County deal—Daphne Sashin, "Disney, Osceola Can't Agree on the Indians over Tax Issue," *Orlando Sentinel*, Sept. 19, 2006.

p. 211 "would have had some problems with that"—interview, Larry Pendleton, Tallahassee, Fla., Feb. 21, 2007.

p. 212 Cape Coral history—city-produced video, available at www.capecoral.net/about.

p. 212 Redfish Point and lot prices—www.flguide.com/cape/history.

p. 213 "on our way to being the second largest city" and all subsequent Feichthaler quotes—interview, Eric Feichthaler, Cape Coral, Fla., Feb. 23, 2006.

p. 214 "city doesn't have infrastructure" and all subsequent Day quotes—interview, Tim Day, Fort Myers, Fla., Feb. 28, 2006.

p. 214 "huge body of information out there" and all subsequent Jackson quotes—interview, Mike Jackson, Cape Coral, Fla., Mar. 1, 2006.

p. 215 Feichthaler asks Indians to outline spring training needs—"Cleveland Says No to Cape Coral's Springtime Offer; Arizona Move Still a Possibility," online at www.ballparkdigest.com/news/2006archives/aug20_26_2006.htm.

p. 215 "do you want spring training" and all subsequent Dalke quotes—interview, Brian Dalke, Goodyear, Ariz., Mar. 9, 2007.

p. 215 talks with Drayton McLane and Arte Moreno—Dalke interview.

p. 216 Goodyear history and population figures—www.goodyearaz.gov.

p. 217 "will be unlike any other spring training facility in the valley"—quoted in Paul Hoynes, "Going to Arizona: Tribe Trades Grapefruits for Cacti," Cleveland *Plain Dealer*, Dec. 22, 2006.

p. 217 construction and maintenance costs—Memorandum of Understanding, by and between the City of Goodyear and the Cleveland Indians Baseball Company Limited Partnership, Regarding the Goodyear Ballpark Village Complex, Sept. 27, 2006.

p. 217 Dalke's letter to major league teams—Brian Dalke files.

p. 218 Stefanov visit to Goodyear—Dalke interview.

p. 218 "location is superb"—"Cleveland Indians Paul Dolan Visits Future Spring Training Site," City of Goodyear press release, Nov. 1, 2006.

p. 219 White Sox attempt to get Indians to Tucson—Patrick Finley, "White Sox Approached Indians about Tucson," *Arizona Daily Star*, Dec. 22, 2006.

p. 220 details on AZSTA/MCSD agreement; "whatever revenue they had left"— interview, Ted Ferris, Glendale, Ariz., Mar. 4, 2007.

p. 220 "We're tapped out"—quoted in Carrie Waters, "$80 Mil for Baseball Taps Out Sports Authority," *Arizona Republic*, Dec. 22, 2006.

p. 220 "heard that before"—interview, Nick Gandy, Orlando, Fla., Jan. 2007.

Chapter 16

p. 222 "now a major league city"—interview, Rick Baker, St. Petersburg, Fla., Feb. 23, 2007.

p. 223 "about expanding our business"—telephone interview, Michael Kalt, Aug. 24, 2007.

p. 223 "not pursuing it"—Baker interview.

p. 224 Hurricane Charley damage—Patrick Whittle, "Rebuilding in the Footprint of Hurricane Charley," *Sarasota Herald-Tribune*, Aug. 13, 2007.

p. 224 background of Charlotte County Stadium—interview, Laura Kleiss Hoeft, Port Charlotte, Fla., Aug. 21, 2007.

p. 224 "show people the economic impact" and subsequent Kleiss Hoeft quotes— Kleiss Hoeft interview.

p. 226 "I'll sign a *thirty*-year lease"—quoted in interview, Jeff Maultsby, Sarasota, Fla., Apr. 1, 2006.

p. 226 background of Reds/Sarasota deal—various clippings, *Sarasota Herald-Tribune*, Oct. 2006–Apr. 2008.

p. 227 Reds called Vero Beach—interview, Joe Baird, Vero Beach, Fla., Aug. 24, 2007.

p. 227 "a great addition"—Doug Sword, "Why Red Sox Have Hearts Aflutter," *Sarasota Herald-Tribune*, Aug. 12, 2008.

p. 227 petition signatures—www.gopetition.com/petitions/reject-public-funding-for-new-ball-park.html, and gopetition.com/online/19770.html.

p. 228 "can't accommodate the demand"—quoted in Nick Carfardo, "Alternative May Be Springing Up in Sarasota," *Boston Globe*, May 1, 2008.

p. 228 "We're playing catch-up"—telephone conversation with Nick Gandy, Aug. 13, 2008.

p. 228 unavailability of state money—telephone interview, Larry Pendleton, Aug. 15, 2008.

p. 229 "big can of worms"—Pendleton telephone interview.

pp. 229–30 FAA and Fort Lauderdale—"Fees Increase May Force Orioles Out of Spring Training Home," *Sports Business Daily*, June 2, 2008.

p. 230 Orioles and Vero Beach—interviews, Joseph Baird, Vero Beach, Fla., Aug. 24, 2007; Feb. 19, 2008. Baird never publicly disclosed the identity of the team with which he was negotiating. That it was the Orioles was widely reported in the *Indian River Press Journal* and confirmed by a private source.

Chapter 17

p. 233 "Destination-point opportunities"—telephone interview, Ed Beasley, Mar. 7, 2007.

p. 234 "I can understand" and subsequent Baird quotes—interview, Joe Baird, Vero Beach, Fla., Aug. 24, 2007.

p. 235 Cook and DuPage counties—press release, W. P. Carey School of Business, Arizona State University, July 23, 2001, online at http://129.219.60.118/top/pressrelease_display.cfm?num=328.

p. 235 one in seven . . . trace roots to Chicago—interviews, John Kaites, Phoenix, Ariz., Mar. 4, 2008; and Scott Reifert, Tucson, Ariz., Mar. 9, 2008.

p. 235 "something very jarring to me" and all subsequent McCourt quotes—interview, Frank McCourt, Los Angeles, Calif., May 12, 2008.

p. 236 "buying him dinner" and all subsequent Kaites quotes—Kaites interview.

p. 238 $300 million of private ancillary development—letter, Rightpath Limited Development to Ed Beasley, Nov. 12, 2006. Rightpath promised 1.1 million square feet of mixed-use development adjacent to the spring training complex. The $300 million figure was arrived at by multiplying 1.1 million square feet by $300, a conservative cost-per-square-foot estimate for commercial construction.

p. 238 deal was structured and subsequent Beasley quotes—Beasley telephone interview.

p. 241 troubles in Abacoa; "If you died and went to hell"—quoted in Dianna Cahn, "Abacoa Town Center Still Hasn't Come into Its Own with Many Stores Empty," South Florida *Sun-Sentinel*, Oct. 16, 2007.

p. 241 $1 billion—City of Glendale, press release announcing memorandum of understanding with White Sox and Dodgers, Nov. 2006.

p. 242 fan cost index—teammarketing.com/fancost. The numbers assume an average spring training ticket price of $15, and reflect the average cost for a family of four to attend a major league baseball game. Both the White Sox and Dodgers are well above the major league average in the fan cost index.

p. 242 thirty-five times—transcript of author interview with Frank McCourt, Los Angeles, Calif., May 12, 2008.

p. 243 "It's an economic decision" and subsequent O'Malley quotes—interview, Peter O'Malley, Los Angeles, Calif., May 15, 2008.

Chapter 18

p. 244 original schedule; Baseball Players' Association restrictions—interview, Craig Callan, Vero Beach, Fla., Mar. 15, 2008.

p. 246 "when this ends…, that all goes away"—interview, Bill DeLury, Vero Beach, Fla., Mar. 17, 2008.

p. 247 "not leaving because we don't like it"—Tommy Lasorda, postgame press conference, Vero Beach, Fla., Mar. 16, 2008.

p. 247 "one door will close" and Lasorda's thoughts on morning of final game—Lasorda pregame press conference, Vero Beach, Fla., Mar. 17, 2008.

p. 248 "wasn't tired, but I felt like I was"—Lasorda pregame press conference.

p. 248 "hope that I get the same feeling"—Lasorda pregame press conference.

p. 248 license plates—Russ Lemmon, "'Blue' Best Describes Final Day at Dodgertown," *Indian River Press Journal*, Mar. 18, 2008.

p. 249 borrow a wrench—Karen Crouse, "Rich Memories in the Last Day at Dodgertown," *New York Times*, Mar. 18, 2008.

p. 249 reporters descended on fans—news accounts on www.ESPN.com and in *Indian River Press Journal*, *Los Angeles Times*, *Los Angeles Daily News*, *New York Times*, and *USA Today*.

p. 249 Erskine's memories of first game—interview, Carl Erskine, Vero Beach, Fla., Mar. 17, 2008.

p. 249 "wed to Dodgertown"—Erskine interview.

p. 250 final game details—author observation, Mar. 17, 2008.

Epilogue

p. 255 Cincinnati's St. Patrick's Day uniforms—Marc Okkonen, *Baseball Uniforms of the 20th Century* (Sterling, 1991), pp. 8, 34.

p. 255 "40 percent of your attendance"—interview, Robert Brinton, Mesa, Ariz., Mar. 4, 2008.

p. 255 Roland Hemond selling players—interview, Scott Reifert, Tucson, Ariz., Mar. 6, 2008.

p. 256 Billy Martin's injury—John Lardner, "The Great Spring Training Nonsense," *Saturday Evening Post*, Feb. 28, 1953, STNBL.

p. 257 Dee talks about spring training road trips—interview, Mike Dee, Fort Myers, Fla., Feb. 23, 2006.

p. 258 "funny thing about spring training"—interview, Charles Steinberg, Los Angeles, Calif., May 12, 2008.

p. 258 "Go team, go!"—author observation, Apr. 1, 2006.

p. 258 "what we work for most of the year"—interview, Jeff Maultsby, Sarasota, Fla., Apr. 1, 2006.

Index

O'Malley, Walter, 43, 67–74, 164, 178, 182, 184, 190, 239, 244, 246, 247, 254
O'Malley, Kay, 68, 247
Oakland Athletics, 123, 168–169, 175, 176, 199, 202, 245
Oakland Oaks, 166
Ocala, Fla., 164–165
Ojeda, Bobby, 206
Olin, Steve, 206
Orange County (Fla.), 106, 210
Orlando, Fla., 34, 36, 40, 117–118, 137, 145
Ortiz, David, 88
Osceola County Stadium 112–113
Osceola County, Fla., 86–87, 101–107, 109–114, 186, 210–211, 218

Palm Springs, Calif., 168, 175
Parker, Dan, 50
Parks, Rosa, 59, 65
Parmer, Bud, 105–108
Patterson, Dwight, 165–168
Payne Park, 227
Pearson, Dan, 141–142, 143n, 145–146
Pendleton, Larry, 84, 211–212, 229
Peoria, Ariz., 85, 172–175, 190, 197, 202, 203, 216
Perry, Floyd, 138
Perry, William, 54
Pesky, Johnny, 4
Peterson, Fritz, 97n
Pettite, Andy, 148
Philadelphia Athletics, 21, 24, 36, 123, 249
Philadelphia Phillies, 5, 11, 24–25, 27, 29, 36, 65, 79, 91, 164, 186, 208, 245n
Philadelphia Stars, 50
Phoenix Municipal Stadium, 175, 200, 202, 245
Phoenix, Ariz., 8, 76, 163–165, 170, 216, 240, 257
Pies, Ron, 169, 174–175, 190–191, 195
Pima County (Ariz.), 192
Pinal County, Ariz., 236
Pinellas County, Fla., 80
Pittsburgh Courier, 50–60, 64

Pittsburgh Crawfords, 50
Pittsburgh Pirates, 3, 23, 119, 131, 225
Pizarro, Juan, 60
Plant City, Fla., 9, 83, 87, 169, 193
Polk County (Fla.), 136, 143, 211
Pompano Beach, Fla., 83, 112
Port Charlotte, Fla., 8–9, 83, 87, 185, 223–225, 232
Port St. Lucie, Fla., 4, 9, 75, 131, 146, 169, 240, 257
Porter, Phillip, 81–84
Posada, Jorge, 148
Posner, Victor, 144, 146
Povich, Shirley, 50
Power, Vic, 59
Powers, Jimmy, 46, 50
Praeger, Emil, 67–68
Puckett, Kirby, 122–123

Queen Creek, Ariz., 236

Rabenecker, Rob, 116
Raglani, Anthony, 251
Ramirez, Manny, 88
Rampersad, Arnold, 56
Randolph, Steven, 251
Range, Paul, 150
Raymond, Bugs, 20
Red Sox Nation, 92, 125
Reese, Pee Wee, 247
Reichler, Joe, 63, 65
Reinsdorf, Jerry, 134, 193, 234–238
Remy, Jerry, 109
Rendevous Park, 167–168
Renteria, Edgar, 155
Rice, Grantland, 27, 33
Rice, Jim, 96
Richards, Paul, 148
Richmond Braves, 158, 160
Ricke, Alan, 134–135
Rickenbacker, Eddie, 44
Rickey, Branch, 24, 43–46, 67, 147–148, 245–246; and Jackie Robinson, 51–54
Ripken, Cal, 230

St. Louis Browns, 24

St. Louis Cardinals, 31–33, 36, 61, 63–64, 65, 75, 79, 119, 173, 189, 223

St. Lucie County (Fla.), 112, 225

St. Lucie West, 240

St. Peter, Dave, 120, 124–126

St. Petersburg *Evening Independent*, 25–26

St. Petersburg Times, 79

St. Petersburg, Fla., 22–34, 35, 61–64, 79, 115, 164, 222–223, 225

Stack, Ed., 139

Stahl, Chick, 93–94

Stahl, Julia, 94

Stavres, Michael, 208–210

Steinberg, Charles, 3, 6–7, 91–92, 98–99, 101, 257

Steinbrenner, George, 79

Stengel, Casey, 31, 33, 119

Stoneham, Horace, 163–165

Stovey, George, 10

Stuart, Fla., 45

Sullivan, Ted, 13, 29, 250

Sun City, Ariz., 108, 164

Sunday, Billy, 12–13

Surprise, Ariz., 8, 144, 196–200, 203, 216

Swain, Robert, 61, 63

Tampa Bay Rays, 9, 135, 145, 194, 222–225

Tampa, Fla., 29, 76, 79, 113, 226, 229

Taylor, Rex, 180

Team Marketing Report, 242

Tebbetts, Birdie, 63

Tempe Diablo Stadium, 175, 200, 202

Tempe Diablos, 168

Tempe, Ariz., 169, 170, 216

Terry Park, 118–119

Texas Rangers, 8, 112, 185, 194, 197, 224, 232

Thaxton, Jon, 227

Thomas A. White Company, 240

Thompson, Fresco, 47–48, 73

Tighe, Jack, 151

Tilley, Cory, 181

Tinker Field, 119–120, 124

Tinker, Joe, 119–120

Tomlin, James, 252

Topping, Dan, 33, 61

Toronto Blue Jays, 79, 185, 186, 194

Torre, Joe, 246

Tourist Development Tax (Fla.) (aka TDT, bed tax), 104, 106–107

Tresh, Mike, 49n

Triandos, Gus, 5

Tucson Electric Park, 86, 219, 234–235

Tucson, Ariz., 5, 7, 85, 131, 163–165, 173, 176, 192–193, 206 234–236, 239, 242, 245, 258

Turner, Ted, 150–152

Tweed, William Marcy (Boss), 11

Unglaug, Robert, 93

United States Specialty Sports Association USSSA, 87

University of Phoenix Stadium, 240, 241

Varitek, Jason, 88

Veeck, Bill, 61, 63, 163–165

Verducci, Tom, 74, 75

Vero Beach *Press Journal*, 69, 75

Vero Beach, Fla., 5, 43–48, 67, 71–77, 81, 83, 99, 145, 177–189, 220, 226, 230–232, 238, 242–243, 244–252

Viera, Fla., 8, 113, 199, 240

Vincent, Fay, 170–171

Vonderhorst, Harry, 16

Wachtel, Edward, 64

Wagner, Honus, 33

Walker, Moses Fleetwood, 10

Walsingham, William, 68

Walt Disney World, 8, 75, 80, 88, 103–104, 110, 129, 137, 140, 141, 144, 147, 151–162, 186, 210, 211–212, 218, 226

Walters, Barbara, 96

Ward, Monte, 17

Washington Nationals, 156